# Education and Information Technology Annual 2015:

# A Selection of AACE Award Papers

Edited by

Theo J. Bastiaens, Ph.D.

Gary H. Marks, Ph.D.

Published by

AACE-Association for the Advancement of Computing in Education

Education and Information Technology Annual 2015: A Selection of AACE Award Papers
(ISBN # 978-1-939797-15-5) is published by
AACE, PO Box 719, Waynesboro, NC 28786, USA
E-mail: info@aace.org
© Copyright 2015 by AACE
www.aace.org  Available at http://www.aace.org/bookshelf.htm

Introduction

The Association for the Advancement of Computing in Education (AACE), http://AACE.org, founded in 1981, is an international, not-for-profit, educational organization with the mission of advancing Information Technology in Education and E-Learning research, development, learning, and its practical application.

AACE serves the profession with international conferences, high quality publications, leading-edge Digital Library (http://EdITLib.org), Career Center, and other opportunities for professional growth.

We are proud to present to you this selection of 25 award winning papers from AACE's conferences (http://AACE. org/conf). This year's selection includes papers from the annual conference of the Society for Information Technology & Teacher Education (SITE) in Jacksonville, Florida, the World Conference on Educational Media & Technology (Ed-Media) in Tampere, Finland and the World Conference on E-Learning (E-Learn) in New Orleans, Louisiana. The decision to nominate a conference paper for an award was made by peer reviewers. All authors were honored during the conference and received a certificate that serves as testimony to their outstanding research and contribution to the conference.

This AACE finest of 2015 book groups the award winning papers in four parts. These four parts provide a timely overview and record of topics that are of primary interest in educational technology this year.

We hope that the reader enjoys this selection as much as we enjoyed working with these cutting-edge scholars. It is the third year that we publish this edition. We are grateful for all the feedback and all the nice comments we got on the 2012, 2013 and 2014 book. We look forward to many new future editions of AACE's award papers.

Thank you very much for your support and participation in AACE events and activities.

Theo J. Bastiaens, Gary H. Marks

Part 1

Pedagogy

In part 1 of this collection the focus is on the pedagogy. In chapter 1 the authors report teachers' perceptions toward the relationships between pedagogical use of emerging technologies and classroom technology infusion. Understanding the relationship between learning theory and technology was considered important because educational practices are rationalized based on proven learning principles and processes. A self-reported questionnaire was used to gather data from 313 full- and part-time nursing teachers in a Taiwanese Nursing Institute during the 2012-2013 academic year. The results of the study revealed that many of the teachers who took part in this study believed in using learning theories as a foundation for selection technology for instruction. Nevertheless, a substantial number of teachers were not sure that they used learning theories to inform their selection of basic software technology for instruction. Also a reasonable proportion of teachers acknowledged that they did not consider learning principles as the based for applying software applications into instruction.

The purpose of the presented study in chapter 2 is to look at how practicing teachers integrate technology-based instruction involving the study of number concepts, geometry, and statistic and probability, during their masters program. Though results showed significant improvement, there is a need for district support in the form of one-to-one technology for all students if technology is to become a seamless student tool.

In Chapter 3 the authors investigate the contribution of field experience and the reflection-on-practice process on Pre-service Teachers' TPACK. Pre-service teachers (PSTs) designed and implemented three technology-based lessons, primarily with GeoGebra. They were observed during the lesson and interviewed before and after each lesson implementation to reflect on their teaching. Five stages in the process of developing TPACK- recognizing, accepting, adapting, exploring, and advancing were used to evaluate PSTs' performance. The qualitative analysis of the data revealed that PSTs TPACK levels changed progressively throughout the study. Three components; the aim of the lesson, the questions used, and the role of the teacher provided important insights to determine the change in the TPACK levels.

In Chapter 4 authors Baker and Schmidt state that the adaption of teaching/learning strategies appropriate for the multigenerational online classroom is a challenge for educators. The pedagogy found in the online classroom shifts the focus from a teacher-centered learning approach to a student-centered learning approach. Four generations of students who could be present in the online classroom are identified and described. Literature reveals that each generation has its own set of values, ideas, beliefs, expectations, ethics, and culture. Educators must understand these differences in order to better understand the learning needs of the students to provide various teaching/learning strategies to promote optimal student outcomes.

Despite the central role that well organized and structured course content plays in engaging learners, authors Norton and Hathaway point, in Chapter 5, to the absence of guidelines for organizing content in ways that meet course learning goals. Recognizing the need for a design solution and, perhaps, the need for a new design framework, design patterns are proposed as an alternative. After describing the elements of a design pattern framework, the authors examine two design cases, demonstrating how the design pattern framework is an applicable approach to structuring course content.

Although expert technology integration planners exist, designing meaningful technology-integrated learning remains a challenge for teachers. To address this problem, the purpose of Davis case study in Chapter 6 was to examine how experts plan for technology integration. The conceptual framework for the study drew from information processing theory to combine two existing constructs resulting in a unique construct called the teacher planning problem space (TPPS). Participants included a purposeful sample of six technology-integrating experts. Data collection included a survey, interviews and technology artifacts related to innovative lessons. These items were interpreted using qualitative content analysis methods and presented as a single case. The preliminary results confirmed the influence of several external factors on planning as well as demonstrated some patterns in how experts planned for technology integration.

In Chapter 7 author Ogunbase presents research on pedagogical design and pedagogical usability of web-based learning environments (WBLEs). The research examines the socio-cultural perspectives of the ways people learn and learner's preferred style of learning and identifies the supposed 'best' types of learning technologies and approaches when need to achieve optimum effectiveness in education process.

Authenticity is an important characteristic of learning experiences and contributes to transfer of learning into practice. Maintaining authenticity in the face of changes in the eventual environment of practice can be challenging. Chapter 8 describes the evolution of an authentic assessment task in a teacher preparation course in response to changes in the program offering and in the wider educational environment. Lessons learned and prospective developments are discussed in light of the effectiveness of the evolution of the task in responding to the changing circumstances.

The flipped classroom is an instructional model in which students are initially exposed to the concepts of the learning contents outside the classroom through the instructor-provided video lectures and other pre-class learning materials, and use the in-class time for student-centered active learning, such as problem solving, collaborative project, and field trip. The pre-class video is widely utilized as a critical pre-class learning material in the flipped classroom instructional model for its media presentation format, easy access, and interest. Authors Long, Logan and Waugh report in Chapter 9 the initial findings from a student survey about their attitudes and preference on the pre-class videos in a undergraduate science course implemented in the flipped classroom model, their perceptions on different formats of pre-class learning materials, including 3 different types of videos and text learning materials. The chapter also reports the students' suggestions on improving the pre-class learning materials.

The purpose of the study in chapter 10 was to investigate the implications of the use of flipped teaching strategy on preservice teachers' learning outcomes, self-efficacy and perception. The investigators Ibrahim and Callaway employed a within-subject design with independent variable: the teaching method (flipped-based (FB) or lecture-based (LB) and two dependent variables: (1) learning outcome (2) students' perception of self-efficacy to integrate technology in teaching. The results showed that there were differences between students' mean test scores and the differences were statistically significant (higher in FB).

---

Part 2

Social Media

Part 2 stresses the design, development, use and evaluation of social media. In chapter 11 the authors believe that there is a need to investigate the role of, and best practices for, social media use in graduate school programs from an institutional perspective. Graduate students and faculty in the Michigan State University Educational Psychology and Educational Technology (MSU EPET) doctoral program established the Social Media Council (SMC) to provide leadership around social media efforts. Drawing from that experience, the authors propose social media best practices for graduate school programs.

Social media is lauded as a powerful tool for informal learning, and a tool of choice for teenagers. Chapter 12 reports on the findings of a survey of 384 secondary school pupils in the UK (aged 11-17) over a 12 week period. The findings indicate a pervasiveness of social media usage amongst this age group, but variety in the types of engagement and self-reported importance of social media. Usage of social media for learning is dominated by logistical task support (for example, clarifying instructions) and heavily focused around homework activities. However, it appears that this provides a context for deeper engagement and learning around those homework activities. The findings indicate also that social media is being used by this age group to support their learning, but that there is still great untapped potential both in terms of the range of activities discussed, and the number of pupils engaging.

Author Carlson presents in chapter 13 an e-mentoring program called EMERGE. It is meant to enhance both career awareness and academic achievement in science, technology, engineering, and mathematics (STEM) for disadvantaged 9th grade girls. Carlsons' goal is to nurture persistence and academic achievement in economically / culturally disadvantaged female learners. She reports on assessment (instruments and collection) for the first cohort of EMERGE participants. Both quantitative and qualitative data indicate that EMERGE was a success and that the program had lasting effects on the students' academic achievement, personal growth, and career choice.

Chapter 14 reports the findings of a case study on teachers' practices in guiding students on a Wikipedia writing assignment in information literacy (IL) instruction. The point of departure is the tension between traditional teacher-centred pedagogical practices and learner-centred assignments. The concept of the Wikipedia writing assignment was developed by a team of literature teachers. A history teacher applied the assignment in her class and made it possible to collect comparative data from another subject. Guided Inquiry – a research-based teaching model for information literacy instruction – was used as an analytical framework to compare two case courses. The findings characterize the black box problem in designing and guiding student-centred learning assignments: the teacher mainly focuses on introducing the assignment and assessing the outcome. However, an emerging approach emphasizing the guidance during the assignment process was also identified in one of the case courses.

In Chapter 15 authors Glassett and Shaha examined year two of an online on-demand professional development in multiple states and districts. Using a quasi-experimental design, the study sought to ascertain whether student gains were sustained in the second year of program participation. Student achievement was examined through randomly matched participating and non-participating schools within districts and states and between districts and states and focused on standardized reading and math scores. Multivariate analysis and effect size calculations verified gains over both years of implementation for participating schools, districts, and states over non-participating PD sites use of Internet-based, on-demand professional learning for improving teacher effectiveness and sustained impacts on student performance.

The authors in chapter 16 present a case study on designing a web-portal that supports the social inclusion of a specific user group, called the LITERACY-portal. LITERACY is an on-going European wide research project creating an online-portal for dyslexic users. The chapter discusses the specific design steps taken to create a portal that fits the needs of its targeted user-group as well as methods and strategies to include users into the design process.

Chapter 17 explores Adaptive Structuration Theory through the cross-cultural collaboration of an online radio station. Students in separate locations used social media and online tools for the purposes of design, implementation, analysis, and evaluation of an online radio station while in a mediated environment. Specific expectations involve successful cross-cultural collaboration involving social media for the purposes of communication and the nexus of the application to Adaptive Structuration Theory.

---

Part 3

Mobile Learning

Authors Banister and Reinhart summarize in Chapter 18 the challenges facing the United States in educating its youth. The dropout rate in the past decades has been staggering, hovering around the 70% mark, with students of color and in lower socio-economic circumstances posting an even higher rate. Perhaps more troubling are the indicators that students who are staying in school until high school graduation are largely disengaged and disenfranchised with their experiences. However, educators are now beginning to embrace the promise of ubiquitous digital technologies in the classroom. Their study examines the practice of adopting mobile devices in K-12 environments in a geographic region of the Midwestern United States. The findings suggest that active learning environments, addressing personalized needs and providing evidence of student competencies, may be accomplished effectively by integrating mobile technologies more prominently in K-12 classrooms.

In Chapter 19 author Rikala focusses on the evaluation process of a nature tour mobile application in a Finnish basic education setting. The idea of the mobile application is to help recording and comparing nature observations and arouse children's interest of nature. The feasibility and learning experiences were evaluated through a framework which includes the core characteristics of mobile learning. The data were collected with teacher and student surveys. The results of the study showed that the pedagogical practices have a strong influence on the mobile learning activity, mobile learning process, as well as mobile learning experience. The clear pedagogical goal made the mobile learning activity more organized and helped the teacher to guide the students to observe nature more goal oriented. The students were motivated, engaged and were concentrating on the task.

Over the past two years the University of Johannesburg embarked on a journey to introduce the use of mobile devices into the classroom to support 21$^{st}$ century teaching and learning. Author Amory's reflective case study in chapter 20 explores the development and use of an appropriate framework to support learning with technology that is aligned to student and staff skill and professional development, a redesign of the support environment to provide just-in-time support, and development of tools for use by mobile devices and infrastructural and policy changes. It is argued that the introduction of mobile devices into teaching and learning is a disruptive event that is part of a radicle innovation. Individuals supported by institutional managerial processes, rather than the managerial processes themselves, drive the innovation in order to create an ecosystem for the use of mobile devices in the classroom.

---

Part 4

Gaming

Gamification is a concept in education that has become more then a buzzword. Given the growing popularity of digital games as a form of entertainment, educators are interested in exploring using digital games as a tool to facilitate learning. The purpose of the study in chapter 21 is to examine game-based learning by describing a learning environment that combines game elements, play, and authenticity in the real-world for the purpose of engaging students' learning of science and enhancing student motivation. The authors discuss the design of the environment and present research conducted. The findings demonstrate that the design of an engaging, interactive environment using a games-based approach can help students have fun while learning.

In Japanese upper secondary schools, students are required to perform "Exploration Activities" in science. However, it is doubtful whether these activities contribute to raising students' interest in learning science or help foster a positive attitude toward utilizing the learning outcomes of science in daily life, because of teachers' tendency to emphasize preparation for college entrance examinations and insufficient examples in government authorized textbooks. The authors believe that it is necessary to develop an appropriate example lesson and framework of instruction to cultivate students' scientific problem-solving abilities for daily life. In this framework, they consider that students' utilization of scientific ways of viewing and thinking should be promoted, and script knowledge of problem-solving for Exploration Activities should be taught. Therefore, in the study in chapter 22, they developed a gaming instructional material for earthquake disaster prevention using the proposed design framework.

In chapter 23 author Salamin briefly reviews the researches related to serious games and describes a specific case, 'the Gademavo game'. Serious games represents a good example of a tool welcomed and appreciated by students stemming from the Digital Natives, while at the same time assuring progression in knowledge acquisition. The Gademavo game, developed by the e-learning Center HES-SO Cyberlearn, aims at providing students in the tertiary sector, with the competence expected for solving problems and decision-taking. The game relies on a space and graphic metaphor closely related to the professional contexts aimed at, and can be customized to the required courses.

In Chapter 24 the authors explored the use of virtual worlds to facilitate student learning in the geosciences. A Second Life island was designed, and they programmed modules covering concepts related to mountain weather and sea breeze to be used in middle and high school classrooms. These virtual world modules engaged students, via their avatars, in real-world virtual experiences. Participants reported gaining a better understanding of and interest in these concepts. Students improved their knowledge of these concepts with statistical significance. While the use of Second Life proved to be successful overall during the study period, issues arising from the resources and requirements of public schools have prompted us to move to an OpenSimulator that allows for greater customization of virtual worlds.

In chapter 25 authors Gose and Menchaca state that people play video games. Many play seriously not just as a hobby. Yet educators either criticize players or resist including games in their curricula. Wouldn't it be great to harness the enthusiasm that already exists for players into educational settings? Their study actually asked game players to identify video game genres and explain what they learned from playing games. Twelve main genres were identified. These genres were: role-playing games, massively multiplayer online role-playing games, first person shooter, sports, puzzle, real time strategy, action, turn based, simulation, fighting, kinetic controlled, and casual. In addition, the study identified 19 learning constructs. The learning constructs were: coding/computer programming, conflict management, communication skills, creating a community, crafting, critical thinking, attention to detail, building management, hand-eye coordination, how to be competitive, interpersonal skills, map awareness, conduct research, economics, reading comprehension, resource management, strategy, spatial thinking, and time management.

# TABLE OF CONTENTS

## PART 1 PEDAGOGY

**Chapter 1** Faculty's Perceptions toward the Relationships between Pedagogical Use of Emerging Technologies and Classroom Technology Infusion
Weichieh Wayne Yu, Chunfu Charlie Lin, Jenny Wang, Chia-Hao, Ho Chang, Mei-Hsin Ho - Taiwan ...................................................................................................23

**Chapter 2** Mathematical Content, Pedagogy, and Technology: What It Can Mean to Practicing Teachers
Beth Bos & Kathryn S. Lee - USA ...................................................................................31

**Chapter 3** An Investigation of a Pre-Service Elementary Mathematics Teacher's Techno-Pedagogical Content Knowledge within the Context of Teaching Practices
Esra Balgalmış & Erdinç Çakıroğlu - Turkey, Kathryn Shafer - USA ...............................41

**Chapter 4** Adapting Teaching/Learning Strategies for the Multigenerational Online Classroom
Darlene Baker & Angela Schmidt - USA .........................................................................49

**Chapter 5** Using a Design Pattern Framework to Structure Online Course Content: Two Design Cases
Priscilla Norton & Dawn - USA .......................................................................................57

**Chapter 6** Teacher Planning Problem Space of Expert Technology Integrating Teachers
Erin Davis - USA .............................................................................................................67

**Chapter 7** Pedagogical Design and Pedagogical Usability of Web-based Learning Environments: Comparative Cultural Implications between Africa and Europe.
Adewunmi Obafemi Ogunbase - Finland .......................................................................73

**Chapter 8** From Creation to Curation: Evolution of an Authentic 'Assessment for Learning' Task
Peter R Albion - Australia ...............................................................................................85

**Chapter 9** Students' Perceptions of Pre-class Video in the Flipped-Classroom Instructional Model: A Survey Study
Taotao Long, Joanne Logan, Michael Waugh - USA ......................................................95

**Chapter 10** Students' Learning Outcomes and Self-efficacy Perception in a Flipped Classroom
Mohamed Ibrahim & Rebecca Callaway - USA ............................................................103

## PART 2 SOCIAL MEDIA

Chapter 11 What We've Got here is Failure to Communicate:
Social Media Best Practices for Graduate School Programs
Joshua M. Rosenberg, Colin A. Terry, John Bell, Virginia Hiltz, Tracy Russo - USA ................. 113

Chapter 12 Perceptions of School Children of Using Social Media for Learning
Robert Blair, David Millard & John Woollard - UK .................................................................... 119

Chapter 13 Using Social Networking to Mentor 9th-grade Girls
for Academic Success and Engineering Career Awareness
Patricia A. Carlson – USA ............................................................................................................. 129

Chapter 14 Guiding Students in Collaborative Writing of Wikipedia Articles – How to
Get Beyond the Black Box Practice in Information Literacy Instruction?
Eero Sormunen & Tuulikki Alamettälä - Finland ......................................................................... 139

Chapter 15 Lessons learned from a two year implementation project: Sustaining
Student Gains with Online On-demand Professional Development
Kelly Glassett & Steven Shaha - USA ........................................................................................... 147

Chapter 16 Designing a web-portal supporting the social inclusion of a specific user
group. A case study of the LITERACY-portal
Dominik Hagelkruys & Renate Motschnig - Austria .................................................................... 155

Chapter 17 Convergence and Divergence: Accommodating Online Cross-Culture
Communication Styles
Susan Simkowski & Bradley E. Wiggins – USA .......................................................................... 165

## PART 3 MOBILE LEARNING

Chapter 18 Using Digital Resources to Support Personalized Learning Experiences in
K-12 Classrooms: The Evolution of Mobile Devices as Innovations in Schools in
Northwest Ohio
Savilla Banister & Rachel Reinhart - USA .................................................................................... 173

Chapter 19 Evaluating the Nature Tour Mobile Learning Application
Jenni Rikala - Finland .................................................................................................................... 179

Chapter 20 Design and implementation of strategies and artifacts to support
ubiquitous computing in and outside the classroom: A reflective case study
Alan Amory - South Africa ............................................................................................................ 187

## PART 4 GAMING

Chapter 21 Using a Game-Based Approach to Design a Rich Media Learning Environment
Min Liu., Jason A. Rosenblum, Lucas Horton, & Jina Kang – USA ..................................... 199

Chapter 22 Development of a Gaming Instructional Material and Design Framework for "Exploration Activities" in Science
Hodaka Taguchi & Toshiki Matsuda - Japan ..................................... 213

Chapter 23 Serious game Gademavo:
How to enhance students' ability in taking decisions in a complex world
Anne-Dominique Salamin - Switzerland ..................................... 223

Chapter 24 Learning Geosciences in Virtual Worlds:
Engaging Students in Real-World Experiences
Reneta D. Lansiquot, Janet Liou-Mark & Reginald A. Blake - USA ..................................... 233

Chapter 25 Video Game Genres and What is Learned From Them
Eddie Gose & Michael Menchaca - USA ..................................... 241

# AUTHORS AND EDITORS CONTACT INFORMATION

Chapter 1 Faculty's Perceptions toward the Relationships between Pedagogical Use of Emerging Technologies and Classroom Technology Infusion
Weichieh Wayne Yu, Chunfu Charlie Lin, Jenny Wang, Chia-Hao, Ho Chang, Mei-Hsin Ho, Taiwan. Email: jamiemeetsworld@gmail.com

Chapter 2 Mathematical Content, Pedagogy, and Technology: What It Can Mean to Practicing Teachers
Beth Bos & Kathryn S. Lee, USA. E-mail: bb33@txstate.edu

Chapter 3 An Investigation of a Pre-Service Elementary Mathematics Teacher's Techno-Pedagogical Content Knowledge within the Context of Teaching Practices
Esra Balgalmış,&Erdinç Çakıroğlu, Turkey, Kathryn Shafer, USA. Email: besra@metu.edu.tr

Chapter 4 Adapting Teaching/Learning Strategies for the Multigenerational Online Classroom
Darlene Baker & Angela Schmidt, USA .E-mail: dbaker@astate.edu

Chapter 5 Using a Design Pattern Framework to Structure Online Course Content: Two Design Cases
Priscilla Norton & Dawn Hathaway, USA. E-mail: pnorton@gmu.edu

Chapter 6 Teacher Planning Problem Space of Expert Technology Integrating Teachers
Erin Davis, USA. E-mail: elesdavis@gmail.com

Chapter 7 Pedagogical Design and Pedagogical Usability of Web-based Learning Environments: Comparative Cultural Implications between Africa and Europe.
Adewunmi Obafemi Ogunbase, Finland. E-mail: Adewunmi.ogunbase@uta.fi

Chapter 8 From Creation to Curation: Evolution of an Authentic 'Assessment for Learning' Task
Peter R Albion, Australia. E-mail: Peter.Albion@usq.edu.au

Chapter 9 Students' Perceptions of Pre-class Video in the Flipped-Classroom Instructional Model: A Survey Study
Taotao Long, Joanne Logan, Michael Waugh, USA. E-mail: tlong11@utk.edu

Chapter 10 Students' Learning Outcomes and Self-efficacy Perception in a Flipped Classroom
Mohamed Ibrahim and Rebecca Callaway, USA. E-mail: mibrahim1@atu.edu

Chapter 11 What We've Got here is Failure to Communicate:
Social Media Best Practices for Graduate School Programs
Joshua M. Rosenberg, Colin A. Terry, John Bell, Virginia Hiltz, Tracy Russo
USA. E-mail: jrosen@msu.edu

Chapter 12 Perceptions of School Children of Using Social Media for Learning
Robert Blair, David Millard, John Woollard, UK. E-mail: Robert.Blair@soton.ac.uk

Chapter 13 Using Social Networking to Mentor 9th-grade Girls
for Academic Success and Engineering Career Awareness
Patricia A. Carlson, USA. E-mail: carlsonp@rose-hulman.edu

Chapter 14 Guiding Students in Collaborative Writing of Wikipedia Articles – How to Get
Beyond the Black Box Practice in Information Literacy Instruction?
Eero Sormunen & Tuulikki Alamettälä, *Finland*. E-mail: eero.sormunen@uta.fi

Chapter 15 Lessons learned from a two year implementation project: Sustaining Student
Gains with Online On-demand Professional Development
Kelly Glassett &Steven Shaha. USA. E-mail: kelly.glassett@schoolimprovement.com

Chapter 16 Designing a web-portal supporting the social inclusion of a specific user group.
A case study of the LITERACY-portal
Dominik Hagelkruys, Renate Motschnig, Austria. E-mail: dominik.hagelkruys@univie.ac.at

Chapter 17 Convergence and Divergence: Accommodating Online Cross-Culture
Communication Styles
Susan Simkowski & Bradley E. Wiggins, USA. E-mail: susan.simkowski@uafs.edu

Chapter 18 Using Digital Resources to Support Personalized Learning Experiences in K-12
Classrooms: The Evolution of Mobile Devices as Innovations in Schools in Northwest Ohio
Savilla Banister & Rachel Reinhart, U.S.A. E-mail: sbanist@bgsu.edu

Chapter 19 Evaluating the Nature Tour Mobile Learning Application
Jenni Rikala, Finland. E-mail: jenni.p.rikala@jyu.fi

Chapter 20 Design and implementation of strategies and artifacts to support ubiquitous
computing in and outside the classroom: A reflective case study
Alan Amory, South Africa. E-mail: aamory@uj.ac.za

Chapter 21 Using a Game-Based Approach to Design a Rich Media Learning Environment
Min Liu., Jason A. Rosenblum, Lucas Horton, & Jina Kang, USA. E-mail:
Mliu@austin.utexas.edu

Chapter 22 Development of a Gaming Instructional Material and Design Framework for "Exploration Activities" in Science
Hodaka Taguchi & Toshiki Matsuda, Japan. E-mail: taguchi@et.hum.titech.ac.jp

Chapter 23 Serious game Gademavo:
How to enhance students' ability in taking decisions in a complex world
Anne-Dominique Salamin, Switzerland. E-mail: adominique.salamin@hes-so.ch

Chapter 24 Learning Geosciences in Virtual Worlds:
Engaging Students in Real-World Experiences
Reneta D. Lansiquot, Janet Liou-Mark & Reginald A. Blake, USA. E-mail : rlansiquot@citytech.cuny.edu

Chapter 25 Video Game Genres and What is Learned From Them
Eddie Gose & Michael Menchaca, USA. E-mail: gose@hawaii.edu

Editors

Theo Bastiaens is professor of Educational Technology at the Fernuniversität in Hagen, Germany and part time professor at the Open University, The Netherlands. He is a member of the AACE board of directors. E-mail: Theo.Bastiaens@fernuni-hagen.de

Gary Marks is CEO and founder of AACE. E-mail: info@aace.org

# EdITLib.org
## The Leading Digital Library Dedicated to Education & Information Technology

## DOES YOUR LIBRARY SUBSCRIBE?

The EdITLib digital library is the premier aggregated and multimedia resource for peer-reviewed research on the latest developments and applications in Educational Technologies and E-Learning.

**Subscribe today to access**
100,000+ articles and
16,000 dissertations written by
200,000+ international authors covering
30+ years of advancements in IT in Education!

- Special Topic Books
- Conference Papers
- Presentation Slides
- Conference Talks
- Journal Articles
- Webinars
- Videos

Abstracts are available open access so you can try the Digital Library at no cost!

Individual subscriptions $19/month or $150/year
Libraries $1995/year

### Academic Journals including:

- Journal of Educational Multimedia and Hypermedia
- International Journal on E-Learning (Corporate, Government, Healthcare, & Higher Education)
- Journal of Computers in Mathematics and Science Teaching
- Journal of Online Learning Research
- Journal of Interactive Learning Research
- Journal of Technology and Teacher Education
- Contemporary Issues in Technology & Teacher Education (electronic)

### Conference proceedings including:

- **EdMedia** – World Conference on Educational Media & Technology
- **E-Learn** – World Conference on E-Learning in Corporate, Healthcare, Government, and Higher Education
- **SITE** – Society for Information Technology and Teacher Education International Conference
- **Global Learn** – Global Conference on Learning and Technology
- **Global TIME** – Global Conference on Technology, Innovation, Media & Education

**NEW!**

- Curated ERIC indexed publications on Educational Technology

- Relevant Content from Proquest Dissertations Just Added

### Newest content additions:

**e-Books:**
- Handbook of Games and Simulations in Teacher Education
- Adding Some TEC-VARIETY: 100+ Activities for Motivating and Retaining Learners Online

**Conference Books:**
- Education and Information Technology 2014: A Selection of AACE Award Papers

**Journals:**
- Journal of Open, Flexible, and Distance Learning

... and many more titles!

Like us on Facebook: facebook.com/editlib
Follow us on twitter: twitter.com/editlib

**Association for the Advancement of Computing in Education**
P.O. Box 719, Waynesville, NC 28786 • Email: info@aace.org • aace.org

# Invitation to Join

The Association for the Advancement of Computing in Education (AACE) is an international, non-profit educational organization. The Association's purpose is to advance the knowledge, theory, and quality of teaching and learning at all levels with information technology.

This purpose is accomplished through the encouragement of scholarly inquiry related to technology in education and the dissemination of research results and their applications through AACE sponsored publications, conferences, and other opportunities for professional growth.

AACE members have the opportunity to participate in Special Interest Groups (SIGs), high-quality peer-reviewed publications, and conferences.

Join with fellow professionals from around the world to share knowledge and ideas on research, development, and applications in information technology and education. AACE's membership includes researchers, developers, and practitioners in schools, colleges, and universities; administrators, policy decision-makers, professional trainers, adult educators, and other specialists in education, industry, and government with an interest in advancing knowledge and learning with information technology in education.

# Membership Benefit Highlights

- Gain professional recognition by participating in AACE sponsored international conferences
- Enhance your knowledge and professional skills through interaction with colleagues from around the world
- Learn from colleagues' research and studies by receiving AACE's well-respected journals and books
- Receive a subscription to the professional periodical Journal of Online Learning Research (JOLR) [digital]
- Access EdITLib-Education & Information Technology Digital Library, a valuable online resource that is fully searchable and covers 30+ years of academic journals and international conference proceedings.
- Receive discounts on multiple journal subscriptions, conference registration fees, and EdITLib Subscriptions.
- AACE Social Media enables you to connect with colleagues worldwide!

**AACE Blog:**
blog.aace.org

**AACE Facebook:**
facebook.com/aaceorg

**AACE Twitter:**
twitter.com/aace

**aace.org**

# AACE Journals

Abstracts for all journal issues are available at www.EdITLib.org

## Education & Information Technology Digital Library — Electronic

The EdITLib is your research and instructional source for peer-reviewed articles and multimedia (100,000+) on the latest research, developments, and applications related to all aspects of Educational Technology and E-Learning from 100s of journals and international proceedings.

## International Journal on E-Learning
(Corporate, Government, Healthcare, & Higher Education)
(IJEL)　　　　ISSN# 1537-245　　　　Quarterly

IJEL serves as a forum to facilitate the international exchange of information on the current theory, research, development, and practice of E-Learning in education and training. This journal is designed for researchers, developers and practitioners in schools, colleges, and universities, administrators, policy decision-makers, professional trainers, adult educators, and other specialists in education, industry, and government.

## Journal of Educational Multimedia & Hypermedia
(JEMH)　　　　ISSN# 1055-8896　　　　Quarterly

Designed to provide a multidisciplinary forum to present and discuss research, development and applications of multimedia and hypermedia in education. The main goal of the Journal is to contribute to the advancement of the theory and practice of learning and teaching using these powerful and promising technological tools that allow the integration of images, sound, text, and data.

## Journal of Interactive Learning Research
(JILR)　　　　ISSN# 1093-023X　　　　Quarterly

The Journal's published papers relate to the underlying theory, design, implementation, effectiveness, and impact on education and training of the following interactive learning environments: authoring systems, CALL, assessment systems, CBT, computer-mediated communications, collaborative learning, distributed learning environments, performance support systems, multimedia systems, simulations and games, intelligent agents on the Internet, intelligent tutoring systems, micro-worlds, and virtual reality-based learning systems.

## Journal of Technology and Teacher Education
(JTATE)　　　　ISSN# 1059-7069　　　　Quarterly

A forum for the exchange of knowledge about the use of information technology in teacher education. Journal content covers preservice and inservice teacher education, graduate programs in areas such as curriculum and instruction, educational administration, staff development, instructional technology, and educational computing.

## Journal of Computers in Mathematics & Science Teaching
(JCMST)　　　　ISSN# 0731-9258　　　　Quarterly

JCMST is the only periodical devoted specifically to using information technology in the teaching of mathematics and science. The Journal offers an indepth forum for the exchange of information in the fields of science, mathematics, and computer science.

## Journal of Online Learning Research
(JOLR)　　ISSN# 2374-1473　　　　Quarterly

The Journal of Online Learning Research is a peer-reviewed, international journal devoted to the theoretical, empirical, and pragmatic understanding of technologies and their impact on primary and secondary pedagogy and policy in primary and secondary (K-12) online and blended environments.

## CITE — Electronic Journal
(CITE)　　　ISSN# 1528-5804　　　　Quarterly

An electronic publication of the Society for Information Technology and Teacher Education (SITE), established as a multimedia, interactive electronic counterpart of the Journal of Technology and Teacher Education.

# AACE Conferences

Details for conferences are available at **www.aace.org/conf**

*The exchange of ideas and experiences is essential to the advancement of the field and the professional growth of AACE members. AACE sponsors conferences each year where members learn about research, developments, and applications in their fields, have an opportunity to participate in papers, panels, poster demonstrations and workshops, and meet invited speakers.*

## SITE 2015
**26th INTERNATIONAL CONFERENCE** — SOCIETY FOR INFORMATION TECHNOLOGY AND TEACHER EDUCATION

**March 2-6, 2015**
**Las Vegas, Nevada**

This conference, held annually, offers opportunities to share ideas and expertise on all topics related to the use of information technology in teacher education and instruction about information technology for all disciplines in preservice, inservice, and graduate teacher education.

## Global Learn 2015
Global Conference on Learning and Technology

**April 16 & 17, 2015**
**Berlin, Germany**

Global Learn is an international conference with the mission of furthering the advancement and innovation in learning and technology. As the educational world becomes increasingly global, new ways to explore, learn, and share knowledge are needed.

## EdMedia 2015
World Conference On Educational Media & Technology

**June 22-24, 2015**
**Montréal, Québec, Canada**

This annual conference serves as a multidisciplinary forum for the discussion of the latest research, developments and applications of multimedia, hypermedia and telecommunications for all levels of education.

## E-Learn 2015

World Conference on E-Learning

**October 20-23, 2015**
**Kona, Hawaii**

E-Learn is a respected, international conference enabling E-Learning researchers and practitioners in corporate, government, healthcare and higher education to exchange information on research, developments and applications.

# Membership Application

You can also apply online at aace.org/my/membership/

## Membership Options

### Professional Membership

- Subscription to 1 AACE Journal (Digital, See journal list under Library Subscriptions)
- Full online access to multiyear back issues of that journal
- Discount conference registrations and proceedings
- Discount subscriptions to additional journals
- Access to the AACE Career Center and Job Board
- All the benefits of AACE Membership.

**$125**

### Student Membership

- All the same benefits of a Professional Membership
- Offered at a discount for students
- MUST be enrolled as a full-time student in an accredited educational institution and provide school information below

**$45**

### Professional Membership PLUS
**EdITLib** — The *Leading* Digital Library Dedicated to Education & Information Technology

- All the same benefits of a Professional Membership
- PLUS 1-year subscription to the EdITLib with 100,000+ peer reviewed journal articles, conference papers and presentations, videos, webinars and much more.

**$175**

### Student Membership PLUS
**EdITLib** — The *Leading* Digital Library Dedicated to Education & Information Technology

- All the same benefits of a Professional Membership
- PLUS 1-year subscription to the EdITLib
- Offered at a discount for students
- MUST be enrolled as a full-time student in an accredited educational institution and provide school information below

**$75**

### Virtual Membership (New Option!)

- **Registration as a virtual participant** for the following events:
  - EdMedia – World Conference on EdMedia & Technology (Value $225)
  - E-Learn – World Conference on E-Learning (Value $225)
- **Conference proceedings** for AACE events, accessible in EdITLib – Education and Information Technology Digital Library
- **Full access** to EdITLib - The Leading Digital Library Dedicated to Education & Information Technology (Value $150)
- **AACE Face-to-Face Conference Registration discounts**

**$395 (Value $600)**

### Purchase Additional Journals

- Professional & Student Memberships include a subscription to 1 AACE Journal (Digital, See journal list under Library Subscriptions)
- Additional journals can be added to your membership

- Please choose ONE option:
  - ☐ Add 1 Journal  $125 prof / $45 student
  - ☐ Add 2 Journals  $180 prof / $70 student
  - ☐ Add 3 Journals  $235 prof / $95 student
  - ☐ Add 4 Journals  $290 prof / $120 student
  - ☐ Add 5 Journals  $345 prof / $155 student

### Library/Institution Subscriptions

- Libraries may purchase subscription to AACE print Journal(s) and/or the EdITLib

- ☐ International Journal on E-Learning (IJEL) — $195
- ☐ Journal of Educational Multimedia and Hypermedia (JEMH) — $195
- ☐ Journal of Computers in Math and Science Teaching (JCMST) — $195
- ☐ Journal of Interactive Learning Research (JILR) — $195
- ☐ Journal of Online Learning Research (JOLR) — $195
- ☐ Journal of Technology and Teacher Education (JTATE) — $195
- ☐ EdITLib – Education & Information Tech. Library (electronic) — $1995

*Additional shipping charge of $15 per journal per year for non-U.S. addresses*

## Applicant Information

Name: _____  E-mail: _____
Address: _____  City: _____  State: _____
Postal Code: _____  Country: _____  ☐ New Member  ☐ Renewal  Membership #: _____
If applying as a student please provide School/Institution Name: _____  Expected Graduation Date: _____
Select Journal(s) to receive: (*Membership includes 1 journal.*)  ☐ IJEL  ☐ JEMH  ☐ JCMST  ☐ JILR  ☐ JTATE

## Method of Payment (US Dollars)

**Enclosed:** ☐ Check (U.S. funds & bank, payable to AACE)  ☐ Purchase Order *(PO must be included plus $10 service charge)*
☐ Bank Wire *(Wire info must be included plus $25 service charge)*
**Credit Card:** ☐ MasterCard  ☐ VISA  ☐ AMEX  ☐ Discover

**TOTAL: $_____**

Card # _____  Card Exp. Date ___/___  Signature: _____

**Return to: AACE** P.O. Box 719, Waynesville, NC 28786 USA • E-mail: info@aace.org • www.aace.org

# PART 1 PEDAGOGY

## 1. Faculty's Perceptions toward the Relationships between Pedagogical Use of Emerging Technologies and Classroom Technology Infusion

Weichieh Wayne Yu[1]*, Chunfu Charlie Lin[2], Jenny Wang[2], Chia-Hao, Ho Chang[1], Mei-Hsin Ho[1]

[1]Department of Nursing, Chronic Diseases & Health Promotion Research Center,
Chang Gung University of Science & Technology, Chiayi, Taiwan

[2]Department of Applied Foreign Languages, National Formosa University, Yuling County, Taiwan

## Introduction

Schools and scholars readily agree that infusing technology in both educational contents and methods of delivery is highly necessary in order to prepare students for industrial and business workplace skills. Therefore, it has become imperative to train and equip teachers with technological skills and methods including techniques to use technology to deliver instruction. The recognition of the importance of technology infusion has led to the demand to provide teachers with current technological skills have given rise to the acquisition of various hardware and software technologies. However, sometimes the knowledge of pedagogy upon which technology integration is rationalized is not properly addressed. This is critical because emphases on technology integration in teachers' training programs might not have received adequate attention among some of the segments of teachers, especially the older teachers. While teachers may receive faculty development training periodically, such training may not adequately address the theoretical framework that guides the selection of instructional strategies and methods upon which technology integration is based.

Pedagogical and technological knowledge mainly refers to the understanding of the processes and methods including practices through which teaching and learning are conducted, managed and assessed (Shulman, 1986). Koehler & Mishra (2008) have attained that effective technology integration practice was to understand content pedagogy which describes the subject discipline to be learned; pedagogical knowledge which deals with the strategies, principles and processes of learning. It also refers to technological knowledge which addresses teachers' ability to select and apply suitable technologies for specific instruction taking into consideration the need of the learner and lesson objectives of the lesson; including the understanding of how the learning contents and technology interact and influence each other. Technology is a fluid infrastructure which transforms with constant rapidity and complexity. The rapid transformation and changes in educational technology tend to put teachers at a disadvantage, particularly teachers who were trained before technology became a buzz word in educational establishments. Koechler and Mishra (2009) observed that:

> Many teachers earned degrees at a time when educational technology was at a very different stage of development than today. It is, thus, not surprising that they do not consider themselves sufficiently prepared to use technology in the classroom and often do not appreciate its value or relevance to teaching and learning. Furthermore, teachers have often been provided with inadequate training for this task (p. 62).

The argument is that the understanding of the relationship between technology infusion and pedagogical knowledge represents the foundation and a road map through which technology integration can be successfully implementation. According to Honey & Moeller (1990), the vital aspect of technology integration is teachers' understanding of the pedagogical principles to address technology integration. Also, Hasselbring, Barron & Risko (2000) remarked that teachers may desire to use computers for instruction and may gain sufficient computer literacy but remain deficient in the acquisition of the pedagogical knowledge required to effectively use technology to facilitate instruction. Whestone & Carr-Chellman (2001) maintained that teachers acknowledged that computers are important in supporting teaching and learning, however, they fail to realize the necessity of implementing technology integration using pedagogy as foundation knowledge.

Also, Pierson (2001) echoed the idea that technology integration involves the utilization of technological skill and pedagogical knowledge to support and facilitate instruction.

The focus of this study is on how emerging technologies, such as mobile technologies, cloud technologies, etc. chosen by the teachers, to play a role in today's class and make technology integration a proven reality. Two fundamental questions under study were: Have teachers mastered and consolidated the skills in these emerging technologies in a manner that creates confident in a manner that helps them to use in the instructional setting? Are teachers able to integrate emerging technologies into teaching and learning using pedagogical principles as a base for making appropriate and suitable selection of technology based on the instructional objectives?

Piaget's definition of effective learning is incremental, from the simple to the complex. While it is neat to make effort to embrace emerging technologies which just cannot exclude social and interactive media, it is vital that teachers master basic technologies that are used for personal and for business. Yet, teachers seem to be less confident in using them and teaching students how to use them. As succulently stated by Gunter & Baumbach (2004), technology integration "requires a good foundation in computer literacy, information literacy and integration literacy…" (p.194). Koc & Bakir (2010) maintained that the availability of technology in the classroom does not ultimately suggest that technology integration is being implemented; the authors believed that teachers need training. It appears that teachers need training not only on more sophisticated type of technology but also on the basic literacy skills because teachers need a thorough understanding of the processes of pedagogy to guide technology integration.

*Pedagogy & Emerging Technologies*

Emerging technologies such as mobile and cloud technologies, or Internet technology in an conglomerate term have become a great tool for teaching and learning. But are teachers able to use these resources to truly enrich their teaching materials or to use different technologies to transform their classroom into virtual authentic classroom? Proper use of the emerging technologies will allow teachers to explore the world as a learning community and to create awareness of current issues in a global scale. A good teacher is required to keep abreast of news and information as they emerge to educate his/her students on the new developments on the disciplines of interest, including emerging research knowledge. Part of the effort to integrate technology into instruction is to be able consolidate the technology skills that have been acquired and being able to infuse it into teaching and learning using pedagogy as well as the ability to enrich classroom instruction using the internet. While there is an increase in the use of computer and the World Wide Web (WWW) for assignment, record keeping and assignments; "less than 10 percent of teachers reported using computers or the internet to access model lesson plans or to access research and best practices (US Department of Education, Office of educational Research and Improvement, 2000, p.1). The findings of a study carried out by Limayem & Hirt (2000) revealed that teachers in their study tend to introduce technology to learners and leave "students to their own devices," the authors claim that this "will not be sufficient" (p. 7). This further illustrates that some teachers may not have the ability to use digital resources readily at hands to enrich teaching and learning in a way that is profitable to be teachers and students. Although, technology has been introduced into education for decades now, yet as Koc (2005) pointed out that " majority of teachers do not feel well prepared to integrate technology into their teaching" (p. 3). The observation of Vannatta & Beyerbach (2000) in Koc (2005) delineated the problematic nature of technology integration among teachers by stating "that technology integration must be connected to course content, objectives and assignments, and addressed much earlier in the teacher education programs" (p. 12). Unfortunately, most technology professional development programs do not adequately address the importance of pedagogical principles in technology integration training. Therefore, the problem of this study is that teachers' understanding of the importance of using pedagogical knowledge as foundation for using emerging technologies to support instruction remains unclear; such uncertainty does not inspire confidence among teachers. Internet resources can improve teaching and expand learning materials, nevertheless, teachers have shown less enthusiasm to use internet resources properly to enrich instruction as well as provide opportunity to engage in exploratory learning with their student. The following research questions were developed to guide this study:

1. What percentage of teachers believes that they consider the use of pedagogical theories as a foundation for selecting technologies to support instruction?

2. Are there any differences among teachers based on years of teaching experience in their perceived ability to use pedagogical knowledge as a base for using emerging technologies to support instruction?

## The Study

The purpose of this study was to investigate teachers' perceptions toward the relationships between pedagogical use of emerging technologies and classroom technology infusion. Understanding the relationship between learning theory and technology was considered important because educational practices are rationalized based on proven learning principles and processes. The goal is to provide data to technology trainers and specialists to help them develop appropriate professional training materials and address teachers' needs during technology profession training in a way that connects pedagogical knowledge and technology. The idea was to identify participants' weaknesses and address those weaknesses during professional development training. Quite often, most technology professional training is carried out without addressing specific needs of the trainees.

*Methodology*

In this study, a self-reported questionnaire was used to gather data from the accessible population for the study was approximately 353 full- and part-time nursing teachers in a Taiwanese Nursing Institute during the 2012-2013 academic year. The faculty taught primarily undergraduate classes and possessed necessary knowledge and skills in seven (7) specialized areas in nursing practices: Fundamental Nursing, Clinical Medicine, Internal Medicine/Surgery, Intensive Care, Public Health/Palliative Care, Psychiatrics, and Obstetrics, Gynecology & Pediatrics. The researchers used a convenient sampling technique to select the subjects for the study. In the end, 313 teachers participated in this study. As seen in Table 1, the participants varied in their age, gender, positions, as well as their experience of using computers for instruction. The questionnaire was validated by professors with expertise in pedagogy and technology integration. The internal consistency of the instrument was established using Cronbach's alpha and it stood $r = 85$, $p. \leq .05$. The primary purpose of the 5-point Likert scale questionnaire administered to the participants was to assess participants' understanding of the use of pedagogical principles as a base to implement technology integration including assessing teachers' use of the emerging technologies to expand instructional materials. Data for research questionnaire was collected using a 5-point Likert scale namely, "SA" for strongly agree (5-point scale), "A" for agree (4-point scale, "N" for neutral (3-point scale), " D" for disagree (2-point scale) and "SD" for strongly disagree (1-point scale). Percentages, means and standard deviation were employed to analyze teachers' responses. Correlational statistics were used to seek if relationship existed among teachers in their responses to questionnaire items based on their demographic, independent variables of gender, age, years of teaching experience salary and type of school where teachers taught.

## Findings

| Demographic Variables | Frequencies | Percentages |
|---|---|---|
| **Gender** | | |
| Male | 91 | 29% |
| Female | 221 | 71% |
| **Age** | | |
| 20-25 years | 36 | 12% |
| 26-30 years | 6 | 2% |
| 31-35 years | 40 | 13% |
| 36-40 years | 53 | 17% |
| 40-45 years | 33 | 11% |
| 46-50 years | 38 | 12% |
| 51-55 years | 52 | 17% |
| 56 and above | 55 | 18% |
| **Experience** | | |
| 5 years or less | 109 | 35% |
| 6-10 years | 52 | 17% |
| 11-15 years | 44 | 14% |
| 16-20 years | 29 | 9% |
| 21-26 years | 35 | 11% |
| 27 years and above | 44 | 14% |

**Table 1**: Distribution of Teachers by Demographic Variables and Percentages

Research Question #1: What percentages of teachers believe that they consider the use of pedagogical theories as a foundation for selecting technologies to support instruction?

Frequencies and percentages for each scale were calculated to determine the distribution of teachers for each Likert rating scale as shown in Table 2 below. In questionnaire item #1, 56 or 18% of the participants strongly agreed that they use learning theories as a foundation for selecting technology for instruction; 133 or 42% agreed with this statement. However, the results showed that 83 or 27% were not sure (undecided) regarding whether or not they consider learning theories as they make instructional decision for their students. Also, 31 or 10% teachers disagreed and 10 or 3% strongly disagreed with the statement in research questionnaire #1. In questionnaire item #10, only 88 or 28% of the respondents strongly agreed, whereas 155 or 50% agreed that they use technology for teaching in a manner that could be used to solve real problem; 49 or 16% remained undecided, 15 or 5% disagreed with the statement contained in questionnaire #10. Moreover, 87 or 28% of the participants strongly agreed with the statement #11 in the questionnaire, while 136 or 46% of the faulty members agreed, 55 or 18% undecided, 27 or 9% disagreed and 8 or 3% strongly disagreed.

| Questionnaire Items | SA | | A | | N | | D | | SD | |
|---|---|---|---|---|---|---|---|---|---|---|
| | f | % | f | % | f | % | f | % | f | % |
| Q1: I use learning theories as a base for applying technology into instruction. | 56 | 18 | 133 | 42 | 83 | 27 | 31 | 10 | 10 | 3 |
| Q2: I consider lesson objectives when I select technologies for instruction. | 107 | 34 | 159 | 51 | 23 | 7 | 18 | 6 | 6 | 2 |
| Q3: I do not consider instructional methods as I select technology to support instruction. | 4 | 1 | 18 | 6 | 36 | 12 | 143 | 46 | 112 | 36 |
| Q4: I do not consider learning styles when I choose technology for instruction. | 2 | 1 | 18 | 6 | 26 | 8 | 141 | 45 | 126 | 40 |
| Q5: I consider students' pace of learning when I select technology to support instruction | 99 | 32 | 165 | 53 | 30 | 10 | 12 | 4 | 7 | 2 |
| Q6: I consider methods of evaluation when I choose technology to support instruction. | 98 | 31 | 148 | 47 | 41 | 13 | 18 | 6 | 8 | 3 |
| Q7: When I select follow-up activities, I do not consider the type of technology to match the follow-up activities. | 10 | 3 | 17 | 5 | 48 | 15 | 150 | 48 | 88 | 28 |
| Q8: I consider students' developmental stage when I select technology for instruction | 105 | 34 | 11 | 4 | 32 | 10 | 11 | 4 | 154 | 49 |
| Q9: When I choose software for instruction, I do not consider if it is user friendly | 10 | 3 | 19 | 6 | 41 | 13 | 120 | 38 | 123 | 39 |
| Q10: As I plan for instruction, I consider how the technological skills taught will be used to solve real life problems. | 88 | 28 | 155 | 50 | 49 | 16 | 15 | 5 | 6 | 2 |
| Q11: As I teacher, I use technology as a tool for teaching problem-solving skills. | 87 | 28 | 136 | 43 | 55 | 18 | 27 | 9 | 8 | 3 |

*F= frequencies*

**Table 2:** Frequencies & percentages of teachers' perceptions of the use of pedagogical theories as a foundation for selecting technologies to support instruction

Research Question #2: Do differences exist among teachers based on years of teaching experience in their perceived ability to use pedagogical knowledge as a base for using emerging technologies to support instruction?

Out of the 11 questionnaire items, statistical significant differences were found to exist among the respondents in four of the questionnaire items based on the teachers' years of teaching experience. In questionnaire item #1, *I use learning theories as a base for applying technology into instruction* (Table 3), significant differences were found among teachers, $F(10, 303) = 3.119$, $p < .01$. Further tests were conducted using Tukey HSD and the results showed that teachers who had between five years or less years of experience (M = 4.22), including those teachers who had between six and 10 years (M = 4.25) and those teachers with 11-15 years of teaching experience (M = 4.30) as well as those with 21-26 years *agreed* with statement contained in questionnaire item #1. However, teachers with 27 years teaching experience and above were *undecided* (not sure) (M = 3.70) regarding questionnaire item #1. In questionnaire item #4, the result of the ANOVA tests revealed that significant differences existed among teachers with different years of experience, $F(10, 303) = 4.650$ $p < .01$. Post Hoc tests were used to locate where the differences were found and the findings indicated that teachers who had five years or less experience, six to 10 years of experience and 21 to 26 years of experience were *undecided* (not sure) (M = 3.67) with the statement: *I do not consider learning styles when I choose technology for instruction.* But teachers with 27 years and above *agreed* (mean score 4.65).

In questionnaire #6, the result of ANOVA showed a significant differences among those participants involved in this study, F(10, 303) = 3.615, p< .01. Teachers with five years of teaching experience or less (M = 4.17); teachers who had experience 6-10 years of experience (M = 4.20); teacher with 11-5 years of teaching experience (M = 4.14) *agreed* with the statement recorded in questionnaire #6 but teachers with 21-26 of experience and 27 and above were *undecided* concerning the statement in questionnaire item #6.

There were statistical significant differences in teachers responses to research questionnaire item #10 (Table 6), F(10, 303) = 4.151, p. < .001. The result of the Tukey HSD tests indicated that teachers who had worked for five years or less including those teachers with 6-10 years of experience, 11-15 years of experience and those teachers with16-20 were *agreed* (M = 4.13) that as they *plan for instruction, they consider how the technological skills taught will be used to solve real life problems.* But teachers with 27 years of experience and above were undecided (M = 3.75) regarding questionnaire item #10.

| Questionnaire Items (Dependent Variables) | Groups | Sum of Squares | df | Mean Squares | F | Sig. |
|---|---|---|---|---|---|---|
| Questionnaire Item #1: I use learning theories as a base for applying technology into instruction. | Between Groups Within Groups Total | 13.101 250.343 263.444 | 10 303 313 | 2.620 .840 | 3.119 | .009 |
| Questionnaire Item #4: I do not consider learning styles when I choose technology for instruction | Between Groups Within Groups Total | 11.461 166.736 178.197 | 10 303 313 | 2.292 .560 | 4.650 | .001 |
| Questionnaire Item #6 I consider methods of evaluation when I choose technology to support instruction. | Between Groups Within Groups Total | 13.427 222.101 235.528 | 10 303 313 | 2.685 .743 | 3.615 | 003 |
| Questionnaire Item #10 As I plan for instruction, I consider how the technological skills taught will be used to solve real life problems. | Between Groups Within Groups Total | 13.716 198.271 211.987 | 10 303 313 | 2.743 .662 | 4.151 | 001 |

**Table 3:** ANOVA results of teachers' pedagogical knowledge as a base for using emerging technologies to support instruction based on teachers' years of teaching experience

## Discussion

The results of the study revealed that many of the teachers who took part in this study believed in using learning theories as a foundation for selection technology for instruction as demonstrated in Table 2. Nevertheless, a substantial number of teachers were not sure that they used learning theories to inform their selection of basic software technology for instruction. Also a reasonable proportion of teachers acknowledged that they did not consider learning principles as the based for applying software applications into instruction. The findings revealed that the use of basic software applications to support instruction still remains problematic. In research questionnaire item #1, only 18% recorded strongly agree response while 28% agreed with the statement in questionnaire item #1. Twenty-seven percent of the participants were unsure; 31 or 10% of the teachers disagreed. When the number of teachers who were not sure about their practice in using learning theories as a base for selecting emerging technologies to facilitate instruction and those teachers who acknowledged that they did not consider learning theories, it became apparent that teachers in the school system needed help in implementing basic technology integration. This could represent one of the problems with technology integration because some teachers do not consider learning theories which could provide them with the rationality for choosing and using technology to support teaching and learning. Selecting technology for instruction arbitrarily or in a vacuum would definitely hinder technology integration.

This finding mirrors the result of a study carried out by Mouza (2011) who argued that teachers did not possess pedagogical content knowledge to implement technology integration. Littrell, Zagumny, and Zagumny (2005) pointed out that teachers still lacked the skill to use technology to promote teaching and learning in a meaningful way. Koehler & Mishra (2009) maintained that the heart of good technology integration lie with the recognition of the relationship between technology and pedagogy. Unfortunately, a sizeable proportion of the teachers who were involved in the resent research did not seem to recognize such relationship.

## References

Gunter, G., & Baumbach, D. (2004). Curriculum integration. In A. Kovalchick & K. Dawson (Eds.),Education and technology: An encyclopedia. Santa Barbara, CA : ABC-CLIO, Inc.

Hasselbring, T., Barro, L. & Risko, V. (2000). Literature review: Technology to support teacher development. Presented at the National Partnership for Excellence and Accountability in teaching (NPEAT). Retrieved February 05, 2012, from http://www.aacte.org/Programs/Research/EdTechPrep.htm

Honey, M. & Moeller, B. (1990). Teachers' beliefs and technology integration: Different values, different understanding. New York: Center for Technology in Education.

Koc, M. & Bakir, N. (2010). A needs assessment survey to investigate pre-service teachers' knowledge, experiences and perceptions about preparation to using educational technologies. Turkish Online Journal of Educational Technology – TOJET, 9(1), 13-22. Retrieved from www.csa.com.

Koc, M. (2005). Implications of learning theories for effective technology integration and pre-service teacher training: A critical literature review. Journal of Turkish Science Education, Volume 1, Issue 1, May

Koehler, M. J. & Mishra, P (2008). Introducing TPACK in AACTE Committee on innovation and technology (eds.) Handbook of technological pedagogical content knowledge for educators (pp. 3-29). New York: Rutledge.

Koehler, M. J. & Mishra, P. (2009). What is technological pedagogical content knowledge. Contemporary Issues in Technology and Teacher Education, 9(1), 60-70.

Limayem, M. & Hirt, G.S. G. (2000). Internet-based teaching: How to encourage university students to adopt advanced inter-based technology. Proceedings of the 33$^{rd}$ Hawaii International Conference on system science.

Littrell, A. B., Zagumny, M. J., & Zagumny, L. L. (2005). Contextual and Psychological predictors of instructional technology use in rural classrooms. Educational Research Quarterly, 29(2), 37.

Mouza, C. (2011). Promoting Urban Teachers' Understanding of Technology, Content, and Pedagogy in the Context of Case Development. Journal of Research On Technology In Education, 44(1), 1-29.

Pierson, M. E. (2001). Technology integration practice as a function of pedagogical expertise. Journal of Research on Computing in Education, 33(4), 413-430.

Shulman, L. (1986) Those who understand: Knowledge growth in teaching. Educational researcher, 15(2), 4-14.

US Department of Education (2000).Teacher Use of Computers and internet in public schools. National Center for Education Statistics, Office of the Educational Research and Improvement.

Vannatta, R. A., & Beyerbach, B> (2000). Facilitating a constructivists' vision of technology integration among education faculty and pre-service teachers. Journal of Research in Computing in Education, 33, 132-148.

Whestone, L. & Carr-Chellman (2001). Preparing pre-service teachers to use technology: Survey results. Tech Trends, 45(4), 11-17.

# 2 Mathematical Content, Pedagogy, and Technology: What It Can Mean to Practicing Teachers

Beth Bos & Kathryn S. Lee, Texas State University, USA

## Introduction

Technology has a natural drawing power for today's youth. It stimulates their interest, curiosity, and creativity. To harness this energy and direct it towards learning mathematics teachers embrace information computer technology (ICT) as a formative power. Teachers need experiences in using technology to go deeper into the mathematics, to direct student interest toward exploring mathematics to problem-solve, reason and prove, strengthen communication and transform a student's view of mathematics. The following study takes a longitudinal look at the results of a professional development program focused on elementary teachers and their development of a deeper understanding of mathematics through the use of technology and the design of instructionally sound mathematics lessons.

## Literature Review

According to the TIMSS 2011 International Results in Mathematics American schoolchildren continue to lag behind major global competitors in mathematics exams (Mullis, Martin, Foy, & Arora, 2012). Despite U.S. progress on some of those tests, students in Singapore, South Korea, Japan and Finland, among others nations, outperformed U.S. fourth- and eighth-grade students on the 2011 TIMSS. The nation's fourth-graders made some progress on the mathematics exam since it was last given in 2007, but U.S. scores on the other exams were statistically unchanged. Asian students have long dominated the math and science exams, dating as far back as 1995, and the current results show they not only earned higher scores, but also a larger number of them performed at the highest levels. In fourth-grade math, for example, 43% of students in Singapore scored "advanced," compared with 13% of their U.S. counterparts. In eighth-grade math, 47% of Korean students scored at the top level as compared to 7% of U.S. students (Mullis, Martin, & Arora, 2012).

The lack of preparation and interest in mathematics has major consequences in higher education. Only about one-third of bachelor's degrees earned in the United States are in a science, technology, engineering or mathematics (STEM) field, compared with approximately 53% of first university degrees earned in China and 63% of those earned in Japan. More than one-half of the science and engineering graduate students in U.S. universities are from outside the United States (National Science Board, 2012).

Two meta-analyses on computer technologies in mathematics education showed encouraging results and credit part of their success to pragmatic constructivist teaching approaches (i.e., problem-based, inquiry-oriented and situated cognition) and suggest that appropriately designed computer technologies can play a role in supporting and encouraging students as they learn (Hattie, 2009; Li & Ma, 2010). Project Tomorrow, a nonprofit education organization, evaluated use of mobile phones with internet access in a program during the 2009-2010 school year and found that not only did mathematics scores increase, but teachers changed their manner of instruction and students were more engaged than before (Project Tomorrow, 2012). Technology can bring together the NCTM's process standards, or best practices, with the use of today's engaging technologies.

In a recent study it was found that high achievement in mathematics was associated with (a) high levels of mathematics confidence, (b) strongly positive levels of affective engagement and behavioral engagement, (c) high confidence in using technology, and (d) a strongly positive attitude to learning mathematics with technology. Low levels of mathematics achievement were associated with (a) low levels of mathematics confidence, (b) strongly negative levels of affective engagement and behavioral engagement, (c) low confidence in using technology, and (d) a negative attitude to learning mathematics with technology (Barkatsas, Kasimatis, & Vasilis Gialamas, 2009). In some cases, the use of virtual manipulatives in mathematics has been shown to increase student understanding despite their achievements levels. There are multiple affordances within each virtual manipulative application (applet), as noticed in another study using virtual manipulatives, and one or more of these affordances may be more influential and beneficial for one achievement group while another affordance (within the same virtual manipulative applet) may be more influential and beneficial for another achievement group (Moyer-Packenham & Suh, 2012).

"Integration of technology is more about the pedagogy of good instruction and less about knowledge of how the technology works" (Earl, 2002, p. 8). We know that adequate *pedagogical integration* of digital technologies is a critical factor for instructional success. Technology will not reach its potential in maximizing teaching and learning without pedagogical integration (Conlon & Simpson, 2003; Cuban, Kirkpatrick, & Peck, 2001; Niess, 2007). Additionally, in order to pedagogically integrate a technology, teachers must first perceive and understand the affordances of the specific technology and then relate the affordances to their instructional goals during lesson planning (Angeli & Valanides, 2009). The challenge for mathematics teachers is to leverage technology affordances of digital tools in their classroom. Leveraging begins with *cognitively* integrating these affordances with teachers' knowledge of specific mathematical tasks and instructional guidance. Technology affordances that teachers construct or activate are important for planning the use of technology in class within a problem-based instructional learning model. Problem-based instruction creates an atmosphere for reasoning and critical thinking and teamed with technology can be very powerful (Donnelly, 2010).

## Conceptual Model

TPACK, a conceptual model used to help teachers understand the relationship between technology, pedagogy and content (mathematical) knowledge, assists in holistically viewing the relationships involved in integrating technology into learning and instruction (Mishra and Koehler, 2006).

Many researchers, beginning with Koehler and Mishra (2005), advocate that one way to learn about the complexities of teaching with technology is to engage in the design process (Koehler, et al., 2011). As Koehler et al. (2011) explain, "through the design process, learners must constantly work at the nexus of content (what to teach), pedagogy (how to teach it), and technology (using what tools)" (p. 151).

## Theoretical Framework

In the past few decades, a constructivist discourse has emerged as a powerful model for explaining how knowledge is produced in the world, as well as how students learn. For constructivists like Kincheloe (2000) and Thayer-Bacon (1999), knowledge about the world does not simply exist out there, waiting to be discovered, but is rather constructed by human beings in their interaction with the world. "The angle from which an entity is seen, the values of the researcher that shape the questions he or she asks about it, and what the researcher considers important are all factors in the *construction* of knowledge about the phenomenon in question" (Kincheloe, 2000, p. 342). Thayer-Bacon (1999) invokes a quilting bee metaphor to highlight the fact that people are socially and culturally embedded, rather than isolated individuals constructing knowledge. To assert that knowledge is constructed, rather than discovered, implies that it is neither independent of human knowing nor value free. Indeed, constructivists believe that what is deemed knowledge is always informed by a particular perspective and shaped by various implicit value judgments (Gordon, 2009).

According to Windschitl (1999), constructivism is based on the assertion that learners actively create, interpret, and reorganize knowledge in individual ways. "These fluid intellectual transformations," he maintains, "occur when students reconcile formal instructional experiences with their existing knowledge, with the cultural and social contexts in which ideas occur, and with a host of other influences that serve to mediate understanding" (p.752).

## Methods

A quasi-experimental design was used for the modified TPACK Survey by Schmidt, Baran, Thompson, Koehler, Shin, and Mishra (2009), and a qualitative method, Lyublinskaya and Tournaki's (2011) TPACK Levels Rubric, was used to assess use of technology as found in the teachers' lesson plans. The samples were carefully selected to represent kindergarten through sixth grade teachers who had at least three years of teaching experience and had students classified as *at-risk* of dropping out of school as determined by Texas Education Agency (TEA) criteria (Public Education Information Management System [PEIMS], 2011-2012). By design the study represented a wide range of elementary teachers (age, nationality, type of school environments) who all taught at-risk students. The study addressed the following research questions:

1) What effects are noticed about teachers' attitude toward the use of technological, pedagogical, and content (mathematical) knowledge and the integration of technology before, directly following participation in a mathematics content class enhanced with technology, and a year after the courses were completed?

    H1: Teachers' attitude toward the integration of technology using TPACK will improve over the period of treatment and will be maintained over an extended period of time.

2) What effects emerged in comparing teachers' lesson plans over a series of three semesters using Lyublinskaya and Tournaki's (2011) TPACK Levels Rubric?
H2: Lesson plans will show advancement in the TPACK Levels and improved use of best practices.

## Participants

The population studied included 45 practicing teachers enrolled in a professional development program with an emphasis on elementary mathematics. The teachers ranged in age from 22 to 60 years old and taught in five different school districts having at least 50% or more at-risk students as identified by TEA. The cohort's ethnicity was 3% Asian, 10% Black, 27% Hispanic, and 60% White; and gender 7% male, 93% female. Teachers taught in urban, suburban and rural areas of Central Texas.

## Treatment

The study's focus centered on three semesters where number theory, geometry, and probability and statistics were taught using various forms of computer related technology. Students were taught about mathematical fidelity and analyzed elementary applets for both mathematical and pedagogical fidelity (Bos, 2011). Did the application appear to be procedural or did it increase their awareness of the patterning and logic involved? Did the application only serve as motivational or did it engage the participant as learners and doers of the mathematics through exploring rich word problems? Was it used to replace pencil and paper tasks or was it used to get students to think and reflect on past mathematical knowledge structures? Is the application related to a mathematical concept and does the action on the object make sense of the mathematics? After the application was examined teachers were asked to find applications they could use in their classroom to strengthen the teaching of mathematics. This proved to be more difficult than they thought and participants came to the conclusion that using technology effectively in teaching mathematics was more difficult than they realized.

Instructional time was spent on posing questions with more than one right method to solve. The interaction centered on participants' dialogue as they rationalized their thinking, often arguing over strategies and solutions. The instructor did not offer solutions and instead posed more questions to be considered. Beyond rich problems based on mathematical content the teachers worked in cooperative groups to develop rich problems and tasks for their students. Participants in the course operated in assigned groups to arrive at what their students would perceive as a relevant problem. Participants would encapsulate their problem into one driving question related to their students' environment to be resolved through a multi-disciplined approach. With the driving question at the center, participants brainstormed the various cognitive avenues students might take and the information their students would need to solve the problem. A wiki was used as a platform for the participants to collaborate on lesson plans and use as a presentation tool for their instructional unit that included their driving question, concept map, project calendar, lesson plans, assessment, and resources as illustrated at www.ci5303.pbworks.com.

Over the course of the second semester on geometry, GeoGebra, graphing calculators, Google Sketch Up, and Patty Paper were used to explore basic constructions, transformations, rotations, dilations, and three dimensional shape manipulations. The teachers explored Van Hiele's (1999) stages of development (visualization, analysis, informal deduction, deduction, rigor) in terms of understanding where students are and how to move them to the deduction stage or possibly the rigor stage, the highest level of thought. Problem-based units were to be designed with a geometry theme around a real life problem. Units ranged from designing quilts and miniature golf courses to planning an eco-safe playground.

In the third semester the Guidelines for Assessment and Instruction in Statistics Education (GAISE) Report: A Pre-K-12 Curriculum Framework guided probability and statistics instruction (Franklin et al., 2007). The teachers learned to help their students develop an understanding of data, number relationships, probability, and graphs with **TinkerPlots® Dynamic Data™ Exploration** software. **TinkerPlots** is designed for students to learn from visual representations of data, and its drag-and-drop interface makes it easy to learn. The teachers planned lessons from measuring climate change to designing a successful school carnival. At the end of the semester, the teachers presented their instructional units and peer-evaluated their units using the International Society for Technology in Education's (2008) National Educational Technology Standards for Teachers (NETS-T) as a guide.

## Data Sources

The TPACK Survey by Schmidt, Baran, Thompson, Koehler, Shin, and Mishra (2009) was used to obtain data. The self-reported survey was designed for pre-service teachers and has been used by both pre-service and in-service teachers. Though the survey claims to determine technology knowledge, pedagogical knowledge, and content knowledge, because the data is self-reported the researchers have used it as indicating participant attitude toward the indicators. In the original test all core subject areas are represented. Because our focus was only on mathematical knowledge content the other subject areas' content were omitted. The TPACK Survey was administered during the teachers' first semester of the program, their last semester of the 36-hour mathematics specialist program, and one year after completion of the program.

Lyublinskaya and Tournaki's (2011) TPACK Levels Rubric was developed based on the TPACK framework for technology integration in the classroom where teachers progress through five progressive levels in each of four components of TPACK as identified by Niess, van Zee, & Gillow-Wilese (2010). The developers organized the rubric as a matrix where each cell represented a specific TPACK level (one of the four components of TPACK). Thus, each row of the rubric represented a specific component of TPACK and each column of the rubric represented a specific level of TPACK. For each cell of the matrix Lyublinskaya and Tournaki developed two specific performance indicators that were consistent with qualitative descriptors developed by Niess, van Zee, & Gillow-Wilese (2010) and the principles for a practical application of technology developed by Dick and Burrill (2009). The relationship between TPACK components and the TPACK levels rubric is highlighted in Table 1.

**Table 1.** TPACK Components and TPACK Levels Rubric

| TPACK Components | Component Descriptor | TPACK Levels Rubric |
|---|---|---|
| Technology knowledge (TK) | Understanding of technology tools | |
| Content knowledge (CK) | What is known about a specific subject (mathematics) – Number Concepts, Geometry, Probability and Statistics? | |
| Technological content knowledge (TCK) | What is known about the affordances to represent or enhance content? | |
| Pedagogical knowledge (PK) | Teaching methods and processes. (i.e. problem-based, inquiry-oriented, concept attainment, and situated cognition) | Knowledge of instructional strategies and representations for teaching and learning subject matter topics with technologies |
| Pedagogical content knowledge (PCK) | Pedagogy specific to a particular subject area. | Knowledge of curriculum and curricular materials that integrate technology in learning and teaching mathematics; |
| Technology pedagogical knowledge (TPK) | Understanding how technology supports particular teaching approach | An overarching conception about the purposes for incorporating technology in teaching subject matter topics. |
| Technology Pedagogical Content Knowledge | | Knowledge of students' understandings, thinking, and learning in subject matter topics with technology |

The purpose of the TPACK Levels Rubric is to assess teachers' TPACK level based on qualitative data collected from teachers, such as lesson plans. The instrument is not intended for direct data collection. The following scoring procedure is applied when using the rubric. The possible range of scores for each component is 0 – 5, where the component score can be an integer (both performance indicators are met) or half-integer (one out of two performance indicators are met). The score is assigned for each component independently.

The TPACK Levels Rubric, used in this study for evaluating lesson plans, was tested for reliability and validity. Content validity was addressed by employing two TPACK experts. The experts were both researchers who were involved in the initial development of the TPACK conceptual framework for mathematics educators. They reviewed the rubric and provided written comments in response to three specific free-response questions about the rubric. The developers revised some of the rubric's items according to the experts' comments. In order to test for inter-rater reliability, two different experts in the field used the revised rubric to score the 45 documents (13 lesson plans with supplemental TI-Nspire documents, 13 narratives of lesson presentations during professional development, and 19 narratives of classroom teaching observations). Each expert was provided with specific instructions and explanations on using the rubric. Both experts found the rubric to be easy to use with all artifacts provided to them for scoring. The range of correlations between the scores of the two experts on the same components was from $r = 0.613$ to $r = 0.679$ $p < .01$. Correlations that examined whether there was a relationship among the four components of the rubric for each expert were also found statistically significant, i.e., the range of correlations for Expert 1 was from $r = .85$ to $r = .94$ $p <.01$ and for Expert 2 was from $r = .93$ to $.97$ $p <.01$. The significant correlations between the four components of TPACK could mean that teachers move to a higher TPACK level only after they achieve the previous level on all components (Lyublinksaya & Tournaki, 2011). The rubric was modified to work with Web 2.0 and other computer related technologies as stated in this paper.

## Results

To measure attitude about knowledge in the TPACK domains the researcher administered the TPACK survey (Schmidt, et al., 2009) three times by way of a web-based survey once at the beginning of the program (pretest), at the end of the program (posttest), and a year after the program ended (posttest 2).

**Table 2.** Paired *t*-test

|  | Pre | | Post | | Post2 | | ANOVA for Pre Post | | |
|---|---|---|---|---|---|---|---|---|---|
| Categories | M | SD | M | SD | M | SD | t | df | d |
| TK | 3.67 | .73 | 4.00 | .72 | 3.91 | .81 | 2.91* | 89 | .41 |
| MK | 3.57 | .72 | 4.10 | .69 | 4.22 | .67 | 3.46* | 44 | .73 |
| PK | 3.99 | .95 | 4.61 | .49 | 4.60 | .54 | 5.65** | 89 | .82 |
| PCK | 3.80 | .61 | 4.63 | .61 | 4.47 | .50 | 2.71* | 29 | 1.36 |
| TPK | 3.68 | .68 | 4.22 | .52 | 4.35 | .59 | 3.21* | 59 | .90 |
| TPCK | 3.70 | .84 | 4.24 | .80 | 4.24 | .80 | 5.47** | 41 | .66 |

TK =Technology Knowledge, MK = Mathematical Knowledge, PK = Pedagogical Knowledge, PCK = Pedagogical Content Knowledge, TPK = Technology Pedagogical Knowledge, Technology Pedagogical Content Knowledge.
* Significant at $p < .01$,     ** Significant at $p <.001$

As shown in Table 2, results of matched-pairs *t*-test yield a statistically significant improvement in all knowledge areas of the matched-pairs t-test for technological pedagogical content (mathematical) knowledge and TPACK domains. A year after the program ended, the participants were surveyed for a third time (Post2 data). The results were very similar to the Post Test data used to calculate the ANOVA *t* value.

## TPACK Levels Rubric

A qualitative analysis of 155 lesson plans written by the teachers in the program was conducted with four coders rating the use of technology using Lyublinskaya and Tournaki's TPACK Levels Rubric (2011). The results showed teacher growth in the use of technology (TPACK) over the three-semester sequence (mean first semester .98, second semester 2.25, and third semester 3.74 out of a total of 5). An ANOVA was conducted yielding an F score of 21.41 and a $p < .001$.

According to the modified Lyublinskaya and Tournaki's rubric (2011) during the first semester technology was used for motivation, rather than actual subject matter development. This would be considered the *Recognizing Level*. Technology was not used for inquiry tasks. During the first semester of the professional development program in-service teachers were taught about technology in terms of mathematical and pedagogical fidelity and the role of technology as a tool to develop concepts. Class assignments included critiquing the interactive activities found at the National Library of Virtual Manipulatives, Mathplayground, and National Council of Teachers of Mathematics' Illuminations. These first semester students were hesitant to try concept related technology and were under no pressure to add technology to their lesson, opting out for using it to motivate students. During the second semester the technology activities included inquiry tasks; the teachers focused on students' thinking while students were using technology on their own (*Adapting Level*). During this level technology was used as a replacement for non-technology based tasks with traditional representations and was used for learning new knowledge by students. In their lesson plans, the teachers focused on students' thinking of mathematics and other multidisciplinary topics including science, while students themselves were using technology–both for learning new knowledge and reviewing prior knowledge. In the third semester of the professional development program curriculum, the larger part of technology use was by students to explore and experiment with the technology for new knowledge and for practice (*Exploring Level*). The teacher served as a guide for student learning focusing on students' mathematics and conceptual understanding. Technology activities were built around learning objects that explicitly promote student reflection – especially the posing of questions for sense making. In this same semester inservice teachers reviewed the teaching of statistics, practicing with *Tinkerplots* and graphing calculators with their cohorts in the program. In their subsequent lesson plans, the teachers had the students use technology to explore and experiment to gain new knowledge by making connections through doing inquiry activities. The third semester coding indicated that the inservice teachers advanced to the beginning of the Exploring Level. The inter-rater reliability was 85% using four raters – two practicing teachers and two Associate Professors.

## Data Analysis

After the internal consistency and reliability were checked on the TPACK survey a paired $t$-test was run using SPSS and the results were examined. The post-test experienced increases that lead to the use of a ANOVA to determine the $t$ score to assess whether the means of two groups were **statistically** different from each other and $d$ score, the effect size, were noteworthy. In using the TPACK Levels Rubric to determine the level of advancement in integrating TPACK into lesson plans an ANOVA was used. All indicators showed statistical significance.

The results of the study address the research questions. The first research question was "What effects are noticed about teachers' attitude toward the use of technological, pedagogical, and mathematical knowledge and the integration of technology before, directly following participation in a mathematics content class enhanced with technology, and a year after the class was completed?" The results show improvement in teacher's attitude toward technology knowledge, mathematical knowledge, pedagogical knowledge, pedagogical content knowledge, technological content knowledge, and technological pedagogical content (mathematical) knowledge even a year after the completion of the MMT program. The significant $t$ scores and effect sizes indicate improvement. The design of the TPACK model is to have all the contributing parts (TK, MK, PK, PCK, TPK) lead to an improvement in TPCK. The significant gains indicate a transformation of positive attitudes toward the use of TPACK rejecting the null hypothesis allowing us to accept hypothesis one. Teachers' attitude toward the integration of technology using TPACK improved through the use of the treatment and this growth appeared to be consistent to the survey responses a year after the program's completion.

The second research question asked, "What effects emerged in comparing the lesson plans over a series of three semesters using Lyublinskaya and Tournaki's (2011) TPACK Levels Rubric?" The lesson plan rubric results confirm that participants progressed in the use of TPACK in their lesson plans and also learned to apply correct pedagogies, including the use of best practices and processes to use technology to enhance learning. Lesson plans were examined and the results indicate advancement from Recognize to the Exploration Stage in use of the TPACK model. Rejecting the null hypothesis, the lesson plans show advancement in the TPACK Levels and show improved use of best practices.

## Limitations

The study is limited by the broad approach taken to describe the integration of technology using the TPACK model. Yet it is because of the broad spectrum of knowledge bases that makes TPACK a universal and powerful framework.

Within the TPACK survey instrument the TCK domains relied on one question to provide evidence of this domains; therefore, the reliability and internal consistency could not be determined creating threats to reliability and internal validity. Since data from the TPACK survey were self-reported the researcher used the results to determine the teacher's attitude about the nature of the TPACK domain. The TPACK Levels Rubric was used to support the overall design of the study and counter threats to reliability and internal validity by providing another indicator of the use of the TPACK domains by the target sample. However the objectivity of raters may have posed a threat to validity due to their own experience and expectations.

The TPACK Levels Rubric showed significant change in the teachers understanding and use of technology, but the ratings also indicate teachers had significant room to improve to the Advance Level. This could be related to the lack of one-to-one technology in the teachers' classrooms.

## Discussion

The research in this study confirmed the findings of Desimone (2011) and Darling-Hammond and McLaughlin (2011) that professional development should be ongoing and intensive. "Professional development needs to be content focused, require active learning, and should be coherent and fit in with other goals within the school environment" (Desimone, 2011, p. 69). "It must be connected to and derived from teachers' work with their students. It must be sustained, ongoing, intensive, and supported by modeling, coaching, and the collective solving of specific problems of practice" (Darling-Hammond & McLaughlin, 2011, p. 82). Teacher professional development is undergoing a paradigmatic shift that suggests the benefits of an intensive and sustained training program similar to the university-school district partnership addressed in this study.

The problem-based approach to studying mathematics set the stage for the teachers' critical thinking. Teachers were required to communicate in their groups, look for connections, and build on each other's thinking. The teachers in the masters program learned that mathematics is messy, noisy, and that persistence and flexibility are essential to mathematical pursuits as they struggled with challenging questions in class. The teachers' problem-based approach to learning that they experienced in the program transferred to their own classes as one teacher reported, "I let my students answer other students' questions now and I watch. I let them know they are capable to think through problems without me interrupting their thought process."

## Conclusion

Evidence supports the belief that technology, pedagogy, and mathematical content can be taught to elementary teachers in ways that (a) support their understanding of students' learning and thinking about mathematical concepts with technology; (b) change their conception of how technology tools and representations support mathematical thinking; (c) provide instructional strategies for developing lessons with technology. Though technology may not be the complete solution to developing student's mathematical understanding, it can change the way teachers teach, provide visual models, and encourage students' active construction of their mathematical understanding. This is accomplished through fostering the use of various representations within mathematics, making connections, communicating cognitive processes, and supporting problem solving and reasoning. Additionally, adequate time is essential to preparing instructional lessons with appropriate pedagogy and based on conceptually and flexible procedural oriented technology.

Experienced teachers have a level of conceptual knowledge and experience that pre-service teachers do not, but, as noted in this study, it took time and more experience with technology tools in mathematically rich environments for them to trust and feel comfortable with the mathematical power of technology. Discussion and constant self-evaluation helped. Developing the instructional strategies for cultivating lessons with technology required modeling and using the technology in their own classrooms before they felt comfortable integrating the technology in their instructional units. The more exploratory the teachers were in their own classrooms the more comfortable they became in relinquishing some control and trusting their students to ask better questions, explore, and make connections through the use of technology. Also of importance is the lasting change to teachers' pedagogy and technology as shown in the results of the administration of the TPACK survey a year after the completion of the program.

# References

Angeli, C., & Valanides, N. (2009). Epistemological and methodological issues for the conceptualization, development, and assessment of ICT-TPCK: Advances in technological pedagogical content knowledge (TPCK). *Computers & Education, 52*(1), 154-168.

Barkatsas, A., Kasimatis, K., & Vasilis Gialamas, V. (2009). Learning secondary mathematics with technology:Exploring the complex interrelationship between students' attitudes, engagement, gender and achievement. *Computers & Education, 52*(3), 562–570. http://dx.doi.org/10.1016/j.compedu.2008.11.001

Bos, B. (2011). Teachers preparation using TPACK when fidelity of treatment is defined. *Contemporary Issues in Technology and Teacher Education, 11*(2), 167-183. AACE. Retrieved February 1, 2014 from http://www.editlib.org/p/33182.

Conlon, T., & Simpson, M. (2003). Silicon Valley versus Silicon Glen: The impact of computers upon teaching and learning: A comparative study. *British Journal of Educational Technology, 34*(2), 137-150.

Cuban, L., Kirkpatrick, H., & Peck, C. (2001). High access and low use of technologies in high school classrooms: Explaining an apparent paradox. *American Educational Research Journal, 38*(4), 813-834.

Darling-Hammond, L., & McLaughlin, M. W. (2011). Policies that support professional development in an era of reform. *Phi Delta Kappan, 92*(6), 81-92.

Desimone, L. M. (2011). A primer on effective professional development. *Phi Delta Kappan, 92*(6), 68-71.

Dick, T., & Burrill, G. (2009). *Technology and teaching and learning mathematics at the secondary level: Implications for teacher preparation and development.* Paper presented at the Annual Meeting of Association of Mathematics Teacher Educators, Orlando FL.

Donnelly, R. (2010). Harmonizing technology with interaction in blended problem-based learning. *Computers & Education, 54*, 350-359.

Earle, R.S. (2002). The integration of instructional technology into public education: Promises and challenges. *ET Magazine, 42*(1), 5-13.

Franklin, C., Kader, G., Mewborn, D., Moreno, J., Peck, R., Perry, M., & Scheaffer, R. (2007). *Guidelines for Assessment and Instruction in Statistics Education (GAISE) Report: A Pre-K-12 Curriculum Framework.* Alexandria, VA: American Statistical Association. Retrieved from http://www.amstat.org/education/gaise/GAISEPreK12_Intro.pdf

Gordon, M. (2009). Toward a pragmatic discourse of constructivism: Reflections on lessons from practice, *Educational Studies, 45*, 39-58.

Hattie, J. (2009). *Visible learning: A synthesis of over 800 meta-analyses relating to achievement.* New York, NY: Routledge.

Hill, C. J., Bloom, H. S., Black, A. R., & Lipsey, M. W. (2007). *Empirical benchmarks for interpreting effect sizes in research.* New York, NY: MDRC.

International Society for Technology in Education. (2008). *National educational technology standards for teachers 2008.* Retrieved from http://www.iste.org/standards/nets-for-teachers/nets-for-teachers-2008

Kincheloe, J. (2000). From positivism to an epistemology of complexity: Grounding rigorous teaching. In J. Kincheloe & D. Weil (Eds.), *Standards and Schooling in the United States, An Encyclopedia, Volume Two,* pp. 325-396. Santa Barbara, CA: ABC-CLIO.

Koehler, M. J. & Mishra, P. (2005). What happens when teachers design educational technology? The development of Technological Pedagogical Content Knowledge. *Journal of Educational Computing Research. 32*(2), 131-152.

Koehler, M. J., Mishra, P., Bouck, E. C., DeSchryver, M., Kereluik, K., Shin, T. S., & Wolf, L. G. (2011). Deep play: developing TPACK for 21st century teachers. *International Journal of Learning Technology, 6*(2), 146-163.

Li, Q., & Ma, X. (2010). A meta-analysis of the effects of computer technology on school students' mathematics learning. Educational Psychology Review. *22*(3), 215-244.

Lyublinksaya, I., & Tournaki, N. (2011). The effects of teacher content authoring on TPACK and on student achievement in algebra: Research on instruction with the TI-Nspire handheld. In R. N. Ronau, C. R. Rakes, & M. L. Niess (Eds.), *Educational technology, teacher knowledge, and classroom impact: A research handbook on frameworks and approaches* (pp. 295-322).Hershey, PA: IGI Global. doi:10.4018/978-1-60960-750-0.ch013

Mishra, P., & Koehler, M. H. (2006). Technological pedagogical content knowledge: A framework for teacher knowledge. *Teachers College Record, 108*(6), 1017-1054.

Moyer-Packenham, P. S., & Suh, J. M., (2012). Learning mathematics with technology: The influence of virtual manipulatives on different achievement groups. *Journal of Computers in Mathematics and Science Teaching, 31*(1), 39-59.

Mullis, I.V.S., Martin, M.O., Foy, P., & Arora, A. (2012). TIMSS 2011 International Results in Mathematics. Chestnut Hill, MA: TIMSS & PIRLS International Study Center, Boston College.

National Council of Teachers of Mathematics. (2013). *Standards overview.* Retrieved from http://www.nctm.org/standards/content.aspx?id=26798

National Research Council. (2001). *Adding it up: Helping children learn mathematics.* Washington, DC: National Academy Press.

National Science Board. (2012). *Preparing the next generation of STEM innovators: Identifying and developing our nation's human capital.* Retrieved from http://www.nsf.gov/nsb

National Science Foundation, National Center for Science and Engineering Statistics. (2013). Women, minorities, and persons with disabilities in Science and Engineering. Retrieved from http://www.nsf.gov/statistics/wmpd/tables.cfm

Neufeld, B., & Roper, D. (2003). *Coaching: A strategy for developing instructional capacity*. Cambridge, MA: Education Matters. Retrieved from http://www.annenberginstitute.org/Products/Coaching.php

Niess, M. (2007). Reflections on the state and trends in research on mathematics teaching and learning: From here to Utopia. In F. Lester (Ed.), *Second handbook of research on mathematics teaching and learning*, (pp. 1293-1311). Greenwich, CT: Information Age Publishing.

Niess M. L., Suharwoto, G., Lee, K., & Sadri, P. (2006). *Guiding inservice mathematics teachers in developing TPCK*. Paper presented at the American Education Research Association Annual Conference, San Francisco, CA.

Niess, M. L., van Zee, E., & Gillow-Wilese, H. (2010-11). Knowledge growth in teaching mathematics/science with spreadsheets: Moving PCK to TPACK through online professional development. *Journal of Digital Learning in Teacher Education, 27*(2), 42-52.

President's Council of Advisors on Science and Technology (2010). *Prepare and inspire: K-12 science, technology, engineering, and math (STEM) education for America's future, Working group report*. U.S. Government: Washington, D. C. Retrieved from http://www.whitehouse.gov/administration/eop/ostp/pcast/docsreports

Project Tomorrow. (2012). *Learning in the 21$^{st}$ Century mobile devices + social media = personalized learning*. Retrieved from http://www.tomorrow.org/speakup/MobileLearningReport2012.html

Public Education Information Management System [PEIMS]. (2011-2012). *EO919 At-Risk-Indicator-Code*. Retrieved from http://ritter.tea.state.tx.us/weds/index.html?e0919

Schmidt, D. A., Baran, E., Thompson, A. D., Mishra, P., Koehler, M. J., & Shin, T. S. (2009).Technological pedagogical content knowledge (TPACK): The development and validation of an assessment instrument for pre-service teachers. Journal of Research on Technology in Education, 42(2), 123-149.

Thayer-Bacon, B. (1999). The thinker versus a quilting bee: Contrasting images. *Educational Foundations, 13,* 47-65.

Van Hiele, P. M. (1999). Developing geometric thinking through activities that begin with play. *Teaching Children Mathematics, 5*(6), 310-16.

Windschitl, M. (1999). The challenges of sustaining a constructivist classroom culture. *Phi Delta Kappan, 80,* (10), 751-755.

# 3 An Investigation of a Pre-Service Elementary Mathematics Teacher's Techno- Pedagogical Content Knowledge within the Context of Teaching Practices

Esra Balgalmış, Erdinç Çakıroğlu Department of Elementary Education Middle East Technical University Turkey, Kathryn Shafer, Department of Mathematical Sciences, Ball State University, USA

## Problem of the Study

Technology plays an ever-increasing role in the lives of elementary school students, dynamic technology-supported instruction presents an opportunity to enhance mathematical reasoning and explore various conjectures of pre-service elementary teachers. Graphing calculators and dynamic software packages, such as Geogebra, Geometer's Sketchpad are vital in raising student awareness, challenging their conceptual understanding and motivating the synthesis of mathematical notions (Hollebrands, 2007, Kaput & Thompson, 1994; Peressini & Knuth, 2005). Construction of mathematical objects, creating models and conducting interactive explorations are available via GeoGebra by dragging objects, tracing points, changing parameters and measuring objects. Pre-service teachers (PSTs) should be challenged to reorganize their subject matter content and how to use educational technology on the development of that subject itself as well as on teaching and learning that subject (Niess, 2005; Koehler & Mishra, 2005). In order to be an effective teacher, pre-service teachers need to know fundamental concepts, knowledge, skills, and attitudes for applying technology in educational settings (NETS•T, 2008, p.1). This perspective suggests that teacher preparation programs must provide numerous experiences to engage the pre-service teacher in investigating, thinking, planning, practicing, and reflecting (Niess, 2005). To respond to this issue, the lead author designed a technology-based field experience based on the (SiTI) model (Hur, Cullen & Brush, 2010). Before participating in the field experience three PSTs had completed a course about how to use dynamic geometry software in mathematics education. This course provided concrete experiences and developed a community of learners (two guidelines of the SiTI model).

## Background

Research shows PSTs' reported pedagogical beliefs are typically not consistent with their instructional practices (Lawless, & Pellegrino, 2007). The question of how PSTs can transform the theoretical knowledge to the practice is a problematic issue in teacher education program (Bobis, 2007). Literature indicates that field experience provide PSTs an authentic contexts for thinking about, designing, implementing, and assessing the impact of integrating technologies in learning mathematics and connecting theory to practice (Wenthworth, Waddoups & Earle, 2004; Niess, 2006; Zeichner, 2008,). Darling-Hammond, (2009) stated that the field experience course supports PST to learn from practice in practice. She claimed that it is impossible to teach how to teach powerfully by asking them (PSTs) to imagine what they have never seen or to suggest they "do the opposite" of what they have observed in the classroom (p. 42).

## The Study

Firstly, Niess, Lee, and Sadri (2007) defined a five level developmental processes for TPACK. In 2009, in the Association of Mathematics Teacher Educators' (AMTE) Technology Committee presented this five level model to illustrate the integration of technology in teaching and learning mathematics. This model published by Niess, Ronau, Shafer, Driskell, Harper, Johnston, Browning, Özgün-Koca and Kersaint (2009) is based on Rogers' (1995) model of the innovation-decision process. This TPACK development model for mathematics teachers can be used in describing and evaluating their TPACK growth (McBroom, 2012).

The five stages in this model are recognizing, accepting, adapting, exploring, and advancing. This model consists of four themes; curriculum and assessment, learning, teaching, and access. As teachers progress along with this model from the level of recognizing, accepting, adapting, exploring, to advancing, TPACK forms and expands for each of the four major themes (Niess et al., 2009). This model can assist in identifying the level of teachers' knowledge related to integrating technology into teaching and in providing insights into knowledge growth (McBroom, 2012). A TPACK level rubric developed by Lyublinskaya and Tournaki (2011) based on this developmental model was used to determine PSTs' TPACK level in the analysis of data collected in this study.

A methodology used to support the development of TPACK is found in the Situated Technology Integration (SiTI) model (Hur, Cullen & Brush, 2010). The SiTI model extends the workshop format of TPACK professional development to include aspects of TPACK that occur within the broader context of the classroom. An emphasis on reaction and beliefs regarding the meaningful implementation of technology is emphasized in the guidelines (italics were added by the researchers).

SiTI Guidelines:
- Provide Concrete Experiences: To assist pre-service teachers in understanding the relationship between theory and practice, various examples and concrete experiences should be provided.
- Promote Reaction: To facilitate knowledge construction, *in-depth and ongoing reaction* should be promoted with assistance from teacher educators.
- Assist in Application: *To help pre-service teachers apply knowledge learned in real situations, opportunities to observe expert teacher's classrooms and chances to utilize knowledge in actual classrooms* should be included.
- Create Communities of Learners: To assist pre-service teachers in examining prior beliefs, sharing new ideas with peers and other educators should be encouraged.
- Develop Technological Pedagogical and Content Knowledge: To successfully integrate technology into their future classes, pre-service teachers should be called on to *develop plans to use their technological knowledge* in a meaningful way in relation to their content and classroom teaching knowledge (p. 167).

In accordance with "promote ongoing reaction" in SiTI guidelines, Shön (1987) proposed the reflective practice to teacher education. In order to assist PSTs in development of TPCK reflection on practice activity is needed.

The main goal of this study was to explain the change in a PSTs' progress at the usage of techno-pedagogical knowledge during their field experiences. With this aim, the research questions guiding the study were the following questions:
1. What are PSTs' TPACK levels in different teaching experiences?
2. Are any changes and adaptations made by PST in their TPACK level development through of the implementation of three technology-based lessons during a field experience?

## The Importance of the Study

This study creates a learning environment in which PST has opportunities to discuss their own real classroom practices and learn by implementing technology-based lesson, and get prepared for their future teaching. The significance of this study arises from the need of teacher development in terms of knowledge of technology used for effective mathematics teaching in Turkey. This study contributes to the limited literature on the TPACK studies in Turkey. While the new elementary mathematics curriculum demands teachers to use educational technology in their teaching, this experience might help them get ready for technology-based teaching environments.

## Method of the Study

In the current study, it is aimed to provide rich and holistic descriptions of the participants' TPACK in mathematics within the context of their field experience teaching episodes through the collection and analysis of qualitative data. In the direction of this aim, the data of evidence of PSTs' improvement in strategies they used to integrate technology in mathematics, ways of dealing with problems, their reactions to this process were gathered through qualitative methods. The design of the study is a case study. Data was collected through four different sources; interviews, observation notes, PST's documents and videotape. This researcher was particularly interested in analyzing the nature of multiple source of information to describe the case.

## Participants and Data Collection

The participants of the study were chosen by purposive sampling method since purposeful sampling strategy in order to reach subjects who will provide rich information about the research question. The aim of the study is investigating the evaluation of PST' technology integration in mathematics education in their field experience instead of generalizing the results to the population. To state in detail, the two interrelated benchmarks are taken into consideration to select the participants as criterion. The first benchmark is PST's prior enrollment into the technology-based geometry course. The second benchmark is PSTs' enrollment into the field experience course. More specifically, the participants of the study should have two courses, which are elective ELE 430 Exploring Geometry with Dynamic Geometry Applications course and ELE 435 School Experience course. The field experience course did not include the three lesson implementations designed in this study. Three of the PSTs agreed to participate in the study.

To collect data, an interview and observation protocol were prepared and provided expert opinion about its usability in this context. A face-to-face semi-structured 8 interview protocols were conducted with each participant individually. Interviews with each PST was conducted both in the department of elementary education and practice school that is natural and familiar to the participants and in the separate room provided by the administrations. Interviews conducted in a conversational method and tape recorded with participants' permission. Researcher asked questions and waited for a clear answer for each question from each participant. When it is necessary, questions were repeated or explained to the interviewee. Additionally during these interviews, PST shared their opinion about how much percent they reach the course objectives, what kind of behaviors that they want to improve to use dynamic geometry program effectively and an explanation about their future teaching plan via dynamic geometry. The duration of the semi-structured interviews were 30 minutes.

Participants were interviewed before each teaching sessions to have information about their expectation about the lesson implementation. In the interview the PSTs shared information about the each step of the technology based activity; starting, middle, closing, extension (optional) and assessment. They explained teaching procedure, which mathematical concept they would teach via technology, what kind of pedagogical (inquiry) questions they were planning to ask in the lesson. They shared their plan about how they would support students' mathematical understanding and their expectations related to students reactions to the technological activity. Finally, the PSTs gave technical information about the technological activity. Participants were interviewed after each teaching sessions to have information about their self-evaluation about the lesson implementation. PST shared their opinion about the implementation of technological activity whether it is implemented as it planned. They explained teaching procedure includes the actions and questions that they asked during the class. They evaluated students' performance. They were asked to give information about their satisfaction about their teaching, handling with drawbacks, classroom and time management. Since interviewees may reflect their selective perceptions (Patton, 2002) in the interview, this data should be supported with another data sources.

In addition to interviews, observation method was used to collect data. The aim of the observations was to make an interpretation about change in PSTs' TPACK. Therefore, conducting observations beside the interview seem crucial in means of going deep into the setting, activities and practices PSTs engaged in. The observation protocol allowed a detailed description of the classroom behavior. It addressed how PSTs engage students in a technology-based activity. The observation protocol helped the researcher focus on the particular behavior of the PSTs. How professionally PSTs implemented their lesson plan. When and how PSTs used GeoGebra activity in the lesson? How PSTs guided students to use technology? What did PSTs actually do during the second and third lesson implementation different than previous implementations? Is there any observed evidence of change in their TPACK throughout the study. After preparing the observation protocol, the expert opinion was taken, experienced in qualitative study and TPACK, to ensure peer review.

In addition to main data sources PSTs' lesson plans, reaction paper prepared for ELE 435 and ELE 420 courses and students' reaction papers related to PSTs' implemented lesson were reviewed in the study. First additional data source was lesson plan. PSTs were required to prepare lesson plans for each technology based lesson implementation. Each PST developed three lesson plans based on national curricula in different mathematics topics. It was required from PSTs to prepare three detailed lesson plans with an technology based activity to teach a particular mathematics topic provided by the classroom teacher. Secondly, reaction paper prepared by PST was used. PSTs were required to write reaction papers for ELE 435 and ELE 420 courses based on their experiences in teaching practice. Although this study was not a part of these courses if participants wrote their perceptions about their implementation in the scope of this study, these papers were used as an additional data sources. Third additional data source was student reaction paper.

## Data Analysis

The data were analyzed through the qualitative methods. The main data sources of this study were; interview transcribes, videotaped lesson implementations, observation notes and documents (lesson plan, reflection papers). In order to answer first research question, what are PSTs TPACK levels in three different teaching implementations? The development in PSTs' performance were evaluated with the help of observation notes, video records and interviews. The TPACK levels rubric developed by Lyublinskaya and Tournaki (2011) was used to determine PSTs' TPACK level. This rubric includes five levels in Niess et al. (2009) to rate PSTs' usage of technology in teaching mathematics. These levels are recognizing, accepting, adapting, exploring and advancing. Recognizing level of TPACK is the first and lowest level to use educational technology in teaching, while advancing level of TPACK is the fifth and highest level. Following Lyublinskaya and Tournaki (2011) rubric items for each level, the researcher utilized the behavior of the PSTs and classified these units into predetermined categories. For instance, dynamic geometry program provides PSTs a spectrum of teaching tools that let them model, demonstrate, hide which mathematical concepts they want to teach. An important feature of dynamic geometry program is modeling real-life problems. Real-life problems are presented in a mathematical context to help students apply math to everyday practices. The researcher checked whether students be given opportunities to search for the solution of the problem from various data sources. The second research question of the study was to what extent do PSTs develop their TPACK through of the implementation of three technology-based lessons in a field experience? In order to answer this research question, the change in PSTs' performance was assessed via observation notes, video records and interviews. First of all, each lesson implementation was described via descriptive field notes and video records, then each implementation was evaluated via reflective filed notes based on the TPACK Levels rubric (Lyublinskaya & Tournaki, 2011). Then the associate professor, collaborated in the assignment of categories previously, reviewed the evaluation of PSTs for each implementation and validated the PSTs' performance level based on the TPACK levels rubric (Lyublinskaya & Tournaki, 2011) proposed by the researcher.

## Validity of the TPACK Levels Rubric

To analyse data TPACK levels rubric was used. The rubric was tested for reliability and validity (Lyublinskaya & Tournaki, 2011). Content validity was ensured by employing two TPACK experts; both researchers who were involved in the initial development of the TPACK conceptual framework for mathematics educators. The range of correlations between the scores of two experts on the same components was from $r = 0.613$ to $r = 0.679$ $p < .01$. Correlations that examined whether there was a relationship among the four components of the rubric for each expert were also found statistically significant, i.e., the range of correlations for Expert 1 was from $r = .85$ to $r = .94$ $p < .01$ and for Expert 2 was from $r = .93$ to $.97$ $p < .01$.

In the present study, TPACK levels rubric was used to assess PSTs' performance in technology-based lesson implementations. In order to complete inter-rater reliability of the lesson implementations researcher asked a rater, who is experts in the content, pedagogy and technology of the lessons implementations and fluent in Turkish, to watch the video-records and lesson descriptions and rate the rubric. Before rating process, researcher explained how to use the rubric to rate the lesson implementation and then they discussed the meaning of each criterion. Some of the example artifacts were rated and discussed to agree on criteria of the rubric. She rated each lesson implementations based on the four component of TPACK independently. Then, the pearson product-moment correlation coefficient was calculated to determine the degree of consistency between independent raters. An acceptable level of reliability using a Pearson correlation is .70 (Multon, 2010). The Pearson correlation calculated for the present study was $r(34) = .73, p < .01$. There is a 73 % consistency between researcher and rater's scores.

# Results

Since there is a space prohibition, this paper reports results from for one of the three PSTs (Pelin, pseudonym) studied. Pelin implemented three lessons with sixth and eighth grade students at a public elementary school in Ankara. Pelin's teaching showed evidence of change in terms of technology usage levels from the first implementation to the third based on the TPACK Levels Rubric. In her implementations, Pelin chose objectives aligned with the national curricula and employed educational technology as a teaching tool to address mathematics topics in field experience course. These three lesson implementations showed that she has the basic technological, pedagogical and content knowledge to design technology-based activities, and implement in elementary school. Pelin didn't construct any technology-based activity, which required advance technical skills, to create. This might be because of the she has limited technical knowledge to create these activities via technology. In addition, it was possible to implement her all three activities without educational technology via physical manipulatives.

Since Pelin used educational technology with different aims in her three lessons. Brief information was give for each lesson. The combination of technology, pedagogy and content was in basic level in the first lesson. In the first lesson, the usage of educational technology was not very crucial. Technology was not used to teach a specific mathematics concept. The purpose of using educational technology in teaching was only drill and practice. This was a teacher-directed lesson. The nature of the activity wasn't available to ask inquiry questions. The technology-based activity used in the lesson was limited to transfer mathematical content to students via technology. Nevertheless, the technology-based activity was required technical skills to construct via spreadsheets. Pelin constructed this activity by herself. Therefore, Pelin's has technical knowledge to construct a spreadsheet activity. When it is compared with the first lesson the usage of educational technology was very crucial in the second lesson. The technology-based activities used by Pelin in the lessons were fit with the lesson objectives. Although the technology-based activity didn't require advance technical skills to construct, they were applicable to have students reach the lesson objectives.

In the second lesson the combination of technology, pedagogy and content was more professional than previous lesson. She combined technology; pedagogy and content knowledge to create technology based teaching activities in a way that led students to a deeper and conceptual understanding of mathematics topics. It was a student center lesson. She posed questions to have students' sense with mathematical concepts linked with GeoGebra representations. Students were actively engaged into the class discussions. Students explored triangle inequalities and angle-side relationships via GeoGebra program. To reach the general overview, students shared their ideas about the relationship between these geometrical concepts and tested their conjectures via GeoGebra. After the explorations, students constructed a mathematical conjecture and they were appeared to develop conceptual understanding about these geometrical rules. The selection of technology-based activities to teach mathematics topics was fit with the content in the second implementation. Pelin didn't construct the technology-based activity, which requires advance technical skills to construct by herself for this lesson. Even if Pelin didn't construct the technology-based activity, her combination of technology, pedagogy and content was professional. The way to teach this topic via technology was successful. Pelin used dynamic nature of the GeoGebra program to have students discover geometric meaning of algebraic identities in the third lesson. The selection of technology-based activities to teach this mathematics topic was fit with the content. Her teaching showed evidence that she has basic pedagogical knowledge to transfer mathematical content via GeoGebra technology to the students.

The evidence in the Pelin case showed that through the implementation of three technology-based lessons in a genuine classroom context PSTs made changes to their technology based teaching and TPACK levels over the course of the three lessons in accordance with the TPACK levels rubric developed by Lyublinskaya and Tournaki (2011). The aim of the technology-based activity is an important factor in determining the role of the teacher and the type of the questions that the teacher needs to ask in a technology based lesson.

At the end of the three technology-based lesson, PSTs were interviewed about their general opinion about using technology in teaching. In the next sections, detailed information of the participants gathered from last interviews was reported. According to Pelin's opinion educational technology is a tool for teacher to help students make abstract mathematical concepts concrete in their mind. She stated that educational technology provides active participation of students into the class discussion. However, possible technical problems in educational technology cause time consuming. Therefore teachers should take precautions for unexpected situations while designing a technology-based lesson.

In her opinion, in this technology age teaching methods should be mixed with educational technology. She reported that, the technology-based courses in teacher training program, specifically ELE 430 contributed her knowledge to use educational technology in teaching mathematics effectively. After that, technology-based teaching experience helped her to notice her potential to use educational technology in teaching. She believes that from the first implementation to the third there was a progress in her performance. However, she didn't fell ready to teach mathematics via technology in her future teaching. There were two reasons for this idea. First of all, she needs more technology-based courses, which includes technical skills and teaching methods related to effectively usage of educational technology in teaching. She advises teacher-training programs to include more technology-based courses. Secondly, using educational technology in teaching hasn't been very common in our education system, yet. According to her observations in collaborative schools, teacher never use educational technology in their teaching. Students have no idea about dynamic geometry programs, as well. For her second implementation at the beginning of the lesson she spent time to give information about GeoGebra menu. Therefore she had a concerns related to usage of educational technology in her future teaching. To implement technology-based lessons she expects from her future school to include technological equipment, technology user teachers and students. In the interview she stated that, the more she implement technology-based lesson, the more she used educational technology effectively. The following section includes excerpt from reflection papers of Pelin. In one of the assignments of ELE 435 course, Pelin reflected on her experiences in this study. One of the questions of that assignment required PSTs to write their opinions about the most educative experience for them. Although this study was not a part of the ELE 435 course In her reaction paper prepared for ELE 430 course Pelin describe her implementations as most educative experiences for her.

## Discussion

The first overarching goal of this qualitative case study was to investigate the possible changes and adaptations in PST's TPACK in field experience course. To reach this goal, multiple sources of data interviews, observations and documents were used. To participate in this study primarily criterion was enrolment of ELE 435 course, to select participants familiar with the educational technology. The focus of ELE 435 course was modeling an effective usage of dynamic geometry program in mathematics education to set the context and purpose for technology usage.

Situated Technology Integration (SiTI) guidelines (Hur, Cullen & Brush, 2010) explain the role of teacher educator in field experience course to support the development of TPACK with novice teachers, provided a framework for the study. To be aligned with the SiTI guidelines, first of all, researcher utilized the SiTI guidelines and provided opportunities for PSTs to have concrete experiences with educational technology in real classroom context.

Zeincher (2008), claimed that teaching practices help PSTs develop the professional vision and skills in this process. Mouza and Wong (2009) also claimed that teachers learn from their practice in their TPACK-based case development strategy. In parallel study, Hixon and So (2009) stated that technology-based lesson implementations are critically important to develop PSTs' TPACK, since the construction of technology-based activity and practiced it in real classroom context gave chance PSTs to pilot their ability. In the teaching activities PSTs assessed the appropriateness of their lesson design in classroom use and noticed the basic requirement for teaching mathematics via technology (Hixon & So, 2009; Zeincher, 2010). During these technology-based teaching experiences processes PSTs were observed and videotaped by researcher. To challenge PSTs about their teaching experience reflection-in-action processes was applied.

The implementation of technology-based lessons in real classroom context has resulted in substantial change in PSTs' TPACK levels. The all three cases showed evidence of change in terms of technology usage levels from the first implementation to the third based on the TPACK Levels Rubric (reference your dissertation here). The first common theme that emerges from the analysis is that through the use of technology in their teaching and reflection-in-action process, PSTs' TPACK level was increased from the first implementation to the third. Case Pelin also supported this claim, since she exhibited substantial change in the success of technology-based lesson implementation throughout the study. While in the first implementation the purpose of using educational technology in teaching was only drill and practice, in the third lesson the purpose of using educational technology in teaching was to have students discover geometric meaning of algebraic identities via exploration. She posed questions to have students' sense with mathematical concepts linked with GeoGebra representations. Students were actively engaged into the class discussions.

## References

Bobis, J. (2007). Empowered to teach: A practice-based model of teacher education. In J. Watson & K. Beswick (Eds.), *Proceedings of the 30th Annual Conference of the Mathematics: Essential Research, Essential Practice* (Volume 1, pp. 61-70). Austrelasia: MERGA.

Darling-Hammond, L. (2010). Teacher education and the American future. *Journal of Teacher Education, 61*(1-2), 35-47.

Hixon, E., & So, H.-J. (2009). Technology's role in field experiences for preservice teacher training. *Educational Technology & Society, 12* (4), 294–304.

Hollebrands, K. F. (2007). The role of a dynamic software program for geometry in the strategies high school mathematics students employ. *Journal for Research in Mathematics Education, 38*(2), 164-192.

Hur, J. W., Cullen, T., & Brush, T. (2010). Teaching for application: A model for assisting pre-service teachers with technology integration. *Journal of Technology and Teacher Education, 18*(1), 161-182.

Kaput J. J., & Thompson, P. W. (1994). Technology in mathematics education research: The first 25 years in the JRME. *Journal for Research in Mathematics Education, 25*(6), 676-684.

Koehler, M. J., & Mishra, P. (2005). Teachers learning technology by design. *Journal of Computing in Teacher Education, 21*(3), 94-102.

Lawless, K. A., & Pellegrino, J. W. (2007). Professional development in integrating technology into teaching and learning: Knowns, unknowns, and ways to pursue better questions and answers. *Review of Educational Research, 77*(4), 575-614.

Lyublinskaya, I., Tournaki, E. (2011) The Effects of Teacher Content Authoring on TPACK and on Student Achievement in Algebra: Research on Instruction with the TI-Nspire Handheld. In R. Ronau, C. Rakes, & M. Niess (Eds.), *Educational Technology, Teacher Knowledge, and Classroom Impact: A Research Handbook on Frameworks and Approaches.* (pp. 295-322) Hershey, PA: IGI Global.

Multon, K. D. (2010). Interrater reliability. N. J. Salkind (Eds.), *Encyclopedia of Research Design* (pp.627-29). Thousand Oaks, CA: SAGE Publications.

McBroom, E. S. (2012). *Teaching with dynamic geometry software: A multiple case study of teachers' technological pedagogical content knowledge.* (Unpublished Doctoral Dissertation). Texas State University, Department of Mathematics, San Marcos, USA.

National Educational Technology Standards for Teachers (NETS.T). (2008). *ISTE national educational technology standards for teachers.* Retrieved on Jun, 2012 from http://cnets.iste.org/teachers/t_stands.html.

Niess, M. L. (2005). Preparing teachers to teach science and mathematics with technology: Developing a technology pedagogical content knowledge. *Teaching and Teacher Education, 21* (5), 509-523.

Niess, M. L. (2006). Guest Editorial: Preparing teachers to teach mathematics with technology. Contemporary Issues in Technology and Teacher Education, 6(2), 195-203.

Niess, M. L., Lee, K., & Sadri, P. (2007). *Dynamic spreadsheets as learning technology tools: Developing teachers' technology pedagogical content knowledge (TPCK).* Paper presented at the annual conference of American Education Research Association (AERA), Chicago, IL.

Niess, M. L. , Ronau, R. N., Shafer, K. G., Driskell, S. O., Harper, S. R., Johnston, C., Browning, C., Ozgun-Koca, S. A., & Kersaint, G. (2009). Mathematics teacher TPACK standards and development model. *Contemporary Issues in Technology and Teacher Education,* [Online serial], 9(1).

Peressini, D., & Knuth, E. (2005). The role of technology in representing mathematical problem situations and concepts. In W. J. Masalski & P. C. Elliott (Eds.), *Technology-Supported Mathematics Learning Environments, Sixty-Seventh Yearbook.* (pp. 277-290). Reston, VA: NCTM.

Rogers, E. M. (1995). Diffusion of innovations. New York, Free Press.

Schön, D. A. (1983). *The reflective practitioner: Professionals in action.* New York: Basic Books Inc. Publishers.

Thompson, D., & Kersaint, G. (2002). Editorial: Continuing the dialogue on technology and mathematics teacher education. *Contemporary Issues in Technology and Teacher Education, 2*(2), 136-143.

Wenthworth, N., Connell, M. L., & Earle, R., (2004). Technology integration into a teacher education program. In. N.,Wenthworth, R., Earle & M. L., Connell (Eds.), Integrating information technology into the teacher education curriculum: Process and products of change (pp.1-14). USA: The Haworth Press, Inc.

Zeichner, K. (2008). Where should teachers be taught? Settings and roles in teacher education. In M., Cochran-Smith, S., Feiman-Nemser, D. J., McIntyre & K., Demers (Eds.), *Handbook of research on teacher education: enduring questions in changing contexts (pp. 259-388).* New York: Routledge & ATE.

# 4 Adapting Teaching/Learning Strategies for the Multigenerational Online Classroom
Darlene Baker & Angela Schmidt, Arkansas State University, USA

## Introduction

Adapting teaching/learning strategies appropriate for the multigenerational classroom is a challenge for educators (Billings & Kowalski, 2004). The pedagogy found in the online classroom shifts the focus from the traditional teacher-centered learning approach to a student-centered learning approach (Hallis, 2008, O'Neill & McMahon, 2005). Four generations of students who could be present in the graduate online classroom are identified and described. However unlikely, a Traditionalists could be attending graduate school, but primarily Baby Boomers, Generation Xers, and the Millennials will make up the culture of the online classroom. Several articles have been written on educating the multigenerational student in the workforce. Limited research is available that explores the multigenerational student in online classes. Literature reveals that each generation has its own set of values, ideas, beliefs, expectations, ethics, and culture. Educators must understand these differences in order to better understand the learning needs of the students to provide various teaching/learning strategies to promote optimal student outcomes. This paper will briefly discuss the differences found among the four generations, address the learning needs of the four generations, and present examples of generation appropriate teaching/learning strategies in the online classroom (Garcia & Qin, 2007; Johnson & Romanello, 2005; Smucny, 2010, Notarianni, et al (2009).

## Growth of the Multigenerational Graduate Student Population

Multiple factors have contributed to the increase in the multigenerational students learning together in graduate higher education. These include:
- Delay in education due to the high cost of a college degree, raising or starting a family
- People are living longer due to advances in healthcare, greater access to healthcare information and services, and also an increase in life expectancy
- Online education availability
- Increased number of graduate students
- Economic downturn which has led to unemployment and an uncertain economic climate
- Pursuing a second degree to make a career change

(Johnson & Romanello, 2005; Saucny, 2012; McCraw & Martindale, 2012).

## Student-Centered Learning

The pedagogy found in the online classroom shifts the focus from a traditional teacher-centered learning approach to a student-centered learning approach. The student-centered approach is effective in online learning by having technology based learning activities, cooperative learning such as using small group discussion, the pursuit of theory based knowledge through problem solving, critical thinking, and research (Hallis, 2008; O'Neill & McMahon, 2005). **Table 1** provides information on teacher-centered vs student-centered learning.

| Teacher-centered Learning "What do I want to teach?"* | Student-centered Learning "What do students need to know?"* |
|---|---|
| Power with the teacher | Power with the student |
| Passive student learning | Active student learning |
| Low level of student choice | High level of student choice |

| | |
|---|---|
| Teacher is lecturer | Teacher is facilitator of learning |
| Promotes recall, memorization, and repetition | Promotes understanding |
| Passively receives information from the lecturer | Responsible and accountable for learning |
| Teacher controls content and delivery | Student-centered control of content with guidance from the teacher |
| Communication is teacher to student | Communication emphasis teacher/student, student/student interaction |
| | Increased sense of autonomy |
| | Mutual respect between student and teacher |
| Assessment is quantitative | Assessment is qualitative and quantitative |

**Table 1 Teacher-centered Learning vs Student-centered Learning**

(*Candela et al, 2006; ONeill & McMahon, 2005; Hallas, 2008; Ferris, 2009; Wright, 2011; Schell & Janicki, 2012; Kee & Kwak, 2013)

In order to maximize student-centered learning, educators need to develop student learning outcomes that align with program outcomes; select appropriate assessment measures, both formative and summative, to accomplish the student learning outcomes; then adapt teaching/learning strategies appropriate to meet the student learning outcomes (Candela, et al, 2006). Assessment results are then utilized to improve online student learning and re-evaluate the effectiveness of the teaching/learning strategies (Hallis, 2008). According to McDonald (2014), assessment is vital to obtain valid and reliable information concerning student achievement.

**Generations Defined**

According to Strauss and Howe (2012), generations are a group of people moving through time with similar values, ideas, beliefs, expectations, ethics, and culture. Each time period has key historic events that shape the attitudes and values based on similar life experiences during critical developmental years (Marconi, 2012; Hannay & Fretwell, nd).

Four generations of students could be present in the online graduate classroom. However unlikely, a Traditionalist could be attending graduate school, but primarily Baby Boomers, Generation Xers, and Millennials. Each generation will be briefly described. **Table 2** provides an overview of the defining events, core values, and famous people of the four generations of learners.

| | Famous People | Defining Events | Core Values |
|---|---|---|---|
| **Traditionalists** (1925-1945) (Silent, Veterans) | Mick Jagger Tina Turner Dick Cheney Teddy Kennedy Elvis Presley Elizabeth Taylor | Pearl Harbor Korean War Great Depression Women's right to vote Prohibition New Deal Technology of the era—radio | Adheres to rules Loyalty Hard work Faith in institutions Respect authority Duty before fun |
| **Baby Boomers** (1946-1964) (Me generation) | Bill Clinton Hillary Clinton Jay Leno | Vietnam Civil rights Kent State | Want to make a difference Spend now, worry later Competitive |

| | Prince Charles<br>Steven Spielberg<br>Laura Bush<br>George W. Bush<br>Oprah Winfrey | Assassinations of JFK, RFK, MLK<br>Walk on moon<br>Sexual revolution<br><br>Technology of the era—television | Optimistic<br>Equal opportunities<br>Equal rights<br>Personal gratification |
|---|---|---|---|
| **Generation Xers**<br>(1965-1980)<br>(Gen X, Generation X) | Michael Jordan<br>George Clooney<br>Brad Pitt<br>Julia Roberts<br>Tom Cruise<br>Lance Armstrong<br>Venus Williams<br>Barak Obama<br>Bill Gates | Challenger disaster<br>Fall of Berlin Wall<br>Chernobyl<br>Watergate<br>Corporate downsizing<br>Iran hostage situation<br>Gulf war<br>Roe vs Wade passed<br><br>Technology of the era—personal computer | Balance<br>Diversity<br>Entrepreneurial<br>Fun<br>Independent<br>Resourceful<br>Suspicious of Boomer values<br>Techno literacy |
| **Millennials**<br>(1981-2000)<br>(Net Generation, Gen Y) | Mary Kate and Ashley Olsen<br>Mark Zuckerberg<br>Prince Williams<br>Prince Harry<br>LeBron James<br>Serena Williams<br>Chelsea Clinton | Columbine<br>9/11<br>Rodney King riots<br>Oklahoma city<br>Virtual classrooms<br>Desert Storm<br><br>Technology of the era—internet | Extreme fun<br>Realistic<br>Loyal<br>Civic duty<br>Optimistic<br>Highly tolerant<br>Like personal attention<br>Techno savvy<br>Multitaskers |

**Table 2 Characteristics of Four Generations of Learners**
Table complied from: (McCready, 2012; Johnson & Romanello, 2005; Smucny, 2010; Billings & Kowalsk, 2004; Marconi, 2012; and Gibson, 2009).

**Traditionalist**

The Traditionalists are also known as the Silent or Veteran generation. Born between 1925 and 1945, this generation grew up during the Great Depression and World War II. The Traditionalists have been described as unimaginative, unadventurous, cautious, and withdrawn (Johnson & Romanello, 2005). This generation adapts and accepts easily rather than rebels. The Traditionalists are hard workers, have respect for authority, are highly loyal and highly disciplined. To this generation, education was just a dream (Gibson, 2009; McCraw & Martindale, 2012). Key historic events include Pearl Harbor, Korean War, Prohibition, and women's right to vote. The technology of the era included the radio, 78 rpm records, dial telephones, and party lines. Some of the most recognizable people of this generation include Mick Jagger, Teddy Kennedy, and Elvis Presley (McCready, 2012; Johnson & Romanello, 2005; Smucny, 2010; Billings & Kowalsk, 2004; and Marconi, 2012 and Gibson, 2009).

**Baby Boomers**

The Baby Boomers are also known as the me generation. Born between 1946 and 1964, the Baby Boomer was born post World War II. This generation is a large population moving through history that needed to revise their parent's generation. However, they grew up respecting their Traditionalist parent's values (Bishop, 2009). Baby Boomers are motivated, competitive, optimistic, and have a great work ethic. To the Baby Boomers, education is a birthright and was highly encouraged by their parents. Key historic events include the Civil Right movement, the assassination of John F. Kennedy, Robert F. Kennedy, and Martin Luther King, and the walk on the moon. Technology of the era included the transistor radio, television, mainframe computers, 33 and 45 rpm records, and touch-tone phones (McCraw & Martindale, 2012; Smucny, 2010).

Some of the most recognizable people of this generation include Bill and Hillary Clinton, Prince Charles, George and Laura Bush, and Oprah Winfrey (McCready, 2012; Johnson & Romanello, 2005; Smucny, 2010; Billings & Kowalsk, 2004; and Marconi, 2012 and Gibson, 2009).

**Generation Xers**

Generation Xers are also known as Gen X, and Generation X. Born between 1965 and 1980, this generation is primarily offsprings of Baby Boomers. Generation Xers were born amidst divorce, living in single parent homes and became known as latch-key kids. This generation became independent, resourceful, self-reliant, and suspicious of Baby Boomer values. Generation Xers view education as something to be endured to acquire a job and financial security. Key historic events include the Challenger disaster, fall of the Berlin Wall, Watergate, Gulf War, and Roe vs Wade. Generation Xers grew up playing video games and using personal computers (Gibson, 2009). Technology of the era included compact disc, personal computers, and email (McCraw & Martindale). Some of the most recognizable people of this generation include Michael Jordan, Lance Armstrong, Barak Obama, and Bill Gates (McCready, 2012; Johnson & Romanello, 2005; Smucny, 2010; Billings & Kowalsk, 2004; and Marconi, 2012 and Gibson, 2009).

**Millennials**

Millennials are also known as the Net Generation and Gen Y. Born between 1981 and 2000, the Millennials were raised by older Baby Boomers and Generation Xers who were termed helicopter parents with structured time and activities. Many Millennials are from blended families, raised by parents who embraced safety, family, and doing the right thing. This generation feels very close to their parents. The Millennials are multitaskers, positive, assertive, civic minded, and moral. Millennials accept authority, are rule followers, and are comfortable with a culturally diverse world (Gibson, 2009). Historic events include Columbine, 9/11. Oklahoma City bombing, and Desert Storm. The Millennials are comfortable with technology and focus on work/life balance. This generation grew up with computers, the internet, and a world of information readily available 24/7 (Johnson & Romanello, 2005). Technology of the era included MP3 players, cell phones, PDAs and the internet. Some of the most recognizable people of this generation include Mark Zuckerberg, Prince William, LeBron James, and Chelsea Clinton (McCready, 2012; Johnson & Romanello, 2005; Smucny, 2010; Billings & Kowalsk, 2004; and Marconi, 2012 and Gibson, 2009).

**Learning Needs of the Four Generations**

According to the literature, the differences found among the four generations influence learning (Billings & Kowalski, 2004). **Table 3** provides an overview of differences as evidenced by approaches to learning, and learning preferences/activities.

| | **Approaches to Learning** | **Learning Preferences/Activities** |
|---|---|---|
| **Traditionalists** (1925-1945) (Silent, Veterans) | "Tell me what to do"* | Task oriented<br>Adaptable<br>Conforms<br>Face to Face contact<br>Detailed instruction<br>Memorization<br>Sequential learning<br>Tell them you appreciate their experiences |
| **Baby Boomers** (1946-1964) (Me generation) | "Show me what to do"*<br>"Want to know exactly what they need to do to make a certain grade"** | Good communication skills<br>Great work ethic<br>Comes prepared for class<br>On time |

| | | Motivation to succeed<br>Conscientious and willing to accept help<br>Experiential learning<br>Clear guidelines<br>Learn through lectures and note taking<br>Detailed handouts<br>Very concerned with grades<br>Enjoy positive reinforcement for their efforts<br>Responds well to feedback<br>Communicate they are valued and needed |
|---|---|---|
| **Generation Xers**<br>(1965-1980)<br>(Gen X, Generation X) | "Why do I need to learn this?"*<br>"Education must be endured, a means to an end (job and financial stability)"** | Results driven<br>Want things presented in straightforward manner<br>Want to learn information in easiest and quickest way—Distance Learning a must<br>Only want to learn what will benefit them directly—study guides and test reviews before the test<br>Reasonable to allow leisure time priority over schoolwork<br>Want points attached to their assignments<br>Enjoy flexible learning times<br>Self-directed learner<br>Need feedback frequently and be specific<br>Learn best by solving problems |
| **Millennials**<br>(1981-2000)<br>(Net Generation, Gen Y) | "Connect me to what I need"* | Open to new ideas<br>At ease with group activities<br>May have difficulty with individualized thinking<br>Demand immediate feedback<br>Experiential activities<br>Learn immediately from their mistakes<br>Active learners<br>Simulation<br>Creative activities<br>Collaborative testing<br>Want extensive orientation<br>Want immediate feedback<br>Voice clear expectations<br>Provide structure<br>Provide respect |

**Table 3 Learning Needs of the Four Generations**
Table complied from (McCready, 2012; **Johnson & Romanello, 2005; *Smucny, 2010; Billings & Kowalsk, 2004; and Marconi, 2012; Gibson, 2009; Billings, Skiba, & Connors, 2005).

**Traditionalist**

The Traditionalist prefers face-to-face interaction, well written notes and instruction. The focus for this generation is on memorization. This generation is task oriented and adaptable. It is important for the educator to let them know their life experiences are appreciated. The Traditionalist also may lack self-confidence (Marconi, 2009).

## Baby Boomers

The Baby Boomers would prefer to have organized lectures and take notes face-to-face rather than have self-learning modules on the web. This generation prefers detailed handouts. Baby Boomers may struggle with computers, however they will accept help. This generation is grade conscious and want to know exactly what it takes to make a certain grade (Johnson & Romanello, 2005). Baby Boomers are willing learners and are committed to life-long learning. The educator needs to be aware that Baby Boomers are motivated by learning, learn best when life experiences can be tied to subject matter, enjoy positive reinforcement for their efforts, and respond well to feedback (Johnson & Romanello, 2005; Marconi, 2012; Notarianna, et al, 2009).

## Generation Xers

Generation Xers are result driven. This generation wants information presented straight forward and in the easiest and quickest way possible. Learning is best done independently, on their own time and on their own terms. Time is precious and leisure time is as important as time spent on academics. The Generation Xers learn quickly and efficiently and learn best by solving problems. The educator needs to know that this generation wants detailed study guides and detailed test review before the test. The Generation Xers only want to learn what will benefit them directly. They want points attached to assignments or the assignment is not important enough to do. They also want instant results and frequent and specific feedback. Generation Xers see class assignments as something necessary to obtain a degree (Johnson & Romanello, 2005; Marconi, 2012; Notarianna, et al, 2009).

## Millennials

Millennials learn much differently than previous generations. This generation is computer savvy and prefers to gather information from the internet. Millennials are goal oriented and have a strong sense of identity. They are multitaskers who demand immediate feedback and get frustrated if they do not get it quickly. This generation needs lots of praise. The Millennials are used to getting ribbons and trophies for first, second, third, and fourth places. The educator needs to know that Millennials like group activities, games, collaborative testing, and simulations. New technology should be used whenever possible. They learn immediately from their mistakes. Millennials are creative, innovative, and like interactive exercises (Marconi, 2012; Johnson & Romanello, 2005; Johanson, 2012; Gibson, 2009; Notarianna, et al, 2009).

## Similarities

Although there are differences among the generations, important similarities do exist that are beneficial to the online educator. These include a need for communication and feedback, a need to be included and heard, a need for social interaction, the need for effective technology, and quality from the teacher. Some teaching/learning strategies that capitalize on these similarities include: (1) promoting an active and collaborative learning environment, (2) developing strategies to create a personal connection with the students, and (3) effectively facilitating online learning (Billings & Kowalski, 2004; McCraw & Martindale, 2012; Schell & Janicki, 2012; Hannay & Fretwell, nd).

## Teaching/Learning Strategies that Capitalize on Similarities

The educator assumes learners are motivated, self-directed individuals. However, educators also realize that students differ in motivation, ways of learning, personal development, life experiences, and performance. Educators with a student-centered focus recognize that each learner is a unique individual and a variety of teaching/learning experiences must be provided to help each student reach their full potential (Candela, et al, 2006; Billings, Skiba, & Connors, 2005).

**Active and Collaborative Learning Environment**

- Group work
- Group discussion
- Interacting with course content
- Peer assessment
- Case studies
- Poster sessions
- Podcast
- You Tube and Facebook

**Student-Faculty Interaction**

- Introduction exercise
- E-mail
- Discussion boards
- Chat rooms
- Blogs
- Wikis
- Online office
- Student led discussions

**Facilitating Online Learning**

- Develop expert computer skills
- Timely feedback, feedback, feedback
- Challenge the student at every opportunity
- Use a variety of effective technology

(Revere & Kovach, 2011; Cantrell, O'Leary, & Ward, 2008; Gibson 2011; Parker & Wasset, 2010)

**Conclusion**

Educators should never stereotype or make assumptions about students based on generational age. The literature reports that exposure to technology may be more important than age in terms of teaching and learning (Smuncy, 2010; McCraw & Martindale, 2012) Other variables may affect online learning as well including the learning style of the student, study habits, cultural differences, geographic area, and socioeconomic status. It is important for educators to be aware of their own biases about each generation. Generational differences should not be viewed as right or wrong but just as different. This will guide the educator in developing a variety of teaching/learning opportunities that cross the multigenerational barrier (Smuncy, 2010; Johnson & Romanello, 2005).

# References

Billings, D. & Kowalski, K. (2004). Teaching learners from varied generations. *The Journal of Continuing Education*, 35 (3), 104-105.

Billings, D. M., Skiba, D. J. & Connors, H. R. (2005). Best practices in web-based courses: Generational differences across undergraduate and graduate nursing students. *Journal of Professional Nursing*, 21 (2), 126-133.

Candela, L, Dalley, K, & Benzel-Lindley, J. (2006. A case for learning-centered curricula. *Journal of Nursing Educaion*, 45 (2), 59-6.

Cantrell, S. W., O'Leary, P., Ward, K. S. (2008). Strategies for success in online learning. *Nursing Clinics of North America*, 43 (4), 547-555.

Ferris, S. P. (2009). Teaching and learning with the net generation. Presentation at the Lilly East Conference.

Garcia, P. & Qin, J. (2007). Identifying the generation gap in higher education: Where do the differences lie? *Journal of Online Education, 3 (4)*. Retrieved from http://www.innovateonline.info/pdf/vol3_issue4/Identifying_the_Generation_Gap_in_Higher_Education-__Where_Do_the_Differences_Really_Lie_.pdf

Gibson, S. E. (2009). Intergenerational communication in the classroom: Recommendations for successful teacher-student relationships. *Nursing Education Perspectives.* 30 (1), 37-39.

Hallas, J. (2008). Rethinking teaching and assessment strategies for flexible learning environments. Proceedings Ascilite Melbourne.

Hannay, M. & Fretwell, C. (nd). The higher education workplace: Meeting the needs of multiple generations. *Research in Higher Education Journal*.

Howe, N. N. & Strauss, W. (2012). what is a generation. *Lifecourse Associates*, retrieved from http://www.lifecourse.com/

Johanson, L. (2012). Teaching the millennial generation: Considerations for nurse educators. *Nurse Educator*, 37 (4), 173-176.

Johnson, S. J. & Romanello, M. L. (2005). Generational diversity: Teaching and learning approaches. *Nurse Educator,* 30 (5), 212-216.

Ke, F. & Kwak, D. (2013). Constructs of student-centered online learning satisfaction of a diverse online student body: A structural equation modeling approach. *Journal of Educational Computing Research,* 48 (1), 97-122.

Marconi, M. A. (2012). What about me? Addressing generational diversity. Retrieved from http://www.rochester.edu/diversity/assets/pdf/annualconference/Workshop%20C2-%20Schlegel%20207-%20Maria%20Marconi.pdf

McCraw M. A. & Martindale, T. (2012). Instructing multi-generational students. Paper University of Memphis.

McDonald, M. E. (2014). *The Nurse Educator's Guide to Assessing Learning Outcomes.* Burlington, MA: Jones and Bartlett Learning.

Notarianni, M. A., Curry-Lourenco, K., Barham, P., & Palmer, K. (2009). Engaging learners across generations: The Progressive Professional Development Model. *The Journal of Continuing Education in Nursing,* 40 (6), 261-266.

O'Neill, G. & McMahon, T. ( 2006). Student-centered learning: What does it mean for students and lecturers? *Immerging Issues in the Practice of University Learning and Teaching.* Dublin: AISHE.

Parker, E. B. & Wassef, M. E. (2010). Flexible online learning options for graduate nursing students. *Nurse Educator,* 35 (6), 243-247.

Schell, G. P. & Janicki, T. J. (2012). Online course pedagogy and the constructivist learning model. *Journal of the Southern Association for Information Systems,* 1 (1), 26-36.

Smuncy, D. (2010). Bridging multigenerational gaps in the online classroom. *Online Learning Magazine for UMUC Faculty* retrieved from http://deoracle.org/online-pedagogy/teaching-strategies/bridging-multigenerational-gaps-in-the-online-classroom.html

Wright, G. B. (2011). Student-centered learning in higher education. *International Journal of Teaching and Learning in Higher Education, 23 (3), 92-97.*

# 5 Using a Design Pattern Framework to Structure Online Course Content: Two Design Cases

Priscilla Norton & Dawn Hathaway, George Mason University, USA

## Introduction

In their examination of learners' perceptions of online learning, Peltier, Schibrowsky, and Drago (2007) found that course content was the "number one driver of perceived quality of the learning experience" (p. 149). They recommended that designers of online courses concentrate on course structure and content and acknowledged that developing the right course structure must be accomplished prior to course delivery. The importance of course structure was echoed by Song, Singleton, Hill, and Koh (2004) who concluded, ". . . there is a need for effective instructional design for online courses. The design should focus not only on the technological aspects of the course, but also on the goals, objectives, and expectations for the learner" (p. 69). Recommendations for how to organize online course content are scarce, and the few available recommendations rely on traditional design models. Similar to the models of Tyler (1969) and Taba (1962), Savenye, Olina, and Niemczyk (2001) proposed guidelines for designing online courses that include analyzing the context, learners, and goals, developing online instructional materials, and conducting formative evaluations and revisions of the course. In their discussion of the development of online instructional materials, they stated that "organization is critical in an online course" (p. 377) and recommended that course materials be organized into easily accessible and viewable chunks of information. They offered no advice on *how* to determine appropriate content chunks, learner activities, or the sequence of content nor how to facilitate cognitive presence - "the exploration, construction, resolution and confirmation of understanding through collaboration and reflection in a community of inquiry" (Garrison, 2007, p. 65).

While online course designers share common concerns across contents such as the need to choose appropriate technologies, to address dimensions of online learning interactions, and to create assessment strategies, course content learning goals vary widely. Course content learning goals, for instance, might center on understanding a process (e.g. the leadership process or the accounting process), a skill (e.g. mathematical computation or using a word processor), a body of knowledge (e.g. the history of Victorian England or laws governing special education), or a theory (e.g. behaviorist, constructivist, and/or cognitivist theories of learning). And, it is likely that distinct content learning goals necessitate different content structures. When we began designing online courses, we found it difficult to identify guidelines for structuring content in the literature related to instructional design and online learning. This absence of explicit and comprehensive guidelines made it difficult to conceptualize ways in which to meet course learning goals despite the central role that well organized and structured course content plays in engaging learners with content.

After extensive review of the literature on design, design thinking, and the design process, we happened upon the concept of design patterns reflected in the work of architects, computer programmers, and web developers. While rarely applied to educational practice, those who have considered the ways in which the concept of design patterns might inform the educational community (e. g. Goodyear et al., 2004; Mor & Winters, 2007; Weisburgh, 2004) generally view the concept as a vehicle for "externalizing knowledge to allow accumulation and generalization of solutions and to allow all members of a community or design group to participate in discussion relating to the design" (Mor & Winters, 2007, n. p.). Similarly, Goodyear et al. (2004) considered the notion of design patterns to be a vehicle for "sharing educational design experience" (p. 449). Offering perhaps the most concise rationale supporting the role of design patterns, Weisburgh (2004) concluded, "Patterns represent an approach to document how experts approach problems or opportunities in their fields in a way that allows others to emulate their thought processes, approaches, and solutions" (n. p.). Thus, educational interest in design patterns generally centers on the archiving and sharing of expertise and serves as a strategy for harvesting and implementing best practices in order to provide a guide for implementing solutions.

We have come to understand the notion of design patterns not only as an archival strategy but, perhaps more importantly, as an analytical framework to guide thoughtful consideration of educational design problems. In our experience, a design pattern framework offers an alternative to traditional design models or, at least, an approach that extends our ability to consider the design component in ADDIE. As an analytical framework, using the design pattern framework enables designers to reframe their design problem, to conceptualize a generalized, reusable solution, and to consider that design solution in the larger context of the overall course design. In this way, designers gain insight into their design problem and are able to capture the essence of the problem and its solution.

## Understanding Design Patterns

A design pattern is a description of a problem that occurs over and over again in a field of practice and then presents the core of the solution to that problem in such a way that the solution can be used "a million times over, without ever doing it the same way twice" (Alexander, Ishikawa, Silverstein, Jacobson, Fiksdahl-King, & Angel, 1977, p. x). "A design pattern names, abstracts, and identifies the key aspects of a common design structure" (Gamma, Helm, Johnson, & Vlissides, 1995, p. 3), making it reusable for recurring design problems. "Patterns communicate insights into design problems, capturing the essence of the problems and their solutions in a compact form" (Van Duyne, Landay, & Hong, 2007, p. 19). Exemplifying the use of design patterns, Alexander et al. (1977) identified 253 patterns to inform the work of architects in their efforts to create physical spaces that work for people. One design pattern, *A Place to Wait*, recognized that wherever people are required to wait there are inherent problems such as wasted time and a sense of demoralization at "hanging around, waiting, doing nothing" (p. 708). The problem then is how to design physical spaces where people wait that minimize these concerns. The solution, according to the *A Place to Wait* design pattern, is twofold. One, the waiting space should be infused with possible enjoyable activities. And, two, the waiting space should provide some places that are quiet and do not draw out the anxiety of the wait.

Similarly, in the field of computer science, Gamma et al. (1995) described 23 design patterns used by computer programmers to design object-oriented software. They describe programmers' use of these reusable patterns to

> . . . solve specific design problems and make object-oriented designs more flexible, elegant, and ultimately reusable. They help designers reuse successful designs by basing new designs on prior experience. A designer who is familiar with such patterns can apply them immediately to design problems without having to rediscover them. (p. 1)

Finally, in web site design, design patterns are used by web developers to establish a common language for articulating an infinite variety of web designs. They are used by web developers as tools to better understand target audiences, help design sites that target audiences find effective and easy to use, shorten development schedules, and reduce maintenance costs. Van Duyne et al. (2007) identified 13 such pattern groups, each with varying numbers of related patterns. For example, the *Creating a Powerful Homepage* family of patterns is used to scaffold the creation of homepages that deserve serious attention and accommodate the rich diversity of the target audience and their needs. "This pattern group describes how to design a powerful home page to fit the needs of your customers [target audience]" (p. 267) and then addresses related patterns that solve related design problems such as building site identity and brand, making a positive first impression, seducing with content, and balancing space for brand against space for navigation.

A design pattern is generally expressed through four essential elements: a pattern name, a description of the problem, the core of the solution, and the pattern's consequences and context (Gamma et al., 1995).

- *Pattern Name:* A pattern name is a handle used to describe a design problem, its solutions, and consequences. Naming a pattern makes it both explicit and useful as a shorthand reference to the solution. It supports design at a higher level of abstraction and enables designers to communicate, document, and discuss the solution, making it easier to think individually or collectively about designs.
- *Description of Problem:* The description of the problem explains both the problem and its context. Sometimes, the problem description includes a list of conditions that must be met before it is appropriate to apply the pattern.

- *Core of the Solution:* The solution is an abstract description of the design solution, not a concrete description of a particular design implementation. It specifies the elements that "make up the design, their relationships, responsibilities, and collaborations" (Gamma et al., 1995, p. 3) as well as how a general arrangement of elements solves the problem. The solution is stated in the form of an instruction and generally followed by a visual representation of the solution in the form of a diagram (Alexander et al., 1977).
- *Pattern's Consequences:* A description of the consequences presents results, costs and benefits, and impacts of applying the pattern. It situates the design pattern within the context of its use. As Alexander et al. (1977) wrote, "No pattern is an isolated entity" (p. xiii). Thus, the consequences element facilitates a designer's ability to link a particular design pattern to other patterns and to additional contextual considerations.

Architectural design patterns are instantiated as walls and doors; programming design patterns are instantiated in terms of codes, objects, and interfaces; and web site design patterns are instantiated as a collection of deliverable web pages. Nevertheless, all design patterns are expressions of solutions to problems in a context. Simply put, a design pattern is a generic solution to a recurring problem within a particular field of practice. And, while established design patterns may serve as guidelines in multiple contexts, efforts to construct patterns that reflect the four essential elements may serve as a design methodology.

## Using a Design Pattern Framework

### Design Case One

Several years ago, we accepted the challenge of designing a graduate online summer course for practicing K-12 teachers that focused on understanding and using Harris' (1997-98) 18 telecollaborative project types. Grouped under the umbrella of web-based learning activities, these 18 types serve to guide K-12 teachers' use of the Internet. Understanding these telecollaborative project types supports K-12 teachers' ability to choose existing and/or design new "powerful educational environments, or spaces for learning and teaching, which are constructed, decorated, and used in customized and ever changing ways . . ." (n. p.). Thus, Harris (1997-98) described these 18 telecollaborative project types as design tools that teachers can use for "reinvention; the process of taking something like a new tool or idea and making it our [their] own in its application" (n. p.). Figure 1 presents Harris' categorization of web-based activities.

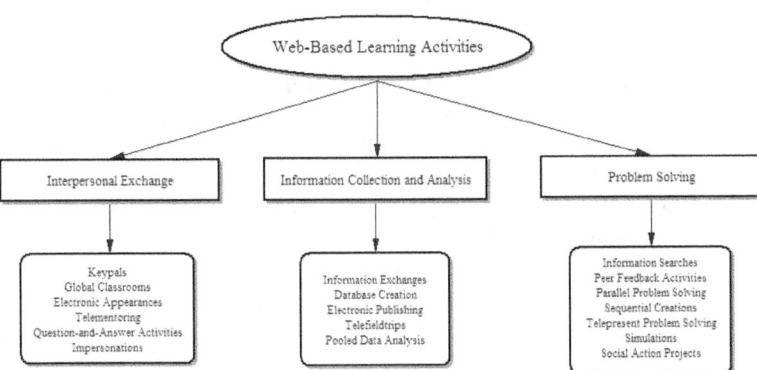

Figure 1. Web-based Learning Activities. This figure represents Harris' (1998) categorization of web-based learning activities as 18 telecollaborative project types organized by three genres.

**The Design Problem**

To make informed decisions about content structure, our temptation (molded by our knowledge of traditional design processes) was to begin with the specifics of our particular course content, focusing on the parts that make up the whole. This led to examination of the content to identify the parts and to create an appropriate order, asking if content should proceed from simple to complex or complex to simple, from part to whole or from whole to part. The first and second essential design pattern elements in the design pattern framework suggested that we step away from the particulars of the content (in our case the 18 telecollaborative project types) and redirect our attention toward naming and describing the content problem in ways that recognized how our problem represented a class of recurring content problems. In this way, our design process began by naming, abstracting, and identifying the key aspects of common content problems so that we could articulate the core of a potentially reusable solution.

Using the design pattern approach, we recognized that our content problem was similar, for instance, to that of English teachers required to teach rhetoric – the art of persuasion. Rhetorical instruction is often designed around three general categories of persuasive techniques – ethos, pathos, and logos and a series of nested concepts (see Figure 2). Similarly, learners who study international conflict resolution learn about deterrence, open warfare, guerilla warfare, diplomacy, negotiation, imperialism, isolationism, and economic sanctions.

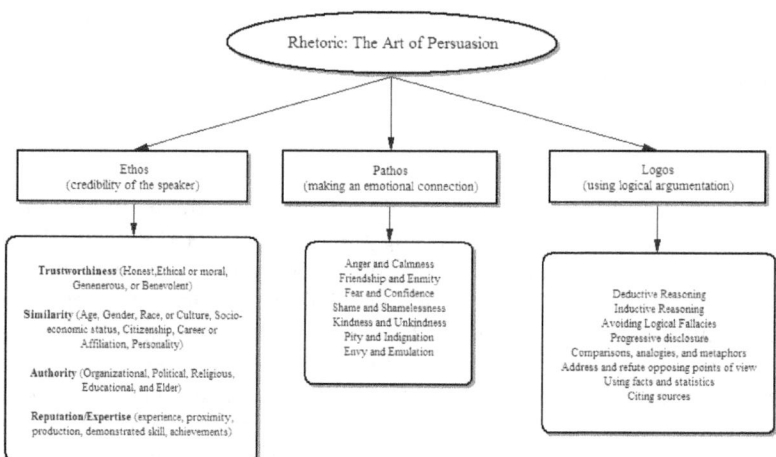

Figure 2. Rhetoric: The Art of Persuasion. This figure presents persuasive techniques grouped as ethos, pathos, and logos under the umbrella abstraction, rhetoric.

When we stepped back from the specifics of Harris' 18 telecollaborative project types, we recognized that our learning goals centered on facilitating learners' ability to distinguish between the nuances of nested concepts under an umbrella abstraction and to understand the ways in which each offered a unique affordance (possibilities and constraints) for shaping practice not on the concepts themselves. We were able to name the pattern, *Concepts Nested Under an Umbrella Abstraction*, and articulate a more insightful description of our actual design problem.

> ***The Problem***: *What is an appropriate content structure to support learners' ability to distinguish between concepts nested under an umbrella abstraction and to choose and use these nested concepts to inform problems of practice?*

**The Core of a Solution**

Restating the problem allowed us to more clearly understand the actual nature of the design problem and led to our ability to move to the third essential design pattern element – conceptualizing a solution. We understood that the solution would be embedded in the activities we selected but that those activities should not focus on the 18 telecollaborative project types as discrete knowledge components. Rather, appropriate activities would be directed towards learners' ability to distinguish between the unique affordances of each telecollaborative project type in order to choose and use the appropriate telecollaborative project type to inform practice.

Activities are the strategies and practices that engage learners in "doing" or "knowing." These activities create opportunities for learners to master learning goals – they are the means to an end. When activities are set in the context of an assignment, those "assignments hold the potential to make learning and teaching more focused and relevant because in the crafting process teachers must be deliberate and highly aware of the context, content, and charge involved in an assignment" (Dougherty, 2012, p. 7). Activities should be organized into larger activity structures - "recurring functional sequences of actions" (Lemke, 1987, p. 219), repeated across content and learning situations. As well as organizing instruction, activity structures "play an important role in the type of cognitive activity" (Arnold & Ducate, 2006, p. 42) to engage learners. Thus, if an activity structure is to facilitate meaningful actions, it must be structured to influence thinking in a critical and reflective manner "where interaction and reflection are sustained; where ideas can be explored and critiqued: and where the process of critical inquiry can be scaffolded and modeled" (Garrison & Cleveland-Innes, 2005, p. 134).

Bloom's Revised Taxonomy - remembering, understanding, applying, analyzing, evaluating, and creating (Anderson & Krathwohl, 2001, pp. 67-68) informed our ability to describe thoughtful activity structures that engaged learners in **reasoning about concepts** as opposed to remembering generalized definitions of those concepts. Using the taxonomy, we were able to state the core of the design solution as an activity structure comprised of four sequenced actions (Figure 3). We stated the solution as:

***The Solution***: *To facilitate online learners' ability to distinguish between concepts nested under an umbrella abstraction in ways that inform problems of practice, use a content structure that engages learners in a recurring activity structure that includes reasoning from example, reasoning from experience, synthesizing reasoning, and reasoning about problems of practice.*

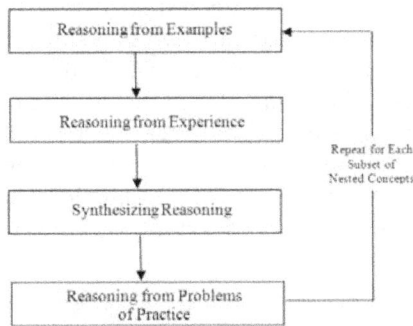

Figure 3. *Concepts Nested Under an Umbrella Abstraction*. This figure presents a visual representation of the activity structure at the core of the solution.

The first reasoning activity in the sequence engages learners in thoughtful actions centered on *reasoning from examples* of a subset of nested concepts. These activities encourage learners to interpret, infer, and identify shared features across representative examples and features that make each concept unique (understanding) as they critique and judge each concept's potential affordances (possibilities and constraints) for practice (evaluating). The second reasoning activity challenges learners to *reason from experience* – to participate in experiential models that represent the application of concepts. In reasoning from experience, learners act in ways that push them to implement and execute instances of concepts (applying) as they continue to critique and judge the impact of each concept's potential affordances (possibilities and constraints) for practice (evaluating). In the third reasoning activity, learners *synthesize their reasoning* by organizing, outlining, and structuring knowledge gained from prior activities (analyzing) as they plan, design, and construct a product (creating). In the final reasoning activity, learners' *reason about problems of practice* as they examine instances of the concepts applied to practice and critique those examples as potential "educational environments or spaces for learning and teaching" (Harris, 1997-98, n. p.)

(evaluating). Once learners have selected a representative example that has applicability to their practice (applying), they invent and plan a strategy for implementation (creating).

**Pattern Consequences**

The fourth essential design pattern element focused our attention on the need to situate the design solution in the context of other patterns and additional contextual considerations. Although the educational literature rarely expresses online course design using the framework of design patterns, related design issues and potential solutions are well documented and informed our thoughtful consideration of the pattern's consequences. We identified five consequences associated with the *Concepts Nested Under an Umbrella Abstraction* design pattern: the need to create accessible and viewable chunks of information, the need to appropriately select online learning technologies, the need to determine how the design pattern should be situated in relation to the umbrella abstraction, the need to consider and address issues of online learning associated with the dimensions of online learning interactions, and the need to devise assessment strategies.

Using the *Concepts Nested Under an Umbrella Abstraction* design pattern, we constructed our online course. The resulting design was embedded in a 10 week graduate online summer course. The course consisted of 5 modules. The first module introduced the umbrella concept – web-based learning activities; Modules 2, 3, and 4 were structured by the design solution, each module instantiating the activity structure. The final module was dedicated to the individual design project and was used as the primary course assessment. The learning management system, Blackboard 9.1, served as the delivery platform.

**Design Case Two**

Our second opportunity to use a design pattern framework came when the secondary education chair at our University approached us after a series of focus group sessions conducted by the secondary education faculty. While those in the focus group endorsed the quality of our candidates, they identified three areas for improvement: using technology in instruction, working with second language learners, and accommodating students with special needs. The chair approached us to design a course that would strengthen the preparation of our preservice candidates in the domain of technology integration. This request did not surprise us as it echoed the findings of the (Project Tomorrow & Blackboard, 2013) report stating that "principals want new teachers to know how to use technology to create authentic learning experiences for students (75 percent) and how to leverage technology to differentiate instruction (68 percent) before they apply for a position at their school" (p. 5).

**The Design Problem**

While a comprehensive review of the literature is not appropriate in the context of this paper, we identified three important conclusions. First, empirical evidence available to the authors indicated that teacher education programs have not taught new teachers how to use technology effectively (Maddux & Cummings, 2004) and that preservice teachers still lack the ability and knowledge needed to teach successfully with technology (Angeli & Valanides, 2008). Second, literature suggested that teachers feel inadequately prepared to use technology effectively in the classroom, particularly to support teaching and learning activities in their disciplines (Hew & Brush, 2007), and, although teachers are exposed to skills-based, "how to" activities in their preservice programs, there is insufficient effort made to align technology with discipline-specific pedagogy (Brush, et al., 2003)). Third, although many researchers have attempted to identify the best strategies for preservice technology integration instruction, "only a handful of studies have carefully and rigorously pursued the evaluation process. The jury is still out on which strategies work best . . ." (Kay, 2006, p. 395).

We wondered: were we designing five, discipline-based courses (social studies, language arts, foreign languages, science, and mathematics) or were we designing one course centered around concepts and tools related to technology integration? As we pondered this dilemma, it occurred to us that the answer was "yes" – the heart of our design problem centered on the *interaction* of technology integration concepts *and* discipline-specific contexts. In seeking to name and describe our design problem (the first and second essential element of a design pattern), we sought to better understand our design problem by asking in what ways our design problem was representative of a class of recurring problems related to the teaching of content. We recognized that our design problem shared distinct similarities to engineering where general discipline-specific concepts of electricity and electrical circuitry took on unique applications in the fields of architecture or computer engineering – general concepts informed multiple contexts. In education, our design problem was similar to special education where general concepts such as differentiation, inclusion, resource, self-contained, categories of disability, and individual educational plans (IEPs) differentially informed the education of, for example, elementary learning disabled students, secondary students with intellectual disabilities, and middle school students enrolled in classes for the gifted. Our design problem was likewise similar to educational assessment where general concepts such as formative, summative, objective, criterion-referenced, norm-referenced, portfolio, and rubric assessment differentially inform the assessment of young learners, secondary learners, and adult learners to say nothing of the requirements associated with assessing different contents or different skills. We were able to name the pattern, *Disciplinary Concepts Applied Differentially to Many Contexts* and articulate a more insightful description of our actual design problem.

> ***The Problem***: *What is an appropriate content structure that builds learners' understanding of how general disciplinary concepts inform and blend with the design of practice in the learners' context of interest?*

## The Core of a Solution

Restating the problem as a recurring design problem allowed us to more clearly understand the actual nature of the design problem and led to our ability to move to the third essential design pattern element – conceptualizing a solution. As in Design Case One, we understood that the solution would be embedded in the activities we selected but that those activities should not focus on general disciplinary concepts (in our case, technology as a discrete set of skills, tools, or concepts). Rather, appropriate activities should be directed towards learners' ability to *integrate* general disciplinary concepts (in our case, technology integration skills, tools, and concepts) with learners' ability to design for practice in their context of interest (social studies, language arts, foreign languages, science, or mathematics classrooms).

Once again, this paper is not the context for a comprehensive review of literature but our review led us to three central conclusions which shaped our solution. First, it is necessary to organize content in ways that reflect practice within a particular context. A field of practice is governed by a body of disciplinary knowledge - a distinctive way of thinking not about facts but evidence, inquiry, and problem-solving (Tishman, Perkins, & Jay, 1995). A disciplinary approach draws attention not only to information as an end in itself but to a means to better-informed practice (Gardner, 2009). Second, learning to practice in a context is most effective when it occurs in an authentic context (Mishra and Koehler, 2007). That is, opportunities to learn are best contextualized in practice as opposed to a more traditional decontextualized approach where practice happens after learning instead of as part of learning. Third, unless the connections between discipline-specific concepts and practice in a particular context are explicitly demonstrated, learners are not able to transfer the knowledge and skills gained to their own practice (Brzycki & Dudt, 2005), Thus, learners need to experience and reflect on models of practice to be able to transfer formal learning to applied contexts (Bullock, 2004). Together, these three considerations provided the backdrop for the activity structure which formed the core of our solution (Figure 4).

> ***The Solution***: *To create a content structure that builds learners' understanding of how general disciplinary concepts inform and blend with the design of practice in the learners' context of interest, use a content structure that engages learners in a recurring activity structure that includes a conceptual design challenge, a design experience, analysis of design examples, and a situated design challenge.*

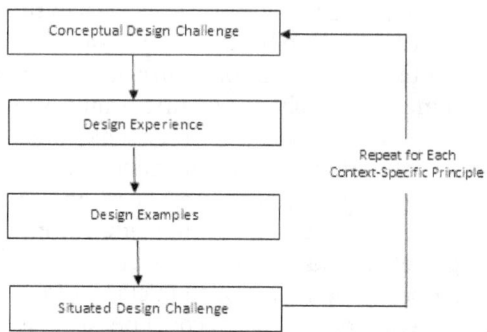

Figure 4. The Solution. This figure represents the activity structure which defines the content structure embedded in the design solution.

The first activity, a conceptual design challenge, builds explicit connections between general disciplinary concepts and principles that guide practice. The learner is challenged to produce a product that demonstrates the ways in which concepts inform and blend with an authentic practice. For example, social studies preservice candidates are asked to review readings and web resources to prepare a presentation to colleagues about the ways in which technology can be integrated with historical research. The second activity, a design experience, engages learners in a completing an instance of practice informed by disciplinary concepts and principles of practice. For example, language arts teachers take on the role of 11th grade language arts students and create a podcast as part of a series on word usage. The third activity, design examples, asks learners to analyze and critique case studies of practice informed by both the general disciplinary concepts and the principles that guide practice. For example, language arts candidates reflect on how two cases studies (using iAnnotate to comprehend informational text and creating infographics as an instance of writing), discussing with fellow learners and reflecting on the ways in which these examples model technology integration concepts and language arts writing standards. The fourth activity, situated design challenge, challenges students to develop a plan of practice – to use their emerging knowledge to shape real-life situations. For example, science candidates are asked to design an instance of practice bridging technology integration concepts with stability and change standards by focusing on the creation of a lesson to teach the interactions between organisms in an ecosystem for a biology unit.

**Pattern Consequences**

The fourth essential design pattern element focused our attention on the need to situate the design solution in the context of other patterns and additional contextual considerations. Although the educational literature rarely expresses online course design using the framework of design patterns, related design issues and potential solutions are well documented and informed our thoughtful consideration of the pattern's consequences. We identified four consequences associated with the *Disciplinary Concepts Applied Differentially to Many Contexts* design pattern: the need to identify a course structure that allowed students to be associated with course materials and activities related to their context of interest (in essence a way to facilitate five courses with a single structure), the need to appropriately select online learning technologies, the need to determine how the design pattern should be situated in relation to the general disciplinary concepts (a way to teach the concepts before addressing the ways in which they inform practice, the need to consider and address issues of online learning associated with the dimensions of online learning interactions, and the need to devise assessment strategies.

Using the *Disciplinary Concepts Applied Differentially to Many Contexts* design pattern, we constructed an online course for preservice secondary education students. We chose an online format so that we could group students by context of interest. The resulting design was embedded in 10 modules. The first four modules completed by all learners introduced and explored the general disciplinary concepts associated with technology integration. Modules 5 through 10 implemented the activity structure in the solution for each of the contexts of practice (social studies, language arts, foreign languages, science or mathematics). Each module was organized using the activity structure from the solution as well as the standards from each context (e.g. historical thinking for social studies, the 5C's for foreign languages, the NCTM standards for mathematics, the Common Core Standards for Language Arts, and the Next Generation Science Standards for science). Module 10 targeted synthesis and evaluation requiring students to reflect on the general disciplinary concepts and the ways in which they informed and blended with their practice. The learning management system, Blackboard 9.1, served as the delivery platform.

## Conclusion: Adopting Design Patterns as a Design Framework

We have adopted the process of constructing design patterns shaped by consideration of the four essential elements as a design framework. It has enabled us to create content structures that support learning goals. Using a design pattern framework based on systematic consideration of the four essential elements of a design pattern has shifted our attention from the specifics of instruction to thoughtful consideration of design by adding depth to our creative design process. Using the four essential elements of design patterns as a framework scaffolds the design process and benefits design work in at least four significant ways:

- First, rather than focusing attention on the objectives of a design, the framework pushes designers to step away from overt details, to rethink a design by broadening their approach, and to situate the design problem in the context of recurring design problems. Once the larger representative design problem is discovered/acknowledged/articulated, it is possible to draw on a wider range of situations and design experiences to identify shared concerns and to uncover related design requirements. As a result, identifying shared concerns helps to define the essential requirements necessary to develop a deeper solution.
- Second, with an understanding of the essential requirements of a design solution, designers are better able to articulate their design challenges and search for literature that might inform their ability to conceptualize and more clearly understand the ways in which the requirements might be met. This informs the designer's ability to state the core of a solution as an instruction.
- Third, once designers are able to state a solution as an instruction, it becomes possible to use that instruction as an actionable guide. Since the instruction refers to the solution of a recurring design problem and not to a solution for a particular problem, the solution statement serves to guide designers' efforts by reducing infinite and unstructured possibilities to structured possibilities. By helping to shape the playing field of their imaginations, creative options are not limited but revealed.
- Fourth, as specified by the design pattern framework, the need to include pattern consequences as part of a design pattern description emphasizes the need to situate design solutions in context. Design consequences point to a clear path for reflecting on what additional considerations the design must address and how those considerations are related to the design pattern.

## References

Alexander, C., Ishikawa, S., Silverstein, M., Jacobson, M., Fiksdahl-King, I., & Angel, S. (1977). *A pattern language*. NY: Oxford University Press.

Anderson, L. W., & Krathwohl, D. R. (Eds.). (2001). *A taxonomy for learning, teaching and assessing: A revision of Bloom's Taxonomy of educational objectives* (Complete edition). New York: Longman.

Angeli, C., & Valanides, N. (2008, March). *TCPK in preservice teacher education: Preparing primary education students to teach with technology*. Paper presented at the AERA annual conference, New York.

Arnold, N., & Ducate L. (2006). Future foreign language teachers' social and cognitive collaboration in an online environment. *Language Learning & Technology, 10*(1): 42–66. Retrieved from http://llt.msu.edu/vol10num1/pdf/arnoldducate.pdf

Brush, T, Glazewski, K., Rutowski, K., Berg, K., Stromfors, C., Van-Nest, M. H., … Sutton, J. (2003). Integrating technology in a field-based teacher training program: The $PT_3$ @ ASU projects. *Educational Technology Research & Development, 51*(1), 57-72.

Brzycki, D., & Dudt, K. (2005). Overcoming barriers to technology use in teacher preparation programs. *Journal of Technology and Teacher Education, 13*(4), 619-641.

Bullock, D. (2004). Moving from theory to practice: As examination of the factors that preservice teachers encounter as they attempt to gain experience teaching with technology during field placement experiences. *Journal of Technology and Teacher Education, 12*(2), 211-237.

Dougherty, E. (2012). *Assignments matter: Making the connections that help students meet standards.* Alexandria, VA: ASCD.

Gamma, E., Helm, R., Johnson, R., & Vlissides, J. (1995). *Design patterns: Elements of reusable object-oriented software.* NY: Addison-Wesley.

Gardner, H. (2009). *Five Minds for the Future.* Boston, MA: Harvard Business Review Press.

Garrison, D., & Cleveland-Innes, M. (2005). Facilitating cognitive presence in online learning: Interaction is not enough. *American Journal of Distance Education, 19*, 133-148.

Garrison, D. (2007). Online community of inquiry review: Social, cognitive, and teaching presence issues. *Journal of Asynchronous Learning Networks, 11*(1), 61-72.

Goodyear, P., Avgeriou, P., Baggetun, R., Bartoluzzi, S., Retalis, S., Ronteltap, F., & Rusman, E. (2004). Towards a pattern language for networked learning. In S. Banks, P. Goodyear, V. Hodgson, C. Jones, V. Lally, D. McConnell & C. Steeples (Eds.), *Networked learning 2004* (pp. 449-455). Lancaster, UK: Lancaster University.

Harris, J. (1997-1998, December-January). Wetware: Why use activity structures? *Learning and Leading with Technology, 25*, 13-17. Retrieved from http://www.fsu.edu/~imsp/silent_invaders/new_weeds/educators/mining_internet.html

Harris, J. (1998). *Virtual architecture: Designing and directing curriculum-based telecomputing.* Eugene, OR: International Society for Technology in Education, University of Oregon.

Hew, K., & Brush, T. (2007). Integrating technology into K-12 teaching and learning: Current knowledge gaps and recommendations for future research. *Educational Technology Research & Development, 55*(3), 223-252.

Lemke, J. L. (1987). Social semiotics and science education. *The American Journal of Semiotics, 5*(2), 217- 232.

Kay, R. (2006). Evaluating strategies used to incorporate technology into preservice education: A Review of the literature. *Journal of Research on Technology in Education, 38*(4), 383-408.

Maddox, C., & Cummings, R. (2004). Fad, fashion, and the weak role of theory and research in information technology in education. *Journal of Technology and Teacher Education, 12*(4), 511-533.

Mor, Y., & Winters, N. (2007). Design approaches in technology enhanced learning. *Interactive Learning Environments, 15*(1), 61-75.

Mishras, P., & Koehler, M. J. (2007). Technological pedagogical content knowledge (TPCK): Confronting the wicked problems of teaching with technology. In R. Carlsen, K. McFerrin, J. Price, R. Weber, & D. Willis (Eds.), Proceedings of Society for Information Technology & Teacher Education International Conference 2007 (pp. 2214-2226). Chesapeake, VA: AACE.

Peltier, J. W., Schibrowsky, J. A., & Drago, W. (2007). The interdependence of the factors influencing the perceived quality of the online learning experience: A causal model. *Journal of Marketing Education, 29*, 140-153.

Project Tomorrow, & Blackboard K-12 (2013). *Learning in the 21st century: Digital experiences and expectations of tomorrow's teachers.* Retrieved from http://www.tomorrow.org/speakup/tomorrowsteachers_report2013.html

Savenye, W., Olina, Z., & Niemezyk, M. (2001). So you are going to be an online writing instructor: Issues in designing, developing, and delivering an online course. *Computers and Composition, 18*, 371–385.

Song, L., Singleton, E. S., Hill, J. R., & Koh, M. H. (2004). Improving online learning: Student perceptions of useful and challenging characteristics. *The Internet and Higher Education, 7*, 59-70.

Taba, H. (1962). *Curriculum: Theory and practice.* New York: Harcourt, Brace.

Tishman, S., Perkins, D., & Jay, E. (1995). *The thinking classroom: Learning and teaching in a culture of thinking.* Needham Heights, MA: Allyn and Bacon.

Tyler, R. (1969). *Basic principles of curriculum and instruction.* Chicago: University Of Chicago Press.

Van Duyne, D., Landay, J., & Hong, J. (2007). *The design of sites: Patterns for creating winning web sites* (2nd ed.). NY: Prentice Hall.

Weisburgh, M. (2004). *Documenting good education and training practices through design patterns.* Retrieved from http://ifets.ieee.org/discussions/discuss_june2004.html

# 6 Teacher Planning Problem Space of Expert Technology Integrating Teachers
Erin Davis, Georgia State University, USA

## Introduction

The ways teachers use instructional technology has the potential to change the quality of teaching and learning but, too often, efforts to create change have resulted in the isolation of technological practices rather than incorporating them into teaching and learning (Earle, 2002, p. 11); hence the "islands of innovation" phenomenon in which innovative pedagogical practices are found among 15% or less of the teacher population at a particular school (Forkhosh-Baruch, Mioduser, Nachmias, & Tubin, 2005; Tubin, Mioduser, Nachmias, & Forkosh-Baruch, 2003). In general, innovation is not a clearly defined concept, and innovation with technology in an educational setting is even more complex (Forkhosh-Baruch et al., 2005). Innovation refers to *technology-supported innovation* and is defined as pedagogical solutions supporting a shift from traditional educational paradigms (teacher-centered) toward emergent ones based on fostering learner-centered processes (Forkhosh-Baruch et al., 2005; Mioduser, Nachmias, Tubin, & Forkosh-Baruch, 2003; Pelgrum, Brummelhuis, Collis, Plomp, & Janssen, 1997). Educators who use technology to implement more learner-centered processes rather than traditional paradigms are innovators: teachers who view growth and change as an integral part of their profession and are willing to swim against the tide of conventional operating procedures (Dede, 1998). In 2010, Public Broadcasting System (PBS) and The Henry Ford created the Teacher Innovator Award (TIA) to recognize these innovators who use digital media to enhance student learning as educators ("2012 Teacher Innovator Awards," 2013). These award winners are examples of expert teachers who lead the charge of educational change in technology integration.

Expert teachers behave differently than their novice counterparts and often possess: 1) automaticity and routinization (e.g. Berliner, 2001; Leinhardt & Greeno, 1986; Sternberg & Horvath, 1995), 2) flexibility in teaching (e.g. Berliner, 2001; Leinhardt & Greeno, 1986), 3) quick and accurate judgment, and meaningful pattern recognition (e.g. Berliner, 2001; Leinhardt & Greeno, 1986; Peterson & Comeaux, 1987; Sternberg & Horvath, 1995), and 4) a specialized knowledge specific to the domain of expertise (e.g. Berliner, 2001; Peterson & Comeaux, 1987; Shulman, 1987; Sternberg & Horvath, 1995). These characteristics are evident in how a teacher prepares to teach a lesson as well as actually teaches it (John, 2006). Without acknowledging the expertise teachers bring to their classrooms, there is little hope of integrating technology into teaching and learning (Cuban, 2003). Technology integration requires:

> "an understanding of the representation of concepts using technologies; pedagogical techniques that use technologies in constructive ways to teach content; knowledge of what makes concepts difficult or easy to learn and how technology can help redress some of the problems that students face; knowledge of students' prior knowledge and theories of epistemology; and knowledge of how technologies can be used to build on existing knowledge to develop new epistemologies or strengthen old ones (Koehler & Mishra, 2009, p. 66)."

Ertmer, Gopalakrishnan, and Ross (2001) defined expert technology-integrating teachers as those who use technology in learner-centered constructivist environments, characterized by Becker and Riel (1999) as activities that are designed around interests, practiced in authentic contexts, and focused on understanding complex ideas. Affirming this notion of expert technology-integrating teachers, Tubin et al. (2003) referred to them as islands of innovation in a sea of traditional practices: initiated and sustained by a small group of leading figures that face the challenge of implementing novel pedagogical solutions characterized as student-centered, process-oriented, and learning-by-doing.

Although the TIA recognizes expert technology integrating teachers every year, designing meaningful technology-integrated learning remains a challenge for teachers. In a 2010 survey of over 3000 teachers, only 29% reported using computers during instructional time (Gray, Thomas, & Lewis, 2010). Gorder (2008) found that teachers used technology for professional productivity and to facilitate and deliver instruction rather than integrating it. Other researchers (e.g. Cuban, 2006; Groff & Mouza, 2008; Wang & Reeves, 2004; Zhao, Pugh, Sheldon, & Byers, 2002) affirmed disappointing levels of technology integration. The purpose of this study is to describe the planning strategies these expert teachers use in designing technology-integrated instruction to address teachers' aforementioned challenge with technology in teaching and learning.

## Conceptual Framework

Teaching with technology has been referred to as a complex, unpredictable, and ill-structured problem to solve and the teacher is a problem-solving expert (Koehler & Mishra, 2009; Mishra & Koehler, 2006). According to Calderhead (1984), planning was a *place* where teachers translated course requirements, institutional expectations, their beliefs, and ideologies of education into guides for action. From this perspective, the act of planning for instruction served as a strategy for solving the complex problem of teaching with technology. The conceptual framework of this study drew from two information processing theory constructs: a *problem space* (Simon & Newell, 1971) and a *process model of teacher planning* (Yinger, 1980). A *problem space* referred to the "fundamental organizational unit of all human goal-oriented symbolic activity" (Newell, 1979, p. 4). Reasoning, problem solving, and decision making were captured in appropriately defined problem spaces (Bickhard & Terveen, 1996). Yinger's (1980) *process model of teacher planning* focused on "deliberate information-processing involved in planning, from an initial idea to its execution in the classroom (p. 113)," and emphasized discovery and design. The resulting conceptual framework is the *teacher planning problem space* (TPPS), which is made of the *planning task environment* and the *planning problem space* (see **Error! Reference source not found.**).

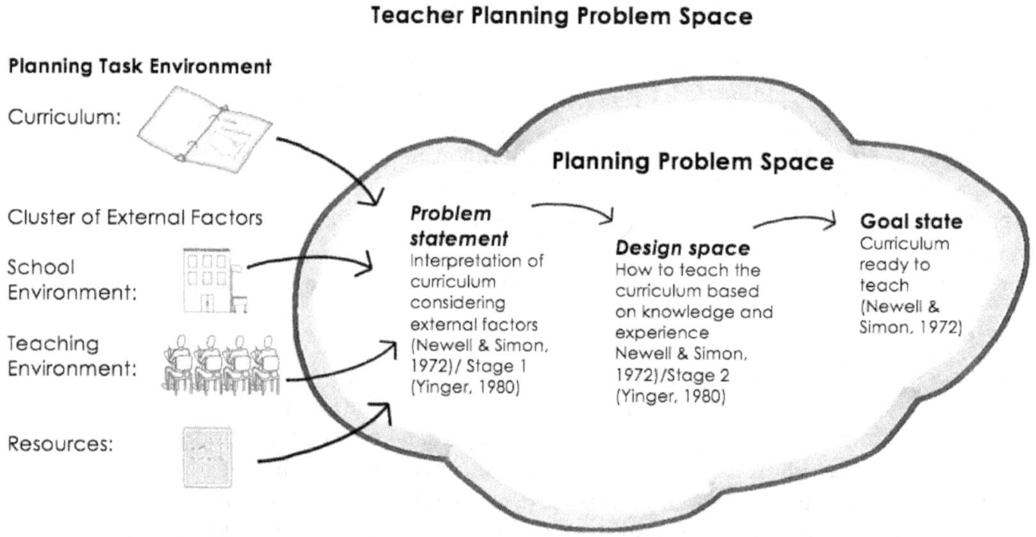

*Figure 1.* The *teacher planning problem space* is a combination of Simon and Newell's (1972) notion a *problem space* and Stage 1 and Stage 2 of Yinger's (1980) *process model for teacher planning*. The combination of a *search space* and Stage 2 was renamed to *design space*. Images, © 2014 Common Craft®.

Yinger (1980) identified external influences, which make up the *planning task environment* such as teaching environment, school organization, the curriculum, technology and non-technology resources, and student characteristics. The internal processes in the *planning problem space* provide an overarching structure with which to examine the mental "space" where teachers do most of their planning. Because much of expert teachers' planning is not written down (John, 2006), they remain as internal processes only to be revealed during the act of teaching. These internal processes or conceptual components of the teacher planning problems space include the knowledge and experience that are indicated by a repertoire of ideas and routines that influence the direction of the planning process (Yinger, 1980). Experience contributes to an expert's use of established routines, grouping strategies, subject matter content knowledge, and pedagogical strategies for representing subject matter content in ways in which their non-expert counterparts do not. Routines not only increases efficiency but also serves to expand the teacher's ability to deal with unpredictable elements (Leinhardt & Greeno, 1986). Yinger (1980) does not reference Simon and Newell's (1972) notion of *problem space* in his planning model. However the two constructs in combination provide an excellent lens for studying teacher planning as a problem-solving endeavor.

## Research Questions

The research questions associated with this objective are:
1. How do expert teachers plan for technology integration?
2. What factors of their *teacher planning problem space* influence planning?

## Methods

This research study used qualitative content analysis methods within the context of a case study to investigate complex units of study consisting of multiple variables with potential importance to understanding the phenomenon (Merriam, 1988). As teachers planned for technology integration, they attempted to solve ill-structured problems, considering multiple variables such as curriculum, physical classroom, class size, time available to teach, resources, individual student characteristics, teacher knowledge and experience, decisions regarding how best to represent content, and activities to facilitate learning of content. A case study was particularly suited to address teacher planning for technology integration because this design can be used to gain an in-depth understanding of "process rather than outcomes, in context rather than a specific variable, in discovery rather than confirmation" (Merriam, 1998, p. Kindle Location 299). The TPPS provided the analytical framework for this study and how teachers negotiate the TTPS was the unit of study.

### Participant Selection

Participants were purposefully selected from an initial pool of thirty-two TIA winners. The six winners of the Teacher Innovation Award sponsored by PBS Learning Media and The Henry Ford who agreed to participate in the study consisted of three females and three males from the Midwest and South. Pseudonyms were used to protect the identification of the participants. However they were informed that due to the public nature of the award and their own accomplishments as experts, it was impossible to guarantee anonymity. The participants represented a range of teaching experience from four to twenty-one years and four were classroom teachers, while the other two served in instructional technology support roles.

### Participant Activities

Participants were asked to take an online survey and partake in three interviews conducted via videoconferencing. The survey consisted of ten questions to gauge technology integration knowledge, technology resources available, and basic planning strategies. The first interview topic was to review the participant's TIA winning entry to gain insight into planning processes. The second interview was centered around a lesson plan the participant had created for instruction during the data collection period and the third interview involved on-the-spot planning given a particular standard in their respective content areas. Additionally, artifacts (lesson plans, student handouts, and assignments) created as a result of the planning processes were also collected. These items will be collected via email and used to supplement interview data.

## Data Collection and Analysis

Data was collected over an 18-week period starting in August 2013 and ending in December 2013. A variety of data was collected including a survey, interviews, documents, and audio-visual material. The *teacher planning problem space* provided the analytical framework for this study and how teachers negotiate this space is the unit of study. QCA is the most appropriate method for analyzing how expert technology-integrating teacher negotiate the *teacher planning problem space* because it is both contextually focused and flexible. The analysis process was on going throughout the data collection period and managed through the use of a computer-assisted qualitative data analysis software (CAQDAS) program. The researcher used an iterative process to develop codes and categorize concepts from technology artifacts, lesson plans, and transcriptions of interviews, moving from the general to the specific until themes emerged. Three rounds of coding were performed using three different coding methods to analyze the data. The first round was initial or open coding to develop the main coding frame, which was tested and revised according to feedback from a peer reviewer. The second round involved coding according to the conceptual framework and coding for the third round was by gerunds. To maintain subjectivity and increase credibility, the researcher created an audit trail using a research journal, peer review of the research process, and memoing.

## Role of Researcher

As an educator of both students and teachers, the researcher had knowledge of, and experience in what Stake (2000) called the special languages that teachers posses as a result of their experiences in the classroom. As an instructional technology specialist (ITS) for an urban school district, the researcher had the opportunity to observe teachers at all grade levels struggle with or completely ignore technology in their instruction. As a classroom teacher, she faced her own struggles with technology integration. The researcher minimized subjectivity by focusing on the participant's perspective of their experience and attempted to maintain outsider's view by creating an audit trail (Ertmer, Addison, Lane, Ross, & Woods, 1999; Merriam, 2009). The goal of the researcher was to represent the case in this study in a manner that created an extention of the teacher's experience that was relatable to some aspects of all teachers' experiences rather than to generalize planning strategies.

## Results and Discussion

The teacher is the most important element in transforming teaching and learning and determines if technology will be successfully integrated (Chen, 2008; "U.S. Congress. OTA EHR 616," 1995; Wang & Reeves, 2004). Because the teacher is the most important factor, enhancing teachers' technology integrating expertise is important to increasing the likelihood that others will integrate technology. Examples of data and results of the study will be reported during the session. This study added to the already existing body of research on the complex nature of teacher expertise and the contributions that experts can make to assist non-experts. Where it was unique was in terms of the conceptual framework as well as in the focus on the planning process that occurred before the performance of teaching, serving also to update literature on planning to include technology. Bitner and Bitner (2002) claimed that teachers need to conceptualize how the use of programs will facilitate teaching and learning. By examining how expert technology-integrating teachers planned for technology-integrated instruction in a conceptual space, this study provided examples for non-experts. Additionally, teachers need "opportunities to observe models of integrated technology use, to reflect on and discuss their evolving ideas with mentors and peers, and to collaborate with others on meaningful projects as they try out their new ideas about teaching and learning with technology (Ertmer, 1999, p. 54)." This study revealed factors that were related to technology-integrating experts' thoughts, decision-making, and judgments as they planned for instruction.

# References

2012 Teacher Innovator Awards. (2013). from http://www.pbs.org/teachers/innovators/

Becker, H. J., & Riel, M. (1999). Teacher professionalism and the emergence of constructivist-compatible pedagogies. http://www.crito.uci.edu/tlc/findings/special_report2/aerj-final.pdf

Berliner, D. C. (2001). Expert teachers: Their characteristics, development and accomplishments. *International Journal of Educational Research, 35*, 463-482.

Bickhard, M. H., & Terveen, L. (1996). *Foundational issues in artificial intelligence and cognitive science: Impasse and solution* (Vol. 109): North-Holland.

Bitner, N., & Bitner, J. (2002). Integrating Technology into the Classroom: Eight Keys to Success. *Journal of Technology and Teacher Education, 10*(1), 95-100.

Calderhead, J. (1984). *Teachers' classroom decision-making.* New York, NY: Holt, Rinehart and Winston.

Chen, C. H. (2008). Why Do Teachers Not Practice What They Believe Regarding Technology Integration? *The Journal of Educational Research, 102*(1), 65-75.

Cuban, L. (2003). *Oversold and underused: Computers in the classroom.* Cambridge, MA: Harvard University Press.

Cuban, L. (2006). The Laptop Revolution Has No Clothes. *Education Week, 26*(8), 29-29.

Dede, C. (1998). Six challenges for educational technology. *Project ScienceSpace.* Retrieved November 16, 2011, from http://www.learningdomain.com/6_challenges.IT.pdf

Earle, R. S. (2002). The Integration of Instructional Technology into Public Education: Promises and Challenges. *Educational Technology, 42*(1), 5-13.

Ertmer, P. (1999). Addressing first-and second-order barriers to change: Strategies for technology integration. *Educational Technology Research and Development, 47*(4), 47-61.

Ertmer, P., Addison, P., Lane, M., Ross, E., & Woods, D. (1999). Examining Teachers' Beliefs about the Role of Technology in the Elementary Classroom. *Journal of Research on Computing in Education, 32*(1), 54-72.

Ertmer, P., Gopalakrishnan, S., & Ross, E. M. (2001). Technology-using teachers: Comparing perceptions of exemplary technology use to best practice. *Journal of Research on Technology in Education, 33*(5), 1-24.

Forkhosh-Baruch, A., Mioduser, D., Nachmias, R., & Tubin, D. (2005). "Islands of Innovation" and" School-Wide Implementations": Two Patterns of ICT-Based Pedagogical Innovations in Schools. *Human Technology, 1*(2), 202-215.

Gorder, L. M. (2008). A study of teacher perceptions of instructional technology integration in the classroom. *Delta Pi Epsilon Journal, 50*(2), 63-76.

Gray, L., Thomas, N., & Lewis, L. (2010). Teachers' Use of Educational Technology in US Public Schools: 2009. First Look. NCES 2010-040. *National Center for Education Statistics.*

Groff, J., & Mouza, C. (2008). A framework for addressing challenges to classroom technology use. *AACE Journal,, 16(1)*(1), 21-46.

John, P. D. (2006). Lesson planning and the student teacher: re-thinking the dominant model. *Journal of Curriculum Studies, 38*(4), 483-498.

Koehler, M. J., & Mishra, P. (2009). What Is Technological Pedagogical Content Knowledge? *Contemporary Issues in Technology and Teacher Education (CITE Journal), 9*(1), 60-70.

Leinhardt, G., & Greeno, J. G. (1986). The Cognitive Skill of Teaching. *Journal of Educational Psychology, 78*(2), 75-95.

Merriam, S. B. (1988). *Case study research in education: A qualitative approach.* San Francisco, CA: Jossey Bass.

Merriam, S. B. (1998). *Qualitative Research and Case Study Applications in Education: Revised and Expanded from Case Study Research in Education.* San Francisco, CA: Jossey-Bass Education Series.

Merriam, S. B. (2009). *Qualitative research: A guide to design and implementation.* San Francisco, CA: Jossey-Bass.

Mioduser, D., Nachmias, R., Tubin, D., & Forkosh-Baruch, A. (2003). Analysis schema for the study of domains and levels of pedagogical innovation in schools using ICT. *Education and Information Technologies, 8*(1), 23-36.

Mishra, P., & Koehler, M. J. (2006). Technological Pedagogical Content Knowledge: A Framework for Teacher Knowledge. *Teachers College Record, 108*(6), 1017-1054.

Newell, A. (1979). Reasoning, problem solving and decision processes: The problem space as a fundamental category.

Pelgrum, W., Brummelhuis, A., Collis, B., Plomp, T., & Janssen, I. (1997). Technology assessment of multimedia systems for pre-primary and primary schools: European Parliament, Scientific and Technological Options Assessment Panel, Luxembourg.

Peterson, P. L., & Comeaux, M. A. (1987). Teachers' schemata for classroom events: The mental scaffolding of teachers' thinking during classroom instruction. *Teaching and teacher education, 3*(4), 319-331.

Shulman, L. S. (1987). Knowledge and Teaching: Foundations of the New Reform. *Harvard Educational Review, 57*(1), 1-22.

Simon, H. A., & Newell, A. (1971). Human problem solving: The state of the theory in 1970. *American Psychologist, 26*(2), 145-159.

Stake, R. E. (Ed.). (2000). *The case study method in social inquiry.* Thousand Oaks, CA: Sage Publications.

Sternberg, R. J., & Horvath, J. A. (1995). A Prototype View of Expert Teaching. *Educational researcher, 24*(6), 9-17.

Tubin, D., Mioduser, D., Nachmias, R., & Forkosh-Baruch, A. (2003). Domains and levels of pedagogical innovation in schools using ICT: Ten innovative schools in Israel. *Education and Information Technologies, 8*(2), 127-145.

U.S. Congress. OTA EHR 616. (1995). http://www.fas.org/ota/reports/9541

Wang, F., & Reeves, T. C. (2004). Why do teachers need to use technology in their classrooms? Issues, problems, and solutions. *Computers in the Schools, 20*(4), 49-65.

Yinger, R. J. (1980). A Study of Teacher Planning. *The Elementary School Journal, 80*(3), 107-127.

Zhao, Y., Pugh, K., Sheldon, S., & Byers, J. L. (2002). Conditions for classroom technology innovations. *Teachers College record, 104*(3), 482-515.

# 7 Pedagogical Design and Pedagogical Usability of Web-based Learning Environments: Comparative Cultural Implications between Africa and Europe

Adewunmi Obafemi Ogunbase, University of Tampere, Finland

## Introduction

My research focuses on change in teaching learning methods as technology and technology-supported approaches to learning are gaining popularity as ways of improving performance, promoting learning, and positioning educational institutions to adapt to changing situations and increase the quality, effectiveness and efficiency of their operations. The aim of the research is to examine the impact of cultural issues on the appropriate selection and use of technology and technology-supported approaches for learning. In order to address this aim, the following objectives are set: (i) to provide a critical assessment of the factors and cultural issues influencing learning approach involving a WBLE. (ii) To examine the link between the expectations of individual leaner in respect to his/her previous learning experience and the effective use of technology and technology-supported approach for learning. (iii) To develop a systematic culture-focused and learners-centered approach to pedagogical design and use of learning activities and styles based on WBLEs.

This paper will describe the process of data collection using both qualitative and quantitative techniques, and as well shows results of data collected relating it to the theoretical results in pedagogical design and pedagogical usability of e-learning researches. The first part of this paper will highlight literature review in this research area. Second part will highlight the research questions and the theoretical frameworks while the third part will describe the research design and methodology, i.e., the tool used for data collection and participants for data collection and the forth part shows results of the empirical study and its discussion. The conclusive parts of this paper will provide suggestions for pedagogical designers and technical usability WBLE designers in designing effective e-learning environments for Users' cultural context.

## 1. Literature Review on Culture, Pedagogical Design and Pedagogical Usability of Web- based Learning Environments (WBLEs)

Since the radical change from traditional teaching-learning method to use of technology caused by high and continuous improvements in technologies, studies for over a decade have been made into the impacts of culture on use of technology in the primary educational process. Studies into cross-cultural influence on information, communication technology (ICT) in education and web usability have become more popular among ICT and educational technology researchers. Some of these researchers are: Bourges-Waldegg & Scrivener, (1998), Burnett & Buerkle, (2004), Choong, & Salvendy, (1999), Del Gado & Nielsen, (1996), Danet & Herring, (2003). Ess & Sudweeks, (1998 & 2001), Eveland & Dunwoody, (2000), Herring, (1996), Kim & Allen, (2002), Matei & Ball-Rokeach, (2001), Nielsen, (1990), Preece, (2001), Sears, Jacko, & Dubach, (2000), Wheeler, (1998) & Nokaneinen (2004 & 2006). Several other researchers have shown in their studies the relationship between culture & WBLE usability (Chau, Cole, Massey, Montoya-Weiss, & O'Keefe, (2002), Faiola, (2002 &

2004) & Trompenaars, (1997)). Some of these include studies on cross-cultural WBLE design & usability with specific concern for user preferences from behavioural perspective. Some of these researchers are: Barber & Badre, (1998), Honold, (2000), Larson & Czerwinski, (1998), Liu, Lin, & Wang, (2003), Marcus, (2000), Marcus & Gould, (2000), Tractinsky, (1997), Zahedi, van Pelt, & Song, (2001), Taws, (2010) & Lidia, (2007). Numerous studies have identified links between culture, WBLE usability, and user preferences. They have shown how cultural factors affect processes of web related content design & use (Collis, (1999), McLoughlin & Oliver, (2000), Owen et al. (1998), Branden & Lambert, (1999), Chen et al. (1999), & Kum et al. (2000)).

From this brief review of existing studies in cultural differences and learning with WBLE/e-learning, results show that learner from different cultural backgrounds use and think about WBLE in different ways. Researchers such as, Collis, (1999), McLoughlin & Oliver, (2000), Owen et al. (1998), Branden & Lambert, (1999), Chen et al. (1999), and Kum et al. (2000) of this result state that WBLEs needs to be designed in consideration of the needs and learners' learning styles. From their results, they suggested some guidelines and models for doing this, and show that despite such guidelines and models used in considering the needs of culturally different learners, some learners are still disadvantaged when studying with or using WBLEs. My research will be focusing on these studies and their results in respect of African learners that are still disadvantaged when studying with or using e-learning environments and WBLEs.

## 2. Research Questions and Theoretical Frameworks

The research study addresses the following six (6) research questions: RQ 1: Is there a relationship between Usability Attributes and Learners' learning culture? RQ 2: Is there a relationship between Pedagogical Design, Pedagogical Usability and Learners' learning culture? RQ 3: Is there a relationship between Web-based learning environment usability and Learners' learning culture? RQ 4: Is there a relationship between learner's culture and learner's learning styles, that is, any influence of a learner's culture on the learner's learning style? RQ 5: What are the cultural issues influencing Web-based learning environment approach? RQ 6: What are the key strategies for designing Educational Websites or Web-based learning environments considering the learner's culture?

However, in this paper, empirical study will only address the first three RQs through tools use in data collection. The findings of the research will help to reduce or close the gap in use of technology (ICTs-use) for teaching and as a learning process in industrialised countries and in sub-Saharan African countries and other less developed or developing countries. The particular reference of this research will be on learners' cultures in Africa and Europe in use of ICTs for teaching learning purpose.

As contribution, this research into learning cultural differences among these continents will help African learners accommodate the inevitable change in technology teaching-learning methodology. It will also help e-learning environments course designers, educators, researchers and WBLEs technical usability designers to consider cultural issues affecting use of e-learning environments and/or WBLEs.

In order to carry out this research the following theoretical frameworks that are most relevant to the aim of this research are discussed in which this research study is grounded: 1. Nielsen's Attributes; Activity Theory, and Unified Theory of Acceptance and Use of Technology (UTAUT) on usability conceptual framework. 2. Curriculum theories, Instructional Design theories, and Learning theories on pedagogical usability. 3. Activity Centered Design (ACD Model), Objectivist Instructional Design Models (OIDMs), Constructivist Instructional Design Models (CIDMs), Mixed approach to Instructional Design (MID), and Design Approaches of Wallace & Anderson (1993) on pedagogical design. 4. Hofstede's cultural dimensions, Hall's cultural attributes, Nisbett's cultural attributes, and Trompenaars & Hampden-Turner's attributes on cultural issues. 4. Kolb's experiential learning theory & Clark's learning style indicator, Jung & Myers-Briggs learning style theory, Honey & Mumford's learning style model, and Felder-Silverman learning style model on learner's learning style approach.

## 3. Research Design and Methodology: Method and Tool use for data collection

This research is on pedagogical design and pedagogical usability of e-learning environments and cultural issues affecting its uses in teaching and learning approach. In this sense, the research makes use of both qualitative and quantitative techniques (i.e. mixed methods approach) in arriving at defined findings. It combines both participant observations using a designed WBLE for data collection with embedded use of open-ended questions, as qualitative technique. And use of questions in form of a questionnaire (the pedagogical usability survey – Nokelainen's PMLQ Factors) placed in the designed WBLE that asks about the relation that exists between two or more variables, as quantitative technique. Also, this research makes use of some other research models that is used in designing the WBLE used for data collection, such as, Performance Expectancy, Effort Expectancy, Social Influence and Behavioural Intention models (as used by Jeremy Taws, 2010; and Bandyopadhyay & Bandyopadhyay, 2008). These methods and models in relation to this research theoretical framework are used in design of a WBLE that is used to collect data for this research study (see Figure 1).

The WBLE designed consists of questionnaire and were administered to European and African learners in order to know and find how African learners like to study and learn via e-learning environments compared with their European counterparts. The basic reason for this is to know how best and effective learning via WBLE can take place from the perspective of both instructor and learners. The web-platform (Figure 1), which contains three different styles of learning materials and activities, randomly allocates different style of learning materials and activities to participants. Pedagogy designs in the WBLE contain different style of contents and same questionnaire. Participants from different locations in Africa (Gambia, Ghana & Nigeria – 50 respondents) and Europe (England, Finland & Netherlands/Germany – 50 respondents) used the WBLE. They provided their responses to the questionnaire (pedagogical usability survey) and then proceeded to answer questions based on the learning materials (cognitive learning survey). This is purposely to determine how participants from different continents differ in use of technology with respect to their cultural characteristics.

**The Tool:** The tool discuss here is basically a WBLE (web-platform shown in figure 1) designed and launched on the internet that contains questionnaires (Cognitive learning and Affective learning questions). The designed WBLE contains instructions to the learning activities, demographic survey, learning materials (Cognitive learning) and the Pedagogically Meaningful Learning Questionnaire (PMLQ) factors of Nokelainen (2006). There are three types of learning activities (Type I, Type II & Type III) on three different topics (Talking Drum, APA Style & Electronic Cigarette) which are randomly assigned in several combinations with each respondent working on three different types of the learning activities. Type I is basically text only learning activity and the basis of measurement (baseline or reference point). Type II is signaling (modeling) learning activity and Type III is combination of Type I and Type II (mixed model) with some web-links as secondary learning activities. At the beginning of the section, respondent selects their continent and then the WBLE's system randomly routes them through their continent path where they perform activities allocated to them within the WBLE. The questionnaires for respondents and data collection criteria are based on the following:

**General Information of the Respondents –** This consists of two main factors: respondents' differences and cultural beliefs (e.g. Gender & Age, Nationality, Continent of Residence, Education/Courses, and Respect for tradition & Culture). The essence of these factors is to determine or find behavioural cultural dimensions of respondents. That is, where respondents belong to in 'uncertainty avoidance' cultural dimension of Hofstede that is identical to Trompenaars & Hampden-Turner's 'universalism/particularism value attributes. According to Case (2000), these factors are of valuable when picking participants in phenomenography research. **Technical Usability/Design –** This consists of five factors: learnability, efficiency, memorability, errors and satisfaction that are taken from Nielsen's usability attributes (1993 & 2000); 4-E models of Collis & Moonen, (2001), Dumas & Redish, (1993), Guillemette, (1989), Rosenbaum, (1989), Rubin, (1994), Shackel, (1991), and Nokelainen, (2004 & 2006) usability checklists. The essence of these factors and checklists is to find how WBLE can be design to meet learner's learning culture in use of e-learning environment/WBLE. These factors are also used as guidelines for structural design of the activities of the WBLE (The website platform – Figure 1).

**Pedagogical Design/Usability –** This contains six main factors: Learner Control, Added Value, Application, Learner Activity, Value of Previous Knowledge & motivation and 21 questions of PMLQ that are more related to this study. All these are embedded in the WBLE platform (Figure 1). In the WBLE, through observation, respondents worked on all the activities randomly allocated to them by the WBLE within a time limit. And these activities contain questionnaires on demographic survey (cultural & educational background), pedagogical design (learning materials), and pedagogical usability survey (The PMLQ). The method used here to collect data relate to nature and purpose of this research as it focuses on describing and finding learner's learning preferences in terms of learning modes, types of learning activities and learning styles that are issues considered more useful in designing and using WBLE, hence, phenomenographic method is employed. The focus for this research discussion and processes are on learning design and evaluating courses, designing e-modules and technical support for learning Institutions in Africa in particular.

The WBLE which is designed to collect data is shown in Figure 1 below.

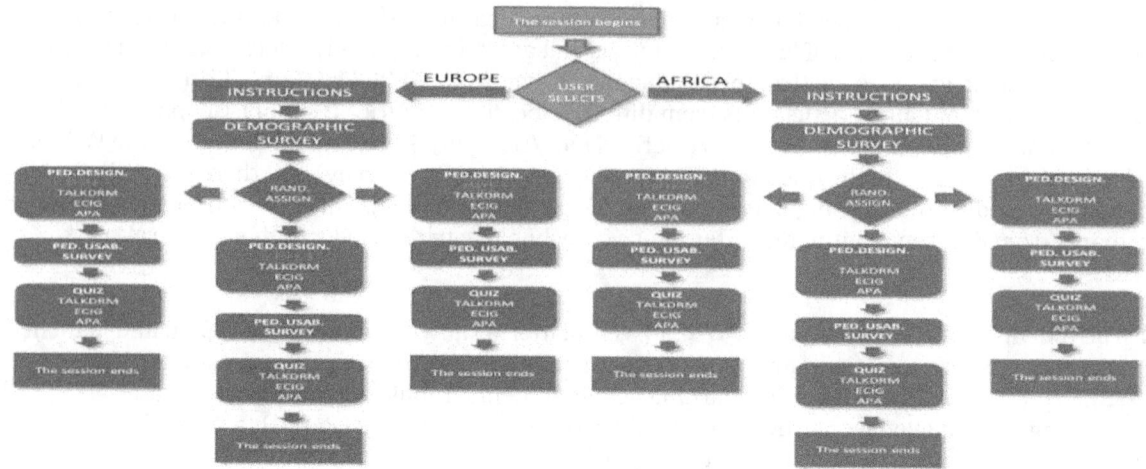

Figure 1: The web-based learning environment (website platform) pictorial structure. Figure 1 above is the designed WBLE that contains instructions to demographic survey, pedagogical design (Cognitive learning) and pedagogical usability survey (PMLQ). At the beginning of the section, respondent selects their continent and then the WBLE's system randomly routes them through their continent path where they perform all activities allocated to them within the web-based learning environment.

**4. Results/Findings and Discussion**

This section shows all results/findings and it only discusses and gives summary of findings from African respondents to the RQs in relation to pedagogical design and pedagogical usability of WBLE. **Results:** The responses to the questionnaires on demographic survey, pedagogical design activities and quizzes, and pedagogical usability PMLQ survey are retrieved from the WBLE's database and results are analysed in Figures 2 to 4 and Tables 1 and 2 below in relation to the research questions (RQs).

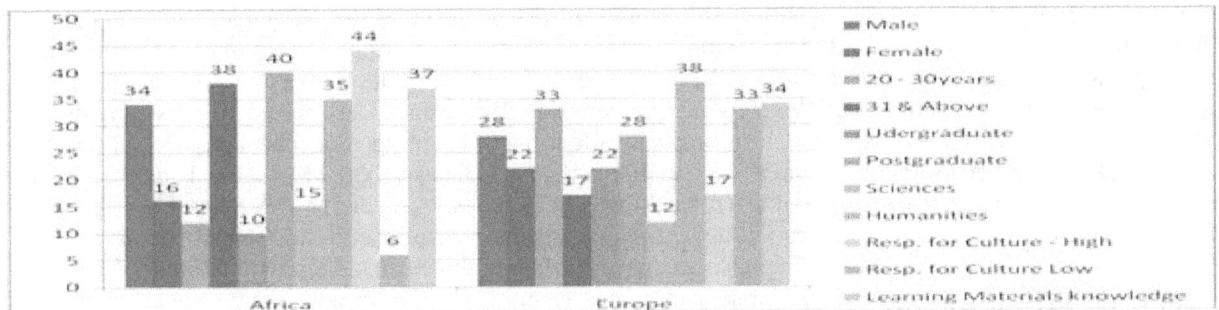

Figure 2: Demographic Survey (Cultural Background) for African and European Respondents

The findings shown in Figure 2 above show that learners from Europe, e.g., with respect for culture and tradition low scores at 33 while African learners shows respect for culture and tradition high score at 44 and 37 previous knowledge of learning materials on the WBLE platform compared with their European counterparts at 34.

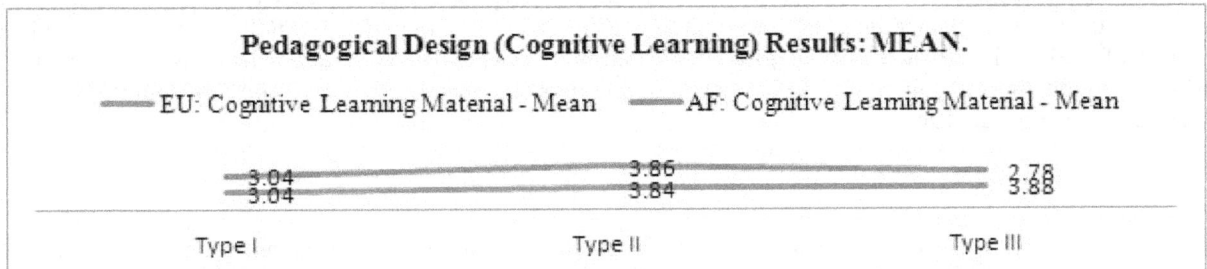

Figure 3: Pedagogical Design (Cognitive Learning) for African and European Respondents

Comparatively from figure 3 above, using the baseline Type I learning activities as parameter of measurement, African learners performed better in Type II (M = 3.86) learning activities while European learners did better in Type III (M = 3.88) learning activities.

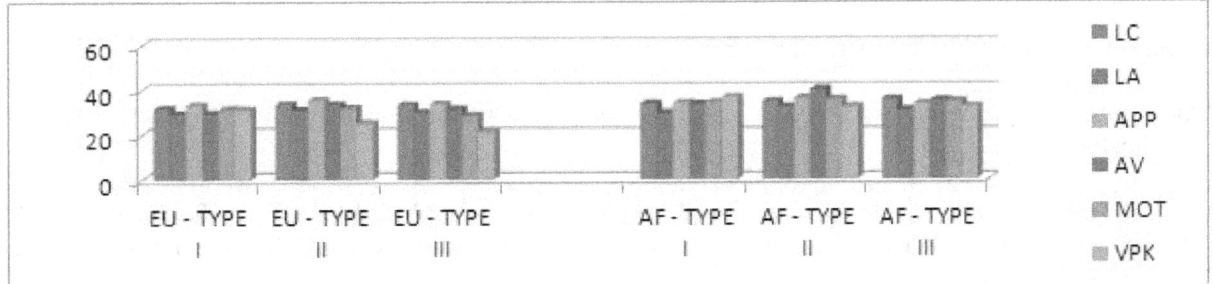

Figure 4: Pedagogical Usability (Affective Learning – PMLQ MEAN for Africa & Europe)
Key: LC = Learner Control. LA = Learner Activity. APP = Applicability. AV = Added Value. MOT = Motivation. VPK = Value of Previous Knowledge.

Figure 4 above clearly shows that both African and European respondents prefer affective learning factors Type

II to Type III with higher responses from African respondents in both Type II & Type III when compared with those of European respondents. However, considering the design of questionnaire and different Types of learning materials in relation to the research objectives, these results from pedagogical usability will be cross checked with those of pedagogical design in the summary of the findings/results to RQs section below. The summary of results using only results from African respondents will be related to RQs on pedagogical design and pedagogical usability of WBLE.

**Discussion:** The empirical results from 100 African and European learners in respect to their learning culture, show that African learners within their learning culture perform better using pedagogically designed WBLE that focus specially more on the following: 1. Learner Control i.e. minimum memory load, meaningful encoding and user control. 2. Motivation i.e. meaningfulness of studies. While their European counterparts highly prefer pedagogically designed WBLE that focus more on Applicability i.e. more activities on learning by doing, and Learner Activity i.e. reflective thinking & problem-based learning. Also, checking overall average of cognitive learning results in Type I, Type II & Type III for African learners, Type I M = 3.04; Type II M = 3.86 & Type III M = 2.78. And those of European learners show: Type I M = 3.04; Type II M = 3.84 and Type III M = 3.88. From these results it can be concluded that African learners in response to their learning culture performed at the lowest in Type III pedagogical design. This is mainly because they would like to use e-learning activities that portray reflective observation and learning based on practical experience i.e., signaling rather than learning activities based on abstract conceptualisation and active experimentation i.e., applicability and learner activity. To conclude this discussion, findings generated through this empirical study to an extent support those findings generated from theoretical studies and hypotheses from previous researches in this perspective of cultural impacts on pedagogical design and pedagogical usability of e-learning environments/WBLE (see Section 1). **Summary of the Findings to the Research Questions (RQs)**

Only the findings from African respondents will be related to the research questions as this research study mainly focus on African learning style and learning culture in relation to pedagogical design and pedagogical usability of WBLE. The purpose is to suggest and recommend best ways and issues to be considered when designing e-learning environments/WBLE by WBLE technical designers and pedagogical designers for effective e-learning activities and e-learning usability in African learners' cultural context.

**RQ 1 & RQ 3 Findings:**

The results here will view technical usability and e-leaning environment usability from pedagogical usability approach. Hence to find RQ 1: the relationship between usability attributes and learner's learning culture and RQ 3: the relationship between WBLE usability and Learners' learning culture. The cultural attributes of African respondents will be correlated with usability attributes/pedagogical usability. These will be:

Usability Attributes/PMLQ Factors I, II & III and LC: 33.85 + 34.85 + 35.70 = M 34.80  LA: 29.56 + 32.20 + 30.80 = M 30.85  APP: 34.08 + 36.24 + 33.80 = M 34.70

Demographic Survey (Cultural Attributes) Sex: 1 = 34 & 2 = 16  Age: n = 50

Respect for culture/tradition: n = 50 PKLM: 37 (High) & 13 (Low) Education: 40 (PG) & 10 (DG) Subject: 15 (Sc) & 35 (Humanities)

AV: 33.60 + 40.20 + 35.10 = M 36.30  MOT: 34.40 + 35.66 + 34.66 = M 34.90  VPK: 36.80 + 32.30 + 32.40 = M 33.83  Table 1 below shows correlation between these variables (pedagogical usability attributes & cultural attributes).

Table 1 Correlations/variables - Ped. Usability, Respect for culture/tradition, Ages, Sex, Education, PKLM & Subjects

| | | Pedagogical Usability | Respect for culture & Tradition | Ages | Sex | Education | PKLM | Subjects |
|---|---|---|---|---|---|---|---|---|
| Pedagogical Usability | Pearson Correlation | 1 | .557 | .551 | 1.000** | 1.000** | 1.000** | -1.000** |
| | Sig. (2-tailed) | | .251 | .257 | . | . | . | . |
| | N | 6 | 6 | 6 | 2 | 2 | 2 | 2 |
| Respect for culture & Tradition | Pearson Correlation | .557 | 1 | -.080 | 1.000** | 1.000** | 1.000** | -1.000** |
| | Sig. (2-tailed) | .251 | | .580 | . | . | . | . |
| | N | 6 | 50 | 50 | 2 | 2 | 2 | 2 |
| Ages | Pearson Correlation | .551 | -.080 | 1 | 1.000** | 1.000** | 1.000** | -1.000** |
| | Sig. (2-tailed) | .257 | .580 | | . | . | . | . |
| | N | 6 | 50 | 50 | 2 | 2 | 2 | 2 |
| Sex | Pearson Correlation | 1.000** | 1.000** | 1.000** | 1 | 1.000** | 1.000** | -1.000** |
| | Sig. (2-tailed) | . | . | . | | . | . | . |
| | N | 2 | 2 | 2 | 2 | 2 | 2 | 2 |
| Education | Pearson Correlation | 1.000** | 1.000** | 1.000** | 1.000** | 1 | 1.000** | -1.000** |
| | Sig. (2-tailed) | . | . | . | . | | . | . |
| | N | 2 | 2 | 2 | 2 | 2 | 2 | 2 |
| PKLM | Pearson Correlation | 1.000** | 1.000** | 1.000** | 1.000** | 1.000** | 1 | -1.000** |
| | Sig. (2-tailed) | . | . | . | . | . | | . |
| | N | 2 | 2 | 2 | 2 | 2 | 2 | 2 |
| Subjects | Pearson Correlation | -1.000** | -1.000** | -1.000** | -1.000** | -1.000** | -1.000** | 1 |
| | Sig. (2-tailed) | . | . | . | . | . | . | |
| | N | 2 | 2 | 2 | 2 | 2 | 2 | 2 |

**. Correlation is significant at the 0.01 level (2-tailed).

This shows that there is positive correlation between pedagogical usability (technical usability and WBLE usability), respect for culture/tradition & age at 0.557 & 0.551 respectively. That is, there is large correlation between the variables ($r = 0.56$ & $r = 0.55$), suggesting quite strong relationship between Usability Attributes/WBLE usability/Pedagogical Usability factors and Cultural Attributes (respect for culture/tradition & age). Hence, variance is $0.557 \times 0.557 = 0.31025$ & $0.551 \times 0.551 = 0.3036$ that indicates 31% & 30% respectively shared variance. This means that these cultural attributes help to explain 31% & 30% of variance in respondents' scores on usability attributes/WBLE usability/pedagogical usability factors. Therefore, the relationship between usability attributes, WBLE usability/pedagogical usability and learner's learning culture in terms of respect for culture/tradition & age as investigated using Pearson product-moment correlation coefficient shows strong, positive correlation between the variables [$r = 0.56$, $n = 50$ & $r = 0.55$, $n = 50$ respectively]. Hence, results show strong relationship between usability attributes, WBLE usability/pedagogical usability and learner's learning culture in relation to respect to culture/tradition and age.

However, other cultural attributes, Sex, Education, PKLM & Subject in relationship with pedagogical usability also show large correlation between the variables ($r = 1.00$). Hence, their variance is $1.000 \times 1.000 = 1$ which indicates 1% shared variance. This means that, these cultural attributes help to explain 1% of variance in respondents' scores on usability attributes/WBLE usability/pedagogical usability factors at significant level $p<0.01$. Therefore, the relationship between usability attributes, WBLE usability/pedagogical usability and learner's learning culture in terms of Sex, Education, PKLM & Subject as investigated using Pearson product-moment correlation coefficient shows large, positive correlation (with exception of cultural attribute: subject that shows large & negative correlation) between the variables [$r = 1.000$ ($r = -1.000$), $n = 2$ at $p<0.01$]. Hence, results also show perfect correlation between usability attributes, WBLE usability/pedagogical usability and learner's learning culture in relation to Sex, Education, PKLM & Subject same as with the theoretical result.

**RQ 2 Findings:**

To find the relationship between pedagogical design, pedagogical usability and learner's learning culture. The cultural beliefs, educational background & learning status of African respondents; pedagogical usability factors; Learner Control, Learner Activity, Applicability, Added Value, Motivation, Valuation of Previous Knowledge; and pedagogical design used. That is, Type I, Type II &Type III learning materials will be correlated as a group of variables. These will be:

**Pedagogical Usability.**

LC: 33.85 + 34.85 + 35.70 = M 34.80 LA: 29.56 + 32.20 + 30.80 = M 30.85 APP: 34.08 + 36.24 + 33.80 = M 34.70 AV: 33.60 + 40.20 + 35.10 = M 36.30 MOT: 34.40 + 35.66 + 34.66 = M 34.90 VPK: 36.80 + 32.30 + 32.40 = M 33.83

**Pedagogical Design**

Type I M = 3.04 Type II M = 3.86 Type III M = 2.78

**Cultural Attributes**

Sex: 1 = 34 & 2 = 16 (n = 50) Age: n = 50  Respect. for cult./tradition: n = 50 PKLM: 37 (High) & 13 (Low) Education: 40 (PG) & 10 (DG) Subject:15 (Sc) & 35 (Humanities)

Table 2 below shows correlation between pedagogical usability, pedagogical design & cultural attributes.

Table 2 Correlations/variables - Ped. Usability, Ped. Design, Respect for culture & tradition, Ages, Sex, Education, PKML, Subjects

| | | Pedagogical Usability | Pedagogical Design | Respect for culture & Tradition | Ages | Sex | Education | PKLM | Subjects |
|---|---|---|---|---|---|---|---|---|---|
| Pedagogical Usability | Pearson Correlation | 1 | -.968 | .557 | .551 | 1.000** | 1.000** | 1.000** | -1.000** |
| | Sig. (2-tailed) | | .162 | .251 | .257 | . | . | . | . |
| | N | 6 | 3 | 6 | 6 | 2 | 2 | 2 | 2 |
| Pedagogical Design | Pearson Correlation | -.968 | 1 | -.287 | -.974 | -1.000** | -1.000** | -1.000** | 1.000** |
| | Sig. (2-tailed) | .162 | | .815 | .144 | . | . | . | . |
| | N | 3 | 3 | 3 | 3 | 2 | 2 | 2 | 2 |
| Respect for culture & Tradition | Pearson Correlation | .557 | -.287 | 1 | -.080 | 1.000** | 1.000** | 1.000** | -1.000** |
| | Sig. (2-tailed) | .251 | .815 | | .580 | . | . | . | . |
| | N | 6 | 3 | 50 | 50 | 2 | 2 | 2 | 2 |
| Ages | Pearson Correlation | .551 | -.974 | -.080 | 1 | 1.000** | 1.000** | 1.000** | -1.000** |
| | Sig. (2-tailed) | .257 | .144 | .580 | | . | . | . | . |
| | N | 6 | 3 | 50 | 50 | 2 | 2 | 2 | 2 |
| Sex | Pearson Correlation | 1.000** | -1.000** | 1.000** | 1.000** | 1 | 1.000** | 1.000** | -1.000** |
| | Sig. (2-tailed) | . | . | . | . | | . | . | . |
| | N | 2 | 2 | 2 | 2 | 2 | 2 | 2 | 2 |
| Education | Pearson Correlation | 1.000** | -1.000** | 1.000** | 1.000** | 1.000** | 1 | 1.000** | -1.000** |
| | Sig. (2-tailed) | . | . | . | . | . | | . | . |
| | N | 2 | 2 | 2 | 2 | 2 | 2 | 2 | 2 |
| PKLM | Pearson Correlation | 1.000** | -1.000** | 1.000** | 1.000** | 1.000** | 1.000** | 1 | -1.000** |
| | Sig. (2-tailed) | . | . | . | . | . | . | | . |
| | N | 2 | 2 | 2 | 2 | 2 | 2 | 2 | 2 |
| Subjects | Pearson Correlation | -1.000** | 1.000** | -1.000** | -1.000** | -1.000** | -1.000** | -1.000** | 1 |
| | Sig. (2-tailed) | . | . | . | . | . | . | . | |
| | N | 2 | 2 | 2 | 2 | 2 | 2 | 2 | 2 |

**. Correlation is significant at the 0.01 level (2-tailed).

The results show that there are strong, negative correlation between groups of variables for Pedagogical Design & Pedagogical Usability at -0.968 (large); Pedagogical Design & cultural attributes of respect for culture/tradition at -0.287 (weak), Age at -0.974 (large), Sex, Education & PKLM at -1.000 (large) each, with exception of Subject that is positive at 1.000 (large). And large, positive correlation between groups of variables for Pedagogical Design & cultural attributes of respect for culture/tradition at 0.557, Age at 0.551, Sex, Education and PKLM at 1.000 each, with exception of Subject that is negative at -1.000.

In sum, these results show large correlations between groups of variables ($r = -0.97$, $r = -0.29$ & $0.56$, $r = -0.97$ & $0.55$, and $r = -1.0^4$ & $1.0^4$), suggesting strong relationship between groups of variables. Hence, variances are: [-0.968 x -0.968 = 0.93702, -0.287 x -0.287 = 0.08237, -0.974 x -0.974 = 0.94868 & $-1.000^4$ x $-1.000^4$ = 1.0] &

[0.551 x 0.551 = 0.3036, 0.557 x 0.557 = 0.31025 & $1.000^4$ x $1.000^4$ = 1.0]. That is, pedagogical design & pedagogical usability at 93.70% with cultural attributes of respect for culture & Age at 8.24% & 94.87% respectively and other cultural attributes (Sex, Education, PKLM & Subject) at 1% also with 31% for respect for culture/tradition & 30% for Age, and other cultural attributes also at 1% as shown in RQ 1 & RQ 3 results.

This means that cultural attributes Age & Respect for culture/tradition help to explain 95% & 8% and 30% & 31% of variance in respondents' scores on pedagogical design and pedagogical usability respectively. Other cultural attributes (Sex, Age, PKLM & Subject) show same results at 1% on pedagogical design and pedagogical usability factors at the significant level $p<0.01$. Therefore, the relationship between pedagogical design, pedagogical usability and learner's learning culture in terms of respect for culture/tradition & age as investigated using Pearson product-moment correlation coefficient shows reasonably strong, correlation between the variables. So also, other cultural attributes, Sex, Education, PKLM & Subject in relationship with pedagogical usability and pedagogical design show large/strong and perfect correlation between the variables.

## 5. Conclusions

Having provided a critical assessment of the factors and cultural issues influencing learning approach involving a web-based learning environment and examined link between the expectations of individual leaner in respect to his/her previous learning experience and effective use of technology approach for learning. And having developed a systematic culture-focused and learners-centered approach to pedagogical design and use of learning activities and styles based on web-based environments as well as described process of data collection and results of data collected. The conclusive parts of this paper will provide suggestions for pedagogical designers and technical usability WBLE designers in designing effective e-learning environments for Users' cultural context. Some of these suggestions based on the empirical findings of this study are as follows:

1. As findings show that activities based work environments are more relevant to African learners and their 'collectivist', uncertainty avoidance and long-term versus short-term time orientation learning cultures, hence, course designers and WBLE designers should consider these facts when designing e-learning environments. The e-course designers and WBLE designers should as well consider the perceived usefulness and perceived ease of use as major determinants of intention to use a technology. This reflects on pedagogical design findings where African learners have comparative advantage on signaling method (Type II) with high learner control affective learning outcome relatively to their least comparative advantage on applicability affective learning outcome in comparison with their European counterparts.

2. The findings show that pedagogical designers and WBLE (technical usability) designers should consider WBLE designs that avoid stress and one that provides exciting and challenging sessions (no dull moments). WBLE users expect e-courses and e-learning environments that embrace different categories of group discussions, and not just discussion, so there can be interactions with instructors (instructor's involvement) and participants on web-based courses and e-learning environments.

3. Pedagogical designers and e-learning environments, technical usability, designers when designing WBLE should ensure that e-learning environments maintain a reasonable power-distance balance between instructors and learners, i.e., authority and non-authority figures.  4. They should provide problems or e-learning tasks that are comfortable and appropriate to the learning values and practices of learners.

5. They should design e-learning so it is connected to learners' cultural values and develop an environment for asking questions and as well allocate time for reflection. Having considered all in this research study-paper on pedagogical design and pedagogical usability of WBLE and its cultural implications in comparison between Africa and Europe, one basic direction for further research will be suggestion in the areas of costs and benefits offered by web-based course environment or e-learning only courses. For examples: 1) what is the cost of the certification or to what extend would the certification be recognised and commensurate positions be given to participants in employment services? 2) The benefits should be clearly highlighted: Who benefits from this? That is, in terms of benefits in the use of technology and technology-supported approaches for learning in respect to instructors and learners interactions via-a-vis the society: a) would teachers become more pedagogically affectionate towards their learners when contacts are web-based and 'faceless'? Or would learners be turned to 'genetically modified seeds'?

# References

Barber, W., & Badre, A. (1998). Culturability: The merging of culture and usability.

Bandyopadhyay, K. & S, (2008). User Acceptance of Information Technology Across Cultures. http://www.swdsi.org/swdsi08/paper/SWDSI%20Proceedings%20Paper%20S456.pdf

Branden, J. B. and J. Lambert (1999). "Cultural Issues related to transnational Open and Distance Learning in Universities: a European problem?" British Journal of Educational Technology 30 (3): 251-260.

Burnett, G. & Buerkle, H. (2004). Information exchange in virtual communities: a comparative study. *Journal of Computer-Mediated Communication*, **9**(2).

Case, J.M. (2000). Students' perceptions of context, approaches to learning and metacognitive development in a second year chemical engineering course. PhD. thesis, Monash University, Melbourne, Australia.

Chau, P. Y. K., Cole, M., Montoya-Weiss, M. and O'keefe, R. M., (2002). "Cultural Differences in the Online Behavior of Consumers,"Communications of the ACM Vol. 45, No. 10: 138-143.

Chen, A., Mashhadi, A., Ang, D., & Harkrider, N. (1999). Cultural issues in the design of technology- enhanced learning systems. British Journal of Educational Technology , 30 (3), 217.

Choong, Y.Y., & Salvendy, G., (1999). Implications for design of computer interfaces for Chinnese users in Mainland China. International Journal of Human Computer Interaction 11/1, 29-46.

Collis B. & Moonen J. (2001); Flexible Learning in a digital world: Experiences and Expectations. Stylus Publishing Inc. 22883 Quicksilver Drive, Sterling VA 20166-2012, USA.

Collis, B. (1999). Designing for differences: Cultural issues in the design of WWW-based course-support sites. British Journal of Educational Technology, 30 (3), 201–215.

Danet, B., & Herring, S. C., (2003). The Multilingual Internet: Language, Culture and Communication in Instant Messaging, Email and Chat. Journal of Computer-Mediated Communication 9 (1).

Del Galdo & Nielsen (1996). International User Interfaces. New York, NY: Wiley. Dumas, J. & Redish, J. (1993). *A practical guide to usability testing.* Norwood, NJ: Ablex.

Ess, C., & Sudweeks, F. (2001). On the edge: Cultural barriers and catalysts to IT diffusion among remote and marginalized communities. New Media & Society, 3(3) 259-269.

Eveland, W. P., & Dunwoody, S. (2000). A test of competing hypotheses about the impact of the World Wide Web versus traditional print media on l e a r n i n g .

Faiola, A. (2004). The second psychology of Vygotsky and Luria: Cross-cultural web design from a cognitive perspective.

Herring, S. C. *(Ed.). (*1996*).* Computer-mediated communication: Linguistic, social, and cross- cultural perspectives.

Guillemette, R. A. (1989). Usability in computer documentation design: Conceptual and methodological considerations. *IEEE Transactions on Professional Communication, 32*, 217- 228.

Honold, P. *(*2000*).* Cultural and context: An empirical study for the development of a framework for the elicitation of cultural influence in product usage. The International Journal of Human- Computer Interaction, 12, 327–345.

Kim, K. S., & Allen, B. *(*2002*).* Cognitive and task influences on web searching behavior.

Kum, C., C. Vanessa, et al. (2000). The Use of Web-Based Learning in Culturally Diverse Learning Environments. AusWeb2K, Southern Cross University, Southern Cross University Press.

Larson, K., & Czerwinski, M. *(*1998*).* Web page design: Implications of memory, structure, and scent for information retrieval. Paper presented at the CHI '98 Human Factors in Computing Systems, Los Angeles.

Lidia Oshlyansky (2007). Cultural Models in HCI: Hofstede, Affordance and Technology Acceptance.

Liu, Y., Lin, F., & Wang, X. *(*2003*).* Education practice and analyzing behaviour of students in a web-based learning environment: An exploratory study from China. Online Information Review, 27*(*2*),* 110–119.

Marcus, A. *(*2000*).* International and intercultural user-interface design. *In* ConstantineStephanidis *(Ed.),* User interfaces for all *(pp.* 47–64*). New York: Erlbaum.*

Marcus, A., & Gould, E. W. *(*2000*).* Crosscurrents: Cultural dimensions and global web user interface design. Interactions.

Matei, S., & Ball-Rokeach, S. *(*2001*).* Real and virtual social ties: Connections in the everyday lives of seven ethnic neighborhoods. American Behavioral Scientist, 45*(*3*),* 550–563.

McLoughlin, C. and R. Oliver (2000). "Designing Learning Environments for Cultural Inclusivity: A Case Study of Indigenous Online Learning at Tertiary Level." Australian Journal of Educational Technology.

Nielsen, J. *(Ed.). (*1990*).* Designing user interfaces for international use: Advances in human factors and ergonomics.

Nielsen, J. (1993). *Usability engineering.* San Diego, CA: Academic Press Nielsen (2000). Designing Web usability: The practice of simplicity. Indianapolis: New Riders.

Nokelainen P. (2006). An Empirical Assessment of Pedagogical Usability Criteria for Digital Learning Material with Elementary School Students. Journal of Educational Technology & Society, 9(2), 178-197.

Nokelainen P. (2004). Conceptual definition of the technical and pedagogical usability criteria for digital learning material. Proceedings of ED-MEDIA 2004, Lugano, Switzerland, 4249-4254.

Owens, E. W. (1998). "Sex and Ethnic related differences amongst High School Students' Technology use in Science and Mathematics." International Journal of Instructional Media Vol 25 (1): 43-55.

Preece, J. *(*2001*)* Online communities: Designing usability and supporting sociability. *N*ew York: Wiley.

Rosenbaum, S. (1989). Usability evaluations vs. usability testing: When and why? *IEEE Transactions on Professional Communication, 32*, 210-16.

Rubin, J. (1994). Handbook of usability testing: How to plan, design, and conduct effective tests. New York, NY: John Wiley & Sons.

Sears, A., Jacko, J., & Dubach, E. M. (2000). International aspects of World Wide Web usability and the role of high-end graphical enhancements. International Journal of Human-Computer Interaction, 12(2), 241–261.

Shackel, B. (1991). Usability - context, framework, design and evaluation. In B. Shackel & S. Shneiderman (2000). Designing the user interface: Strategies for effective human-computer interaction. Reading, MA: Addison-Wesley.

Taws, J., (2010). Cultural Differences and their Influence on Technology Acceptance: An Empirical Study of Taiwanese and Canadian Users.

Tractinsky, N. (1997). Aesthetics and apparent usability: Empirically assessing cultural and methodological issues.

Trompenaars, F. (1997). Riding the waves of culture: Understanding cultural diversity in business.

Wallace, M. D., & Andersen, T. J. (1993). Approaches to interface design. Interacting with computers, 5, 259-278.

Wheeler, D. L. (1998). Global culture or culture clash: New information technologies in the Islamic world -A view from Kuwait. Communication Research. 25, 359-376.

Zahedi, F., van Pelt, W.V. & Song, J. (2001). A conceptual framework for international web design. IEEE Transactions on professional communication, 44(2), 83-103.

# 8 From Creation to Curation: Evolution of an Authentic 'Assessment for Learning' Task

Peter R Albion, University of Southern Queensland, Australia

## Background

Despite 30 years of effort toward change, schooling has not been as substantially changed by information and communication technology (ICT) as other aspects of society (Ertmer & Ottenbreit-Leftwich, 2013). Belland (2009) drew upon the theory of *habitus* to explain why teacher preparation programs might be unsuccessful in moving graduates toward integrating ICT in their classroom practice; it is difficult for a relatively short teacher preparation program to overwrite the understanding of teaching that candidates develop during the previous 12 years of experience as learners in conventional classrooms.

Similarly, Ertmer, Ottenbreit-Leftwich, Sadik, Sendurur, and Sendurur (2012) argued that, in order to move teachers toward more effective integration of ICT, professional development should use the same ICT and pedagogical approaches that teachers are able to use in their classrooms. They reiterated a call for teacher professional development to be offered using authentic approaches.

The implication of these arguments from Belland (2009) and Ertmer et al. (2012) is that widespread change in the practices of teachers with ICT will be facilitated by first implementing the desired changes within programs for teacher preparation and ongoing development. That is, there is a need for teacher education at all stages to offer learning experiences that authentically represent the context within which teachers will be expected to perform.

There seems to be no reason to expect that other aspects of teacher preparation and development should be different. Authenticity in learning experiences for teachers should facilitate transfer of learning to professional practice. The challenge, in a time of rapid change across multiple aspects of schooling, will be to ensure that the learning experiences offered are appropriately authentic and meet other requirements of the particular teacher education context.

This paper describes the evolution of an assessment task within a final year course in an initial teacher preparation program. The task represents a substantial proportion of the total assessment in the course but also functions as a significant learning activity within the course with a dual focus on developing knowledge relevant to the course and dispositions for professional practice. In this respect it may be seen as assessment for learning as much as, or more than, assessment of learning. The evolution of the task will be considered against significant changes in the operation of the bachelor degree program within which the course is placed and in the wider educational environment.

## The changing educational environment

Biological evolution occurs in response to environmental changes. As conditions change then the relative advantages and disadvantages of specific characteristics shift and organisms with more favourable combinations of characteristics are more likely to survive and reproduce. Similarly, educational evolution occurs in response to changes in societal and institutional conditions. In this instance some of the key changes that affected evolution of the course assessment included the increasing abundance of information, increasing focus on learning networks as a site of professional learning, emergence of curation as a professional activity, changes to curriculum and its implementation by education systems, and desire of students for more flexible learning opportunities.

## Abundance of information

Historically information has been scarce and has changed slowly. In the earliest times information was stored in human memory and transmitted orally. The invention of writing changed that but the change caused misgivings for some, including Socrates, who expressed disquiet about the potential of writing to increase forgetfulness and decrease wisdom (Kalantzis & Cope, 2012). Reproduction of handwritten documents was slow and expensive, so copies were rare and information was still conveyed orally by those with access to written copies. When printing was introduced it became possible to produce more copies cheaply but it was still necessary to physically distribute them. Traditional approaches to education developed in this context and can be described as a *pedagogy of scarcity* (Weller, 2011). When access to information is limited, transmissive approaches to learning and teaching by lectures and similar methods makes sense.

Four technological waves have changed the ecology of information (Albion, 2011), which is now expanding and changing very rapidly. For centuries publishing was expensive and restricted to specialists, but in the 1980s desktop publishing enabled almost anybody to print professional looking materials. In the 1990s the World Wide Web made a single electronic copy of a document available globally. In the 2000s Web 2.0 made it easy for anybody to instantly publish material to the world. Now mobile Internet access allows smartphones to access and publish material from anywhere with a mobile telephone connection. As access to information has changed, much else has changed with it. Although we commonly talk about the information economy, a critical difference between information and the material goods of the conventional economy suggests a different possibility:

...if you have any particular piece of information on the Net, you can share it easily with anyone else who might want it. It is not in any way scarce, and therefore it is not an information economy towards which we are moving...There is something else that moves through the Net, flowing in the opposite direction from information, namely attention (Goldhaber, 1997).

In this view, we are living with an *attention economy* rather than an *information economy*. Information is plentiful and, far from being diminished, its value is most often increased by sharing and linking with information available elsewhere. Attention is limited by the time we have available and sources of information compete for a share of our attention. The *pedagogy of scarcity* was based on transmitting scarce information from teacher to learners and is less relevant in an age when information is abundant and easily accessible to all. What we need now is a *pedagogy of abundance* (Weller, 2011).

Based on a traditional understanding of information it was natural to think of education and learning as being about transfer of information from teacher to learner. A constructivist view of knowledge encouraged us to think of learning as building knowledge by extending on the known (Bereiter, 2002). Connectivism (Siemens, 2005) suggested that knowledge may exist in the network as much as, or more than, in an individual and that learning is about making connections. The challenge for educators is to be lifelong professional learners using the power of the network to support user-generated learning (Swanson, 2013) by engaging with professional learning networks and sharing resources through curation.

## Professional Learning Networks

Whether or not they realize it, people have a personal or professional learning network (PLN). We all learn from other people in family, school, or community and they form part of a PLN that has developed without much conscious effort. Teachers, including those in preparation, need to give some serious thought to how to extend and shape a PLN so that it meets their needs most effectively. Warlick (2012) compares developing a personal learning network to cultivating a garden. In a world of abundant and rapidly changing information developing an effective PLN is an important strategy for maintaining professional currency. For teachers, a strong PLN is a way to maintain professional links with distant colleagues and engage in lifelong learning.

A network is typically looser than a group or community. It may include people who are known personally as well as others with whom there is no personal contact but who are followed as sources of information without necessarily engaging in direct exchanges. It may begin with people known in the real world and be extended through social networking services like Facebook, Twitter, or Google+ to include people with whom there is no other connection. Although social networking sites are sometimes derided for being time wasters full of trivia they also support many professional connections.

## Curation

One approach to dealing with the abundance of information on the Internet is *content curation*, a process through which somebody gathers and presents material similarly to how a curator brings together an exhibition in a museum or art gallery. Jarche (2012) linked curation to the processes of personal knowledge management (PKM) that are essential to professionals working with an abundance of information.

Jarche (2012) and Kanter (2011) described curation as having three phases - Seek, Sense, Share. In the Seek phase topics are defined, sources are organized and scanned, and high quality material is captured. In the Sense phase a useful artifact is produced by adding annotations and other writing to place the selected material in context and make sense of it in relation to other material. In the Share phase the artifacts are made available to the professional learning network and comments are offered on artifacts similarly shared by others. Weisgerber (2012) described eight steps rather than three in the curation process – find, select, editorialize, arrange, create, share, engage, track – but her process is essentially similar, especially when viewed alongside the more detailed processes described by Jarche (2012) and Kanter (2011) within each of their phases. Antonio, Martin and Stagg (2012) offered a definition of digital curation as "an active process whereby content/artefacts are purposely selected to be preserved for future access" and suggested that additional aspects such as dissemination via social media and comment by readers were important. Curation as a response to abundance of information is still an emerging practice but the essential features appear to be that it:

> presents high quality content selected for its relevance to a specific topic (seek),
> includes description and comment that adds value to the content (sense), and
> is published so that it is available to, and engages, interested colleagues (share).

As the practice of digital curation has become more common, the processes and tools that are used have evolved. At its most basic, curation could be undertaken using a web search engine and web publishing software for developing and publishing a website to make the curated items available. Curators have appropriated existing tools such as social bookmarking sites, Delicious (delicious.com) and diigo (diigo.com), and media sharing sites, Flickr (flickr.com) and YouTube (youtube.com), to their purposes, adding Twitter (twitter.com) and other channels for dissemination. New tools such as Pinterest (pinterest.com) have been taken up by curators as they have emerged and tools such as Scoop.it (scoop.it) have been developed specifically to support curation. Antonio, Martin, and Stagg (2012) conceptualized the array of digital curation tools as four overlapping areas comprising digital curation surrounded by blogs and microblogs, social bookmarking, and video and image sharing.

## Implementing new curriculum initiatives

In a period of rapid societal change it is not surprising that educational systems are implementing changes. In Australia the past couple of decades have seen a progression from broad agreement among state an federal governments about goals for education (MCEETYA, 1989) toward a national Australian curriculum (ACARA, 2011). In Queensland, the State Education Department has responded to the Australian curriculum by developing the Curriculum into the Classroom (C2C) materials (Education Queensland, 2013) which are described on the website as "digital resource that can be adapted to meet different school contexts" but have been adopted rather than adapted in some schools where they are seen as the definitive interpretation of the curriculum.

The C2C materials are just one, admittedly influential, source of prepared plans available for adaptation, or adoption, by teachers in their classrooms. The World Wide Web now offers a profusion of sites from which lesson plans and teaching resources can be downloaded for use by teachers to support planning for their classes. In addition to sites like the C2C resources developed by Education Queensland (2013), there are marketplaces like Teachers Pay Teachers (teacherspayteachers.com) and many others from which resources can be downloaded and adopted or adapted. While some teachers may still choose to create their own plans and resources based on curriculum requirements it is increasingly likely that most teachers will prefer to begin with existing materials and adapt them to meet their own needs.

## Flexible learning

Most undergraduate students at Australian universities have significant commitments to employment. In 2006, almost 5% were working full-time, 15% were working more than 20 hours per week, and 70% were working an average of 15 hours per week (James, Bexley, Devlin, & Marginson, 2007). Their number also includes a proportion of mature age students likely to have family commitments. In 2006, 45% of teacher education students were 25 years or older and 10% were at least 40 years old (DEST, 2006) and those proportions continue. The availability of students to attend classes is affected by work and family commitments. As a consequence, many are choosing to undertake all or part of their study by distance or online in order to achieve the flexibility they need to meet their other commitments.

The common response from universities is to use Learning Management Systems to facilitate access to study materials and learning activities. From 2001 to 2010 multimodal enrolments (mixed on and off campus) in Australia rose from 4% to 8% (DEEWR, 2011). At USQ the proportion of web-based enrolments increased by more than 400% from 2006 to 2010 (USQ, 2012) and by 2012, up to 70% of students in the 4-year Bachelor of Education were studying at least some subjects online. Students enrolled on campus also access materials and activities online via the LMS. These demographic changes inevitably affect the design of courses and the integrated learning and assessment activities.

## Evolution of the Assessment Task

A previous paper described the evolution of the course, *EDP4130 Technology Curriculum and Pedagogy*, with respect to how its design might be revised with a more explicit focus on development of pre-service teachers' TPACK (Albion, 2012). *Technology* in the course title refers to the subject specified in Queensland (QSA, 2013) and Australian (ACARA, 2013) curriculum documents and might be described as *design and technology* or similar in other jurisdictions. It is more similar to what is widely understood as STEM (Science, Technology, Engineering, and Mathematics) education than to Information Technology, although information and digital technologies do feature in the curriculum documents. This paper takes a more narrow focus on the evolution of the major assessment piece in the course and the contribution that it might make to pre-service teachers' learning specific to the course and technologies education, and to more general development of professional dispositions.

### Year 1

Prior to introduction of the *EDP4130* course in 2011, a technology education course had been offered from 2002 until 2005. Like *EDP4130*, that course was offered in the final year of a four year teacher preparation program. The major assessment piece engaged the entire annual cohort (typically 150 students), working in tutorial classes, in collaboratively developing technology curriculum resources and making them available to all cohort members. The approach was based loosely on the relate-create-donate pattern advocated by Shneiderman (1998) and each student completing the course had the potential to acquire a substantial collection of curriculum materials that could be used in their future classrooms. The task was designed to provide students with a technology challenge to be met through application of the technology design cycle (design-make-appraise or investigation-ideation-production-evaluation in the then national and state curriculum documents). The task also included a requirement to reflect and report on their learning as it related to the technology curriculum. Students appreciated the practicality of the assessment task and the teaching resources that they acquired through it. In some cases that was confirmed by contact from former students a year or more after graduation requesting details of the site where the resources could be accessed.

When *EDP4130* was first offered in 2011 the major assessable task was retained without significant change on the basis of that past success. A significant point of difference between *EDP4130* and the previous course was the mode of offer. The earlier course had been offered each year to about 120 students on the main campus of the university and a further 30 students on a smaller campus about 400 km distant, with both groups taught by traditional face-to-face lecture and tutorial. By 2011, consistent with the factors driving the move toward flexible learning as described above, all undergraduate courses were being offered fully online as well as in face-to-face mode on three campuses. The online class in 2011 numbered about 25 students and was treated as equivalent to a face-to-face tutorial class for the major assessment task. Each tutorial class (or equivalent) was charged with developing a number of sets of curriculum support materials to support 6 to 8 hours of technology curriculum learning over a period of 3 to 4 weeks. The number of sets required for each class varied according to the size of the class, with a set required for every five students. Classes were jointly responsible for negotiating the process of development and typically formed smaller groups and made each responsible for developing a set of materials. As was observed in the previous course, students appreciated the focus on activities that had direct relevance to their professional futures. Management of the development process was generally simple in face-to-face classes that met at least weekly but was more challenging for the online class where communication was mostly by email and asynchronous discussion forums with the option for synchronous links using Wimba or Skype.

## Year 2

Review of the 2011 course offer noted the challenges that all students had encountered with managing the large group activity and the particular challenges for those who were studying online. For the 2012 offer the assessment task was modified so that students were required to develop a plan and associated resources for teaching the technology curriculum but had a choice to work individually or in small groups rather than in a class group with collective responsibility. Consistent with the relate-create-donate model (Shneiderman, 1998) the materials that students developed were still required to be made available to all members of the cohort, thereby maintaining the authenticity of developing an artifact of value for a real audience. In order to preserve the benefits attached to working with the larger group, students were required to develop a personal reference network with which to discuss their materials development and to participate in a studio-style environment (Brown, 2006) so that their work in progress was open for comment by peers. This Virtual Learning Design Studio (VLDS) was mediated through the ePortfolio environment (mahara.org) provided by the university so that students might develop familiarity with the ePortfolio tools that they would be required to use in the following semester.

Most students engaged effectively with the task, although a small proportion delayed engagement with the VLDS until close to the end of semester, thereby minimizing any benefit that they received from comments of their peers. Working individually addressed the issues experienced by online students in the previous offer while retaining the benefits of developing and sharing resources. By the time the course was offered in 2012, the C2C initiative (Education Queensland, 2013) was being implemented in schools. C2C was confined to English, Mathematics, Science and History, and did not directly affect teaching of technology except insofar as one of its characteristics was to focus teaching on single learning areas and discourage integration across the curriculum. However, the emergence of C2C and the increasing availability of other teaching materials rendered the assessment task less relevant because of the move toward adapting teaching materials rather than developing them from scratch. Hence some further rethinking of the task design was required.

## Year 3

Revision of *EDP4130* for the 2013 offer was informed by the environmental changes described above. Rather than requiring students to develop plans and teaching materials from scratch, the design recognized the ready availability of plans and resources on the WWW and required students to curate digital resources that would support learning in some part of the curriculum. By recognizing the availability of resources the course design was moved toward a *pedagogy of abundance* (Weller, 2011). The requirement to engage with a professional learning network (PLN) introduced in the 2012 offer was retained because of the important role that a PLN plays in curation as both source of items to be curated and destination for sharing. The description of the assessment task began by declaring that the focus for the project was to "**curate a publicly accessible collection of online resources relevant to the classroom implementation of technology education in the Australian context**." That was followed by further details about requirements and the assessment criteria.

Because some students in the 2012 offer had reduced the value of the VLDS by delaying their engagement with it, the curation task was developed with two assessable phases. The intention was to ensure that students made a start early in the semester and had opportunity for feedback to ensure that they were on track. The first phase submission was due two weeks after beginning of semester, carried 15% of the semester marks, and required identification of a theme for curation, steps toward development of a PLN, selection of curation tool(s), and presentation of a sample curated item. Table 1 lists the assessment criteria with brief descriptions.

| Criterion | Description |
| --- | --- |
| Theme | Identify and justify a theme for its professional relevance to technology education |
| PLN mechanics | Explain the choice of 2 or more online services as sources of information for curation |
| PLN membership | Explain the choice of 3 to 6 experts as sources of information |
| Curation tool(s) | Explain the selection of a curation system |
| Curation sample(s) | Provide a sample of a curated item with an explanation of the curation process |

**Table 1:** Criteria for first phase of curation assessment

The final phase submission was due as part of the end of semester submission, carried 18% of the semester marks, and addressed criteria related to the content of the collection and its dissemination to a wider audience. Table 2 lists the assessment criteria with brief descriptions.

| Criterion | Description |
| --- | --- |
| Publication | Curated collection published on a professionally presented public site |
| Content of collection | A number of properly attributed items linked to the collection theme |
| Value added | Evidence of selection, editorial comment, contextualisation and critique |
| Curation process | Explanation of the curation process, role of PLN, etc. |
| Audience engagement | Evidence of efforts to promote the collection and of responses and further dissemination |
| Professional learning | What was learned and what is the continuing value of curation for professional growth? |

**Table 2:** Criteria for final phase of curation assessment

At the beginning of semester students were provided with the description of the task and the marking guides for both phases. The course site within the LMS also offered an 18 minute recorded presentation about curation (repeated in class for those attending on campus) and notes addressing the same content. The materials included suggestions about tools that might be suitable for developing and interacting with a PLN and/or for curating digital resources. Tools freely available on the Internet (diigo, Delicious, Twitter, Wordpress, Facebook, Scoop.it, Storify, Pinterest, etc.) were suggested but no specific tools were required and students were informed that they could meet course requirements using tools of their own choice, including those provided through the university.

Students were encouraged to sign up to Twitter and use it to disseminate items they curated. To provide access to the stream of tweets for those who had reservations about social media a Twitter widget displaying all tweets with a #edp4130 hashtag was embedded in the course LMS space and those using Twitter were asked to include the hashtag in relevant tweets. Similarly the RSS tool in the LMS was used to display items posted to a diigo group.

## Student Response to the Curation Task

Student submissions for the first phase of the task confirmed the value of including it as a spur to action and check on directions. Despite the focus statement for the task (see above) and the other activity in the course being directed toward the *Australian Curriculum: Technologies* document (ACARA, 2013) several students declared themes and provided examples that were directed toward ICT integration rather than technologies curriculum. Feedback on the first phase advised those students that ICT integration was important but not the specific subject for the curation task and, in most cases, that clarification assisted them to better direct their work for the second phase. The idea of a PLN and the processes for developing one had been discussed in class but some students identified their PLN with a specific page they had established on a website rather than with the web of contacts that might have been linked to that page. Again they were provided with feedback to refocus their efforts. The most popular curation tool was Scoop.it, which had featured in examples provided to the class, but others selected by students included Pinterest, Facebook, pages in their ePortolio (mahara.org) and websites developed using Weebly (weebly.com), Wix (wix.com) or other tools. Issues identified in this aspect of the first phase work included doubtful relevance or value of items curated, comments that did not appropriately link curated items to curriculum or potential classroom application, and potential technical issues with the tools being used, especially around the lack of capability for organizing a collection of items using tagging, categories or other methods. Feedback provided guidance intended to assist students with better meeting the task requirements in their submissions at the end of semester.

In the submissions at the end of semester it was evident that most students had benefited from feedback on the first phase and had made appropriate adjustments where necessary though some still appeared to be uncertain about their direction. Most of the sites used for curation were well presented but many students failed to include sufficient information about themselves to enable a potential user of their site to confirm their credibility as a source. That would not reduce the basic utility of the curated items but gave no basis for confidence in any comments they offered about curriculum links. The value of the comments offered by student curators on their selected items varied from a perfunctory 'Great resource' or similar to identification of specific sections of curriculum documents and suggestions for use in teaching.

All but a very few students met, or slightly exceeded, the target of one curated item per week, but most of the tools used for curation included some indication of the dates on which items were curated and it was clear from that evidence that almost without exception students had engaged with the activity in the first weeks when preparing the first phase submission and again in a burst late in semester when preparing the final submission. There was little evidence of a sustained pattern of curating across the duration of the semester. Dissemination to their PLNs was similarly concentrated in two periods of peak activity with little sustained effort across the semester. There was some evidence of linkages formed among the students with items curated by one being picked up by others and some students had clearly developed extended professional links with practicing teachers or other professionals via Twitter and other channels as a result of engagement in the curation and PLN activity.

Where students wrote about their learning through the task, most offered positive comments about the value of the activity for developing a collection of teaching resources curated by themselves and colleagues. Some of that might be attributed to writing what they thought would please a marker but much of it appeared to be genuine appreciation of the value of the task, and especially of a developing PLN, for their future as professional educators. A check conducted on a selection of curation sites three months after the end of the assessment task found no activity beyond the required period, suggesting that they were not continuing the activity or at least not in the same spaces.

## Conclusion

As an element of the *EDP4130* course the curation task was intended to provide students with ongoing access to collections of ideas and resources that would support classroom learning linked to the Australian Curriculum: Technologies and assist them with developing an active professional learning network that would have a life beyond the course. On completing the course they should have developed or enhanced their professional presence on the Internet and developed enduring professional links within their own cohort and beyond.

As noted above, the quality of the curated collections varied – both in the selection and curation of items with comments and in the actual presentation on the websites. This probably resulted, at least in part, from lack of exposure to suitable models of curation. Although the desired qualities were explained in course materials and in classes some students evidently had not internalized the appropriate standards for application in their own work. One possible approach to improvement in this area would be to engage students in reviewing a selection of curation sites and discussing the merits of their content and presentation. Such a learning activity early in the semester should help to build consensus about the qualities that make some curated collections more valuable than others. Students could then apply that knowledge in developing their own collections.

Engagement with a PLN, through curation or otherwise, is likely to be most effective if it is consistent to the point of being habitual. The pattern of peaks in curation activity observed around assessment dates indicates that students were not consistently engaged and were therefore unlikely to develop an habitual pattern of activity around interaction with their PLN. One possible solution would be to require that the curation activity demonstrate consistent engagement over the semester. Because students' other commitments vary and a steady stream of curatable items on any topic cannot be guaranteed there would need to be provision for some flexibility but it would still be possible to require demonstration of activity across the semester as part of the assessment.

These changes based on experience will prompt evolution of the assessment task toward a form that is more fit for the prevailing environment. As the environment continues to change it is unlikely that it will ever be a perfect fit but continuing reflection on the environment and experience will ensure that it remains authentic.

## References

ACARA. (2011). *The Australian Curriculum.* Canberra: Commonwealth of Australia (Australian Curriculum, Assessment and Reporting Authority) Retrieved from http://www.acara.edu.au/curriculum/curriculum_design_and_development.html.
ACARA. (2013). *Technologies.* Canberra: Commonwealth of Australia (Australian Curriculum, Assessment and Reporting Authority) Retrieved from http://www.acara.edu.au/curriculum/learning_areas/technologies.html.
Albion, P. R. (2011). Connected learning: What do our widening social networks mean for the future of learning? In A. Dashwood & J.-B. Son (Eds.), *Language, Culture and Social Connectedness* (pp. 89-100). Cambridge: Cambridge Scholars Publishing.
Albion, P. R. (2012). Designing for Explicit TPACK Development: Evolution of a Preservice Design and Technology Course. In P. Resta & R. Rose (Eds.), *Proceedings of Society for Information Technology & Teacher Education International Conference 2012* (pp. 2680-2685). Chesapeake, VA: Association for the Advancement of Computing in Education (AACE).
Antonio, A., Martin, N., & Stagg, A. (2012). Engaging higher education students via digital curation. In M. Brown (Ed.), *Future Changes, Sustainable Futures. Proceedings of ascilite 2012.* Wellington, NZ.
Belland, B. R. (2009). Using the theory of habitus to move beyond the study of barriers to technology integration. *Computers & Education, 52*(2), 353-364. doi: 10.1016/j.compedu.2008.09.004
Bereiter, C. (2002). *Education and mind in the knowledge age.* Mahwah: L. Erlbaum Associates.
Brown, J. S. (2006). New Learning Environments for the 21st Century: Exploring the edge. *Change, 38*(5), 18-24.
DEEWR (2010). *Students: Selected Higher Education Statistics.* Retrieved from http://www.deewr.gov.au/HigherEducation/Publications/HEStatistics/Publications/Pages/2009FullYear.aspx
DEEWR (2011). *uCube - Higher Education Statistics.* Retrieved from http://www.highereducationstatistics.deewr.gov.au/
DEST (2006). *Survey of Final Year Teacher Education Students.* Retrieved from http://www.dest.gov.au/sectors/school_education/publications_resources/profiles/documents/FinalYrTeachStudentsSurveyReport_pdf.htm.
Education Queensland. (2013). *Curriculum into the Classroom (C2C).* Brisbane: The State of Queensland (Department of Education, Training and Employment) Retrieved from http://education.qld.gov.au/c2c/.
Ertmer, P. A., & Ottenbreit-Leftwich, A. (2013). Removing Obstacles to the Pedagogical Changes Required by Jonassen's Vision of Authentic Technology-Enabled Learning. *Computers & Education, 64,* 175-182. doi: 10.1016/j.compedu.2012.10.008

Ertmer, P. A., Ottenbreit-Leftwich, A. T., Sadik, O., Sendurur, E., & Sendurur, P. (2012). Teacher beliefs and technology integration practices: A critical relationship. *Computers & Education, 59*(2), 423-435. doi: 10.1016/j.compedu.2012.02.001

Goldhaber, M. H. (1997). The Attention Economy and the Net. *First Monday, 2*(4). Retrieved from http://firstmonday.org/htbin/cgiwrap/bin/ojs/index.php/fm/article/view/519/440

James, R., Bexley, E., Devlin, M., & Marginson, S. (2007). Australian University Student Finances 2006: Final Report of a National Survey of Students in Public Universities. Retrieved from http://www.universitiesaustralia.edu.au/documents/publications/policy/survey/AUSF-Final-Report-2006.pdf

Jarche, H. (2012). *PKM as pre-curation*. Retrieved from http://www.jarche.com/2012/07/pkm-as-pre-curation/

Kalantzis, M., & Cope, B. (2012). *Socrates on the Forgetfulness That Comes with Writing*. Retrieved from http://newlearningonline.com/literacies/chapter-1-literacies-on-a-human-scale/socrates-on-the-forgetfulness-that-comes-with-writing/

Kanter, B. (2011). *Content curation primer*. Retrieved from http://www.bethkanter.org/content-curation-101/

MCEETYA. (1989). The Hobart Declaration on Common and Agreed National Goals for Schooling in Australia, from http://www.mceecdya.edu.au/mceecdya/hobart_declaration,11577.html

QSA. (2013). *Years 1-9 Technology*. Brisbane: The State of Queensland (The Office of the Queensland Studies Authority) Retrieved from http://www.qsa.qld.edu.au/7299.html.

Shneiderman, B. (1998). Relate-Create-Donate: a teaching/learning philosophy for the cyber-generation. *Computers & Education, 31*(1), 25-39. doi: 10.1016/S0360-1315(98)00014-1

Siemens, G. (2005). Connectivism: a learning theory for the digital age. *International Journal of Instructional Technology & Distance Learning, 2*(1).

Swanson, K. (2013). Professional Learning in the Digital Age: The Educator's Guide to User-Generated Learning. Larchmont, NY: Eye On Education.

USQ. (2012). *University of Southern Queensland 2011 Annual Report*. Toowoomba: University of Southern Queensland.

Warlick, D. (2012). Cultivating Your Personal Learning Network: A Gardener's Approach to Learning (2nd ed.): The Landmark Project.

Weisgerber, C. (2012). *Teaching Students to Become Curators of Ideas: The Curation Project*. Retrieved from http://academic.stedwards.edu/socialmedia/blog/2012/04/16/teaching-students-to-become-curators-of-ideas-the-curation-project-3/

Weller, M. (2011). A Pedagogy of Abundance. *Spanish Journal of Pedagogy*, (249), 223-236.

# 9 Students' Perceptions of Pre-class Video in the Flipped-Classroom Instructional Model: A Survey Study

Taotao Long, Joanne Logan, Michael Waugh, The University of Tennessee – Knoxville, USA

## Introduction

In this paper, the video also refers to video podcasts (Hammersley, 2004; Heilesen, 2010), audiographs (Loomes, Shafarenko, & Loomes, 2002), vodcasts (Vajoczki, Watt, Marquis, & Holshausen, 2010), or webcast (Shim, Shropshire, Park, Harris, & Campbell, 2007), which are video files distributed in a digital format through the Internet for learning using personal computers or mobile devices (McGarr, 2009). Videos can be presented in the form of video clips or screen casts "as in capturing what is on the computer screen, adding a bit of audio narrative, and publishing as multimedia" (Richardson, 2006, p. 111).

In education, videos have become increasing popular among educators worldwide (Zanten, Somogyi & Curro, 2012). Videos have been used to provide learners the access to previous lectures (McGarr, 2009; Griffin, Mitchell, & Thompson, 2009), transmitting the video lectures of special guest speakers or special topics (Wang, Mattick, & Dunne, 2010), explanations of problem solving (McGarr, 2009), providing supplementary materials for a course (McGarr, 2009), summaries of a class (Lee & Chan, 2007; Holbrook & Dupont, 2010), and delivering administrative information to students (Vogele & Gard, 2006; Heilesen, 2010). Some educators put forward an additional application of videos in education that students learn by collaboratively investigating, planning, generating, and sharing their own videos academic-based videos (Kearney & Schuck, 2005; Kearney, 2013).

Video is considered to improve teaching and learning for providing learners "the freedom of choice or control over their environment" (Kay, 2012, p. 823). Additionally, Hew (2009) argued that "the main advantage of podcasting is the simplicity, convenience, and time savings that it offers to learners" (p. 334). In some other studies, learners indicated that videos are enjoyable (Copley, 2007), motivating (Bolliger, Supanakorn, & Boggs, 2010), and helpful to improve understanding (Heileson, 2010; McGarr, 2010; Kay, 2012). Some studies suggested that videos can improve learners' problem solving skills (O'Bannon, Lubke, Beard, & Britt, 2011; Kay & Kletskin, 2012; Vajoczki, Watt, Marquis, & Holshausen, 2010), and can promote online learners' sense of social presence (Lee & Chan, 2007; Borup, West, & Graham, 2012).

The flipped classroom is an instructional model in which the students are exposed to initial learning content before class outside the classroom through instructors' video lectures and other pre-class learning materials, and utilize class time for active learning, such as problem solving, collaborative group work, laboratory experiments, field trip, and product creation, etc (Gannod, Burge, & Helmick, 2008; Gerstein, 2011; Warter-Perez & Dong, 2012). Different from the instructor-centered and lecture-based instructional model, the two main phases of instruction are "flipped" or reversed. In the flipped classroom instructional model, the presentation of initial learning content, which is usually presented to students in a traditional lecture instructional model, is completed before the class meeting via various means, often technology-based or technology-enhanced, and learner-controlled by watching instructor-provided videos or reading text-format learning materials provided by the instructor (O'Neil, Kelly, & Bone, 2012; Knewton, 2012). The in-class time is utilized for students' active learning experience such as problem solving, laboratory experiments, collaborative designing and creating projects (Gerstein, 2011; Strayer, 2012).

Video is always viewed as an important component in the flipped classroom model (Demetry, 2010; Moravec, Williams, Aguilar-Roca, & O'Dowd, 2010). In Demetry's (2010) study with undergraduates, it was demonstrated that watching videos as the pre-class learning experience can stimulate the students' interest in spending outside class time learning the basic concepts. Learners can go through the videos in advance to come prepared for the in-class session to clarify their understanding, and reinforce their learning whenever they would like (Imran, 2013).

With the advances in technology and the prominent development of online video resources, large amount of instructional videos can be accessed to educators to support their instruction, such as Khan Academy, providing open educational video resources on diverse subjects (Khan, 2012). The pre-class learning phase in the flipped classroom instructional model is a kind of personalized instruction, and the aim is to meet the learning needs of individual learners (Davies, Dean, & Ball, 2013). In this sense, how to meet the learners' need and preference is critical in designing, developing, and providing pre-class videos in the flipped classroom instructional model.

This study described a student survey study on the students' attitudes and perceptions on the pre-class videos in an undergraduate science implemented in the flipped classroom instructional model, such as their attitudes towards the experience of learning contents before class via video, and their preference on different types of pre-class videos, plus the text format pre-class learning materials. This study also investigated students' suggestions for improving the pre-class learning videos in order to improve the learning and teaching efficiency.

## Method

This survey study aimed at gaining students' acceptance of the new learning method of learning via watching videos before class meeting time and their perceptions of different types of per-class learning materials, including 3 different types of videos and text format learning materials. Another aim of this study was to examine whether relationship existed between the students' preference on different types of pre-class learning materials and their demographic information, such as grade and major. This study also intended to examine students' suggestions to improve the videos in order to improve their learning interest and efficiency.

## The Course

The course selected for this study addressed the topic of "Water and Civilization". It was an introductory-level course in environmental soil science at a research university in the southeastern US. There were two sections of this course, but the instructor and the syllabus were the same. There was one class per week, and each class lasted for one and half hours.

Before each class meeting, the students were required to watch an instructor-provided video. Most pre-class videos lasted for about 20-30 minutes, but the length of some others varied within 1 hour. Sometimes the students also had to complete some text format reading materials ahead of class. Then the students had to finish an online quiz with 5-8 questions, and they were told in the first class of the semester that the grades of the pre-class quizzes would be calculated in their final grades of the course. During the class time, the students were required to participate in various active learning activities, such as collaborative projects focused on exploration and demonstration, field trips and presentations, and role-play games. There was no post-class homework assignment for each class activity.

The pre-class videos can be classified into 3 types, the *video lecture*, the *movie lecture*, and the *webinar*. Video lecture is a kind of video the instructor taken of his/her own lecture with the support of studio on campus. This kind of video provides the students with the video broadcasting window of the instructor giving lectures and slides presented to the students (Image 1), sometimes the outline of the content is also presented to the students. The slides are flipped with the instructor's giving lecture.

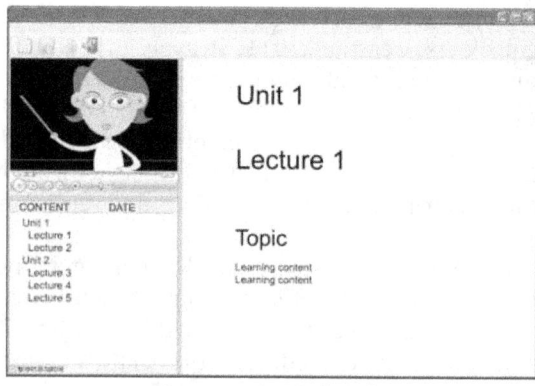

Image 1. Video lecture

Movie lecture is a kind of video not created by the instructor, but are selected and used for his/her class from other websites, such as Youtube and Khan Academy. In this course, the movie lectures were Youtube videos from well-known channels such as National Geography and Nature.

A webinar consists of the audio record of the guest speaker's presentation supplemented with animation, text, images, and charts. In this course, the webinars were guest speakers' presentations.

## Participants

A total of 55 students from the two sections of this course participated in this study. Although this course was an introductory course in environmental soil science, the students were from undergraduates from various majors in agriculture, science and engineering, and medical related majors.

Among the 55 students, 51 participated in this survey. There were 24 (47.1%) students from the agriculture related majors, such as plant science, environmental science, and animal science. Fourteen students (14%) were from engineering majors, such as industrial engineering and electronic engineering. There were 5 (9.8%) students from science, such as mathematics and computer science, and the other 8 students (15.7%) were from medical related majors.

A total of 16 students (31.4%) were sophomores, 14 (27.5%) were juniors, 18 (35.3%) were seniors, and the last 3 (5.4%) students were freshmen.

## Data collection

The survey used in this study was revised based on the survey used in an existing study about students' use of problem-based video podcasts in college mathematics education (Kay & Kletskin, 2012). The survey questions in this study included students' background information, such as major and grade; prior experience of learning through pre-class videos; use of pre-class videos in this course, such as when the students usually viewed the pre-class videos, how many times they visited the videos and the total time length they spent on viewing the video per class. Additionally, the students were asked to rate the helpfulness, easiness, the extent the videos facilitated their understanding of the knowledge, and the facilitation of quizzes through 5-point likert scales in the survey. In the next part of the survey, the students were asked to rank their preferences on the 4 types of pre-class learning materials, including 3 types of videos and text format materials. The students were also asked to explain their perceptions on the four different types of pre-class learning materials and the reasons of their ranking in an open-ended question. The other open-ended questions collected the students' suggestions on improving the pre-class videos in this course.

The anonymous online survey was posted through the survey function on the Blackboard course manage system. An invitation was posted to invite all the 55 students to participate in the survey. They were also informed that an extra five credits would be added into their final grade if they completed the survey. A total of 51 valid responses were received (n=51). The internal validity (Cronbach α) of the closed-ended questions in this survey was 0.85. However, all the items in the survey were analyzed individually in order to gain their detailed insights into the pre-class videos in this course.

## Data Analysis

For the closed-ended questions in this survey, descriptive analysis was used to determine the students' demographic information, their use and general preference on the pre-class learning videos in this course. A correlation analysis was used to examine the relationship between the students' background information and their general preference on the pre-class videos, and the relationship between their background information and their preference on the different types of pre-class learning materials. For the open-ended questions in the survey, a document analysis was used to determine the students' key ideas about their experience and perceptions of learning through viewing the pre-class videos, and their suggestions for improving the videos.

# Results

## General Preference of Pre-class Videos

Although just 21.6% of the students had the experience of learning via watching videos before class in other courses, the students had positive general attitudes towards the pre-class videos they viewed in this course. Overall, 78.4% of the 51 students participated in this study chose "strongly agree" or "agree" when they were asked whether they preferred learning via videos to text format materials. The students rated their preference of using pre-class videos to text materials (Likert scale from 1 to 5) with an average item score of 4.5 (SD = .831). The highest rated features of pre-class videos were helping to understand knowledge, easy to control, and easiness in learning. The other features that the students liked pre-class videos were that the topics were well explained in the video, the videos were helpful for them to complete the quizzes, and useful tips for their learning. From the open-ended question responses, the highest rated features of pre-class videos were that videos were interesting, authentic feeling, and various cultural perspectives provided.

Students also agreed that the quizzes helped them understand the knowledge covered in videos. Among the 51 students completed the survey, 78.4% of rated the quizzes as useful (n=30; 58.4%) or very useful (n=10; 19.6%) for helping them understand the knowledge covered in the pre-class videos. The students rated the helpfulness of the quizzes (Likert scale from 1 to 5) with an average item score of 4.34 (SD = .692).

## Preference on Different Types of Videos

When responding on which one from the four different types of pre-class learning materials, including video lecture, movie lecture, webinar, and text materials, was most helpful for their learning, 43.1% (n=22) of the 51 students chose the option of "video lecture", and 31.4% (n=16) chose the option of "movie lecture". The students' responses showed that webinar was not as well received as the video lecture and movie lecture; only 4 of the 51 students (7.8%) chose the option of "webinar". Moreover, it should be noted that 6 students (11.8%) selected "text format materials" as their favorite type of pre-class learning material.

From the students' responses on the open-ended questions about their perceptions on the four different types of pre-class learning materials, they shared the aspects they liked and disliked about each type of pre-class learning materials.

The video lecture was the type of pre-class learning materials ranked first on students' preference. The features video lectures were liked by the students were that the video lectures were interesting, easy to follow, and convenient for self-control. Another feature was that the video lectures provided the students an authentic classroom learning experience by coordinating the audio and instructor's slides at the same time.

The movie lecture ranked second on the students' preference. Interest was also one of the features they students liked movie lectures. The relaxed environment was an additional feature the students liked. The other features the students liked movie lectures included that students could get to know other perspectives, other cultures and other geographic features via showing the real situations. However, two aspects were the main aspects of movie lectures according to the students' viewpoints, which were that they were sometimes so fast, and not very easy to learn because most of them had no text hints.

As a type of pre-class learning videos, webinar ranked lowest on the students' preference. The reasons that the students thought the webinar were least in promoting their learning were that they were monotonous, boring, and easy to distract. Nevertheless, the students acknowledged that webinar was very informative, and could "show much information in a short time". Although some responses shows that webinar presents much information "in a clear and convincing flow", the monotonous feeling could not give the students a motivating experience.

The previous findings showed that 78.4% of the 51 students participated in this study chose "strongly agree" or "agree" when they were asked whether they preferred learning via videos to text format materials. However, when responding on their perceptions of text format learning materials, the students also admitted that they were helpful in learning. The students argued that although text format learning materials were not as interesting as videos, their features of simplicity, the easiness for students to review and complete quizzes, highlight and take notes, had much advantage over the pre-class learning videos.

## Relationships Between Students' Background and Preference on Videos

Before the study, the researcher originally planned to examine the relationship between the students' background information and their preference on pre-class videos. However, it was out of the researcher's imagination that there were no statistical correlation between the students' majors, grade, and their general preference on videos, plus their preference on different types of pre-class learning materials.

From the correlation analysis, it shows that there was no significant difference between the students' grades and their general preference on pre-class videos with ANOVA analysis of $F (3, 47) = .278$, $p = .841$. The result of one-way ANOVA also showed that there were also not significant difference between the students' majors and their general preference on pre-class videos with $F (3, 47) = .656$, $p = .583$. In addition, there were no significant correlations between the students' majors or grades and their preference on different types of pre-class learning materials with the results of one-way ANOVA of $F (3, 44) = .926$, $p = .436$, and $F (3, 44) = .521$, $p = .670$.

## Students' Suggestions on Improving Pre-class Videos

An open-ended question provided the students with an opportunity to offer their suggestions to improve the pre-class videos for this course in future. Most students suggested that the videos should be shorter and that 20 to 30 minutes was the ideal length in their opinion. In addition, the students showed high interest in the Youtube videos showing the nature and culture in other countries, and the perspectives under other cultural backgrounds, especially the videos from National Geography and Discovery. They expressed their desire to view more videos of these kinds in the pre-class learning phase in future.

Another suggestion the students put forward was that they expected the technical problems would be solved. Some students reflected that the audio and visual effect of some videos was not well enough, and some were not smooth. They expected the improvement on the technical aspects of the pre-class videos in order to have a more engaging pre-class learning experience.

# Discussion

Overall, according to the survey results, the pre-class learning videos were well received by the students. The pre-class learning experience via watching the instructor provided videos were also successful in motivating their learning interest and improving the students' understanding of learning content. The results of this study also provide insights for educators on using pre-class videos in implementing the flipped classroom instructional model in their courses.

## The Flipped Classroom Needs More Than Videos

It was a major finding of this study that as a pre-class learning material in the flipped classroom instructional model, videos can motivate the students' learning interest and improving their understanding on learning content, and it supports some previous studies confirming the pre-class videos are valuable for building students' conceptual understanding and convenience in learning (Demetry, 2010; Dove, 2013; Imran, 2013). However, video was not necessarily essential in the flipped classroom instructional model. The flipped classroom requires more than preparing videos for the students.

First, the essence of the flipped classroom instructional model is that more opportunities and activities can be provided to the students in the in-class time (Dove, 2013). The role of videos is to facilitate students to learn the basic concepts before class. The aim of pre-class learning is to remove lectures from the in-class time, in order to allow better use of the in-class time for student-centered active learning activities.

As a result, the goal of the pre-class videos is to help students be prepared for the in-class learning activities, which are the key component of the flipped classroom model.

Second, the flipped classroom is more like an ideology evolved into empowering students to consume information outside class and demonstrate understanding of the basic concepts of learning content in various ways (Makice, 2011), and it can also understood as an innovative model of teaching and learning which utilizes educational technology and student-centered active learning activities to positively impact the learning environment (O'Neil, Kelly, & Bones, 2012). Any technologies, learning materials, and learning activities, can be utilized in the flipped classroom instructional model if the needs of students could be met and the learning effectiveness could be improved by adopting them, but not limited to video.

Third, in the pre-class learning phase, simply providing the videos is not enough. There should be some other pre-class learning activities to make sure the students have watched the videos and be prepared for the in-class activities. In this study, pre-class quizzes were responded as helpful for the students to understand the knowledge covered in the pre-class videos. Frydenberg (2012) asserted that quizzes are used accompanied with videos as the students' pre-class learning activities in the flipped classroom, for quizzes can motivate students to watch the videos because each quiz counts a small amount toward final grades, and quizzes can help students check their understandings of key concepts prior to doing student-centered, hands-on, active in-class activities. Moreover, quizzes should not be too long, in order not to increase students' burden. In this study, the 5 minutes quizzes were well received by the students. Additionally, encouraging students to take notes when viewing the pre-class videos is an alternative way to make sure the students prepare for in-class activities via viewing the videos.

## Make Videos More Engaging

The length and the quality of the pre-class videos have a great influence on students' engagement to the pre-class learning in the flipped classroom instructional model. The students' responses in the open-ended questions in this study confirmed the finding from Wagner, Laforge and Cripps (2013)' research on teaching an engineering course in the flipped classroom instructional model that videos which can clearly present engineering materials in 10 to 15 minutes were best received by students. The students in this study complained that some videos were too long, and they suggested that the videos not be longer than 20 minutes.

Videos covering the learning content and presenting in a clear flow are always thought of good quality. The biggest difference between the pre-class videos in the flipped classroom model and the video podcasting in other educational settings is that the aim of the pre-class videos in the flipped classroom model is to help the students be prepared for the in-class learning activities, so the coverage of the knowledge and the strategies to make sure the students have be prepared are the critical issues.

In this study, the three different types of videos stood for three different ways of presenting the course content. Different from what was assumed before the study, there was no statistically significant correlation between the students' general preference on the pre-class videos, plus their preference on the different types of the pre-class learning materials, and their background information, especially the major. It could be explained by the fact that this course was an introductory level course in environmental science. The course content, the flipped classroom approach, and the pre-class and in-class learning experience were all new to the students, so it was not probable that their knowledge background in the learning in their own majors would influence their learning in this course.

However, it is notable that educators should consider the students' majors, grades, and the characteristics of the course. For example, in the courses required more on broadening students' visions on the other local regions and other cultures, such as this course, the pre-class videos should be focused on providing students a vivid and intuitional demonstration of the learning content; for the courses focused on abstract theoretical knowledge, such as mathematics, the pre-class videos should be focused on logic and illustrations of examples, in order to facilitate students' understanding.

Another suggestion for making the videos more engaging is to make them more interactive. Here the "interactive" possesses two implications. The first implications means the videos can provide students an authentic environment that the instructor is talking and communicating with them, the same as in the classroom. In this study, the video lecture was ranked highest among the four different types of pre-class learning materials, for it provided the students the experience of hearing the instructor's voice and watching the lessons developed step-by-step on the screen, and the students felt that the instructor was "speaking with them through the video". The other implication is that the videos should be kept on the pace of the students' thinking flow. In this study, the students responded that although they could control playing the videos, they appreciated the videos "they don't need to play forward or retrieve to try to keep pace with the videos". They desired the videos be more focused and highlight the key points with subtitles, and allow them to have time to take note.

For the instructors who have the first trial to make a pre-class video in the flipped classroom, initiating video production represents a significant added workload. Wagner, Laforge, and Cripps (2013) convinced that on average a 15 minutes video required 2 to 3 hours of producing and editing time using extremely user-friendly developed video editing tools. However, once the initial technical and logistical problems are solved, the time spent on creating a video will be significantly reduced, and the completed videos can be saved for future use.

As mentioned previously, the essence of the flipped classroom is that more opportunities can be provided to the students in the in-class time. It is the same way that more opportunities can be provided to the instructors to prepare for their course implemented in the flipped classroom model, both the pre-class phase and the in-class phase. Instructors should make the plan for the preparation according to the requirement of courses, their own technical literacy, and the available resources and supports.

# References

Bolliger, D. U., Supanakorn, S., & Boggs, C. (2010). Impact of podcasting on student motivation in the online learning environment. *Computers & Education, 55*(2), 714–722.

Borup, J., West, R. E., & Graham, C. R. (2012). Improving online social presence through asynchronous video. *The Internet and Higher Education, 15* (3), 195-203.

Copley, J. (2007). Audio and video podcasts of lectures for campus-based students: Production and evaluation of student use. *Innovations in Education and Teaching International, 44*(4), 387–399.

Davies, R. S., Dean, D. L. & Ball, N. (2013). Flipping the classroom and instructional technology integration in a college-level information systems spreadsheet course. Educational Technology Research and Development,

Demetry, C. (2010, October). *"Work in Progress - An Innovation Merging "Classroom Flip" and Team-Based Learning."* Proceedings of 40$^{th}$ ASEE/IEEE Frontiers in Education Conference, Washington, DC.

Dove, A. (2013). Students' Perceptions of Learning in a Flipped Statistics Class. In R. McBride & M. Searson (Eds.), *Proceedings of Society for Information Technology & Teacher Education International Conference 2013* (pp. 393-398).

Frydenberg, M. (2013). Flipping Excel. *Information Systems Education Journal, 11* (1), 63-73.

Gannod, G., Burge, J., & Helmick, M. (2008). Using the Inverted Classroom to teach Software Engineering Using the Inverted Classroom to Teach Software Engineering. Paper presented at *The 30th International Conference on Software Engineering.* Leipsig, Germany

Gerstein, J. (2011). *The Flipped Classroom Model: A Full Picture.* Retrieved from http://usergeneratededucation.wordpress.com/2011/06/13/the-flipped-classroom-model-a-full-picture/

Griffin, D. K., Mitchell, D., & Thompson, S. J. (2009). Podcasting by synchronising PowerPoint and voice: What are the pedagogical benefits? *Computers & Education, 53*(2), 532–539.

Hammersley, B. (2004, February 12). Audible revolution. The Guardian Newspaper, 27. Retrieved from. http://www.guardian.co.uk/media/2004/feb/12/broadcasting. digitalmedia.

Heilesen, S. B. (2010). What is the academic efficacy of podcasting? *Computers & Education, 55* (3), 1063-1068.

Holbrook, J., & Dupont, C. (2010). Making the decision to provide enhanced podcasts to post-secondary science students. *Journal of Science Education and Technology, 20*(1), 233–245.

Imran, M. (2013). Increasing the interaction time in a lecture by integrating flipped classroom and just-in-time teaching concepts. *Journal of learning and teaching,* 7, 1-13.

Kay, R. & Kletskin, I. (2012). Evaluating the use of problem-based video podcasts to teach mathematics in higher education. *Computer & Education, 59,* 619-627.

Kay, R. & Kletskin, I. (2012). Evluating the use of problem-based video podcasts to teach mathematics in higher education. *Computer & Education, 58* (2), 619-627.

Kay, R. H. (2012). Exploring the use of video podcasts in education: a comprehensive review of the literature. *Computers in Human Behavior, 28,* 820-831.

Kearney, M. (2013). Learner-generated digital video: Using Ideas Videos in Teacher Education. *Journal of Technology and Teacher Education, 21*(3), 321-336.

Kearney, M. & Schuck, S. (2005). Students in the Director's Seat: Teaching and Learning with Student-generated Video. In P. Kommers & G. Richards (Eds.), *Proceedings of World Conference on Educational Multimedia, Hypermedia and Telecommunications 2005* (pp. 2864-2871). Chesapeake, VA: AACE. Retrieved September 9, 2013 from http://www.editlib.org/p/20518.

Khan, S. (2012). The one world schoolhouse: Education reimagined. London: Hodder and Stoughton.

Knewton (2012, March 8). *The flipped classroom infographic: A new method of teaching is turning the traditional classroom on its head.* Retrieved from http://www.knewton.com/flipped-classroom/

Lee, M. J. W. & Chan, A. (2007). Reducing the effects of isolation and promoting inclusivity for distance learners through podcasting. *Turkish Online Journal of Distance Education,* 8, 1, 85–104.

Loomes, M., Shafarenko, A., & Loomes, M. (2002). Teaching mathematical explanation through audiographic technology. *Computers & Education, 38*(1), 137–149.

Makice, K. (2011, December 10). *Flipping the Classroom Requires More Than Video.* Retrieved from http://www.wired.com/geekdad/2012/04/flipping-the-classroom/

McGarr, O. (2009). A review of podcasting in higher education: Its influence on the traditional lecture. *Australasian Journal of Educational Technology, 25*(3), 309–321.

O'Bannon, B. W., Lubke, J. K., Beard, J. L., & Britt, V. G. (2011). Using podcasts to replace lecture: Effects on student achievement. *Computers & Education, 57*(3), 1885–1892.

O'Neil, K., Kelly, T., & Bone, S. (2012). We Turned Learning On Its Ear: Flipping the Developmental Classroom. *World Conference on Educational Multimedia, Hypermedia and Telecommunications 2012.* Denver, Colorado, United States.

Richardson, W. (2006). *Blogs, wikis, podcasts, and other powerful web tools for classrooms.* Thousand Oaks, CA: Corwin Press.

Shim, J. P., Shropshire, J., Park, S., Harris, H., & Campbell, N. (2007). Podcasting for e- learning, communication, and delivery. *Industrial Management and Data Systems, 107*(4), 587–600.

Strayer, J. F. (2012). How learning in an inverted classroom influences cooperation, innovation and task orientation. *Learning Environment Research, 15* (2), 171-193.

Vajoczki, S., Watt, S., Marquis, N., & Holshausen, K. (2010). Podcasts: Are they an effective tool to enhance student learning? A case study from McMaster University, Hamilton Canada. *Journal of Educational Multimedia and Hypermedia, 19*(3), 349–362

Vogele, C. & Gard, E. T. (2006). Podcasting for corporations and universities: look before you leap. *Journal of Internet Law, 10*(4), 3–13.

Wagner, D., Laforge, P., & Cripps, D. (2013). Lecture material retention: a first trial report on flipped classroom strategies in electronic systems engineering at the University of Regina. In proceeding of 2013 Canadian Engineering Education Association Conference, Montreal, Canada, June.

Wang, R., Mattick, K., & Dunne, E. (2010). Medical students' perceptions of video- linked lectures and video-streaming. *Research in Learning Technology, 18*(1), 19–27.

Warter-Perez. N., Dong. J. (2012). Flipping the Classroom: How to Embed Inquiry and Design Project into a Digital Engineering Lecture. Proceedings of *American Society for Engineering Education-Pacific South West Section Conference*, San Luis Obispo, CA.

Zanten, R.V., Somogyi, S., & Curro, G. (2012). Purpose and preference in educational podcasting. *British Journal of Educational Technology, 43* (1), 130-138.

# 10 Students' Learning Outcomes and Self-efficacy Perception in a Flipped Classroom

Mohamed Ibrahim & Rebecca Callaway, Arkansas Tech University, United States

## 1. Objective

Although lecture-based teaching strategy (LB) used for decades as an effective way to help students acquire new knowledge (e.g., Hattie, 2009; Schwerdt, 2009), many educators argue that this teaching model is mostly static, passive and not suitable for teacher candidates preparing for extended field experience and careers in teaching. Students reported also that the information delivered during lectures may come too slowly or cover what they already know; other students have trouble taking in information so rapidly, or they may lack the prior knowledge needed to understand the presented content (Goodwin & Miller, 2013).

A growing number of teachers started recently using different teaching strategy through creating flipped or inverted classrooms. This teaching strategy involves moving the lecture content before class and working on homework and hands-on activities during class time. For example, the data from the Flipped Learning Network (2012) indicated that membership on its social media site rose from 2,500 teachers in 2011 to 9,000 teachers in 2012. In the flipped teaching strategy (FB), educators can employ online asynchronous educational video, recorded lectures or readings and spend time in class working on problems or exercises through active, group-based problem solving activities. The learning materials can incorporate multimedia visual representations, such as interactive graphs, photos or animation. During watching the video, lectures or reading the text, students have the chance to control the pace of the multimedia streaming to match their own learning preferences. Students can also watch or listen to recordings of class lectures on their computers, tablets, smart phones, or personal media players outside of class, leaving class time to engage in learning activities that might otherwise assigned as homework (Frydenberg, 2013).

Reports of student perceptions of the FB found to be somewhat mixed, but are generally positive overall. For example, some prior research found that students tend to prefer in-person lectures to video lectures, but prefer interactive classroom activities to lectures (Bishop & Verleger, 2013). Although there is steady increase in the number of teachers who adopt the FB in classrooms, there is little research on the effect of this teaching strategy on preservice teachers. Therefore, the purpose of this study is to examine the implications of the use of flipped classroom teaching strategy on preservice teachers' learning outcomes, self-efficacy and perception in a technology integration course.

## 2. Theoretical Framework

*Cognitive Theory of Multimedia Learning:*

Since the introduction of television, large body of empirical studies on the use of multimedia in education have demonstrated that students not only prefer it over text, but are also more likely to gain deeper learning from multimedia than from words alone (Baggett, 1984; Mayer, 2002, 2003, 2005; Mayer & Moreno, 2002; Salomon, 1984; Shepard, 1967; Wetzel, Radtke, & Stern, 1994). Researchers suggested that because multimedia contain two representations, visual that conveys information about objects and its relation to other objects, and verbal that communicates abstract meaning and special attributes of this information, a combination of both representations should increase the learning effect (e.g., Guttormsen Schar, Kaiser, Krueger, & th, 1999; Lowe, 1999). A major assumption underlying this empirical work is that humans can construct a mental representation of the semantic meaning from either auditory or visual information alone, but when instruction presented in both formats, each source provides complementary information that is relevant to learning (Baggett, 1984).

Cognitive theory of multimedia learning (CTML) (Mayer, 2001), proposed several assumptions regarding the relationship between cognition and learning from dual representation information formats.

Four of these assumptions are particularly relevant to learning from multimedia learning materials. First, the cognitive architecture assumption postulates that the human mind consists of an unlimited, long-term memory (LTM) in which all prior knowledge is stored and a limited working memory (WM) in which new information is processed. Second, the dual-channel assumption proposes that WM has two channels for visual/pictorial and auditory/verbal processing and that the two channels are structurally and functionally distinct (Clark & Paivio, 1991). Third, the limited capacity assumption states that each cognitive channel has limited capacity for information that can be processed at one time (Baddeley, 1986; Baddeley & Logie, 1999). Fourth, the active processing assumption explains that humans actively engage in the cognitive processes to select relevant verbal and non-verbal information from the learning materials, organize the selected information into cognitive structures, and integrate these cognitive structures with the existing knowledge to construct a new (or update an old) mental representation (Mayer, 1996).

*Flipped Classroom:*

Researchers on the flipped classroom do not agree on the type of activity that constitutes the flipped teaching model. For example, some researchers tend to delineate the flipped classroom in a broad definition and suggest that assigning video or reading outside of class and having discussions in class constitutes the flipped classroom. Bishop & Verleger (2013) reject this definition and describe the flipped classroom as an educational technique that consists of two parts: interactive group learning activities inside the classroom, and direct computer-based individual instruction outside the classroom. According to this definition, flipped teaching strategy may use videos or readings as an outside of the classroom activity. For example, Demetry (2010) provides lecture notes for students to read at home prior to the class session, rather than providing video lectures to help meet the goal of increasing "time on task" to complete course-related activities. Other researchers identified flipped classroom as "events that have traditionally taken place inside the classroom, now take place outside the classroom and vice versa" (p.32) (Lage, 2000). Therefore, flipped classroom is based on the idea that students are engaged in group interactive learning activities inside the classroom. To make sure that students watched the videos or completed the reading at home, students can respond to "clicker questions" to report their progress as they work on the exercises (Houston, 2012). Finally, the learning activities as well as the assigned homework in flipped teaching model vary widely between studies. For example, some activities are made up of asynchronous web-based video lectures and closed-ended problems or quizzes, while others consider that the flipped classroom actually represents an expansion of the curriculum, rather than a mere re-arrangement of activities (Bishop & Verleger, 2013).

*Self-efficacy and Learning*

According to social cognitive theory (Bandura, 1997) self-efficacy is a form of self-judgment that influences decisions about what behaviors to undertake, the amount of effort and persistence put forth when faced with obstacles, and finally, the mastery of the behavior. According to Bandura, self-efficacy is not a measure of skill; rather, it reflects what individuals believe they can do with the skills they possess. For example, in discussing self-efficacy in computer use, Compeau and Higgins (1995) distinguished between component skills such as formatting disks and booting up the computer and behaviors individuals can accomplish with such skills, such as using software to analyze data. Thus, preservice teachers' perception of their self-efficacy focuses on what they believe can accomplish with the knowledge they master during their learning. It does not refer to a person's skill at performing specific learning related tasks (e.g. class management, integrate technology in their teaching and mastering a content area). Instead, it assesses a person's judgment of his or her ability to apply knowledge and skills in a broader context.

Preservice teachers participating in a technology integration course learn skills and knowledge of teaching with technology in an actual classroom. Self-efficacy beliefs are a key component for preservice teachers' success in overcoming the fear they may experience in this new area. For example, Compeau and Higgins (1995) empirically show that there is a relationship between computer self-efficacy and computer use. Staples (1999) found that those with high levels of self-efficacy in remote computing situations were more productive and satisfied, and better able to cope when working remotely. Consequently, novice teachers enrolled in a technology integration course are required to develop set of skills to prepare them to teach with technology and to perform successfully a distinct set of behaviors required to establish, maintain and utilize effectively teaching with technology beyond basic personal Internet and computer skills.

**Research questions**

The focus of this study was to investigate the implications of the use of the flipped teaching strategy on preservice teachers' learning outcomes and self-efficacy in a technology integration course. Based on previous studies of CTML and self-efficacy, this study will be guided by the following questions:

(1) Will the flipped teaching strategy improve preservice teachers' learning outcomes compared to lectures-based teaching strategy in a technology integration course?
(2) Will the flipped teaching strategy improve preservice teachers' self-efficacy in a technology integration course?
(3) What is the perception of preservice teachers regarding the use of flipped teaching strategy in a technology integration course?

The first question: Will the flipped teaching strategy improve preservice teachers' learning outcomes compared to lectures-based teaching strategy in a technology integration course? This primary research question was at the heart of the study, as the answer to this question will inform instructors and trainers the effect of the use of flipped teaching strategy on preservice teachers' learning outcomes. In general, prior research found that the flipped teaching strategy resulted in improvement of students' learning outcomes. Other studies, however, found that overall class testing scores do not support that flipping the classroom improved the entire class (Sparks, 2013). Therefore, the result of this study will examine the effect of the flipped teaching strategy on students' learning outcomes in the context of a technology integration course.

The second question: Will the flipped teaching strategy improve preservice teachers' self-efficacy in a technology integration course? According Bandura's social cognitive theory, it is important to assess students believes and ability to apply the knowledge and skills they acquire during a lesson as indication of understanding the learning content (Compeau, 1995). The answer of this question will help instructors and trainers to evaluate the effect of the flipped teaching strategy to improve preservice teachers' self-efficacy to apply the knowledge they acquire in the context of the technology integration course.

The third question: What is the perception of preservice teachers regarding the use of flipped teaching strategy in a technology integration course? The answer of this question attempts to recognize the perception of preservice teachers' toward the use of flipped teaching strategy in the technology integration course. The answer will help instructors and trainers to use the appropriate teaching strategies for students with different learning preferences. Particularly, the question focuses on whether learners will perceive the flipped teaching method positively or not.

**Research Hypotheses:**

In this study, the investigators hypothesize that:

- The flipped teaching strategy will improve preservice teachers' learning outcomes in a technology integration course.
- The flipped teaching strategy improves preservice teachers' self-efficacy in a technology integration course.
- The majority of preservice teachers will prefer the use of flipped teaching strategy in a technology integration course.

## 3. Methods

This study employed a within-subject design to assess the effect of using flipped teaching method on preservice teachers' learning outcome and self-efficacy in technology integration courses. The study has one independent variable: the teaching method (lecture-based or flipped-based method) and two dependent variables: (1) learning outcomes (2) students' perception of self-efficacy to integrate technology in teaching.

The participants were sixty preservice teachers (39 undergraduates, 21 graduates), enrolled in technology integration courses at a midwestern university. Participants were non-science majors and attending three sections: section one: 19 undergraduate students, section 2: 20 undergraduate students and section three: 21 graduate students (10 male, 50 female). Students were from four different majors: 32 in early childhood education, 2 in elementary education, 14 in middle-level education, 9 in high school education and 3 other education major such as physical education or speech/theater. English was reported as the native language of all participants. The average reported age of the participants was 22-25 years (SD = 1.415 years). Participants were 53 White, 4 African American, 1 Hispanic and 1 Asian, among them 4 freshmen, 11 sophomores, 23 juniors, and 22 seniors.

The lessons and activities used in this experiment were adapted from the textbook "Integrating Educational Technology into Teaching" by Roblyer and Doering, Sixth Edition (2012). Participants taught with two different teaching methods: traditional lecture-based method to teach one topic: learning with technology in special education and the flipped-based method used to teach four topics: Technology tools for 21st century teaching, hypermedia tools for 21st century teaching, distance teaching and learning and the role of the internet and developing and using web-based learning activities and teaching

## 4. Materials

All learning materials used in the flipped teaching method, including videos, post-tests and surveys were online as part of the Blackboard course content and released to students every week based on the topic covered in that week. The instrumentations consisted of the following items: demographic survey, 10-question multiple-choice post-test for each of the five learning topics, 10-question 11-level Likert scale to assess students' perceived self-efficacy based on Bandura' measure (Bandura, 2006). All learning measures were selected or developed by the course instructor and were used regularly with students attending the technology integration courses.

*Pre-test*

Demographic survey: This questionnaire was to collect information about the participants' makeup, such as students' gender, years in college, area of specialization and age.

Students' self-efficacy survey (pre and post): This questionnaire designed with 11-point scale ranges from "Cannot do at all" at zero to "Highly certain can do" at 100. Students are asked to answer how confident are they in their belief that they have this ability". For example, in question number three, students were asked the following question: "How certain are you that you can identify and use technology tools and information resources in your content area to increase productivity, promote creativity, and facilitate academic learning. Rate your degree of confidence by recording a number from zero to 100 using the scale given below". Participants could rate their confident by selecting a number starting from zero "Cannot do at all" to 100 "Highly certain can do".

The investigators developed the self-efficacy measure based on Bandura's "Guide to the construction of self-efficacy scales" in (Pajares, 2006). The measure tailored to assess students' ability to integrate technology in their teaching. The initial ratings of the measure indicated that all items adequately reflect and assess the topics covered in all conditions and the scores averaged across the 10 items. Mean for the total sample M = 83.00, SD = 11.30, range = 8.38. The investigators calculated the inter-rater reliability of the measure by intra-class correlation coefficients to evaluate the consistency of the ratings. The reliability for the measure Cronbach's alpha (an estimated of internal consistency) was .92 (across all sections). Further, the investigators used this measure as self-efficacy assessments in other classes related to teaching technology for preservice teachers (face and construct validity). Finally, the investigators examined the measure's scale results and scale results of other concepts in the technology integration courses such as computer- assisted instruction, virtual classroom and course management system, and found that the results of this measure significantly correlated with the results in other concepts and Cronbach's alpha was .88 (criterion-related validity).

*Post-test*

The learning outcome test: This measure consisted of five quizzes cover five different learning topics to elicit participants' retention and transfer of knowledge of these topics. The five topics are: learning with technology in special education (lecture teaching method), technology tools for 21st century teaching, hypermedia tools for 21st century teaching, distance teaching and learning and the role of the internet, developing and using web-based learning activities and teaching (flipped teaching method). The questions of these measures based on the topics covered in this experiment. An example of the multiple-choice question in the topic "learning with technology in special education" is: "Technology offers potential to help address this characteristic, which arises when an individual is unable to fulfill a role due to a limiting condition:" Participants could choose from the following responses: "Impairment, handicap, disability, or deficit". Another example of multiple-choice question in the topic "hypermedia tools for 21st century teaching": "In this system, as originally conceptualized by Ted Nelson, items of information from all over the world could be logically connected with links". Participants could choose from the following responses: multimedia, hypertext, hypercard, linkway. Each correct answer yields 1 point, for a total of 10 points and scores ranged from zero (no correct responses) to 10 (all correct responses) for every quiz.

The retention and knowledge transfer measurements developed by the textbook's author, selected, and reviewed by the course instructor to assess participants' understanding and application of the five topics. The initial ratings of the measures indicated that all quizzes adequately reflected and assessed the five topics covered in this study.

*Materials*

The learning materials used in the present study were five topics to help preservice teachers to integrate technology in teaching. The materials were identical in all sections and released every week with the related activities. There were two different teaching methods: traditional (lecture-based) and flipped. Traditional method was based on lectures and direct teachings conducted by the instructor and the information was delivered during the meeting, while students listen to lectures and learn from them. In this method, the lesson's content and delivery was most important aspect of instruction and students learn knowledge through the assignments completed at home. For example, to teach the topic "learning with technology in special education", the instructor lectured about the topic and used a power point presentation during the class time and covered the following points: Introduction to special education, current issues in the use of technology in special education, effective ways for technology to be integrated into special education and the Tech-PACK needs and challenges in special education. Students in all sections attended the class in a computer lab and worked and submitted their work through computers.

The assignment of this teaching strategy was based on lecture notes and the textbook. The assignment was in form of essay questions and students had to complete all work at home with no help except of their notes. For example, an assignment asked students to review the teaching notes and textbook (pages, 398 -400) regarding impairment, disability and handicap. Students were asked to "explain in no less than 600 word the difference between Impairment, Disability and Handicap with examples for each definition.

In the flipped teaching strategy, the instructor did the following: Students read the chapter or online materials before class (at home). For the difficult points, students asked to watch video or screencast. To insure that students completed the assigned readings or videos, instructor conducted a Q & A in the first five minutes of the class and then the assigned topic introduced in another five minutes. The instructor dedicated the class time for hands-on activities. Students worked through activities related to the assigned topic and with the guidance of the instructor and the support of their peers. In this method, instructor emphasized collaborative learning and students had the opportunity to ask questions to instructor and their peers as well. For example, in the flipped teaching strategy, the instructor started the topic "Distance teaching and learning and the role of the Internet", by asking students questions based on the home reading such as why teachers should develop rationale to use internet or what are some of the internet's problem areas teachers have to address before using the internet for teaching and learning. Students' answers include, accessing sites with inappropriate materials, safety and privacy issues for students, fraud, computer viruses and hacking, and copyright and plagiarism issues. After the Q & A, instructor introduced the topic using short power point presentation and covered the following points: Distance education: an evolving use of the internet, developing an internet use rationale, using and implementing the internet effectively: navigation, searching and storing, communicating and social networking. After the Q & A and the topic introduction, students were guided to complete hands-on activities related to the week's topic. For example, student were asked to develop a WebQuest including: deciding the lesson to be taught through the WebQuest, using Google to collect the information web links, images and videos and finally create a free website for the WebQuest that includes these pages: Introduction, Task, Process, Resource, Evaluation, Conclusion and Teacher Page. During the activity, students were free to ask for help or ask questions from their peers or instructor.

*Procedure*

First, students in all sections completed demographic and self-efficacy surveys. Second, instructor used the flipped-based method to teach four topics in four consecutive weeks to all sections. In the fifth week, instructor used traditional lecture-based method to teach one topic to all sections. At the end of every week students completed a quiz related to the week's topic and at the end of the fifth week, students completed self-efficacy survey (post). All surveys and learning activities presented and submitted through Blackboard.

## 5. Results

Prior to the main analyses, the data was screened for normality, out-of-range responses and systematic patterns of missing values and found that the data is normally distributed and no apparent patterns or clusters emerging.

First question: To answer the first question: Will the flipped teaching strategy improve preservice teachers' learning outcomes compared to lectures-based teaching strategy in a technology integration course?"

To answer this question, the investigators conducted a paired-samples t-test to compare students mean test scores in the two conditions flipped and lecture-based. The analysis show that there were significant differences in the students' mean test scores in all flipped teaching method test scores: Test 1 (M=6.61, SD=1.62), test 2 (M=11.48, SD=4.44), test 3 (M=5.56, SD=1.42), test 4 (M=6.79, SD=1.76) compared to lecture-based mean test scores (M=9.4, SD=1.14) conditions; $t(30)=8.399$, $p = 0.001$, $t(30)= 9.017$, $p = 0.001$, $t(26)= 5.498$, $p = 0.001$, $t(28)= 8.681$, $p = 0.001$. These results suggest that flipped teaching strategy does have positive effect on preservice teachers' test scores in technology integration course. Specifically, our results suggest that when students engage in class activities using the flipped teaching strategy, the test scores improved. Table 1 summarizes the paired-samples t-test results.

*Table 1* The Mean scores and standard deviations for the paired-samples t-test results of the all test in flipped and traditional teaching strategies

| | | Paired Differences | | | | | | | |
| --- | --- | --- | --- | --- | --- | --- | --- | --- | --- |
| | | | | | 95% Confidence Interval of the Difference | | | | |
| | | Mean | Std. Deviation | Std. Error Mean | Lower | Upper | t | Df | Sig. (2-tailed) |
| Pair 1 | Chapter 5_15 | 3.258 | 2.160 | .388 | 2.466 | 4.050 | 8.399 | 30 | .000 |
| Pair 2 | Chapter 6_15 | 8.065 | 4.980 | .894 | 6.238 | 9.891 | 9.017 | 30 | .000 |
| Pair 3 | Chapter 7_15 | 2.222 | 2.100 | .404 | 1.391 | 3.053 | 5.498 | 26 | .000 |
| Pair 4 | Chapter 8_15 | 3.345 | 2.075 | .385 | 2.556 | 4.134 | 8.681 | 28 | .000 |
| *Note:* Means with different subscripts differ significantly at p<.001 | | | | | | | | | |

Second question: Will the flipped teaching strategy improve preservice teachers' self-efficacy in a technology integration course?

To answer the second question, the investigators conducted a paired-samples t-test to compare students' self-efficacy mean scores before and after using the flipped teaching strategy. The analysis show that there were significant differences in the students' self-efficacy mean scores after flipped teaching strategy (M=830.00, SD=113.014) compared to before the use flipped teaching strategy (M=737.30, SD=170.516); $t(36)$= -4.652, $p$ = 0.001. These results suggest that flipped teaching strategy have positive effect on preservice teachers' self-efficacy in technology integration course. Specifically, our results suggest that when students engage in class activities using the flipped teaching strategy, their confidence to apply what they learn improved. Table 2 summarizes the paired-samples t-test results.

*Table 2* The Mean scores and standard deviations for the paired-samples t-test results of students' self-efficacy before and after the use of flipped teaching model

|  | Paired Differences | | | | | | | |
|---|---|---|---|---|---|---|---|---|
|  |  |  |  | 95% Confidence Interval of the Difference | | | | |
|  | Mean | Std. Deviation | Std. Error Mean | Lower | Upper | t | df | Sig. |
| Before - After | -92.703 | 121.213 | 19.927 | -133.117 | -52.288 | -4.652 | 36 | .000 |

*Note:* Significant at $p < 0.001$ level

Third question: What is the perception of preservice teachers regarding the use of flipped teaching strategy in a technology integration course? To answer this question, the investigators collect data from 60 students through answering 12 questions to assess their perception on the flipped teaching strategy. The results were reduced to three answers regarding favoring the flipped teaching model (Agree, Disagree or Neither agree or disagree). The number of responses by agree from the 12 questions were 452 (62.9%), disagree 104 (14.5%) and neither agree or disagree were 163 (22.7%). Figures 1 summarizes statistics of students' responses

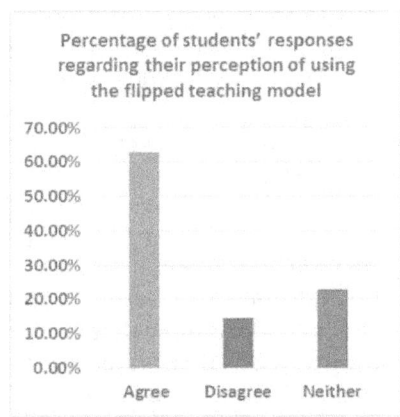

## 6. Scientific or scholarly significance of the study or work:

The main finding of this study is that the use of the flipped teaching strategy indeed has the potential to help preservice teachers to improve their learning outcomes in the technology integration course. This benefit demonstrated by the statistically significant differences in learning outcomes between students taught by flipped and lecture-based teaching strategies, with the highest scores achieved by students in the flipped condition and the least was in the lecture-based condition. The results of the present study support previous findings produced in the context of other content areas and with different population and provide empirical evidence that validates the flipped teaching strategy to improve students' learning outcomes (Sadaghiani, 2012; Sparks, 2013; Walker, 2011). Specifically, the preservice teachers' test scores improved in all tests after they engaged in flipped teaching activities compared to their test scores after lecture-based activities. A possible interpretation of this result is that students during the flipped classroom had the opportunity to work together and engage in hands-on learning activities, which allowed them to participate in authentic and collaborative learning environment. According to prior studies, the effectiveness of the flipped classroom on student learning is due to the additional opportunities for students to collaborate and work on problem solving together (Demetry, 2010; Strayer, 2007).

Furthermore, assigning multimedia learning materials for students to review outside classroom allows them to learn content at their own pace and permits them to view and listen again to those sections that present important or complex concepts (Gibbons Jf, 1977). This interpretation is consistent with prior cognitive research, which noted the positive effect of allowing students to control the pace or stream of learning content. If students lack control over the pace of the learning content, this might burden their limited cognitive resources, especially learning from multimedia materials. According to cognitive theory of multimedia learning (CTML), the human cognitive system can process only small portions of the large amounts of visual and auditory stimuli received. Unlike processing printed text, learners in formal educational contexts typically do not have the opportunity to stop the multimedia presentation and reflect on what they are learning and identify potential gaps in their knowledge. Thus, information processing in this situation frequently requires longer and more intense periods of cognitive and metacognitive activity. Regardless of the amount of information presented in each sensory channel, the learner's working memory (WM) will accept, process, and send to long-term memory (LTM) only a limited number of information units (Attneave, 1954; Jacobson, 1950, 1951). Thus, working memory requires pauses or direct prompting to accept, process, and send to the long-term storage only the most crucial information (Clark, Nguyen, & Sweller, 2006).

Another significant finding of this study is that students' self-efficacy perception was significantly improved after engaging in flipped teaching strategy compared to their self-efficacy perception after lecture-based. This benefit demonstrated by the statistically significant differences in the reported self-efficacy scores after the flipped activities compared to lecture-based, with the highest scores reported by students after the flipped activities and the least was in the lecture-based.

A possible interpretation for this result is that the flipped teaching activities promote students' cognitive engagement and helped them to interact efficiently with learning content than in the lecture-based teaching activities (as reflected by the higher test scores in all tests after flipped teaching strategy) and consequently improved and promoted their self-efficacy perception. This interpretation is consistent with prior self-efficacy research. According to this theory, self-efficacy reflects what individuals believe they can do with the skills they possess and they can accomplish.

Finally, this study found that preservice teachers favor the use of flipped teaching strategy in a technology integration course compared to the lecture-based teaching strategy and this was demonstrated by the statistically significant differences in the number of students who were in favor of the flipped strategy compared to lecture-based, with the highest numbers for the flipped strategy and the least was for the lecture-based (452 vs. 104) or (62.90% vs.14.50%).

A possible interpretation for this result could be found in students' rationalizations in the perception survey. Although the majority of students who preferred the flipped classroom indicated that it promotes collaboration and hands-on activities during the class time, other students have different reasons such as: "had less lecture time", "work at my own pace", "using technology", "being able to interact more with the teacher and being able to ask questions as I worked" and "we do not have to sit and listen to an hour long lecture that goes in one ear and out the other one".

Although opinions tended to be positive, but there were invariably a few students who strongly disliked the change. One very interesting case was a student reported that she dislike the flipped teaching model because "Everyone asking questions. I wasn't able to concentrate and do my work in the classroom. I am a very ADD person. I have to be somewhere without distractions to do well". Although this student reported her dislike of the flipped teaching model, she received higher grades in all the quizzes completed after flipped classes compared to her quiz grade after the lecture-based class.

**References**

Attneave, F. (1954). Some informational aspects of visual perception. *Psychological review, 61*(3), 183-193.
Baddeley. (1986). *Working memory*. Oxford; New York: Clarendon Press ; Oxford University Press.
Baddeley, & Logie. (1999). Working memory: The multiple-component model. In A. Miyake & P. Shah (Eds.), *Models of working memory: mechanisms of active maintenance and executive control*. New York: Cambridge University Press.

Baggett, P. (1984). Role of temporal overlap of visual and auditory material in forming dual media associations. *Journal of Educational Psychology, 76*(3), 408-417.

Bandura, A. (1997). *Self-efficacy : the exercise of control*. New York: W.H. Freeman.

Bandura, A. (2006). Toward a Psychology of Human Agency. *Perspectives on Psychological Science, 1*(2), 164-180.

Bishop, J., & Verleger, M. (2013). *The Flipped Classroom: A Survey of the Research.* Paper presented at the 120th ASEE Annual Conference & Exposition, Atlanta.

Clark, Nguyen, & Sweller. (2006). *Efficiency in learning: Evidence-based guidelines to manage cognitive load*: Pfeiffer.

Clark, & Paivio. (1991). Dual coding theory and education. *Educational Psychology Review, 3*(3), 60.

Compeau, D. R. H. C. A. (1995). "Computer Self-Efficacy: Development of a Measure and Initial Test". *MIS quarterly : management information systems., 19*(2), 189.

Demetry, C. (2010). *Work in Progress - An Innovation Merging "Classroom Flip" and Team-Based Learning.* Paper presented at the the 40th ASEE/IEEE Frontiers in Education Conference, Washington, DC.

Frydenberg, M. (2013). Flipping Excel. *Information Systems Education Journal, 11*(1), 63-73.

Gibbons Jf, K. W. R. D. K. S. (1977). Tutored videotape instruction: a new use of electronics media in education. *Science (New York, N.Y.), 195*(4283), 1139-1146.

Goodwin, B., & Miller, K. (2013). Research Says / Evidence on Flipped Classrooms in Still coming In. *Technology Rich Learning, 70*(6), 78-80.

Guttormsen Schar, S., Kaiser, J., Krueger, H., & th. (1999). Multimedia: the effect of picture, voice & text for the learning of concepts and principles.

Hattie, J. (2009). *Visible learning : a synthesis of over 800 meta-analyses relating to achievement*. London; New York: Routledge.

Houston, M. L. L. (2012). Humanizing the Classroom by Flipping the Homework versus Lecture Equation.

Jacobson, H. (1950). The informational capacity of the human ear. *Science (New York, N.Y.), 112*(2901), 143-144.

Jacobson, H. (1951). The informational capacity of the human eye. *Science (New York, N.Y.), 113*(2933), 292-293.

Lage, M. J. P. G. J. T. M. (2000). Inverting the Classroom: A Gateway to Creating an Inclusive Learning Environment. *Journal of Economic Education, 31*(1), 30-43.

Lowe, R. K. (1999). Extracting information from an animation during complex visual learning. *European Journal of Psychology of Education, 14*(2), 225-244.

Mayer. (1996). Learning Strategies for Making Sense out of Expository Text: The SOI Model for Guiding Three Cognitive Processes in Knowledge Construction. *Educational psychology review., 8*(4), 357.

Mayer. (2001). *Multimedia learning*. Cambridge; New York: Cambridge University Press.

Mayer. (2002). *The promise of educational psychology : Learning in the content areas*. Upper Saddle River, N.J.: Merrill.

Mayer. (2003). The promise of multimedia learning: Using the same instructional design methods across different media. *Learning and Instruction, 13*(2), 125.

Mayer. (2005). *The Cambridge handbook of multimedia learning*. Cambridge, U.K.; New York: Cambridge University Press.

Mayer, & Moreno. (2002). Animation as an aid to multimedia learning. *Educational Psychology Review, 14*, 87-100.

Pajares, F. U. T. C. (2006). Self-efficacy beliefs of adolescents. from http://site.ebrary.com/id/10429529

Roblyer, M. D., & Doering, A. H. (2012). *Integrating Educational Technology into Teaching + Myeducationlab With Pearson Etext*: Allyn & Bacon.

Sadaghiani, H. R. (2012). Online Prelectures: An Alternative to Textbook Reading Assignments. *Physics Teacher, 50*(5), 301-303.

Salomon, G. (1984). Television is "easy" and print is "tough": The differential investment of mental effort in learning as a function of perceptions and attributions. *Journal of Educational Psychology, 76*(4), 647-658.

Schwerdt, G. W. A. C. (2009). *Is traditional teaching really all that bad? a within-student between-subject approach*. Munich: CESifo.

Shepard, R. N. (1967). Recognition memory for words, sentences, and pictures. *Journal of Verbal Learning and Verbal Behavior, 6*(1), 156-163.

Sparks, R. (2013). Flipping the Classroom: An Empirical Study Examining Student Learning. *Learning in Higher Education, 9*(2), 65-70.

Staples, D. S. H. J. S. H. C. A. (1999). A Self-Efficacy Theory Explanation for the Management of Remote Workers in Virtual Organizations. *Organization Science Organization Science, 10*(6), 758-776.

Strayer, J. F. (2007). The effects of the classroom flip on the learning environment a comparison of learning activity in a traditional classroom and a flip classroom that used an intelligent tutoring system. from http://rave.ohiolink.edu/etdc/view?acc%5Fnum=osu1189523914

Walker, J. D. C. S. B. N. (2011). Vodcasts and Captures: Using Multimedia to Improve Student Learning in Introductory Biology. *Journal of Educational Multimedia and Hypermedia, 20*(1), 97-111.

Wetzel, C., Radtke, P., & Stern, H. (1994). *Instructional Effectiveness of Video Media*: Lawrence Erlbaum Associates.

PART 2 SOCIAL MEDIA

# 11 What We've Got Here is Failure to Communicate: Social Media Best Practices for Graduate School Programs
Joshua M. Rosenberg, Colin A. Terry, John Bell, Virginia Hiltz & Tracy Russo,
Michigan State University, USA

## Introduction

Social media provides faculty, staff, and students a platform to interact and share information. In addition, recent research about Twitter (Greenhow & Gleason, 2012), Facebook (Shaltry, Henriksen, Lu, & Dickson, 2013), and social media use among adolescents and adults (Pew Internet, 2013) speaks to the value of integrating social media within teaching and learning. However, there is a need to investigate the role of, and best practices for, social media use in graduate school programs from an institutional perspective. In our experience facilitating an ongoing social media initiative with the Michigan State University (MSU) Educational Psychology and Educational Technology (EPET) doctoral program, the need to establish social media best practices emerged from unclear responsibilities and a lack of cohesion in what was communicated through various social media platforms affiliated with the program. To address these concerns, face-to-face graduate students, hybrid graduate students (who enroll in both face-to-face and online courses), and faculty established the Social Media Council (SMC). The SMC is responsible for providing support and guidance related to the social media presence of the program. Although the particulars are unique to MSU EPET, the best practices and benefits outlined are applicable to graduate school programs in education and other fields, as well as to researchers in the interactions among hybrid and face-to-face students of the same program.

## Literature Review

The increasing prevalence of social media has impacted higher education and the lives of students as they relate to one another, to faculty, and to university administration. Social media has altered the communication between these groups and impacted students' scholarly lives; as dramatic evidence, Barnes and Lescault (2011) found that "100% of universities surveyed use social media to communicate with students, up from 61% in 2007-08" (p. 2). A review of the literature led us to draw three general conclusions about the potential role and benefits of social media from an institutional perspective.

### Social Media Can Build Community

First, social media can build community with students across diverse geographic areas, particularly those in an online or hybrid program; for example, Manago (2012) found that social media helped support "psychosocial needs for permanent relations in a geographically mobile world" (p. 369). Students participating in an online or hybrid program seek community among fellow students, faculty, and administration. Social media, particularly Facebook, have provided a platform through which to build that community: Schwartz (2009) found that, for students, Facebook could serve as "an extension of the classroom, something like a grad-student lounge in which all kinds of connections take place, some routine and some substantial" (p. 2). Manago's (2012) research showed similar findings as college students view Facebook as a tool for procuring social support.

In the MSU EPET program, these findings are routinely found in practice. Each of the hybrid PhD cohorts relies on social media to build and maintain community across very diverse geography. The 2010 cohort relied on regular discussions via Google Hangouts whereas the 2012 cohort built a thriving Facebook page to offer support to one another. The 2012 cohort Facebook page has generated hundreds of professional and personal postings including videos, photos, document attachments, and links. Social media initiatives have also prompted greater community between hybrid and on-campus learners in the form of shared research interests and research opportunities (webinars, lectures, conferences, etc.), thereby breaking down experiential differences between the two student-types.

### Social Media Supports Program Advancement

Social media can significantly support external efforts, such as program advancement. For example, researchers at Johns Hopkins found that "a robust social media campaign, along with such creative features as student-run blogs, can lure prospective students while a stale online presence can turn them off" (Pidaparthy, 2011, p. 2). Pidaparthy (2011) also found that prospective students view social media as providing a sense of what life is really like on campus "whether it's through a virtual tour or Twitter" (p. 2). Research shows that universities are using a mixture of social media platforms to reach prospective students; 98% reported using Facebook, 84% reported using Twitter, and 66% reported using a blog (Barnes & Lescault, 2011). Overall, universities' use of these social media channels to recruit students has been viewed successfully. Barnes & Lescault (2011) reported that 95% of colleges found their Facebook page to be a successful recruiting tool.

The MSU EPET social media efforts highlight the important role of current students cultivating and communicating a program's brand through genuine perspective to potential students and outside constituents. Specifically, MSU EPET social media provides real-time reporting of current students' activities, experiences, and achievements. For example, a group of MSU EPET hybrid students were on-campus for two weeks of practicum-based coursework in the summer of 2013. The students were encouraged to participate in a Twitter campaign using the #EPETsummer and #MSUEPET hashtags to share the unique summer intensive experience. These unfiltered messages provide prospective students with an opportunity to see "behind the scenes," a perspective rarely found in traditional university program literature.

### Social Media Supports Networking and Collaboration

Social media can foster a network that celebrates research accomplishments, connects students with scholars, and fosters collegiality and dialogue between disciplines. Moran, Seaman, and Tinti-Kane (2011) found that "a total of 78% of all faculty report using at least one social media site in support of their professional career activities" (p. 13). Graduate students also connect and converse through the social media channels, thereby broadening their professional network. DiVall (2012) found that initial Facebook pages created for specific classes allowed students to span the classroom to future courses or the professional world as users continued to interact on the page following the close of the class. Perhaps not surprisingly, a 2013 Pew Research Foundation report shows that although Facebook remains the dominant social networking platform, 42% of online adults now use multiple social networking sites (Duggan & Smith, 2013). Ultimately, institutionalized social media creates a community of scholarship, thereby prompting varied and diverse learning experiences (Lai et al, 2007).

MSU EPET's program uses a multi-pronged approach (detailed below). Ideaplay.org, for example, centralizes students' and faculty's blog posts, creating a hub for sharing current studies, interests, and questions while also recognizing successes such as achievements in research. Ideaplay.org has also prompted collaborative writing efforts and future research directions among faculty and students.

In summary, the use of social media has the potential to build community, support program advancement, and support networking and collaboration. Experiences shared from the MSU EPET program offer insight into how universities capitalize on these changing opportunities to connect with students and integrate social media into their academic lives. In the next section, we identify and describe six best practices - establish why, establish how, be authentic, understand privacy, coordinate channels, and engage volunteers - for social media use within graduate school programs.

## Best Practices

### Establish Why

An educational program must first address, either explicitly or implicitly, what function social media will serve for the program. The two options considered in MSU EPET were: A) social media would enable program personnel to express an official perspective for an internal or an external audience (or both), or B) social media would open an authentic window into the life of the program. Option A is a top-down, tightly-organized approach, which portrays a particular image and highlights resources and opportunities consistent with the values and interests of program personnel. Option B is a bottom-up, less-directed approach that prompts a less scripted portal into the program.

Our initial approach in the EPET program was Option A: Full-time employees of the program published to Twitter and Facebook that which was deemed appropriate, useful, and purposeful. The intent was to serve the internal audience (primarily current and past students) while also providing value to prospective students. Following some time with this approach, we were displeased. Very few program individuals were actively engaged or invested in the effort, as the vision, criteria, and purpose were removed and unclear. Communication was sporadic, and communication lacked consistency, purpose, and direction. Given this dissatisfaction, we shifted toward Option B: We engaged students, not solely department personnel, who would actively feed content into the various social media channels. This shift was coincident with our formation of the informal social media council, the members of whom are collectively the authors of this paper. With this change, we also shifted our focus, toward giving the public - including prospective students - a portal into the life within our program. Rather than crafting an intentional message, the social media posts became a real-life sampling of research, news, and events in the program.

**Establish How**

Our bottom-up approach still necessitates considerable intentionality and critique. Specifically, we established consensus on what constitutes appropriate content, social media member responsibilities, and intentionality with concern to the selection and use of various social media portals and their respective affordances. As our practice and experience evolved so did our consensus with policies and best practices. This approach benefitted from faculty oversight and support, analogous to the role of a faculty advisor to a student committee or organization. Moreover, this approach benefitted from traditionally defined roles such as Chair and Secretary, as well as the formation of special interest groups. These initially unwritten policies have slowly formalized as needs, situations, and issues have arisen.

**Be Authentic**

As detailed earlier, instead of crafting a top-down strategy, we sought to show our real-life, both because it would be easier than creating something scripted and because we believed that our day-to-day practices would be valuable to prospective students. This means it is not unusual for council members, through official program channels, to interact or even joke with members of our community, especially others in the EPET program but also those in our department and university. This authentic approach has permitted public opportunities to share program news and events, and also celebrate individual or collective accomplishments and achievements.

In conjunction with being authentic and transparent, we recognized that guidelines for appropriate participation in our program-supported social media channels were necessary. However, we wanted the policy to be as simple and clear as possible. Here is the policy as it stands today: *We expect that all contributors to the resources will do so in a professional manner that is consistent with the values and acceptable use policies of Michigan State University.* Prospective students and outside colleagues often communicate with us through the social media platforms, especially Facebook. Social Media Council members are encouraged to dialogue and converse. Moreover, they are encouraged to appropriately relay questions or inquiries to MSU EPET administration, especially with regards to potential program candidacy.

**Understand Privacy**

The policy of authenticity - and transparency - we have described is not without limits. Instead, we are adamant that being part of a graduate school program involves many acts of private communication. For example, administrative communications pertaining to student or program expectations or requirements would not be applicable or relevant to those outside the program. Furthermore, we acknowledged the need for a virtual place for students to explore new, evolving, and uncertain research ideas without public display. As a result, our program established a weekly EPET Brownbag discussion among students and faculty, which are not broadcasted beyond members of the program. In all, understanding and creating spaces for private and semi-private communication has become an important part of our work.

**Coordinate Platforms**

With many social media platforms available, it was clear to us from the beginning that our different channels needed to work with one another. We chose to coordinate our efforts with each social media channel through periodic meetings with those responsible for each platform: These meetings provide an opportunity to discuss strategies, successes, and challenges, as well as an opportunity to further work with, not against, one another. As part of their stewardship of each channel, council members are asked to consider automatic cross-posting of updates, the general vision and appropriateness of each platform, and the unique affordances and audiences respective to each.. Below are our general guidelines for each platform.

Table 1
*Guidelines for each social media channel.*

| | |
|---|---|
| EPET Hub | An online community primarily for students and faculty within the program to share resources, news, ideas, such as EPET Brownbag speakers. |
| Edutech | The public face of our program (especially for recruiting purposes); this channel is most directly linked to the College of Education at MSU. |
| Ideaplay | A shared, student-run blog for public thinking and exploration on topics related to educational psychology and technology. |
| Facebook | A community page with news, notes, photos, and media about the EPET program, students, and faculty. |
| Twitter | News and notes from the EPET program. In addition, relevant and thought-provoking news from the disciplines of educational psychology and technology. |

The unique affordances provided by Facebook are different, yet equally valuable, to those afforded by Twitter or ideaplay. Facebook best supports photos, semi-brief postings (150 – 300 characters) and linked-users (where program students and faculty can be tagged). Twitter best supports short, quick announcements (140 characters or fewer) and hyperlinked stories on a more routine basis. Adversely, ideaplay.org supports long postings (200+ words), less routine postings, and more in-depth exploration of a particular research topic as presented first-hand by the writer. Regardless of conduit, consideration should be given to the platform's best use, thereby also considering a platform's constraints.

An additional key question was how our social media would relate to official communication and resources of the program. We chose to manage the two initiatives separately. However, we have created an archive within our social media efforts - on the EPET Hub - of official communication and resources. In addition, we have cross-links to http://edutech.msu.edu where official program resources are available. As a result, participant experience, especially for those outside the program, is seamless as official distributions are easily accessed.

**Engage Volunteers**

Generally, most contributions outside those posted by Social Media Council members are voluntary. Some encouragement, however, is often needed. As new ideas and research come to light, council members will often call on faculty and students for assistance/contributions. Faculty instructors and advisors have supported this effort through a "volun-told" approach with their own students. The Social Media Council has found success through the unequivocal value of routine, consistent posting, because when certain platforms have been dormant or less-active, user engagement with the platform drops precipitously. Many of the platforms, including Facebook and ideaplay.org, provide usage reports on a routine (weekly or monthly) basis. To maintain outside interest and engagement, we have found great value in ensuring that the social media platforms are active and engaging for our own students and faculty.

# Conclusion

In this paper, we have discussed the need for institutionalized social media policies, reviewed the extant literature, and identified and described six best practices - establish why, establish how, be authentic, understand privacy, coordinate channels, and engage volunteers - that emerged from our experience facilitating an ongoing social media initiative. In conclusion, we briefly describe the benefits of a social media initiative from the perspective of those involved and their institutions, as well as the potential significance of this work to research. In addition to the general benefits discussed in the literature review, we have identified specific benefits of a social media initiative from the perspective of those involved and their institutions. First, we have found that members of the EPET SMC have found coordinating a social media initiative provides a rich context for learning about social media. This example of learning about technology (social media) through the use of technology has strong support in the extant literature (e.g., Mishra & Koehler, 2006). Second, growth in informal writing is another benefit we have experienced. For the graduate student, writing in a common language based on scholarly ideas mimics formal writing practices without the high stakes associated with formally assessed assignments. Third, similar to growth in informal writing, institutionalizing social media affords opportunities for collaboration. Numerous entry points for faculty and graduate students to engage in collaborative scholarship and write at a lower risk threshold. Fourth, lessons learned from an institutionalized social media effort are immediately available for use outside the program itself. For example, lessons learned from the creation of ideaplay.org were applied to create a faculty teaching and learning Wordpress site (teaching.nmc.edu) at a small, rural community college affiliated with a member of the council. Finally, we have found that an institutionalized social media effort shared between students and faculty speaks to program investment and authorship as well as program advancement.

Our ability to identify but not yet support empirically these speaks to the need for research into social media use and initiatives in graduate school programs. In addition, the unique format of the EPET program directs attention to the lack of research into the interactions among face-to-face and online hybrid students of the same program. As research related to social media has shown, there exists significant value in yielding the unique affordances of various software platforms to the benefit of increased engagement, interest, and dialogue. Student-run institutionalized social media can bolster the student, faculty, and program opportunities related to community, research, recruitment, and engagement. There exists significant value with an institutionalized social media initiative in graduate programs. As noted, such initiatives can cultivate creative and collaborative writing and research. Moreover, such initiatives can foster program community, greater collegiality and scholarship among faculty and students, and further transparency with program accomplishments. These benefits span all audiences from prospective students to current students to tenured faculty. Through persistence and coordination, social media initiatives can provide opportune ways to communicate.

# References

DiVall, M. V, & Kirwin, J. L. (2012). Using Facebook to facilitate course-related discussion between students and faculty members. *American Journal of Pharmaceutical Education, 76*(2), 32.

Duggan, M., & Smith, A. (2013). *Social Media Update 2013*. Retrieved from http://www.pewinternet.org/2013/12/30/social-media-update-2013/

Greenhow, C., & Gleason, B. (2012, October). Twitteracy: Tweeting as a new literacy practice. In *The Educational Forum* (Vol. 76, No. 4, pp. 464-478). Taylor & Francis Group.

Greenhow, C., Robelia, B., & Hughes, J. E. (2009). Learning, teaching, and scholarship in a digital age Web 2.0 and classroom research: What path should we take now?. *Educational Researcher, 38*(4), 246-259.

Lai, C., Yang, J., Chen, F., Ho, C., & Chan, T. (2007). Affordances of mobile technologies for experiential learning: The interplay of technology and pedagogical practices. *Journal of Computer Assisted Learning, 23*(4), 326-337.

Manago, A. M., Taylor, T., & Greenfield, P. M. (2012). Me and my 400 friends: the anatomy of college students' Facebook networks, their communication patterns, and well-being. *Developmental Psychology, 48*(2), 369–80.

Moran, M., Seaman, J., & Tinti-Kane, H. (2011). *Teaching, learning, and sharing: how today's higher education faculty use social media*. Pearson Learning Solutions

Pidaparthy, U. (2011). How colleges use, misuse social media to reach students. *CNN Tech*. Retrieved from http://www.cnn.com/2011/10/20/tech/social-media/universities-social-media/

Shaltry, C., Henriksen, D., Wu, M. L., & Dickson, W. P. (2013). Situated Learning with Online Portfolios, Classroom Websites and Facebook.*TechTrends*, *57*(3), 20-25.

Schwartz, H. (2009). Facebook: the new classroom commons? *The Chronicle of Higher Education*, (February). Retrieved from https://chronicle.com/article/Facebook-The-New-Classroom/48575/

Weick, K., (2000). Organizational Redesign as Improvisation, reprinted in *Making Sense of the Organization,* Wiley-Blackwell.

# 12 Perceptions of School Children of Using Social Media for Learning
Robert Blair, David Millard & John Woollard, University of Southampton, UK

## Introduction

An enthusiasm for the use of Web 2.0 technologies and services, in particular online social media, by school-aged children would appear evident if one looks at the findings of recent surveys. In an investigation of children's media literacy Ofcom (2010) reported that amongst UK children who have access to the Internet at home, 25% in the age range 8 to 12 have an social media profile rising from 15% in 2008. For the age range 12 to 15 the figure rose from 52% to 70% over the same period.

What makes this enthusiasm for the use of social media interesting to educationalists and researchers is the possibility that the affordances of social media may support formal or informal learning (Burden & Atkinson, 2008). If one subscribes to the current dominant theories of learning which hold that learning is a socio-cultural event (Brown & Adler, 2008; Lave & Wenger, 1991; Vygotsky, 1978; Papert, 1980), then it would follow that the collaborative nature of social media provides an ideal support framework for learning (McLoughlin & Lee, 2007). This has been explored in a Higher Education context but there are relatively few studies looking at how school-aged children are using social media for their learning (Ahn, 2011).

This paper explores this question. Utilising professional relationships developed over a number of years in an advisory role the lead researcher was able to gain access to a strongly 'gated' community, i.e. school pupils under the age of 18, to collect survey data about their social media usage, and their attitudes and experiences of using social media for learning. The survey was designed to address the following questions:

How do school children perceive their use of social software in everyday life?
How do school children perceive their use of social software for formal and informal learning?
Does practice match perception in Q1 and Q2 - how is social software actually used by school children?

Our aim is to investigate pupil perceptions of the importance of social media in everyday life and learning whilst touching upon the tensions and challenges of gaining access and consent to working with young and adolescent learners. (Greenhow & Robelia, 2009). The findings contribute to the relatively limited field of knowledge regarding the use of social software by UK (secondary) school-aged children in support of informal, collaborative learning (Lee, McLoughlin, & Chan, 2007).

## Background

It has been observed that the collaborative and communal nature of social software parallels the properties of good models of student centered, active learning (Maloney, 2007). From a constructivist pedagogical perspective the learner interprets what they are told based upon previous knowledge and experience, then transforms the input accordingly, changing their conceptual views based upon conversation and collaboration (Driscoll, 2000). Connectivism is a related pedagogy that gives these connections primacy, and it has been described as a theory of learning for the networked, digital world (Siemens, 2005; Downes, 2006; Louriero & Bettencourt, 2010). In connectivism learner competence is a product of the creation and utilisation of formal connections, so for the learner the capacity to learn is more important than the knowledge currently held by the learner.

Social media therefore appears to hold great promise for learning, but while there have been many studies into the use of social software in support of learning at college and university level there have been relatively few in the compulsory schooling age range (Lee et al, 2007, Ahn, 2011 Whilst some research in the higher and further education sectors indicates that the use of social media can help create a sense of presence, community building and participant interaction (Brady et al., 2010; Lee & McLoughlin, 2010; Naveh et al., 2010), other research findings indicate social media are often regarded by students as having greater importance in identity politics rather than in support of learning (Ellison et al, 2007; Selwyn, N. 2009). In comparison the few studies which have been conducted with school aged children and adolescents have been mostly concerned with issues such as privacy, safety and identity (Livingstone & Brake, 2010), those concerned with education have mostly taken a literary perspective of learning in which practices such as creating media have been the focus of attention (Greenhow & Robelia, 2009; Ito et al, 2008; Jenkins, 2006).

Nevertheless, it is important to understand how school-aged children use social media, and how they see it as a tool for learning. This is because learners' perceptions of the possibilities and uses of social software tools may differ significantly from the perceptions and intentions of educators, and a more informed understanding of user perceptions may offer a greater chance of success in the design and use of social software for learning (Dron, 2007).

Our work is similar to Selwyn's (2009) study investigating university students' Facebook activity in which they found that much of students use of social media to support learning centred upon discussion of learning experiences, logistical support and formal learning objectives. Luckin et al's (2009) also investigated adolescent students perception and use of Web 2.0 social media in formal and informal learning contexts through investigation of the uses to which social media were put. Luckin discovered little evidence of high level learning activities through collaborative or peer assistance, yet when facilitated by a teacher the learners appeared more willing to engage in higher level thinking skills such as evaluation and creation. Our study is different in that it explores not only the ways in which social media is used but also why it is used and how that use is perceived by students.

## Methodology

Unlike conducting research with participants who are over the age of 18 recruiting participants who are of school age is a difficult stage in the research process (Alderson, 2004; Sinclair, 2004). Issues of approach (Hood et al, 1996), access through gatekeepers (Butler & Williamson, 1994) and consent (Cree et al., 2002; Hill et al., 2004; Masson, 2004; Miller, 2000) can appear to frustrate the research process leaving researchers feeling dependent upon the goodwill of organisation's to cooperate (Aldgate and Bradley, 2004). Our approach was to use the lead researcher's experience as a classroom teacher and moderator, and to utilise existing professional relations with departments of ICT in a group of six UK secondary schools, our sample can therefore be considered one of convenience. School leaders were invited to participate in the study who would then act *in loco parentis* for the school pupil population with respect to the parental consent required for participants under the age of 18.

Due to the potential size of population sample, access to an online questionnaire or e-survey was selected as the most appropriate tool for data collection (Couper, 2000). The survey consisted of 8 sections including participant consent, use of social media, educational use of social media, and learning and sharing knowledge. From discussion with serving classroom teachers several factors affecting research instrument design were recognised early in the process. It was realised that as the participants could vary greatly in terms of reading ability and comprehension skills the survey design would require great care to accommodate this variation. To help participant understanding the questions would be couched in 'student speak'. Another important aspect to consider was the time required to complete the survey, as participant schools were asked to conduct surveys during timetabled classroom lessons, the content of which were planned in advance and accounted for the entire lesson time. Due to these time restrictions the questions were kept to the minimum required to gain baseline data for further qualitative research.

The survey questions were classed as high level e.g. "how do you perceive the use of social software in supporting informal learning?" or a supporting low level such as "have you ever used social software to help a friend with something they didn't understand in class?". This was to determine whether reported perceptions matched the stated uses of social software. An example could be that the participant may answer that they do not perceive social software to be important in support of learning, if they then proceeded to give examples of having supported or been supported through the use of social software perhaps their understanding of the first question was inaccurate or the use of social software was commonplace and taken for granted. In an attempt to maintain participant interest, and as a measure of validation, the answer options varied through each section from simple yes/no to drop-down options, radio button or multiple choice / multiple selection. Participants were given the opportunity to add comments if they felt that an important point has been missed or comment upon the survey in general.

Conducting research with school pupils as participants in the school setting is recognised as being fraught with difficulty (Greenhow and Robelia, 2009), not least of which is gaining access to the participants' school environment. The research instrument developed in this project was designed to be administered by school teachers during timetabled lessons without the need for researcher presence. Though addressing the issue of researcher presence in the classroom the drawback was dependence upon teacher willingness to administer the online survey.

In design of the survey instrument several steps were taken to ensure internal validity (Gray, 2009). Once the initial questions were drafted each question was subject to internal peer review (Cresswell, 2007). Then during informal usability style testing with volunteer participants at a local school the relevance of each question was discussed and participant comments noted for action if deemed necessary. Finally the study was submitted and granted ethics approval by the University of Southampton ethics board (Ethics number 5942).

Once the surveys had been taken the raw data collected was cleaned in three stages to ensure that further analysis would produce meaningful results. The first stage was removal of participant records who had not agreed to take part in the survey (and had thus left the survey early). Next was removal of participants' records who reported that they did not use social media. These participants were given the opportunity, if they wished, to explain why they did not use social media for further analysis. The third stage of data cleaning consisted removal of records with questions answered in a meaningless way (either no selection, or more than one answer selected).

Quantitative questions were typically answered via a Likert scale, these were plotted and error bars calculated to show significant results. The Qualitative data results consisted of the reported examples of participants providing or receiving help with their learning through social media. After a first reading of the comments initial codes were developed to describe a range of intentions and activities. Following a second reading, 14 days after the first reading of the comments, a set of high level themes were developed to give one interpretation of common themes and as a measure of intra-coder reliability (Neuendorf, 2008; Krippendorff, 2004).

## Results and Analysis

In total 383 pupils responded to the survey across 17 classes in six different schools. Of these 71 were excluded from the study due to incomplete or poorly formed answers, of the remaining 312 pupils, 144 left qualitative comments as well as providing quantitative data. The first section of the survey investigated pupils' perceptions of the importance of social media or social networking sites (SNS), participants were asked "do you think that social media is important in everyday life ?", with 3-point likert answer options: 'very important', 'sometimes' or 'not important at all'. Fig 1. Gives an overview of the answers received, grouped by academic year. It indicates little change in average perception of importance as pupils progress through academic years, although there is a small spike in 'very important' answers in year 7 (11 years old) and another in 'not important' answers from year 10 (14 years old). We also analysed the replies by gender and year group, which revealed greater variance (Fig 1, top right and bottom right). Responses from female pupils indicates that social media gains importance between year 8 (12 years old) with 20% of females reporting that social media is very important to 70% in year 10 (14 years old) after which levels of importance start to fall. But for male pupils instead of falling in year 8 levels of importance appear to peak at 45% then fall to 20% only rising slightly in year 11. These trends act to cancel each other out, and on average across all years, 31% of respondents reported that social media was very important, and a further 62% described it as important. However 7% described social media as not important at all, this challenges the popular views of the ubiquity of social media use and importance amongst young people, and echoes similar findings amongst University-aged students that challenges the idea of Digital Natives (Jones et al, 2010).

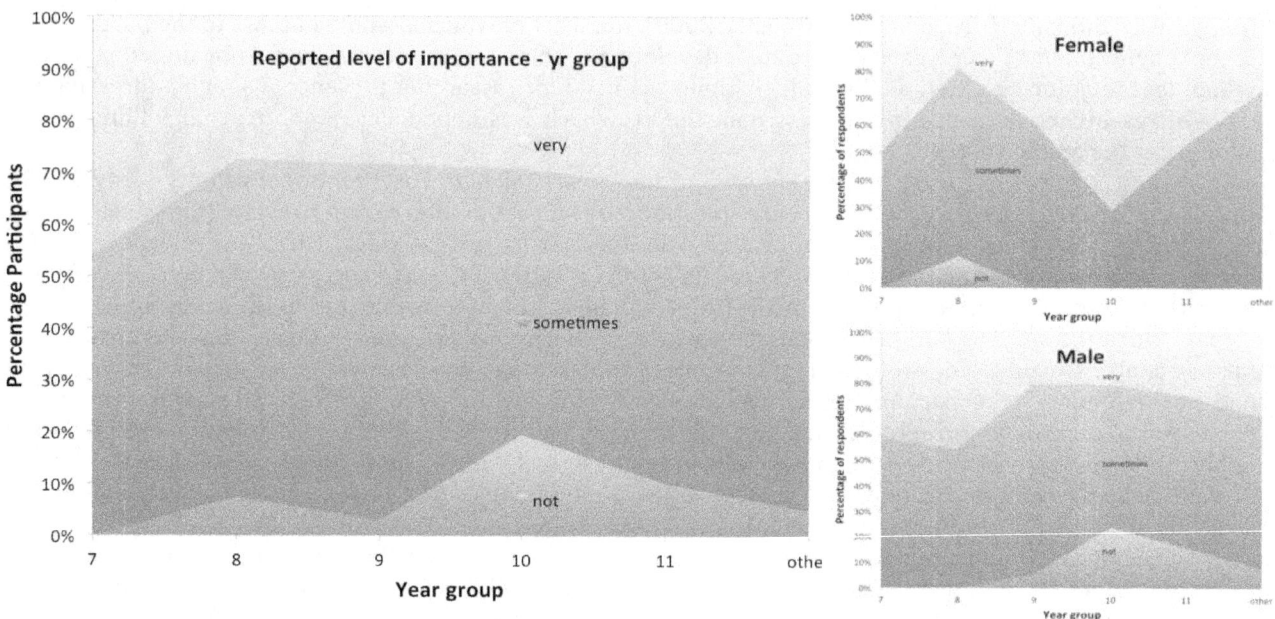

**Fig 1.** Reported level of importance of social media in everyday life by year group
(Left: Overall, Top Right: Female, Bottom Right: Male)

Other possible indicators of the level of importance reported by participants were time spent online, number of social network site friends and the number of groups of which participants were a member. Results of data collected for participant time spent online on a daily and weekly basis followed quite closely the reported levels of importance. When questioned about group memberships and number of friends the analysis produced some unexpected results. In both cases the way in which pupil's answered the question about perceived importance of social media seemed to have little effect on their number of friends or group membership. However, although nearly 40% of the sample responded that they were not a member of any group, in the most popular 2-5 groups range the percentage of those who apparently perceived social media as not important in everyday life was, surprisingly, almost 20% greater than for other groups (Fig. 2). This may be some artifact of the patterns of use amongst more experienced users, and requires further investigation.

The questionnaire also asked pupils which social media systems they used, and how frequently they used them. We were concerned that an open question might confuse younger children (who might not be aware of what we meant by social media) so the participants were asked to answer this in relation to 11 named systems. These included the most well known social networks (Facebook, Twitter and MySpace), curation style sites (Tumblr and Pintrest), photo sharing (Instagram and Flickr), Q&A (ask.fm), in-game communities (Minecraft), and sites popular with younger users (Bebo and SnapChat).

The data collected is shown in Fig 3. There seems to be three categories of application depending upon popularity and frequency of use: (1) popular and used frequently: Facebook, Twitter, Instagram and Snapchat (2) popular but used infrequently: Minecraft, Ask.fm and Tumblr (3) unpopular and used infrequently: Bebo, Flickr, Pinterest and Myspace. These categories remained constant even when participant responses were grouped by year, by reported level of perceived importance in everyday life, or length of time accounts had been held. It is interesting to note that the general age limit stated in terms and conditions for use of the social media listed (apart from Minecraft), was year 9 (age 13). As participants had submitted demographic data in the form of gender and academic year group it became clear that age limits were not generally being adhered to as some pupils in year 7 (age 11), reported holding accounts for over three years.

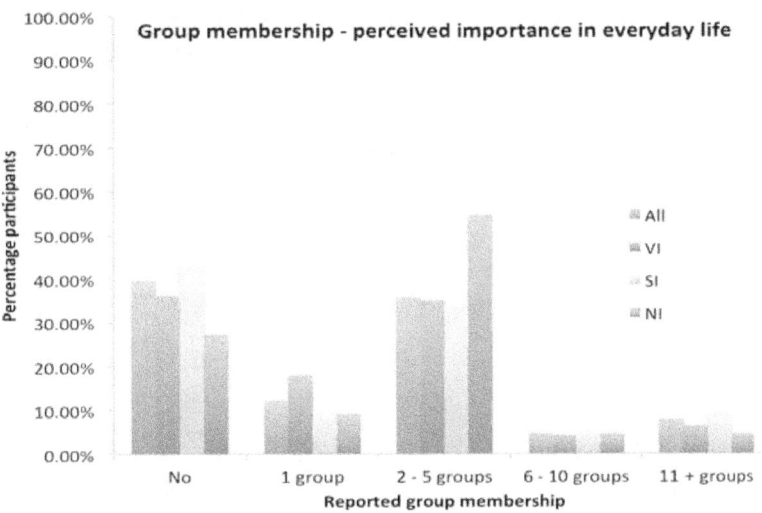

**Fig. 2** Percentage of respondents and group membership

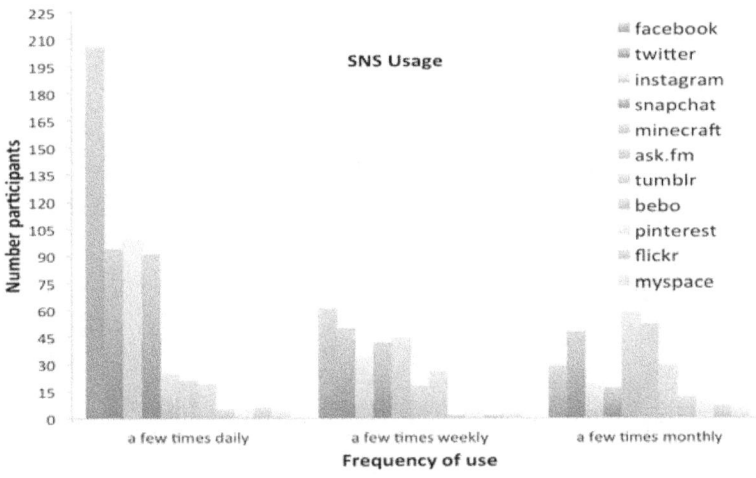

**Fig 3.** Reported Social Neworking System (SNS) frequency of use

Looking at social media uses participants were asked to place a value on the likelihood of using social media for a particular task, a value of five for the most important '*I only use social media for this reason*', and a value of one for the least important '*I will rarely use social media for this reason*'. Fig 4 shows the results; it is clear that 'talking to friends' was regarded as significantly more important than 'talking to relatives', and almost twice as important as 'organising events', 'sharing knowledge', 'taking part in discussions' or 'helping with schoolwork'. Analysis of responses by gender and year group yielded comparable results with few significant differences noted. This indicates that pupils are either not using social media for more advanced interactions (such as learning), or are not aware that they are doing so. This is explored further in the qualitative analysis below.

To determine if there was a difference between reported perception of the importance of social media in everyday life and in support of learning participants were asked how important they perceived social media to be in collaborative, informal learning and knowledge sharing when in lessons and out of school. The chart below (Fig. 5) shows little difference in the three reported perceptions of social media when used *in lessons* and reveals a general ambivalence whatever the enthusiasm was for social media in other areas of life. However, when asked to consider the importance of social media *outside of lessons* to support learning those participants who perceived social media as least important in everyday life unexpectedly regarded it with greater importance for learning. Further investigation is required to see whether this is because frequent users of social media do not see it as a special tool, and therefore fail to report it as being used for learning, or whether their patterns of behaviour are set by everyday use, whereas less-frequent users have less established patterns of behavior and are thus more open to other uses.

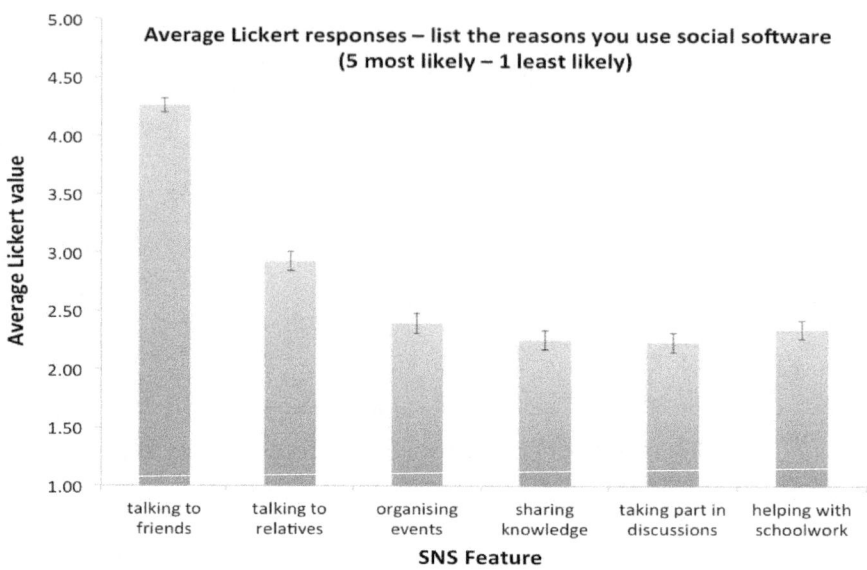

**Fig. 4** Average values given for reasons for using social media (5 most likely – 1 least likely)

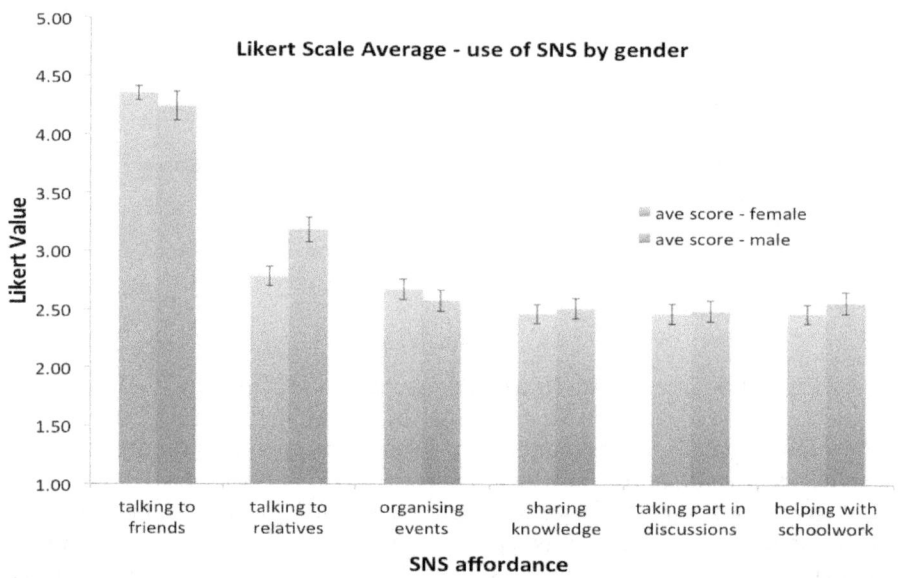

**Fig. 5** Perceived importance of social media in collaborative, informal learning and knowledge sharing

In additional to this quantitative data, we also gathered qualitative data directly about pupil's experiences. The participants were asked if they could give an example of an occasion they have been helped or had helped a peer through social media. The participants were also directly asked their opinion about the use of SNS to support learning out of school. The optional responses were: 'it is a good idea', 'I'm not bothered', 'I don't mix school work with fun'. By crosschecking these responses with the examples given we can begin to see whether perceptions of usefulness (the direct question) are actually a good reflection of experiences (the examples).

Table 1 shows the data about how students responded and about how this maps to the examples they shared. As one would expect those participants who thought that use of social media to help with school work was a good idea reported relatively high instances of receiving (64%) or providing (65%) help. Even amongst pupils who did not think social media should be mixed with schoolwork there was some reporting of examples (8% for help given, 11% for help received). It is interesting to note that amongst those that reported that no help had been observed (153 no help received, 139 no help given) a significant proportion (62 no help received, 53 no help given) still reported examples, this represents a certain ambiguity in self-reporting in 40% and 38% of cases respectively.

| Participant responses: has helped or been helped by a peer | Helping with school work - what do you think about using social media to help with school work when you are not in school: | | | |
|---|---|---|---|---|
| | Total | It's a good idea | I'm not bothered | I don't mix school work with fun |
| # Initial responses | 298 | 138 | 122 | 38 |
| Received support (yes) | 145 (49%) | 88 (64%) | 50 (41%) | 7 (18%) |
| Received support (no) | 153 (51%) | 50 (36%) | 72 (59%) | 31 (82%) |
| (yes) example given | 52 (17%) | 28 (20%) | 21 (17%) | 3 (8%) |
| (no) example given | 62 (21%) | 18 (13%) | 35 (29%) | 9 (24%) |
| Offered support (yes) | 157 (53% | 90 (65%) | 57 (48%) | 10 (26%) |
| Offered support (no) | 139 (47%) | 47 (35%) | 64 (52%) | 28 (74%) |
| (yes) example given | 60 (20%) | 36 (26%) | 20 (16%) | 4 (11%) |
| (no) example given | 53 (18%) | 14 (10%) | 30 (25%) | 9 (24%) |

**Table 1:** Percentage of students who expressed an opinion about use of social media for learning when not in school and had received or provided help for learning

The examples provided by participants were coded in an effort to develop a general picture of how participants might be using social media to support informal learning. Comments referring to help received by participant were labeled 'in', and those for help that was offered were labeled 'out', Initial codes which developed organically through participant choice of terms and topic, we identified two codes that were concerned with logistics (understanding tasks and accessing school systems materials):

- **administration**: examples related to practical matters associated with school activities (for example passwords and deadlines)
- **homework**: examples related to the support of homework tasks (for example, explaining requirements, passing on copies of materials)

We also identified two codes that were pedagogical and were about interpreting, understanding or discussing the actual material being learned:

- **understanding-homework**: examples related to the understanding of homework materials
- **understanding-lesson**: examples related to the understanding of lesson materials

| Analysis of themes | | | |
|---|---|---|---|
| Themes | Code | Responses (%) | Participant Comments |
| Logistics (114) | Administration (5) | In 3 (2%) | "When Was The homework due in?" |
| | | Out 2 (1.4%) | "what the password is for my maths" |
| | Homework (109) | In 68 (49%) | "They helped with homework as i wasnt here when we got a sheet and he/she told me the questions" |
| | | Out 41 (29%) | "explanation of the homework given to us." |
| Understanding (78) | Understanding-homework (55) | In 13 (9%) | "have had French homework explained and maths homework explained over facebook." |
| | | Out 42 (30%) | "they where stuck on some english homework and i gave them some helpful tips" |
| | Understanding-lesson (23) | In 8 (6%) | "they explaned something to me which we did in a lesson that i didnt get in the lesson" |
| | | Out 15 (11%) | "i explained something to them which we did in a lesson that they didnt get in the lesson" |

**Table 2:** Development of codes and themes from qualitative responses

As the purpose for analysis of the qualitative data was to develop an understanding of how social media was actually being used by the participants, comments from the original (uncleaned) data set were included. The logic behind this being that although a participant may have selected more than one option thus invalidating their record with regard to quantitative data, it would not effect the validity of their qualitative answers. From the original data set 140 (36.5%) 'in' comments and 141 (36.8%) 'out' comments were analysed. Table 2 shows an overview of the themes, codes, and numbers, and includes examples of each code for both In and Out. What immediately stands out is that the majority of examples were about Logistics (114 total) rather than Understanding (78 total). It is also clear that help in understanding concentrates around homework (55) rather than lessons (23). This data indicates that although the primary use of social media is relatively straightforward and task orientated, there are plenty of examples where more advanced engagement is occurring. Understanding the nature of this engagement is important future work. It could well be the case that the conversations occurring around the logistics of homework have established certain norms, and thus enabled secondary conversations around understanding, whereas this mechanism has not applied to other learning activities like lessons.

## Conclusions

Social media is perceived as holding great promise for learning, especially from a constructivist or connectivist perspective. But the majority of work to date looking at how learners use social media for learning has concentrated on adult learners. In our work we have tried to examine how school-aged children engage with social media, perceive its value for learning, and use it for learning. Over a 12 week period 384 pupils (aged 11-17) at six UK secondary schools took part in our online survey investigating their perceptions and use of social media in everyday life and for learning. We set out to investigate three separate questions.

1. How do school children perceive their use of social software in everyday life?

Though school aged children report using social media extensively there is a significant minority (20%) who do not view it as important in their everyday lives. Different social media tools are regarded as having specific uses with only a handful of tools being used by a large number of pupils, and there appears to be very little difference of use irrespective of gender or age. There are gender differences in perceived importance, but these perceptions do not seem to effect actual engagement.

2. How do school children perceive their use of social software for formal and informal learning?

Findings show that low level uses (chatting to friends or relatives) were seen as the most important aspects over more complex uses (such as arranging events or sharing content). In support of learning social media is primarily used for logistical reasons (e.g. managing homework tasks), there is a strong secondary activity around engaging with the content itself, but this is primarily based around homework activity, rather than other school activities such as lessons. This may be because the use of social media for homework logistics provides a social expectation and framework around homework, which is missing for other school work.

3. Does practice match perception in Q1 and Q2 - how is social software actually used by school children?

There is some evidence that self-reported behaviour is not reliable, for example over 40% of students who reported that they did not receive support via social media, still reported examples of this occurring. There also appears to be a reporting bias, in that students reveal more examples of them helping others, than others helping them, and this shows how important it is to ask these kinds of questions from both sides.

We believe that our work will contribute to the still relatively small set of studies looking at how school children both perceive and actually use social media for their learning, and will highlight some of the challenges of working with this age group. Building an evidence base in this area can help to challenge myths about the social media use amongst young people, and provide a platform to build both new skills and new tools to enable school children to use these powerful social media tools more effectively.

## References

Ahn, J. (2011). The effect of social network sites on adolescents' social and academic development: Current theories and controversies. Journal of the American Society for Information Science and Technology, 62(8), 1435-1445.
Alderson, P. (2004) Ethics. In: Fraser, S., Lewis, V., Ding, S., Kellett, M. & Robinson, C. (Eds.) Doing Research with Children and Young People, London: Sage.
Aldgate, J. & Bradley, M., (2004), Children's Experiences of Short Term Accommodation, The Reality of Research with Children and Young People, pp. 67-93. London: SAGE.
Brady, K. P., Holcomb, L. B., & Smith, B. V. (2010). The use of alternative social networking sites in higher educational settings: A case study of the e-Learning benefits of Ning in education. Journal of Interactive Online Learning, 9(2), 151–170.
Brown, J. S., & Adler, R. P. (2008). Open education, the long tail, and learning 2.0. Educause review, 43(1), 16-20.
Burden, K., & Atkinson, S. (2008). Evaluating pedagogical affordances of media sharing Web 2.0 technologies: A case study. Proceedings ascilite Melbourne, 121-125.
Butler, I., H. Williamson (1994) Children Speak: Children, Trauma and Social Work. London: Longman.
Couper, M.P. (2000). Web-based surveys: A Review of Issues and Approaches, Public Opinion Quarterly 64.
Cree, V. E., Kay, H., & Tisdall, K. (2002). Research with children: sharing the dilemmas. Child & family social work, 7.
Creswell, J. W., Clark, V. L. P. (2007). Designing and conducting mixed methods research. Thousand Oaks, CA: Sage publications.
Dron, J. (2007). Designing the undesignable: Social software and control. Educational Technology & Society, 10(3), 60-71.
Ellison, N. B., Steinfeld, C., & Lampe, C. (2007). The benefits of Facebook ''Friends:'' Social capital and college students' use of online social network sites. Journal of Computer-Mediated Communication, 12(4), article 1. Retrieved September 9, 2007 from http://jcmc.indiana.edu/vol12/issue4/ellison.html
Gray, D. E. (2009). Doing research in the real world. Sage.
Greenhow, C., & Robelia, B. (2009). Informal learning and identity formation in online social networks. Learning, Media and Technology, 34(2), 119-140.
Hill, M., Davis, J., Prout, A., & Tisdall, K. (2004). Moving the participation agenda forward. Children & society, 18(2).
Hood, S., Kelley, P., & Mayall, B. (1996). Children as research subjects: A risky enterprise. Children & Society, 10(2), 117-128.
Ito, M., Horst, H., Bittanti, M., Boyd, D., Herr-Stephenson, B., Lange, P. G., & Robinson, L. (2008). Living and learning with new media: Summary of findings from the digital youth project. The John D. and Catherine T. MacArthur Foundation Reports on Digital Media and Learning.
Jenkins, H. (2006). Convergence culture: Where old and new media collide. NYU press.
Jones, C., Ramanau, R., Cross, S., & Healing, G. (2010). Net generation or Digital Natives: Is there a distinct new generation entering university?.Computers & Education, 54(3), 722-732
Krippendorff, K. (2004): Content Analysis: An Introduction to Its Methodology. 2nd edition, Thousand Oaks, CA: Sage.
Lave, J. & Wenger, E. (1991). Situated learning: legitimate peripheral participation. Cambridge, England: Cambridge University Press.
Lee, M. J. W., McLoughlin, C., & Chan, A. (2007). Knowledge creation processes of students as producers of audio learning objects. In S. Wheeler & N. Whitton (Eds.), Proceedings of ALT-C 2007: Beyond control - Learning technology for the social network generation (pp. 116-128). Oxford, England.

Lee, M. J., McLoughlin, C., & Chan, A. (2008). Talk the talk: Learner_generated podcasts as catalysts for knowledge creation. British Journal of Educational Technology, 39(3), 501-521.

Lee, M. J. W., & McLoughlin, C. (2010). Beyond distance and time constraints: Applying social networking tools and Web 2.0 approaches to distance learning. In G. Veletsianos (Ed.), Emerging technologies in distance education (pp. 61–87). Edmonton, AB: Athabasca University Press.

Livingstone, S., & Brake, D. R. (2010). On the rapid rise of social networking sites: New findings and policy implications. Children & society, 24(1), 75-83.

Luckin, R., Clark, W., Graber, R., Logan, K., Mee, A., & Oliver, M. (2009). Do Web 2.0 tools really open the door to learning? Practices, perceptions and profiles of 11–16-year-old students. Learning, Media and Technology, 34(2), 87-104.

Maloney, E. (2007) What Web 2.0 can teach us about learning, The Chronicle of Higher Education, 53.

Masson, J. (2004) The Legal Context', Doing Research with Children and Young People, eds. Fraser, S., Lewis, V., Ding, S., Kellett, M., Robinson, C., London: SAGE.

McGloughlin, C., & Lee, M. J. W. (2010). Personalised and self regulated learning in the Web 2.0 era: International exemplars of innovative pedagogy using social software. Australasian Journal of Educational Technology, 26.

Miller, S. (2000). Researching children: issues arising from a phenomenological study with children who have diabetes mellitus. Journal of Advanced Nursing, 31.

Naveh, G., Tubin, D., & Pliskin, N. (2010). Student LMS use and satisfaction in academic institutions: The organizational perspective. The Internet and Higher Education, 13(3), 127–133.

Neuendorf, K. A. (2008). 5 Reliability for Content Analysis. Media messages and public health: A decisions approach to content analysis, 67.

Ofcom (2010). UK Children's Media Literacy. http://stakeholders.ofcom.org.uk/market-data-research/media-literacy/medlitpub/medlitpubrss/ukchildrensml/children

Papert, S. (1980). Mindstorms: Children, computers, and powerful ideas. Basic Books, Inc.

Selwyn, N. (2009). Faceworking: exploring students' education_related use of Facebook. Learning, Media and Technology, 34.

Sinclair, R. (2004). Participation in practice: making it meaningful, effective and sustainable. Children & Society, 18(2), 106-118.

Vygotsky, L.S. (1978). Mind in society: The development of higher psychological processes. Cambridge, MA: Harvard University Press.

# 13 Using Social Networking to Mentor 9th-grade Girls for Academic Success and Engineering Career Awareness

Patricia A. Carlson, PhD, Rose-Hulman Institute of Technology, USA

## Introduction

EMERGE combines the efficacy of social networking with the maturity, academic talents, and dedication of Rose-Hulman Institute of Technology's junior/senior women students. A two-year pilot program (2008 - 2010) conducted at three Indiana Wabash Valley (U.S.A.) high schools produced excellent outcomes. An adapted version of the program is now in operation as part of an economic development partnership between Rose-Hulman (RHIT) and Shelby County, Indiana. (This version involves five high schools, with separate male and female mentoring groups at each school house.)

EMERGE uses both structured and informal activities to motivate students who have an interest in STEM studies, but who need a cohesive learning environment to achieve the focus and resiliency necessary for academic success.

## E-mentoring – Models and Platforms

Robust, internet-based e-mentoring (tele-mentoring) has been in use for over a decade now (see Perez & Dorman 2001). Beginning with simple email capabilities and growing as the technology evolved, these online exchange programs have proliferated and have reported significant successes. For example, mentoring programs that sustain the interest of African-American males in high school achievement are currently available in a wide variety of forms (Cravens 2003). O'Neill and Harris identify four categories of e-mentoring (Winter 2004-2005):

- *Ask-an-expert*: professionals answer questions on an *ad hoc* basis.
- *Tutoring*: usually a one-to-one exchange based on a rigorous, master-to-apprentice scenario.
- *Curriculum-Based Tele-mentoring*: students pursue in-depth examinations of topics covered in the classroom, guided by their external mentor-expert.
- *A Tele-mentoring Relationship*: exchanges move beyond question-and-answer to achieve goals of broad-based affective and cognitive development.

We have adopted and merged the best practices from these successful approaches in order to use social networking to build powerful mentoring relationships among 9th-grade girls and female undergraduate engineering students at Rose-Hulman.

Early tele-mentoring efforts faced the difficulty of finding an appropriate digital platform for communication and collaboration. For example, noted advocates for constructivism in education, Bereiter and Scardamalia, built a platform (The Knowledge Forum®, see http://en.wikipedia.org/wiki/Knowledge_Forum) to mediate the types of socio-cognitive exchanges needed to nurture electronic learning relationships (2003). Fortunately, today a range of learning management systems (LMS) incorporate the synchronous and asynchronous tools necessary for successful – and secure – e-mentoring. We have selected Moodle (http://www.moodle.org ), an Open Source product that requires no licensing fee and has a number of leading-edge learning mediators. Moodle is part of a movement most commonly called Web 2.0. This refers to Internet-based services -- such as blogging, wikis, podcasting, video-casting, chats, and forums, that help personalize students' learning experiences by focusing on communication and collaboration.

## EMERGE Concept Overview

EMERGE partners 9th-grade girls with Rose-Hulman women students for the duration of an academic year (approximately nine months). A well-defined treatment ensures that the dominant tenor of the e-mentoring is academic achievement, while – at the same time – sustaining the excitement of exploring STEM. The multi-faceted treatment can best be summarized through a graphic (Fig. 1).

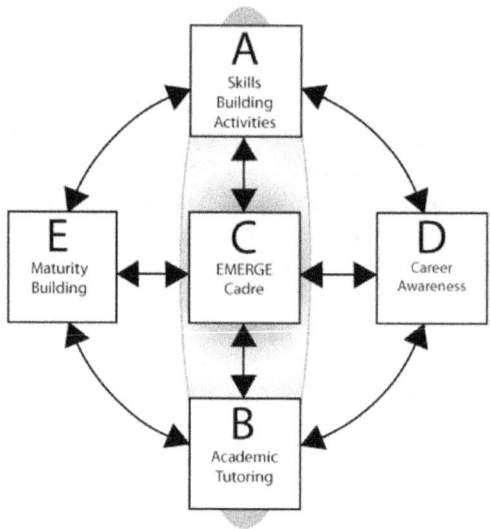

**Figure 1:** Conceptual overview of EMERGE components and objectives

**Area A—Skills Building**: Each small group (~ eight girls and one mentor) complete an agenda of problem-based "challenges" featuring topics that mirror work done at one of the sponsoring companies or developed to merge with the Indiana State Academic Standards. Students learn techniques for spatial/visual, temporal, quantitative, and probabilistic thinking within these active learning modules.

**Area B—Academic Tutoring**: Rose-Hulman undergraduates provide as-needed help with homework issues. Our mentors focus on STEM subjects, but also help with other disciplines. Additionally, the mentors provide advice and practice sessions for taking college admissions tests (such as PSAT, SAT, and ACT).

**Area C—EMERGE Cadre**: Camaraderie lies at the heart of this program. Though most of the interaction takes place in small learning communities, the program also establishes a group identity through EMERGE logos on shirts, backpacks, and school supplies. Creating a cohesive group with a positive image for STEM alleviates many of the negative peer-pressures for STEM achievement that permeate high school cultures.

**Area D—Career Awareness**: Day-long field trips to near-by high-tech organizations (e.g. Crane Naval Weapons Center, Cook Urological, IU Medical School) help to contextualize STEM learning. Rather than simple walk-throughs, we look for venues where a concentration of Rose-Hulman alumni/ae engineering employees can engage the students with hands-on activities. We supplement these trips with online awareness materials from the Society of Women Engineers (SWE) and from Women in Engineering ProActive Network (WEPAN).

**Area E—Maturity Building**: Fundamental changes in routines, pedagogies, and academic demands are especially challenging for some U.S. students as they move from middle school to a high school venue. EMERGE serves as a bridge program to strengthen the socio-cognitive skills require in a more demanding world. We nurture maturity and self-confidence through close bonding with a supportive reference group and a near-age role model.

## Implementation Framework

EMERGE is hosted through PRISM (http://www.rose-prism.org ), a nationally recognized K-12 educational technology hub sponsored by Rose-Hulman and the Lilly Endowment, Inc. for the past eleven years. The tele-mentoring takes place through PRISM's Children's Internet Protection Act-compliant learning management system.

Using the advances of Web 2.0, EMERGE provides a secure means for richly interactive communication and collaboration. Within this private web-space, mentors and mentees can set meeting times, post agendas, update calendars, collect data, share documents and other digital files, vote on issues, and store project materials. Most important are the dialogues and sharing of thoughts enabled by this platform (see Hazari, North & Moreland 2009 and Mesch & Talmud 2006).

### Program Objectives

Two well-proven approaches for improving student retention, increasing academic achievement, and raising career aspirations for young people are (1) mentoring and (2) membership in a cohesive, supportive learning community. One application of social networking – known by its generic term as tele-mentoring – has shown great promise for fulfilling these requirements. D. A. Scigliano's edited collection -- *Telementoring in the K-12 Classroom* – confirms that both researchers and practitioners have established a foundation for understanding e-mentoring's advantages, both inside and outside the classroom (2011). We also examined materials from the *Tele-mentoring Young Women in Science, Engineering, and Computing Project* – among others – to ensure that EMERGE featured a series of effective interventions to promote career awareness at this early stage in a young woman's development (see Bennett, Huper, Tsikalas, Meade, & Honey 1998a; Bennett, Hupert, Tskalas, Meade, & Honey 1998b; Kochan & Pascarelli 2005; Rhodes 2003)

Three major goals guide all activities in the EMERGE program:

- *Academic Success & Career Awareness* – Helping students to adopt a proactive stance on learning and to begin creating their own plan for career and educational choices.
- *Motivation & Maturity* – Helping 9th-grade students develop the socio-cognitive skills to bridge the transition into high school.
- *Subject Matter Tutoring* – Providing a consistent, reliable source of encouragement and advice, including scheduled or as-needed online tutoring for academic subjects and help with homework.

### Pilot Study Model

During a 2008-2010 field testing, the EMERGE professional-level supervisor trained 18 women engineering students at Rose-Hulman in the skills of mentoring. (Participation was by competitive application / interview for these paid positions.) Together, the supervisor and mentors set up small learning communities (typically made up of one college student and from six-to-eight 9th graders). These e-mentoring families stayed together for the entire academic year. Using the powers of social networking, nearly one hundred 9th-grade students remained with the program for their entire freshman year of high school. In February, 2010, EMERGE was named as a finalist in the *Power of Mentoring Awards*, sponsored by College Mentors for Kids (http://www.collegementors.org/ ).

Not to be overlooked, the program also had an impact on the Rose-Hulman women participants. The pilot program mentors went on to attain careers in science / engineering. Most applied for the EMERGE positions because they had genuine altruistic purposes, but they also wished to develop their management, inter-personal, and leadership skills.

### Basic Implementation and Logistics

EMERGE optimally requires a full year cycle. Having a strong working relationship, shared objectives, and a steadfast champion within the high school are all critical to success. Additionally, if local business / industry serve as sponsors, planning and calibration among all constituencies must take place at regular intervals.

Careful planning must also be given to both student populations involved: mentors and mentees. Most school districts have stringent regulations and need several layers of approval before sanctioning a tele-mentoring program. For example, mentors will probably need to undergo a background check and district school boards may need to be consulted before participating students are surveyed or their data used in any fashion. Because the assessment involves human subjects, an Institutional Review Board (IRB) protocol must be followed and agreements signed. Some districts may require mentors to report "alerts," or situations indicating at-home abuse or other improper situations. Thus, the professional supervisor will need to discuss these ethical / legal guidelines with the mentors. Additionally, the professional-level supervisor will need to set up a training and a reporting regiment for the college-level students.

The mentees need to have home access to the Internet, as well as parental permission to participate. (Ideally, an orientation session should be held by the EMERGE supervisor with parents to introduce the various activities and advantages of the program.) Mentees need to be trained on the basic operation / interface of the EMERGE web based platform. EMERGE also blends face-to-face experiences with tele-mentoring, requiring – in the best-case scenario – four comingled events. A "getting- to- know-you" lunch at the beginning and an awards lunch at the end deepen relationships. The program also includes two field trips per year. All activities must be closely monitored by the EMERGE staff to ensure both relational appropriateness and program efficacy.

## EMERGE and STEM Career Awareness

All components of EMERGE encourage the mentees to become the next generation of scientists and engineers. The treatment is exemplary because it combines promoting career awareness with support for academic success. This union of motivation and achievement gives a student not just the *desire* but also the *ability* to pursue a post-secondary degree in STEM.

With each yearly EMERGE cycle, we fine-tune our modules to deliver a more codified treatment. We are currently constructing a collection of outside-the-classroom "challenges" built around specified themes. Our objective is to have a series of online project-based learning modules based on increasingly more complex problems that each group completes under the tutelage of their mentor. These units increase career awareness, build critical thinking skills, and generate self-confidence – all fundamental to success in STEM subjects. With the help of our corporate partners, we are developing "authentic" tasks embedded within real-world scenarios.

For example, the EMERGE program implemented in Shelby County this academic year (2013 - 2014) and last (2012 – 2013) operates as part of an economic development agreement between a range of stakeholders (city / county councils, local industries, and four school districts). For this instantiation, EMERGE showcases learning units based on the types of research / development / manufacturing work being done by four companies connected with the consortium.

Using age-appropriate, non-proprietary content, inquiry-based learning units engage the students and contextualize their studies within real-life careers. Each month has a theme that exposes Shelby County students to local industry partners and connects students to Rose-Hulman mentors (see Figs. 2 and 3). These interactions lay the foundation for a clear path to success. Additionally, we have developed a set of documents (e.g. program flier, parental permission materials, and descriptions for corporate partners) that are available by request.

**Figure 2:** The January theme, Communicating Digitally, was launched with our business partner, Lifeshare Technologies. Both high school and Rose-Hulman mentors learned about Alice, a drag-n-drop, 3D animation program that provides a gentle introduction to computer programming.

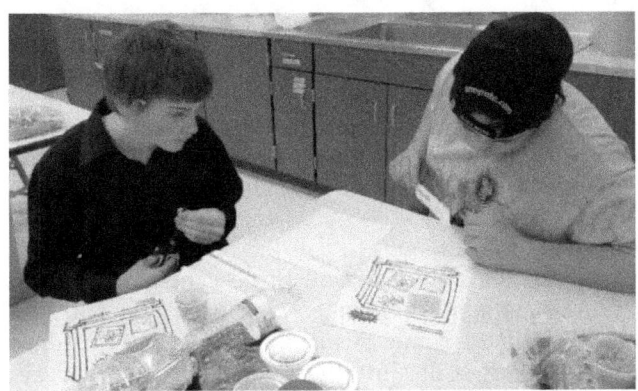

**Figure 3:** February focused on engineering careers and was sponsored by Triumph Controls, LLC. The high school students and mentors worked on a challenge project: to reverse engineer (using only available supplies) a Lifting Machine recently advertised by a hypothetical competitor. In the online environment, mentors answered student questions about engineering careers and course requirements.

## Assessment Results – Pilot Cohort of Young Women

Both cohorts from the EMERGE pilot (2008 – 2009 and 2009 – 2010) were successful. Year one involved Vigo County School Corporation (VCSC), represented by single high school, West Vigo High School (WVHS). In year two, the program involved North High School in Vigo County and Northview High School in neighboring Clay County. In all, approximately 100 9th-graders and 18 Rose-Hulman women students completed the EMERGE pilot program. We use the assessment done for the first cohort – West Vigo High School (WVHS) – to illustrate both program efficacy and the methods of our evaluation model.

WVHS is classified as a rural school house. It is one of three high schools in the district, with the other two being substantially larger (having a student population over 2,000 each). In 2012, WVHS had 32 teachers and 438 students, a 36% drop in student population since 2007. Nearly 50% of the WVHS population is on free or reduced lunch (which serves as a proxy indicator for low socio-economic population); only one-half of the students tested passed the state competency examination for math / language arts in 2009. The school did not make Annual Yearly Progress for 2010-2011 or 2011-2012.

### Assessment Instruments

Two online surveys were administered to this 2008 - 2009 cohort: one at the end of the group's freshman year (2009) and the second at the end of their senior year (2012). We present highlights from both self-report questionnaires.

- *Survey #1 (late May 2009)*: An exit survey contained 22 items, answered on a four-part Likert scale (strongly agree, agree, disagree, and strongly disagree). All 35 mentees from this first year completed the online survey. Questions loaded on the three central goals of the treatment. Table 1 provides sample results from each of the three thematic clusters.

- *Survey #2 (late May 2012)*: Thirty-three of the original 35 participants were still enrolled at WVHS and completed a 34-item exit survey (administered online through the Dean of Students Office). The survey was divided into three types of questions:

- → Profile of STEM engagement (e.g. "How many AP math, science, engineering, and technology courses did you take in high school.") **16 Questions**

- → Questions requiring a narrative answer (e.g. "What do you see yourself doing in five years?") **3 Questions.**

- → Agree/disagree items presented as a five-part Likert scale (e.g. "Participating in EMERGE helped me to improve my academic performance.") **15 Questions.**

The last group of questions loaded on the same three programmatic goals that structured the first survey. Table 2 provides sample results from these fifteen survey items.

**Quantitative Results**

While items in both surveys clustered around three central objectives, the exact questions were tailored for the specific situation. Thus, some of the questions for Survey 2009 and Survey 2012 had a similar focus, but the wording was not exactly the same. Also, Survey #1 (2009) had a four-part Likert scale, while Survey #2 (2012) had a five-part Likert scale. In other words, the first survey did not include a "neutral" category, while the second survey did. These variations preclude inferential statistical comparisons between the two data sets. However, descriptive analysis provides compelling results.

**N = 35**

| Question | Strongly Agree | Agree | Disagree | Strongly Disagree |
|---|---|---|---|---|
| *Cluster #1: Did EMERGE help students adopt a proactive stance on learning and creating their own plans for future career and educational choices?* | | | | |
| Participating in EMERGE has helped me to develop better study habits. | 11.4% | 71.4% | 17.1% | 0% |
| Participating in EMERGE has encouraged me to think about what I want to do when I graduate from high school. | 51.4% | 42.9% | 5.7% | 0% |
| Participating in EMERGE has encouraged me to think more seriously about continuing my education beyond high school. | 62.9% | 34.3% | 2.9% | 0% |
| Participating in EMERGE has helped me to see how important my high school education is to my future. | 51.4% | 48.6% | 0% | 0% |
| *Cluster #2: Did students develop better socio-cognitive skills to help bridge the transition to high school?* | | | | |
| Participating in EMERGE helped me to communicate more clearly with peers and teachers. | 8.6% | 62.9% | 28.6% | 0% |
| Participating in EMERGE helped me improve my skills for working well with others. | 17.1% | 68.6% | 14.3% | 0% |
| Participating in EMERGE helped me handle the demands of my high school environment. | 17.1% | 65.7% | 17.1% | 0% |
| Participating in EMERGE has helped me to be more confident in my own abilities. | 14.3% | 74.3% | 11.4% | 0% |
| *Cluster #3: Did EMERGE provide a consistent, reliable source of encouragement and advice, including support for STEM academic subjects?* | | | | |
| Participating in EMERGE this semester gave me a sense of belonging to a supportive group. | 14.3% | 77.1% | 8.6% | 0% |
| My EMERGE mentor was interested in me, and I could count on her for support / advice. | 28.6% | 51.4% | 17.1% | 2.9% |
| I feel close to the other girls in my EMERGE group. | 34.3% | 60.0% | 5.7% | 0% |
| I would recommend the EMERGE program to a friend. | 40.0% | 60.0% | 0% | 0% |

**Table 1:** Results from EMERGE Cohort A Survey Administered in May 2009

N = 33

| Cluster #1: Did EMERGE help students adopt a proactive stance on learning and creating their own plans for future career and educational choices? | | | | | |
|---|---|---|---|---|---|
| Question | Strongly Agree | Agree | Neutral | Disagree | Strongly Disagree |
| There are great career choices for women in science, technology, engineering, and math. | 45.5% | 48.5% | 6.1% | 0% | 0% |
| Participating in EMERGE influenced my decision to complete high school. | 15.2% | 24.2% | 21.2% | 24.2% | 15.2% |
| The EMERGE program increased my interest in science, technology, engineering, or math as a career choice. | 6.1% | 33.3% | 24.2% | 30.3% | 6.1% |
| Participating in EMERGE helped strengthen my belief that girls can do as well in science, technology, engineering, and math as boys do. | 33.3% | 51.5% | 12.1% | 0% | 3% |
| **Cluster #2: Did EMERGE help build socio-cognitive skills for success in high school?** | | | | | |
| Question | Strongly Agree | Agree | Neutral | Disagree | Strongly Disagree |
| Participating in EMERGE helped me to communicate more effectively with peers and with teachers | 6.1% | 42.4% | 36.4% | 12.1% | 3% |
| Participating in EMERGE helped me to develop skills for handling the demands of a high school environment. | 3% | 30.3% | 51.5% | 12.1% | 3% |
| Participating in EMERGE was very valuable for my personal development. | 9.1% | 39.4% | 33.3% | 18.2% | 0% |
| Belonging to my EMERGE small group helped me to balance school obligations with other activities. | 12.1% | 33.3% | 30.3% | 21.2% | 3% |
| **Cluster #3: Did EMERGE provide a nurturing environment that resulted in stronger academic performance?** | | | | | |
| Question | Strongly Agree | Agree | Neutral | Disagree | Strongly Disagree |
| I would recommend the EMERGE program to others. | 18.2% | 63.6% | 12.1% | 6.1% | 0% |
| Participating in EMERGE helped prepare me for taking college admissions tests (such as the PSAT, the SAT, or the ACT) | 3% | 42.4% | 39.4% | 15.2% | 0% |
| Emerge helped me to be confident in taking harder courses in science, technology, engineering, and math. | 6.1% | 39.4% | 36.4% | 18.2% | 0% |
| Participating in EMERGE helped me to improve my academic performance. | 3% | 42.4% | 36.4% | 15.2% | 3% |

**Table 2:** Results from EMERGE Cohort A Survey Administered in May 2012

Looking at these data from another perspective permits a stronger degree of comparison. For Table 3, we calculated the ratio of respondents selecting agree or strongly agree to those selecting disagree or strongly disagree on both surveys. We report these results for questions that can be considered functional equivalents within the three programmatic goals.

| Cluster #1: Did EMERGE help students adopt a proactive stance on learning and creating their own plans for future career and educational choices? | | | |
|---|---|---|---|
| Pairs | Question | Year | Ratio A / D |
| #1 | Participating in EMERGE has helped me to see how important my high school education is to my future. | 2009 | 27 to 1 |
| | Participating in EMERGE influenced my decision to complete high school. | 2012 | 1 to 1 |
| #2 | Participating in EMERGE has caused me to be more interested in my current science, mathematics, or technology classes. | 2009 | 2 to 1 |
| | The EMERGE program increased my interest in science, technology, engineering, or math as a career choice. | 2012 | 13 to 12 |
| #3 | Participating in EMERGE has made me more confident in my own abilities. | 2009 | 5 to 1 |
| | Participating in EMERGE helped strengthen my belief that girls can do as well in science, technology, engineering, and math as boys do. | 2012 | 28 to 1 |
| **Cluster #2: Did EMERGE help build socio-cognitive skills for success in high school?** | | | |
| Pairs | Question | Year | Ratio A / D |
| #4 | Participating in EMERGE helped me handle the demands of my high school environment. | 2009 | 5 to 1 |

|  | Question | Year | Ratio A/D |
|---|---|---|---|
|  | Participating in EMERGE helped me to develop skills for handling the demands of a high school environment. | 2012 | 11 to 5 |
| #5 | Participating in EMERGE has helped me to balance my time among school work, responsibilities at home, and social activities. | 2009 | 3 to 1 |
|  | Belonging to my EMERGE small group helped me to balance school obligations with other activities. | 2012 | 15 to 8 |
| #6 | Participating in EMERGE helped me to communicate more clearly with peers and teachers. | 2009 | 2 to 1 |
|  | Participating in EMERGE helped me to communicate more effectively with peers and with teachers | 2012 | 28 to 0 |
| *Cluster #3: Did EMERGE provide a nurturing environment that resulted in stronger academic performance?* ||||
| Pairs | Question | Year | Ratio A/D |
| #7 | I would recommend the EMERGE program to a friend. | 2009 | 28 to 0 |
|  | I would recommend the EMERGE program to others. | 2012 | 27 to 2 |
| #8 | Because of EMERGE, I want to take more high school classes that relate to math, science, or technology. | 2009 | 3 to 1 |
|  | Emerge helped me to be confident in taking harder courses in science, technology, engineering, and math. | 2012 | 5 to 2 |
| #9 | EMERGE has helped me to develop better study habits. | 2009 | 3 to 1 |
|  | Participating in EMERGE helped me to improve my academic performance. | 2012 | 5 to 2 |

**Table 3:** Results from Functionally Equivalent Questions on Surveys 2009 and 2012

These results support the claim that EMERGE was highly successful during its inaugural year and also had a lasting, positive impact on the participants.

**Qualitative Results**

Preliminary review of the profile and narrative sections of the 2012 surveys suggests that the EMERGE cohort of 33 was above the averages in all categories for WVHS women graduating that year. However, we underscore two caveats: (1) the school had only incomplete data for some of the 18 qualitative questions we asked, and (2) the graduating class contained 78 women, meaning that nearly 50% were EMERGE participants. We emphasize that of the 35 original members of the cohort, 33 graduated on time and the 2 non-surveyed had moved out of the district. The all-person graduation rate for WVHS in 2012 was 72%,

while the rate for the EMERGE participants was 100%.

**Figure 4:** West Vigo High School students joined EMERGE staff at a 2009 session at Cook Medical's Urological and Women's Health operations near Spencer, IN. The group learned about careers available in engineering and life science fields. Shirts and lanyards helped to establish EMERGE group identity. (Photo provided by Cook, Inc. and used with permission)

Of special note for EMERGE sponsoring companies, we found anecdotal evidence that the content emphasized in the field trip / learning modules of 2008-2009 had an effect on career choices. For the first cohort, we worked with Cook Urological and Women's Heath to showcase STEM/engineering in medicine and health. A group of Rose-Hulman alumni/ae at the Spencer, Indiana facility took us under their wing and helped with a mini-curriculum for life science / bio-medical engineering activities, including a day-long field trip.

Of the 22 EMERGE participants who answered the fill-in question "What are your plans after high school graduation?", 21 will go on to post-secondary education; one will join the military. This represents 64% of the total sample of 33 respondents. (We make the assumption that the eleven students electing not to respond were not going on to higher education.) Of the 21 electing for post-secondary education, 14 specifically indicated a health or medicine-related career choice. (One will attend Rose-Hulman, majoring in bio-medical engineering.) Therefore, of those going on to post-secondary education, 67% selected a career allied with one of the EMERGE treatment's major themes.

## Program Extensions

A lack of funding caused EMERGE to go into hiatus from September 2010 through September 2012. However, we have found renewed interest in e-mentoring when embedded as part of a more comprehensive economic development / workforce enhancement plan for disadvantaged counties in the state. The Shelby County consortium is one example; other counties are also exploring partnerships with Rose-Hulman and EMERGE. Consequently, we are now focusing on incremental improvement in two areas: assessment and dissemination.

### Refine the Assessment Model

EMERGE will build upon its existing approach to improve the assessment framework. Essentially, we will restructure or add in three areas (1) improve the self-report surveys, (2) use focus groups for iterative feedback, and (3) add digital tools for evaluating the electronically logged usage patterns and mentoring exchanges. Essentially, we will look for improvement in assessment on two levels:

- *Program Implementation*: Monitoring outcomes for sustained quality improvement, such as (1) training of student mentors and (2) examining traffic data to determine trends and patterns, (3) isolating best practices from these data, exercises, and exchanges.

- *Program Efficacy:* Mentees and their teachers (in all subjects) will be asked to provide observations on several dimensions for each student's maturation:

    | | |
    |---|---|
    | Self-directed learning | Desire to continue education |
    | Critical thinking | Subject grades |
    | Career and workplace awareness | Science and mathematics comprehension |

### Enable Replication at Other Schools of Engineering

EMERGE not only provides benefits to the students and schools immediately involved, but also serves as a test-bed for refining the core competencies of successful e-mentoring programs. Next year, the EMERGE staff will codify and electronically disseminate program materials so that other engineering institutions may set up their own tele-mentoring program. These items include "how to" guidance for program implementation, such as (1) training of college student mentors and (2) free use of EMERGE's Moodle platform to get started. Also provided will be methods for assessing the program's efficacy.

# References

Bennett, D., Hupert, N., Tsikalas, K., Meade, T., & Honey, M. (1998a). *The benefits of online mentoring for high school girls -- Year 3 evaluation,* Center for Children & Technology, September. Available: http://cct.edc.org/report_summary.asp?numPublicationId=77

Bennett, D., Hupert, N., Tsikalas, K., Meade, T., & Honey, M. (1998b). *Critical issues in the design & implementation of tele-mentoring environments.* Center for Children & Technology, September. Available: http://cct.edc.org/admin/publications/report/09_1998.pdf .

Bereiter, C., Scardamalia, M. (2003). Learning to work creatively with knowledge." In E. D. Corte, L. Verschaffel, N. Entwistle, & J. V. Merrienboer (Eds.), *Powerful learning environments: Unraveling basic components and dimensions* (pp. 73-78). Oxford: Elsevier Science.

Cravens, J. (2003). Online mentoring: Programs and suggested practices as of February 2001. *Journal of Technology in Human Services*, 21 (1/2), 85-109.

Hazari, S., North, A., & Moreland, D. (2009). Investigating pedagogical value of wiki technology. *Journal of Information Systems Education.* 20 (2), 187-198.

Kochan, F., & Pascarelli, J. (Eds.) (2005), *Creating successful tele-mentoring programs.* Greenwich, CT: Information Age Publishing.

Mesch, G. S. & Talmud, I. (2006). Online friendship formation, communication channels, and social closeness. *International Journal of Internet Science*, 1 (1), 29-44.

O'Neill, D. K., & Harris, J. B. (Winter 2004-2005). Bridging the perspective and developmental needs of all participants in curriculum-based tele-mentoring programs. *Journal of Research on Technology in Education*, 37 (2), 111-128.

Perez, S., & Dorman, S. M. (2001). Enhancing youth achievement through tele-mentoring. *Journal of School Health,* 71 (3), 122-123.

Rhodes, J. E. (2003). Online mentoring: The promise and pitfalls of an emerging approach," *National Mentoring Partnership.* Available at: http://www.mentoring.org/research_corner/11_03_online.adp

Scigliano, D. A. (Ed.) (2011). *Telementoring in the K-12 classroom: Online communication technologies for learning.* New York, NY: Information Science Reference.

# Acknowledgements

The EMERGE pilot (2008 – 2010) was funded by a grant from the Fund for the Improvement of Post-secondary Education (FIPSE). The PRISM Project is funded by the Lilly Endowment, Inc. to use networking and new media in support of innovative STEM K-12 education. Any opinions, findings, and conclusions or recommendations expressed in this material are those of the author and do not necessarily reflect the views of the funding agencies.

# 14 Guiding Students in Collaborative Writing of Wikipedia Articles – How to Get Beyond the Black Box Practice in Information Literacy Instruction?

Eero Sormunen, Tuulikki Alamettälä, University of Tampere, Finland

## Introduction

Fluent literacy is a key competence enabling among other things independent learning, continuous development of professional expertise and full participation in the society. The internet revolution has radically broadened the concept of and requirements for literacy towards digital, information, and media literacies. Students are said to be fluent searchers of information since they daily "google" for information. However, recent research shows that most students do not master the basics of effective searching in complex tasks (e.g., Walraven, Brand-Gruwel, & Boshuizen, 2008). Students' skills are quite limited in planning and reformulating queries (Kiili, Laurinen, & Marttunen, 2009), assessing the credibility of information (Kiili, Laurinen, & Marttunen, 2008), and synthesizing information across sources (Sormunen & Lehtiö, 2011).

Pedagogical practices in schools do not keep apace with the rapidly changing media and information environment. Essay-type assignments which require independent acquisition and use of information sources are used to train students' information literacies (IL). Unfortunately, task assignment designs still tend to be traditional, and learning outcomes remain poor (Limberg, Alexandersson, Lantz-Andersson, & Folkesson, 2008). Recent studies (Hongisto & Sormunen, 2010; Limberg et al., 2008) show that teachers focus on the technical aspects of searching and citing information sources, while students' main problems concern developing own questions, assessing information, building meaning from sources, and constructing knowledge for their own texts.

Finland has been a top achiever in the PISA (Programme for International Student Assessment) results on reading literacy (Kuusilehto-Awale & Lahtero, 2014; Niemi, Toom, & Kallioniemi, 2012). Several factors in the Finnish school system have been proposed to explain high outcomes in reading such as university based teacher education (Master's degree required) and the autonomy of schools and teachers in implementing the national curriculum (Kuusilehto-Awale & Lahtero, 2014). Obviously, present pedagogical practices in the Finnish school have shown their effectiveness in literacy education. However, it is another question how these practices scale up in open, internet-dominated information environments which call for new literacies. Studies mentioned above suggest that there might be a gap between the present pedagogical practice and the needs to learn new literacies.

This paper reports the findings of a study on teachers' ways to plan and guide assignments for information literacy instruction. The data was collected in two upper secondary school classes, where students wrote Wikipedia articles as group work. We used Guided Inquiry (Kuhlthau, Maniotes, & Caspari, 2007) - a research-based teaching model for information literacy - as the framework of analysis for present pedagogical practices in IL instruction. The goal was to find out which aspects of the research-based teaching model are exploited also in the present pedagogical practice and which are not.

## Earlier research

Information and related literacies have been studied in different research traditions under various labels such as new literacies, digital literacies and media literacies (see e.g., Bawden, 2001; Lankshear & Knobel, 2011). In this paper we build on the tradition of information literacy and information seeking research – two subfields of information studies. They provide a solid theoretical and empirical basis to study information searching, assessment and use in learning. Information literacies refer to the various forms of competences and social practices which have become essential in the learner's interaction with the information resources shaped by the internet.

In information studies, students' information searching and use has been in the focus of research from the late 1980s. Kuhlthau (1991, 2004) revealed the complexity of information searching in a genuine learning situation. Drawing on the constructivist theories of learning, task-based approach to information seeking, and a long series of empirical studies in different educational contexts, she developed and verified the Information Search Process (ISP) model to characterize learners' information behaviours and experiences of uncertainty at different stages of the learning process. Based on the ISP model, Kuhlthau, Maniotes, & Caspari (2007) developed Guided Inquiry (GI) for information literacy instruction. The framework has been evaluated in a few classroom studies (Chu, Chow, Tse, & Kuhlthau, 2008; Chu, Tse, & Chow, 2011). Recent research on information retrieval has also identified the link between learning and exploratory Web searching. While simple lookup searches (e.g. routine "googling") aim to find facts or single documents providing an answer to the searcher's problem, the goal of exploratory searches is to acquire knowledge and make sense in a process of learning or investigation (Marchionini, 2006). Researchers have identified a range of attributes characterizing exploratory searches: information needs are ill-defined and multifaceted, search outcomes cannot be specified in advance, and various search strategies needs to be attempted and different types of sources interpreted (Wildemuth & Freund, 2012). The challenge for educating students in information literacies is that students, as expressed by (Vakkari, 2010), should learn the principle that "... the solution to a problem is created, not found".

Our earlier study on students' behaviour in a Wikipedia writing assignment revealed differences between two classes in (1) how students used sources (Sormunen, Heinström, Romu, & Turunen, 2012), (2) how student groups collaborated (Sormunen, Tanni, & Heinström, 2013), and (3) what learning experiences they reported (Heinström & Sormunen, 2013). We also found that the teachers interacted differently with students which might be one reason for variation in students' behaviours and experiences. Overall, teachers tended not to intervene the inquiry process after introducing it and paid little attention to supporting students' collaboration during online inquiry (Sormunen, Alamettälä, & Heinström, 2013). In this paper we further elaborate teachers' ways of guiding student groups in their Wikipedia assignment.

## Guided Inquiry (GI)

The underlying idea of the Guided Inquiry framework (Kuhlthau et al., 2007; Kuhlthau, Maniotes, & Caspari, 2012) is that information literacies are best learned by training appropriate information practices in a genuine collaborative process of inquiry. In this line of taught, the goal is that, in addition to information literacies, students learn curriculum content, how to learn (by working with sources), and social skills (collaborative knowledge building).

Guided Inquiry applies two collaborative forums. The whole class - called as an *inquiry community* – is used to introduce and motivate the assignment and share results. Small groups - called as *inquiry circles* - are the main forum of learning activities. Students are guided to enhance their learning by three *inquiry tools*: *inquiry journals* help reflect on personal learning, *inquiry logs* help keep track of and comment important information sources found, and *inquiry charts* help visualize, organize and synthesize ideas. Each inquiry tool is introduced at a pre-defined stage of the assignment and typically applied in all stages after that. The teacher team (e.g. a teacher and a teacher librarian) concentrates on organizing student groups to work collaboratively, explicating learning goals, monitoring the progress of groups and providing active feedback.

The eight stages of Guided Inquiry are illustrated in Table 1. The framework emphasizes (as made obvious by the ISP model) stages 1-4 before actual gathering of sources for the writing stage starts. Students are prepared for information gathering by activities stimulating curiosity and interests, sharing what are known already, discovering and exploring ideas how to study the topic and formulating questions. After these steps students are expected to figure out what topic or problem they are going to study in the inquiry circle and personally, to have a preliminary understanding of their information needs, and to be able to formulate relevant search concepts. Further, they gradually develop more explicit criteria to select sources for use, and read sources more consciously from a specified viewpoint. The underlying aim is that students learn to manage the uncertainty inherent in the construction process of information searching and learning.

**Table 1.** The stages of Guided Inquiry.

| Stage | Goals of core activities | Inquiry tools |
|---|---|---|
| 1. Open | Invitation to inquiry, open minds, stimulate curiosity | Inquiry community introduced |
| 2. Immerse | Build background knowledge, connect to content, | Inquiry circles and inquiry |

|   |   | discover interesting ideas | journals introduced |
|---|---|---|---|
| 3. | Explore | Explore interesting ideas, look around, dip in | Inquiry logs introduced |
| 4. | Identify | Pause and ponder, identify inquiry question, decide direction | Inquiry charts introduced |
| 5. | Gather | Gather important information, go broad, go deep | |
| 6. | Create | Reflect learning, go beyond facts to make meaning, create to communicate | |
| 7. | Share | Learn from each other, share learning, tell your story | |
| 8. | Evaluate | Evaluate achievement of learning goals, reflect on content, reflect on process | |

Guided Inquiry shares the socio-constructivist theory base with the implementations of inquiry learning (inquiry-based, problem-based, project-based learning). Thus, when we are analysing teachers' practices in the GI framework, we examine whether or not teachers apply pedagogical ideas typical of inquiry learning.

## Case study

### Research question

Our aim was to find out through a case study how the present pedagogical practices in Finnish upper secondary schools relate to a teaching model – Guided Inquiry (Kuhlthau et al., 2007) - developed on the basis of extensive research on information searching and use in learning (Kuhlthau, 1991, 2004). We focused on one research question:

*To what extent do teachers' ways to design collaborative Wikipedia writing assignments provide elements similar to the eight stages of Guided Inquiry?*

Our goal is not to evaluate the case courses in terms of learning outcomes but to explore qualitatively to what extent teachers implement the ideas of inquiry learning in information literacy assignments. The results might contribute in introducing justified hypothesis how teachers' pedagogical practices affect students' behaviour in inquiry-type group assignments.

### Case courses

Data were collected from two eight-week courses in an upper secondary school in the city of Tampere, Finland, during the spring term of 2011. Thirty students in ten groups completed a course in Finnish literature, and twenty-eight students in seven groups completed a course in Finnish history. In the literature course, the task was to write an article for the Finnish edition of Wikipedia while the history course used a dedicated school wiki as the writing forum. In both courses, the students were instructed to follow Wikipedia's conventions and requirements for authors. In the literature course each assignment was about a classic Finnish novel. In the history course, the teacher had prepared topics dealing with Finnish history from the period of 1918 to 1939.

The assignment was introduced, written guidelines distributed, groups formed, and the topics for articles were allocated for groups at the first meeting. The second meeting was a training session in the nearby city library. One 30-minute lesson was devoted to library searching and another lesson to Web searching. The librarian knew the students' topics and distributed materials from the library collection for the students. After the visit to the library, the students worked the next five (in the history course four) 90-minute sessions in the computer class to search for information, to select and read sources and to write text for the articles under the teacher's supervision. In the history course a substitute teacher was supervising the class for two sessions instead of the regular teacher.

The case courses were a part of "Tieto haltuun" development project initiated in 2008 to improve teachers' and students' information literacy skills in Tampere upper secondary schools (Sormunen, Eriksson, & Kurkipää, 2012). The concept of writing Wikipedia articles as an information literacy assignment was introduced by a team of teachers in mother tongue and literature (called here *literature teachers* for short). They had used the assignment three times before our case study but the teacher of the case course was personally applying it for the first time. In the history course, the teacher (called here the *history teacher*) was also applying the Wikipedia assignment for the first time. Obviously, the literature teacher had a more favourable position since the assignment concept was originally developed for literature classes, and she could enjoy the help of more experienced literature teachers. However, we regard both case courses as appropriate representatives of information literacy instruction built on teachers' professional practices in the Finnish upper secondary schools.

### Data collection and analysis

The student groups were shortly interviewed by a research assistant during classroom sessions and more thoroughly at the end of the course. Interviews were used to collect data on teacher-initiated teacher/group interactions. The teachers were interviewed before and after the course. All interviews were recorded and transcribed. The research assistant wrote observation memos instantly after classroom sessions to record the overall course of classroom activities. We had access to all course materials including the teachers' written instructions. The materials also included students' progress reports, responses to homework assignments, article drafts, and the teachers' comments on them published in the Moodle learning environment. The data were used to compare the designs of the assignments and their implementation between the literature and history classes.

The interview transcripts were coded thematically (see Boyatzis, 1998) using Atlas.ti software package. We tried to find all instances where students mentioned an interaction with the teacher. Interaction categories were derived from the data and quantified in five main activities (planning group work, planning contents, searching & assessing sources, reading, writing and editing). All interviews and course materials were read systematically to find all details of the assignment designs and teachers' justifications of using a particular design.

### Findings

We present the results of our analysis by reporting the activities the teachers had designed for the assignment related to each of the eight Guided Inquiry stages. Also the ways of exploiting collaborative forums (inquiry community and circles) and inquiry tools (journals, logs and charts) are described. Each section starts with a short reminder of the idea of the stage, and mentions if a collaborative forum or an inquiry tool is to be introduced to students (in *italics*).

**Stage 1: Open.** *The goal of this stage is to introduce the assignment to students, motivate them and stimulate their curiosity. Inquiry community introduced.* Both teachers had prepared written instructions for student groups and introduced them to students during the first classroom session. Teachers allocated students to groups and listed the themes for the articles. In the literature course, the groups were allowed to select the novel on which to work. The history teacher decided how themes were allocated to groups. In the introduction, both teachers focused on the requirements for the written articles, how the students should work in the groups and how to report their progress. No stimulating triggers (e.g., videos), nor classroom/small group discussions were used to motivate students for the task ahead. The first session took a traditional, teacher centred form. Students were not exposed to activities typical of, or in sense of a classroom community (cf. Scardamalia & Bereiter, 2006).

**Stage 2: Immerse.** *The goal is to 'connect to content', activate what is already known, and generate ideas related to the theme. Inquiry circles and journals introduced.* In the history course, the teacher listed 3-5 subtopics for each group to help them comprehend what to write about the imposed theme. The teacher did not activate the groups to explore their own knowledge or to generate ideas how the theme could be approached. In the literature course, each student had to read the novel selected by the group and write a literary essay. Thus literature students were exposed to an activity which moved their attention on the theme before they started to collect information sources for the writing task. Literary essays also built shared knowledge about the novel within the group and probably helped discuss about ideas how to proceed with the assignment.

The teachers allocated students into groups and gave them instructions to work on the assignment. However, they did not explicitly guide student groups (inquiry circles) how to collaboratively 'connect to content' or develop ideas about it. Personal inquiry journals were not introduced but in the literature course literary essays played a similar function in activating students to think about the theme. However, reading a novel and writing an essay do not guide to reflect on personal learning and the activity does not continue across the whole assignment process as the inquiry journal does.

**Stage 3: Explore.** *At this stage students explore interesting ideas how to work with the theme by consulting information sources searched by students or made available by the teacher. Inquiry logs introduced.* In the history course, we could not identify organized activities related to the exploration stage. After the instructions were distributed (incl. the lists of subtopics for each group) and the students participated the teaching sessions in the library, they were expected to start searching information about their themes (i.e., skip to the Gather stage). The literature teacher activated students to explore the writing task ahead by a homework assignment: students had to study and report the writing conventions applied in Wikipedia. Further, the teacher guided student groups to select a well-written Wikipedia article about classic novels and their authors, discuss in the group about the contents, and based on their observations outline a content plan for their own article. The teacher also gave student groups selected information sources (or hints of such sources) to start exploring the theme.

The literature teacher exploited here the idea of inquiry circles by giving student groups a task to study Wikipedia articles and use the outcome in planning their own article. She also understood that at the exploration stage students need to use selected sources to learn basics of the theme. However, students were not advised to use tools (such as inquiry logs) to manage sources found along the process.

**Stage 4: Identify.** *The students should identify the questions to be worked on (focus formation), develop a plan what information needs to be searched, and outline a rough sketch for the text to be written. Inquiry charts introduced.* Writing an encyclopaedic article is not a genuine inquiry task. Rather than formulating research questions the author specifies a topic or a theme about which the article is about. Activities described at the exploration stage (studying some relevant sources, analysing similar articles) help clarifying the plan for the topical content (focus formation), identifying information needs and sketching a content plan.

The history teacher seemed to think that giving a theme title and 3-5 subtopic phrases to students is enough for them to form a focus for each group's article. Thus she did not see the need to expose student groups to guided activities where they collaboratively create their subjective interpretation about the theme. The literature teacher used quite elegantly the task of analysing related Wikipedia articles to direct students groups to discuss and plan the content of the own articles. Teachers did not introduce any tools such as inquiry charts to visualize ideas about the theme.

**Stage 5: Gather.** *Students guided by the teacher and the librarian should collect detailed information from various channels, assess them and select them for further inspection.* In both courses, students participated a teaching and practicing session on library and web searching organized by the local public library. The librarian had in advance collected materials related to the assignment themes and gave them directly to students in the end of the teaching session. Students in the literature course expressed that they were served by useful materials while students in the history course regarded given materials mostly as non-relevant. The session in the library took place early in the assignment process and especially history students were not very familiar with their themes at the time of searching.

The approaches adopted by the teachers in supporting searching for and selecting information sources were quite divergent. The literature teacher distributed actively materials she considered relevant. The history teacher expected students to search independently all sources needed. Guided Inquiry guidelines seem to balance between these extremes. An obvious consequence of "helping too much" was that literature students reported very low learning experience scores in Web searching. History students reported higher learning experiences but even for them learning experiences were lower than they regarded as typical of school assignments (Sormunen, Alamettälä, et al., 2013). The library offered an overall instruction for searching in the library and in the internet. However, both courses lacked activities which support student groups in analysing their themes to identify effective search concepts and strategies, or in reflecting on their search behaviours in an inquiry learning situation.

**Stage 6: Create.** *Students read and reflect on information sources selected and prepare a presentation answering the inquiry question (e.g. term paper, poster) and learn collaboratively.* No signs of activities or guidance related to reading and interpreting sources were observed except a few cases when students asked for help. In the literature course, the teacher required the student groups to upload text drafts onto the school's wiki platform and commented them actively. Most comments dealt with language or citations. However, these interventions activated students during the process to assess their own work. The history teacher did not comment the texts before the final version.

**Stage 7: Share.** *The experiences gained and answers found are shared within the inquiry community.* In the history course, the articles were made available to the class in the wiki forum and the students were expected to read them all to prepare for an exam. In the literature class, student groups gave a short presentation of their article in the classroom. In Guided Inquiry presenting the documentary outcome is only one aspect of sharing in the classroom. Sharing experiences about the process and learning is emphasized as well. This side of sharing experiences was missing in our case classes (however, see stage 8).

**Stage 8: Evaluate.** *Students reflect on the learning process, assess the outcomes and share these experiences with others in the inquiry community.* Students filled in a self-assessment form and gave numerical ratings for various aspects of the article and the assignment process. They also wrote comments on their role and activity in the group work. However, students' learning experiences were not discussed in the classroom. Only the teacher presented overall verbal feedback in the classroom. Guided Inquiry emphasizes the teacher's role in evaluating students' progress and giving feedback during the process. This was very rare in the history class. The literature teacher made interventions more actively but focused mainly on commenting text drafts, i.e., on the end-product rather than the process.

## Discussions and conclusion

Our study collected data from two case courses. Both teachers were using the Wikipedia assignment for the first time but the concept had been tested in literature courses earlier by other members of the teacher team. The history teacher made a pioneer's work in applying the assignment in history. The problems observed in her class suggest that borrowing a successful approach from one subject area might not be successfully transferred to other subject areas without customizing it. For example, in the history class, the themes were selected to match curriculum requirements for content and were apparently too broad to work as Wikipedia articles (to be synthesized by novice writers in history).

The unfavourable position of the history teacher gives us a chance to characterize the gap between the present pedagogical practice and the emerging new pedagogical practice for information literacy instruction. Second, the comparison of the literature course against the Guided Inquiry framework helps us demonstrate how present pedagogical practices may concretely turn into new practices matching better the requirements of information literacy instruction. Further, the results of the case study inform us about the strengths and weaknesses of encyclopaedic writing assignments in IL instruction.

We may consider the history course as a typical case where traditional pedagogical practice is applied to a learner-centred writing assignment based on independent acquisition of information sources. Characteristic to this approach is that the assignment process is seen as a black box: instructions (incl. generic library and web search training) are given as inputs, and the written text is evaluated as the output. The teacher do not identify the possibility to divide the process into stages as zones of intervention (Kuhlthau et al., 2007; Kuhlthau, 2004; Vygotsky, 1978). Especially, the guidance and activities related to the first four stages of Guided Inquiry (Open, Immerse, Explore, Identify) are seriously overlooked. Students face the challenges of Web searching unprepared since they have not developed a focused idea or viewpoint to study the theme of the assignment. Traditional practice in schools do not offer concrete pedagogical means for IL instruction as pointed out by Limberg et al. (2008).

The team of teachers in mother tongue and literature had developed the concept of Wikipedia writing assignment as a pedagogical practice in their curriculum subject. Their approach diverged from the simple black box model by introducing several specific activities for students at the early stages of the assignment similar to Guided Inquiry. For example, the personal exercise to study Wikipedia writing conventions and activating groups to analyse well-written articles before starting to plan their own article were good examples of these. Both activities turn students' attention on important issues that might otherwise be passed without reflection. Also Kiili, Mäkinen, and Coiro (2013) have emphasised the importance of opening the black box and the need for stage specific activities.

In the literature course, students reported high learning experience scores on three items: 1) understanding Wikipedia in general, 2) understanding difference between Wikipedia and other information sources, and 3) skills in source-based writing (Sormunen, Alamettälä, et al., 2013). These are relevant learning outcomes in IL instruction. However, low learning experience scores in Web searching indicated that some other sub-goals mentioned by teachers were not achieved so well. This variation in success suggests that students identified learning to happen when they were challenged by specific activities. On the other hand, routine doing as part of the assignment process (e.g., googling) does not have the same effect.

In a Wikipedia assignment, it is easy to cognitively challenge students in source-based writing and achieve learning goals accordingly. Writing and publishing in Wikipedia is a motivating context for students to practice information searching, assessment of sources and argumentative use of information (see Forte & Bruckman, 2009). However, the limitation of encyclopaedic writing is that it is not intended to generate new knowledge but to synthesize knowledge from existing sources (i.e., a type of literature review). Thus, the Wikipedia assignment is not an optimal tool to practice the core processes of inquiry, such as creative formulation of research questions. In our case course, the teachers did not pay much attention on guiding students in Web searching or critical assessment of sources but this is not a restriction of the Wikipedia assignment *per se* but a decision of the teachers in this particular situation.

Our study was qualitative in nature and based on a sample of two case courses only. The findings should not be generalized without care. At best, the findings could be applied in formulating informed hypotheses to study present practices in information literacy instruction and in evaluating new pedagogical approaches to improve practices. However, we have a strong impression based on various concrete experiences in schools that a black box syndrome is common in designing and guiding IL assignments. The analysis of case courses in the Guided Inquiry framework gave us an opportunity to make these impressions more explicit and concrete.

## References

Bawden, D. (2001). Information and digital literacies: a review of concepts. *Journal of Documentation*, *57*(2), 218–259.

Boyatzis, R. E. (1998). *Transforming qualitative information: Thematic analysis and code development*. Thousand Oaks: Sage.

Chu, S. K. W., Chow, K., Tse, S., & Kuhlthau, C. C. (2008). Grade 4 Students' Development of Research Skills Through Inquiry-Based Learning Projects. *School Libraries Worldwide*, *14*(1), 10–37.

Chu, S. K. W., Tse, S., & Chow, K. (2011). Using collaborative teaching and inquiry project-based learning to help primary school students develop information literacy and information skills. *Library and Information Science Research*, *33*(2), 132–143. doi:10.1016/j.lisr.2010.07.017

Forte, A., & Bruckman, A. (2009). Writing, citing, and participatory media: wikis as learning environments in the high school classroom. *Interational Journal of Learning and Media*, *1*(4), 23–44. doi:10.1162/ijlm

Heinström, J., & Sormunen, E. (2013). Students' collaborative inquiry – relation to approaches to studying and instructional intervention. In I. Huvila (Ed.), *Proceedings of the Second Association for Information Science and Technology ASIS&T European Workshop 2013* (pp. 19–32). Turku: Åbo Akademi University. Retrieved from http://www.abo.fi/sitebuilder/media/29327/aew2013proceedings.pdf

Hongisto, H., & Sormunen, E. (2010). The challenges of the first research paper–observing students and the teacher in the secondary school classroom. In A. Lloyd & S. Talja (Eds.), *Practising Information Literacy: Bringing Theories of Learning, Practice and Information Literacy Together* (pp. 96–120). Retrieved from https://www12.uta.fi/blogs/know-id/files/2010/05/Hongisto_Sormunen_v10_copy.pdf

Kiili, C., Laurinen, L., & Marttunen, M. (2008). Students Evaluating Internet Sources: From Versatile Evaluators to Uncritical Readers. *Journal of Educational Computing Research*, *39*(1), 75–95. doi:10.2190/EC.39.1.e

Kiili, C., Laurinen, L., & Marttunen, M. (2009). Skillful Internet reader is metacognitively competent. In L. T. . Hin & R. Subramaniam (Eds.), *Hanbook of research on new media literacy at the K-12 Level: Issues and challenges* (Vol. II, pp. 654–668). Retrieved from http://www.igi-global.com/chapter/handbook-research-new-media-literacy/35943

Kiili, C., Mäkinen, M., & Coiro, J. L. (2013). Rethinking academic literacies; Designing multifaceted literacy experiences for pre-service teachers. *Journal of Adolescent & Adult Literacy*, *Early View*. doi:doi: 10.1002/jaal.223

Kuhlthau, C. C. (1991). Inside the search process: Information seeking from the user's perspective. *Journal of the American Society for Information Science, 42*(5), 361–371. doi:oi:10.1002/(SICI)1097-4571 (199106)42:5%3C361::AID-ASI6%3E3.0.CO;2-%23

Kuhlthau, C. C. (2004). *Seeking meaning : a process approach to library and information services.* Westport: Libraries Unlimited.

Kuhlthau, C. C., Maniotes, L. K., & Caspari, A. K. (2007). *Guided inquiry. Learning in the 21th century.* Westport: Libraries Unlimited.

Kuhlthau, C. C., Maniotes, L. K., & Caspari, A. K. (2012). *Guided Inquiry design* (p. 188). Santa Barbara: Libraries Unlimited.

Kuusilehto-Awale, L., & Lahtero, T. (2014). Finnish Case of Basic Education for All – With Quality Learning Outcomes. *Journal of Education and Research, 4*(1), 1–18.

Lankshear, C., & Knobel, M. (2011). *New literacies: Everyday practices and social learning* (3rd ed., p. 296). New York: Open University Press.

Limberg, L., Alexandersson, M., Lantz-Andersson, A., & Folkesson, L. (2008). What matters? Shaping meaningful learning through teaching information literacy. *Libri, 58*(2), 82–91. doi:10.1515/libr.2008.010

Marchionini, G. (2006). Exploratory search: from finding to understanding. *Communications of the ACM, 49*(4), 41–46.

Niemi, H., Toom, A., & Kallioniemi, A. (Eds.). (2012). *Miracle of Education. The Principles and Practices of Teaching and Learning in Finnish Schools* (p. 38). Rotterdam: SensePublishers.

Scardamalia, M., & Bereiter, C. (2006). Knowledge building: Theory, pedagogy, and technology. In I. K. Sawyer (Ed.), *Cambridge Handbook of the Learning Sciences* (pp. 97–118). New York: Cambridge University Press.

Sormunen, E., Alamettälä, T., & Heinström, J. (2013). The Teacher's Role as Facilitator of Collaborative Learning in Information Literacy Assignments. In S. Kurbanoğlu, E. Grassian, D. Mizrachi, R. Catts, & S. Špiranec (Eds.), *Worldwide Commonalities and Challenges in Information Literacy Research and Practice SE - 67* (Vol. 397, pp. 499–506). Springer International Publishing. doi:10.1007/978-3-319-03919-0_67

Sormunen, E., Eriksson, H., & Kurkipää, T. (2012). Wikipedia and wikis as forums of information literacy instruction in schools. In R. Gwyer, R. Stubbings, & G. Walton (Eds.), *The Road to Information Literacy: Librarians as Facilitators of Learning* (pp. 310–327). Berlin: De Gruyter Saur. Retrieved from https://www12.uta.fi/blogs/know-id/files/2012/05/Sormunen_Eriksson_Tuulip??_final.pdf

Sormunen, E., Heinström, J., Romu, L., & Turunen, R. (2012). A method for the analysis of information use in source-based writing. *Information Research, 17*(4), paper 535. Retrieved from http://InformationR.net/ir/17-4/paper535.html

Sormunen, E., & Lehtiö, L. (2011). Authoring Wikipedia articles as an information literacy assignment – copy-pasting or expressing new understanding in one's own words? *Information Research, 16*(4). Retrieved from http://informationr.net/ir/16-4/paper503.html

Sormunen, E., Tanni, M., & Heinström, J. (2013). Students' engagement in collaborative knowledge construction in group assignments for information literacy. *Information Research, 18*(3), paper C40. Retrieved from http://informationr.net/ir/18-3/colis/paperC40.html#.UoTV3eJZ7ZU

Vakkari, P. (2010). Exploratory searching as conceptual exploration. In *HCIR 2010: Proceedings of of the Fourth Workshop on Human-Computer Interaction and Information Retrieval* (pp. 24–27). Microsoft Research. Retrieved from http://research.microsoft.com/en-us/um/people/ryenw/hcir2010/docs/papers/Vakkari_fp10.pdf

Walraven, A., Brand-Gruwel, S., & Boshuizen, H. P. A. (2008). Information problem solving: A review of problems students encounter and instructional solutions. *Computers in Human Behavior, 24(3), 24*(3), 623–648. Retrieved from http://www.sciencedirect.com/science/article/pii/S0747563207000325

Wildemuth, B. M., & Freund, L. (2012). Assigning search tasks designed to elicit exploratory search behaviors. In *Proceedings of the Symposium on Human-Computer Interaction and Information Retrieval - HCIR '12* (pp. 1–10). New York, New York, USA: ACM Press. doi:10.1145/2391224.2391228

Vygotsky, L. S. (1978). *Mind in Society* (p. 158). Cambridge: Haward University Press.

**Acknowledgements.** The study was part of the Know-Id project funded by the Academy of Finland (grant no. 132341). The authors thank the teachers of the case courses, the "Tieto haltuun" project in the City of Tampere, and Leeni Lehtiö and Teemu Mikkonen, who took care of the data collection during the case courses.

# 15 Lessons learned from a two year implementation project: Sustaining Student Gains with Online On-demand Professional Development

Kelly Glassett, *School Improvement Network*, Steven Shaha, *University of Utah, USA*

## I. INTRODUCTION

The inconsistent assumptions–that teachers learn only by doing, rather than by helping to define the problems of practice–has its roots in deep philosophical notions about competence, learning, and trust that are at the core of what constituted professional development prior to the turn of the century (Cochran-Smith, 2006). The intervening years between 1957 and 2000 found teachers being told that other people's notions of learning and teaching were more important than their own and that knowledge gleaned from everyday work with students was of little value (Cochran-Smith, 2006). The experts sitting on the outside saw learning as packaged, teaching as a technical thing, and students and teachers as passive recipients of "objective knowledge" (Sarason, 1993).

In our present era of educational reform we have come to understand that teaching as a professional practice is situated in social and physical contexts and that professional development involves creating opportunities for teachers to reflect and interact in the day to day activity of teaching (Borko, Jacobs, Eiteljorg, & Pittman, 2006; Greeno, 2003). The situative nature of teaching and learning posits that "teachers' own classrooms are powerful contexts for learning" (Putnam & Borko, 2000, p. 418). This perspective however, does not limit PD to K-12 classrooms, but includes real examples and artifacts such as video, student work samples, and curriculum materials that afford analysis and reflection.

In 2004 Sherin explained, "Video allows one to enter the world of the classroom without having to be in the position of teaching in-the-moment" (p. 13). Video affords one the ability to capture the rich complexity of classrooms for later analysis and reflection (Brophy, 2004). Classroom videos illuminate particular strategies and aspects of the classroom that might be missed and afford one to reenact the social fabric of a classroom (Clarke & Hollingworth, 2000). By being able to assign certain videos during PD, administrators can target particular ideas around teaching and learning and focus analysis and reflection around particular pedagogical strategies with a shared common experience (Brophy, 2004).

## STATEMENT OF THE PROBLEM

During the past decade, studies related to PD delivered online and on-demand have increased (Shaha & Ellsworth 2013, 2014). Studies have logically verified that level of teacher activity and engagement with online PD affects that correlated impact achieved for student performance – students of teachers with highly active engagement in online PD outpaced the students of teachers reflecting more passive PD participation, such as viewing videos alone, versus downloading and uploading material (Garet et al., 2002; Darling-Hammond 2004; Desimone et al., 2002; King 2002; Santagata, 2009; Shaha & Ellsworth 2013).

Despite recent studies and publically available PD program evaluations, there remains a paucity of substantive, quantitative and rigorous research on the impact of video PD on student performance. Masters et.al, recently commented specifically on the "dearth of scientific research" (Masters et al., 2012). Such is a travesty, given the pressure on administrators and educators to improve the impact teachers have on students. It is particularly alarming that decisions regarding the purchase and implementation in alternative PD offerings remain based primarily on anecdotal credibility, and not upon analysis of student outcomes. Substantially more research is needed to establish quantitatively a compelling link between teacher participation in PD and gains in student performance (**Garet et al. 2001;** Desimone et al. 2002; Shaha et al. 2004; Meiers & Ingvarson 2005; Buczynski & Hansen 2010; Avalos 2011).

Even more rare – arguably completely missing – are studies evaluating any sustained gains for PD participation. In our review of the literature we were completely unable to find a single piece of published research that reflected a follow-up on the impact of PD on the students of participating teachers past the first year of the program.

## REVIEW OF THE LITERATURE

According to the literature base, teacher professional development (PD) seeks to improve classroom practices, increase teacher knowledge, and increase student learning and achievement gains (Borko, Jacobs, Eiteljorg & Pittman, 2006; Fishman, Marx, Best, & Tal, 2003; Loucks-Horsley, Love, Stiles, Mundry, & Hewson,

2003; Mizell, 2010; Shaha et.al., 2004; Wilson & Berne, 1999). Generally speaking, scholars concur that effective PD needs to be on-going, address student learning needs, has application to specific curricula, and addresses knowledge, skills, and beliefs of teachers (Borko, Jacobs, Eiteljorg & Pittman, 2006; Cohen & Hill, 1998; Killion, 2002; Santa, 2004; Wehry, 2001; Young, Dougherty, Lai, & Matsumoto, 1998). Even though scholars generally agree on the goals of PD, until recently there has been less agreement how on how to measure PD in reliable and valid ways (Fishman, et al., 2003).

In recent years there has been increasing interest for integrating video in teacher PD (Boling, 2007). Videos are useful tools for PD; videos allow teachers to see the complexity and richness of a real classroom settings by capturing voices, body language, interactions, and a more realistic picture of the learning environment. Also, videos lend themselves to potentially richer discussions of teacher practices and help teachers connect theory and practice better (Brophy, 2004; Seago, 2004). More specifically though, in our current climate of standards-based learning, video examples of standards-aligned "teaching have become important tools for developing teacher understanding and capacity to apply standards-based learning targets to lessons that embed increased rigor, student collaboration, critical thinking, and precise language" (Leith, 2013, p. 20). Furthermore, Colestock and Sherin (2009) reported teacher viewing of classroom video events as assistive to teachers in learning and implementing strategies, beneficial to professional growth, and encourages teacher reflection. Video examples of classroom practice have also been shown to increase teacher understanding of student perspectives (Colestock & Sherin, 2009; Putnam & Borko, 2000).

Videos focused on specific pedagogical practices have the potential to drive in-depth conversations because they focus teachers' concentration on specific instances of practice (Ball, Ben-Peretz, & Cohen, 2001). For instance, videos support the examination and analysis of teaching strategies, how students think about and question about ideas and concepts, and the "how to" of curriculum enactment (Ball & Cohen, 1999).

Without a doubt, the extant literature on PD has seen an increase in the use of video and video cases for preservice and inservice teachers (Boling, 2007). Video is a useful tool preservice and inservice teachers for a number of reasons; unlike text-based examples, videos allow preservice and inservice teachers a full view of the complexity of a real classrooms by capturing a more realistic picture of the learning environment. This richness affords a potentially for richer discussions of teacher practices and help teachers connect theory and practice better (Brophy, 2004; Seago, 2004). Sherin and van Es (2005) demonstrated that watching video, overtime, for both preservice and inservice teachers increased their ability to interpret the features of classroom teaching.

## II. METHODS

The purpose of this longitudinal research was to perform a second year follow-up on a multi-State study of the comparative impact of PD on the students of participating teachers versus the non-participating schools within the same districts. We leveraged the year-1, pre-versus-post, quasi-experimental study and conducted a second year follow-up study. Our goal was to determine whether school totals for students of teachers in their second year of PD participation experienced similar gains as were quantified in the first pre-versus-post year, or whether those early gains diminished or were improved upon. Restated, we sought to determine whether early gains achieved were sustained, lost or improved upon.

Recent research argues that quantifying improvements in student performance on standardized tests is a rigorous and valid measure of teacher impact on students, and therefore a useful metric for assessing the impact of PD (Buczynski & Hansen 2010; Avalos 2011; Desimone et al., 2002; **Garet et al. 2001;** 2002; Meiers & Ingvarson 2005; Wasik & Hindman 2011). As the costs associated with providing educational offerings are more rigorously scrutinized into the future, the need to demonstrate the impact of PD will become increasingly important (Farnsworth et al. 2002; Lewis et al., 2003; Magidin et al., 2012; Rienties et al., 2013).

The study contrasted gains in performance for schools whose teachers participated in the online, on-demand PD offering (hereafter Schools) versus the remaining schools in the same district whose teachers did NOT participate (hereafter Districts). This study was an extension of a previously executed pre-versus-post study, and involved the addition of a second post-implementation year of data to the preciously analyzed data (Shaha & Ellsworth, 2013).

The study design reflected a quasi-experimental approach (Cook & Campbell 1979): Pre-PD levels of student performance were compared with Year 1 and Year 2 post-implementation, and performance in PD-participating Schools was co mpared with their own corresponding non-participating schools within Districts.

The pre-PD included data from the 2009-2010 school year, and the two post-implementation years – 2010-11 and 2011-12 – were the corresponding data from the subsequent two school years thereafter.

School participation was defined as use of a single commercially-available online, on-demand PD product widely used in the United States (PD 360 ® and Observation 360 ®). This enabled teachers to participate in a full range activities which range instructional videos on teaching techniques, to communities of other users, to posting and downloading PD-related materials. Participation criteria for Schools was defined as a minimum average of 90 minutes per teacher of logged-in time cumulatively school-wide. This minimum was adopted to ensure sufficient PD use to enable that conclusions be drawn regarding PD use beyond mere sign-on alone or minimal usage. Comparison District schools were included with their corresponding districts only if fewer than 25% of schools within a given district were categorized as PD participants. All schools categorized as participating within a district were included only if the school and district each met inclusion criteria.

PD School participation data analyzed were extracted from the data automatically captured by the PD provider (School Improvement Network) as a result of PD use, and corresponding District data from the same sources, including verification off eligibility for including District sample set due to meeting non-PD participation criteria. Student performance data were gathered from publically available web sources for the three consecutive school years. Any data not available online were gathered by telephone requests, all with Institutional Review Board (IRB) approval where such existed. For analyses, student performance data were defined as the sum of the percentages of students rated either proficient or advanced on the respective standardized student performance tests for each school – no changes in testing were noted within the sample for the three consecutive years of data.

The final data set included the same 169 schools in 73 districts and 19 States for the third year of data as was analyzed in the previous 2-year pre-versus-post study. All percent changes reported were calculated as net change in performance, divided by performance for the earlier of the two years: e.g. (Year 2 – Year 1)/ Year 1. Significance for percent change figures was determined by contrasting versus zero change (0.0%) by a t-Test for proportions. All analyses were conducted using SPSS version 17.0 or higher (PASW Statistics, SPSS, 2009, with SAS used for confirmatory purposes when results were close to $p<0.05$). Minimum level of statistical significance was determined a priori at $p<0.05$.

## III. Results
### Mathematics

Student performance levels were contrasted for Schools versus Districts, for pre-PD versus Year 1 post-PD (See Table 1, Figures 1, Shaha & Ellsworth, 2013). For Math, results showed that students of teachers in PD-inclusion Schools experienced a net change of 11.1 percentage points in students classified as Proficient or Advanced versus a 2.6 net change for Districts. That equaled an 18.9% ($p<0.001$) increases in performance year-over-year, versus 4.2% ($p<0.01$) increase over the percent from the previous year for their respective Districts. The percent change for students in PD participant Schools was 4.5 times greater than for their respective Districts. Differences between School and District means in the pre-PD year were marginally significant ($p=0.065$), favoring Districts, and that pattern reversed for Year 1 post implementation ($p=0.085$).

Table 1. Student Math performance for participating schools versus their districts

Math

| | | Pre | Year 1 | | | | | Year 2 | | | | | | | | |
|---|---|---|---|---|---|---|---|---|---|---|---|---|---|---|---|---|
| | | Advanced + Proficient | Advanced + Proficient | Net Change vs. Pre | Effect Size | Pct Change vs. Pre | Significance | Advanced + Proficient | Net Change vs. Year 1 | Effect Size | Pct Change vs. Year 1 | Significance | Net Change vs. Pre | Effect Size | Pct Change vs. Pre | Significance |
| Schools | Mean | 58.4 | 69.5 | 11.1 | 4.2 | 18.9% | p<0.001 | 74.8 | 5.3 | 15.0 | 7.7% | p<0.01 | 16.4 | 5.6 | 28.1% | p<0.001 |
| | StDev | 21.9 | 21.1 | | | | | 23.4 | | | | | | | | |
| Districts | Mean | 62.9 | 65.5 | 2.6 | | 4.2% | p<0.01 | 65.8 | 0.4 | | 0.5% | ns | 3.0 | | 4.7% | p<0.01 |
| | StDev | 20.4 | 20.2 | | | | | 22.3 | | | | | | | | |
| Comparative Net Difference | | -4.5 | 4.1 | | | | | 9.0 | | | | | 13.5 | | | |
| Significance | | p=0.065 | p=0.085 | | | | | p<0.001 | | | | | p<0.001 | | | |
| Net Difference in Change | | | 8.4 | | | 14.7% | | 5.0 | | | | | 13.5 | | | |
| Significance | | | p<0.001 | | | p<0.001 | | p<0.01 | | | | | p<0.001 | | | |

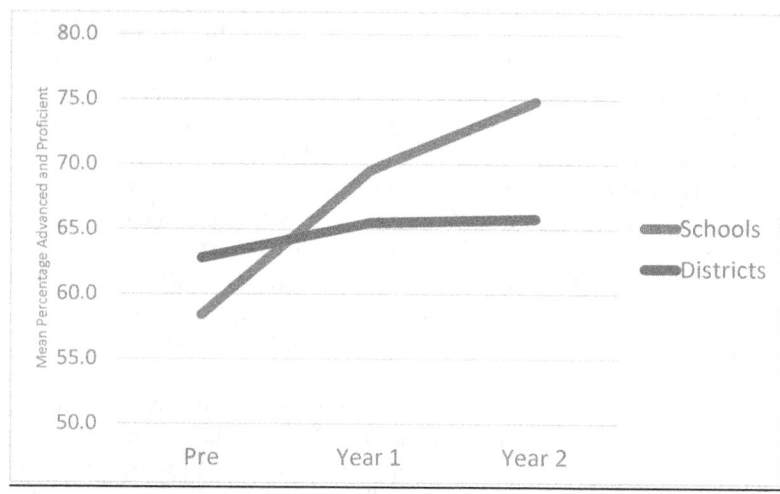

Figure 1: Comparative pre versus post performance for Math proficient and advanced

Next the student performance data were compared for Schools versus Districts for gains between Year 1 post-PD and Year 2 post-PD. For Math, results showed that students of teachers in PD-inclusion Schools experienced an additional net change of 5.3 percentage points in improved student performance, versus a 0.4 net change for Districts. That equaled a 7.7%% (p<0.01) increases in performance year-over-year, versus 0.4% (not significant, hereafter ns) increase over the percent from the previous year for their respective Districts. The growth for students in PD participant Schools was 15.5 times greater than for their respective Districts.

Finally, results showed that students in the School group net change of 16.4 percentage points in improved student performance when contrasting Year 2 with the pre-PD baseline, versus a 3.0 net change for Districts. That equaled a 28.1% (p<0.001) increases in performance by Year 2 over baseline, versus 4.7% (p<0.01) increase for their respective Districts. The growth for students in PD participant Schools was 5.6 times greater than for their respective Districts.

**Reading**

Student performance levels were contrasted for Schools versus Districts, for pre-PD versus Year 1 post-PD (See Table 2, Figure 2, Shaha & Ellsworth, 2013). For Reading, results showed that students of teachers in PD-inclusion Schools experienced a net change of 10.3 percentage points in students classified as Proficient or Advanced versus a 1.6 net change for Districts. That equaled an 18.1% (p<0.001) increases in performance year-over-year, versus 2.6% (p<0.01) increase over the percent from the previous year for their respective Districts. The percent change for students in PD participant Schools was 6.4 times greater than for their respective Districts. Differences between School and District means in the pre-PD year were marginally significant (p=0.079), favoring Districts, and that pattern reversed for Year 1 post implementation (p=0.063).

Table 2. Student Reading performance for participating schools versus their districts
Reading

|  | Pre | Year 1 | | | | | Year 2 | | | | | | | |
|---|---|---|---|---|---|---|---|---|---|---|---|---|---|---|
|  | Advanced + Proficient | Advanced + Proficient | Net Change vs. Pre | Effect Size | Pct Change vs. Pre | Significance | Advanced + Proficient | Net Change vs. Year 1 | Effect Size | Pct Change vs. Year 1 | Significance | Net Change vs. Pre | Effect Size | Pct Change vs. Pre | Significance |
| Schools Mean | 56.9 | 67.2 | 10.3 | 6.4 | 18.1% | p<0.001 | 74.1 | 6.9 | 3.2 | 10.2% | p<0.001 | 17.2 | 4.7 | 30.2% | p<0.001 |
| StDev | 22.4 | 22.1 | | | | | 19.9 | | | | | | | | |
| Districts Mean | 61.2 | 62.7 | 1.6 | | 2.6% | p<0.01 | 64.9 | 2.2 | | 3.5% | p<0.01 | 3.7 | | 6.0% | p<0.01 |
| StDev | 21.1 | 20.7 | | | | | 17.4 | | | | | | | | |
| Comparative Net Dif | -4.3 | 4.5 | | | | | 9.2 | | | | | 13.5 | | | |
| Significance | p=0.079 | p=0.063 | | | | | p<0.001 | | | | | p<0.001 | | | |
| Net Difference in Change | | | 8.7 | | 15.5% | | | 4.7 | | | | 13.5 | | | |
| Significance | | | p<0.001 | | p<0.001 | | | p<0.01 | | | | p<0.001 | | | |

Figure 2: Comparative pre versus post performance for Reading proficient and advanced

Student performance data were next contrasted for Schools versus Districts for Year 1 post-PD and Year 2 post-PD. Results showed that students of teachers in PD-inclusion Schools experienced an additional net change of 6.9 percentage points in improved student performance, versus a 2.2 net change for Districts. That equaled a 10.2% (p<0.001) increases in performance year-over-year, versus 3.5% (p<0.01) increase over the percent from the previous year for their respective Districts. The growth for students in PD participant Schools was 3.2 times greater than for their respective Districts.

Finally, results showed that students in the School group net change of 17.2 percentage points in improved student performance when contrasting Year 2 with the pre-PD baseline, versus a 3.7 net change for Districts. That equaled a 30.2% (p<0.001) increases in performance by Year 2 over baseline, versus 6.0% (p<0.01) increase for their respective Districts. The growth for students in PD participant Schools was 4.7 times greater than for their respective Districts.

**Asymptotic Pattern**
The graphics depicting the findings for both Mathematics and Reading each portray an interesting corroborative pattern. While growth continues in the second year of data, the amount of year-over-year gain decreased versus that achieved in the first year. Statistically, an asymptotic pattern is expected: Levels of students classified as Proficient plus Advanced cannot not exceed 100%. Therefore as that upper limit (i.e. ceiling) is approached, the year-over-year gains will statistically slow as they asymptotically near the ultimate goal.

**IV. Discussion and Conclusions**
Past research, although embarrassingly limited in volume and rigor, has provided some basis for understanding the impact of PD its first year of pre-versus-post implementation. Even less is available regarding online, on-demand professional development for pre-versus-post interpretation. And finally very, very few represent multi-State, high-sample-size analyses quantifying PD impact. In that context, still woefully fewer studies exist offering substantive quantitative evidence of the impact of PD into subsequent years as substantiation of sustainment. We believe this may be the first such study.

This multi-state, quasi-experimental study provides quantitative, compelling evidence of the impact of on-demand, Internet-based PD for enhancing teacher efficacy as measured by changes in student performance on standardized tests. First-year post-implementation gains showed that participation in the online, on-demand PD offering resulted in 4.5 times and 6.1 times greater gains for math and reading, respectively, for participating schools versus their respective, comparable district populations. In the second year, advantages were sustained with 5.3 times and 3.2 times greater gains for participating schools versus their district peers. Thus favorable trends persisted, and continued improvements were sustained.

As with all quasi-experimental research, interpretation of these findings involves some extrapolation beyond the ideal controlled conditions of strict experimental research. It remains nearly impossible in education to study comparative student gains within environments with rigorous control-versus-treatment conditions. Therefore it will also remain challenging to firmly establish cause-and-effect conclusions based on the quasi-experimental design and naturalistic settings in which this study was achieved. However, the evidence remains compelling.

This may be the first-ever study of a two-year follow-up quantifying the sustained impact of online, on-demand PD on student performance. It surely is one of very, very few studies establishing the sustained effect of any systematic PD on student performance contrasting comparable student populations in a large sample, multi-State design. Bottom line the data clearly and substantively indicate that continued PD participation results in sustained gains, and even continued additional gains, as teachers apparently leverage what they learn. Whether this is explained by acquisition of knowledge and skills from PD participation, or simply improved attention and focus on the part of classroom teachers, will remain unclear. Yet establishing such an explanatory nuance is likely less important than the formulaic conclusion that sustained participation in PD across years is correlated with sustained improvements in student performance.

## References

Avalos, B. (2011). Teacher professional development in teaching and teacher education over ten years. *Teaching and Teacher Education, 27*(1), 10-20. doi:10.1016/j.tate.2010.08.007

Bahr, D. L., Shaha, S. H., Farnsworth, B. J., Lewis, V. K., & Benson, L. F. (2004). Preparing tomorrow's teachers to use technology: attitudinal impacts of technology-supported field experience on preservice teacher candidates. *Journal of Instructional Psychology, 31*(2), 88-97.

Benson, L. F., Farnsworth, B. J., Bahr, D. L., Lewis, V. K., & Shaha, S. H. (2004). The impact of training in technology assisted instruction on skills and attitudes of pre-service teachers. *Education, 124*(4), 649-663.

Bongiorni, S. (2004). All in the timing. *The Greater Baton Rouge Business Report.*

Buczynski, S., & Hansen, C. B. (2010). Impact of professional development on teacher practice: Uncovering connections. *Teaching and Teacher Education, 26*(3), 599-607. doi:10.1016/j.tate.2009.09.006

Cook, T. D., & Campbell, D. T. (1979). Quasi-experimentation: Design & analysis issues for field settings. Boston: Houghton Mifflin Company.

Darling-Hammond, L. (2004). Standards, accountability, and school reform. *Teachers College Record, 106*(6), 1047-1085.

Desimone, L. M., Porter, A. C., Garet, M. S., Yoon, K. S., & Birman, B. F. (2002). Effects of professional development on teacher's instruction: Results from a three-year longitudinal study. *Educational Evaluation and Policy Analysis, 24*(2), 81-112.

Farnsworth, B., Shaha, S., Bahr, D., Lewis, V.. & Benson. L. (2002). Preparing tomorrow's teachers to use technology: Learning and attitudinal impacts on elementary students. *Journal of Instructional Psychology, 29*(3).

Garet, M. S., Porter, A. C., Desimone, L., Birman, B. F., & Yoon, K. S. (2001). What makes professional development effective? Results from a national sample of teachers. *American Educational Research Journal, 38*(4), 915.

Guskey, T. R. (2002). Professional development and teacher change. *Teachers and Teaching, 8*(3), 381-391. doi:10.1080/135406002100000512

Hirano, H., & Makota, F. (Eds.). (2006). *JIT is flow: Practice and principles of lean manufacturing* (ISBN 0-9712436-1-1 ed.) PCS Press, Inc.

Ingvarson, L., Meiers, M., & Beavis, A. (2005) "Factors Affection the Impact of Professional Development Programs on Teachers' Knowledge, Practice, Student Outcomes & Efficacy" *Australian Council for Educational Research.* 13(10), January 2005.

King, K. P. (2002). Identifying success in online teacher education and professional development. *The Internet and Higher Education, 5*(3), 231-246. doi:10.1016/S1096-7516(02)00104-5

Latham, N., & Vogt, W. P. (2003). Do professional development schools reduce teacher attrition? Evidence from a longitudinal study of 1,000 graduates. *Journal of Teacher Education, 58*(2), 153-167.

Lewis, V. K., Shaha, S. H., Farnsworth, B., Benson, L., & Bahr, D. (2003). The use of assessment in improving technology-based instruction programs. *Journal of Instructional Psychology, 30*(2).

Magidin, d. K., Masters, J., O'Dwyer, L. M., Dash, S., & Russell, M. (2012). Relationship of online teacher professional development to seventh-grade teachers' and students' knowledge and practices in English language arts. *The Teacher Educator, 47*(3), 236-259. doi:10.1080/08878730.2012.685795

Masters, J., Kramer, R. M. d., O'Dwyer, L., Dash, S., & Russell, M. (2012). The effects of online teacher professional development on fourth grade students' knowledge and practices in english language arts. *Journal of Technology and Teacher Education, 20*(1), 21-46.

Ohno, T. (Ed.). (1988). *Just-in-time for today and tomorrow* (ISBN 0-915299-20-8 ed.) Productivity Press.

Rienties, B., Brouwer, N., & Lygo-Baker, S. (2013). The effects of online professional development on higher education teachers' beliefs and intentions towards learning facilitation and technology. *Teaching and Teacher Education, 29*(0), 122-131. doi:10.1016/j.tate.2012.09.002

Ruffa, S. A. (2008). Going lean: How the best companies apply lean manufacturing principles to shatter uncertainty, drive innovation, and maximize profits. *AMACOM (American Management Association)*.

Santagata, R. (2009). Designing video-based professional development for mathematics teachers in low-performing schools. *Journal of Teacher Education, 60*(1), 38-51.

Sebastian, J., & Allensworth, E. (2012). The influence of principal leadership on classroom instruction and student learning: A study of mediated pathways to learning. *University Council for Educational Administration, 10*, 626-663.

Shaha SH, Ellsworth H (2013). Multi-State, Quasi-experimental Study of the Impact of On-demand Professional Development on Students Performance. *International Journal of Evaluation and Research in Education (IJERE)*. Vol.2, No. 4.

Shaha SH, Ellsworth H (2014). Quasi-Experimental Study on the Impact of Online, On-Demand Professional Development on Educators in Title I Schools. *Effective Education Journal*.

Shaha, S. H., Lewis, V. K., O'Donnell, T. J., & Brown, D. H. (2004). Evaluating professional development: An approach in verifying program impact on teachers and students. *Journal of Research in Professional Learning, 1*(1), 1.

Wasik, B. A., & Hindman, A. H. (2011) Improving Vocabulary and Pre-Literacy Skills of at-Risk Preschoolers through Teacher Professional Development. *Journal of Educational Psychology 103*(2), 455-69.

Villegas-Reimers, E. (2003). Teacher professional development: an international review of the literature. Paris: International Institute for Educational Planning.

# 16 Designing a web-portal supporting the social inclusion of a specific user group. A case study of the LITERACY-portal

Dominik Hagelkruys, Renate Motschnig, University of Vienna, Austria

## Introduction

"The International Dyslexia Association" states that about 15-20% of the world's population have a language-based learning disability. 70-80% of these arise from deficits in reading, with dyslexia being the most common cause of reading, writing and spelling difficulties (The International Dyslexia Association, 2007). Often these difficulties also influence the social lives of affected persons. "Dyslexia International" states that the "academic and psychological consequences of unaddressed dyslexia are devastating" and "a prime cause of school drop-out, marginalization and social exclusion. Studies show that dyslexic people are over-represented in prisons, among adolescents who commit suicide, and among people suffering from mental illnesses, including depression" (Dyslexia International asbl).

"I don't read. I simply never could."
"Grammar in my emails is never correct and it cost me my job."
"I'm even ashamed to write an illness note to my kid's teacher."

These three are only a few examples of problems in people's daily lives in today's world overloaded with textual information. All three have one factor in common – *dyslexia*. These comments were collected by the LITERACY-project (ONLINE PORTAL FOR E-LEARNING AND SUPPORTING SOCIAL INCLUSION OF PEOPLE WITH DYSLEXIA) during its research process and clearly showcase its mission: to create an online portal for e-learning and supporting social inclusion of people with dyslexia.

The LITERACY-project is an on-going European wide research project, which started in March 2012 and will run for three years. It is funded by the European Commission and aims to support adults and teenagers > 16 years of age with dyslexia (or limited reading literacy) and to improve their social inclusion. Its goal is to provide an ICT solution which will enable dyslexic youth and adults to acquire learning skills, accommodation strategies and methods for succeeding at literacy related tasks at work and at home. The ICT solution, an internet portal, has been designed to enable users with dyslexia to operate independently online, by providing interactive services like for example:

- Comprehensive analysis of one's strengths and weaknesses and based on it
- personalized e-learning tools and assistive technology and
- a community zone with a specialized human-computer interface – helping users to socialize in ways they find meaningful.
(LITERACY Project, 2012)

By tracing the goals, design decisions, strategies and the structure of the "LITERACY-Portal", this paper discusses how a web-portal can be designed to support the social inclusion of a specific user group through the means of the portal itself,. The focus of this case study (Yin, 2009) is on the goals, principles and processes informing the design of such a web-portal in order to meet the needs of its specific user group. An essential aspect is the role of user-involvement in the different steps of a human-centered design process (Norman, 2002). Furthermore strategies and methods that help users to strengthen their skills and social inclusion through the means of the portal will be considered.

## The LITERACY-portal

The LITERACY-project aims to create an advanced web-portal that targets the specific needs and problems of dyslexics. Its goal is to "empower and support dyslexic youth and adults to help themselves succeed in literacy related achievements, ultimately strengthening their success and inclusion in school, university, work and their social lives" (LITERACY Project, 2012).

The portal consists of different areas that target specific needs of dyslexic users and support them in various ways. This means that the portal will not only provide e-learning programs, assistive technologies and training activities. It will also include valuable information on how to master problematic everyday life tasks and an area for active communication with experts and peers. In order to make the learning and usage experience as positive as possible, the users will be provided with personalized recommendations, including tips, e-learnings, brain trainings, assistive tools and interesting articles, based on an "intelligent" assessment process. In the following a screenshot of the preliminary portal-interface can be seen:

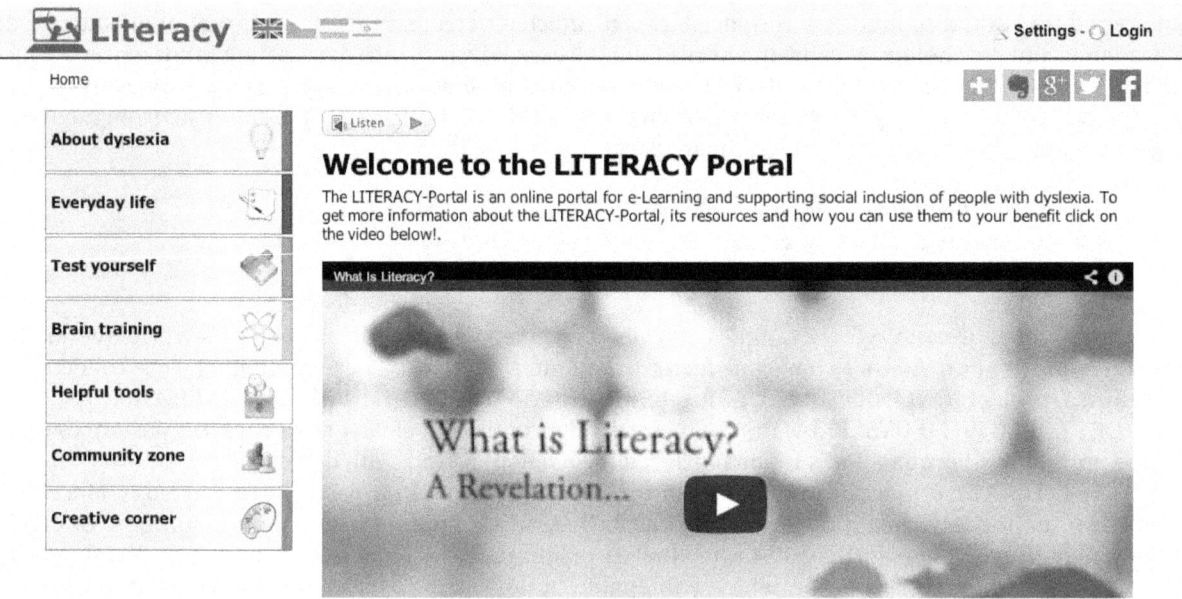

Figure 2: The LITERACY-portal

The portal serves users with seven main areas: About dyslexia, Everyday life, Test yourself, Brain training, Helpful tools, Community zone and Creative corner.

The "About dyslexia" area provides general information about dyslexia, its symptoms, its benefits and what it means to a person's life.

Through the "Everyday life" part of the portal, users get information about how to deal with everyday life tasks, like for example orienting oneself in traffic, applying for jobs or presenting oneself in an interview situation. This area is aimed to provide helpful tips and solutions for everyday life situations that might be problematic for dyslexics in form of e-learning materials. The various e-learnings are designed in an interactive, appealing and engaging way that is easily accessible for dyslexic users.

The assessment part of the portal, "Test yourself", gives users the opportunity to enhance their learning experience with the portal. Through a three step-assessment procedure the individual strength and weaknesses of a specific user are analyzed. Subsequently, users are provided with a "sub-set"-of the information, tips, tools and trainings provided by the portal that fit their specific profile. This will allow users to benefit from the portal in an even more effective way.

Through the "Brain training" area the portal-users get access to a set of training tools and learning games, that was compiled by dyslexia-experts from Israel, Hungary and the Czech Republic. The various trainings and games are intended to improve different cognitive skills like attention, accuracy, memory or literacy.

The "Helpful tools" section contains a set of assistive tools and helpful software that are considered to be beneficial for dyslexic users. The tools were chosen by experts from the fields of ICT, dyslexia and usability.

The LITERACY-portal also provides its users with a multi-layered community area, the "Community Zone. It not only establishes connections to the most popular social media and social networking platforms but also offers an independent forum and chat module. Comment sections for specific areas of the portal are intended to contribute to an active user community.

The research of the LITERACY-project shows that dyslexics tend to be very creative persons. Therefore the portal provides the "Creative corner", an area to be expressive through digital tools and even to be artistic. The Creative corner introduces users to creative tools, software and websites that can be used alone or in collaboration with others.

## Design Principles

As one of the main goals of the LITERACY-portal is to support the social inclusion of its specific user group through the means of the web-service itself, the implementation of a suitable and adequate design of the portal interface and structure was of high priority. Therefore some guiding concepts had to be set in place. The LITERACY-consortium decided to follow three main principles: keep it simple, make it accessible and make it fun.

**Keep it simple (for everyone)**

<u>Cognitive load:</u> The cognitive load describes the amount of information and interactions that need to be processed by a user. Keeping the cognitive load low needs to be one of the main-goals, as it directly affects many other design-related goals. If the cognitive load is too high, the user will not be able to process the important information. Therefore everything besides the information (i.e. the navigation etc.) needs to be as simple as possible. The improvements regarding this goal will be directly affected by the achievements of the other goals.

<u>Consistency:</u> An easy and also important way to reduce the cognitive load is to be consistent regarding the design of the portal. This includes a clear navigation which is easy to use and understand but also a color-design that stays consistent throughout the whole portal and provides a secure and known frame the user can rely on.

**Make it accessible**

<u>Retrieving information:</u> It is always important to provide a simple and easy design for the users. In the case of the LITERACY-portal it has to be accessible for different types of users, especially for dyslexics. Unfortunately the user group of dyslexics is not very consistent itself, so the portal has to provide content and services for a wide range of potential user-profiles and preferences. To make this possible the content and services need to be accessible through different types of communication channels and some channels might even need to be combined. An initial step would be to provide alternative methods to retrieve information. This could mean to provide text-alternatives for images or a text-to-speech-solution for a paragraph of textual information. Furthermore the whole portal should adhere the main requirements of accessibility to make it usable with different types of assisting technologies.

<u>Responsive design:</u> Although the research-proposal of the LITERACY-project does not mention a mobile version of the platform, it surely is beneficial to choose a responsive design approach for the LITERACY-portal. It does not affect the "normal" desktop-version of the portal-design in any way and ultimately allows for easy adaptation of the portal to the use via smart phones or tablets by just adding specific style-sheets.

<u>Presentation of content:</u> In order to present the actual contents of the LITERACY-portal in a fitting and easily accessible way, different style guides provided by external experts in dyslexia and web-design, like for example the British Dyslexia Association (http://www.bdadyslexia.org.uk/), Davis Dyslexia Association International (http://www.dyslexia.com) or dyslexic.com (http://www.dyslexic.com) were used as a reference and extended by experts from the fields of usability, accessibility, dyslexia and psychology.

**Make it fun**

<u>User-autonomy:</u> Users should be able to use the portal by themselves with little to no instructions and without any constrictions. This also includes the visual appearance of the portal. The user should be able to alter the visual elements of the portal, (i.e. color-themes, font, etc.).

<u>Human-Computer-Interaction:</u> The communication and interaction between the system and the user is a very important part of the design of the portal. The output of the system needs to be clear and easy to

understand as well as motivational and encouraging. On the other side the user needs adequate possibilities to interact with the system and to provide his input. A sophisticated, intelligent and engaging way of communication will make the portal fun and easy to use and will essentially improve the success of the users while using the portal.

## Human Centered Design

In the development of a web-based tool such as the LITERACY-portal, there is an increasing awareness of the fact that early user involvement is a key success factor. Taking this into account, the so-called "human-centered design" (HCD) process, which suggests a number of useful interventions that guide the process of including users, was chosen for the project.

The international standard ISO 9241-210: Human-centered design for interactive systems describes human-centered design as an "approach to systems design and development that aims to make interactive systems more usable by focusing on the use of the system and applying human factors/ergonomics and usability knowledge and techniques". It further elaborates that usable "systems can provide a number of benefits, including improved productivity, enhanced user well-being, avoidance of stress, increased accessibility and reduced risk of harm" (ISO 9241, 2010). These benefits make this approach ideal for the LITERACY-project.

The basic philosophy behind human-centered design is that "the user shouldn't suit the product, the product should suit the user". To achieve this goal, it is necessary to know the user and his needs and interests deeply. This necessity formed human-centered design into a process that consists of short incremental development phases, prototyping, and collection of feedback of real future users already at the early stages of design. More details about human-centered design can be found in the already mentioned international standard ISO 9241-210 and the topic is also thoroughly advocated in Donald Norman's "Design of everyday things" (Norman, 2002).

The LITERACY-project chose to use the HCD approach as user-inclusion was deemed to be a major success factor for the overall portal. Different individuals of the targeted user-group were invited to participate in multiple testing sessions and evaluations and their inputs directly contributed not only to the design but also to the planning of subsequent testing sessions.

**Inclusion of users and experts**

The LITERACY-consortium conducted a series of testings of design artefacts such as the interface or menu structure, and also introduced other measures like interviews and surveys, in order to create an interface and portal design that fits the needs of the specific user-group. The following paragraphs contain a brief overview over the major steps taken so far and display the outcomes and the impact of each step on the overall portal design.

Before the initial steps of the human-centered design process, personas, task analysis and context analysis, even started a knowledge base was created through an extensive literature and online research. Additionally the design team arranged for meetings with dyslexics, stakeholders and experts of the field to collect even more inputs. This thorough preparation process made it possible to set realistic design goals and create personas, as well as a task and context analysis for the planned portal. These initial steps would function as a foundation for all following steps of the design process.

In the next step dyslexic test-users were presented with five different types of menu-designs, which were pre-selected by experts from the fields of dyslexia, pedagogy, usability and psychology. The most popular menus chosen were the classic vertical menu and a menu consisting of buttons arranged in a grid. Additionally card sortings, in which the participants were asked to arrange cards with menu-items into categories, were conducted. The results of these testing sessions were thoroughly analyzed and served as the source for the first clickable prototypes of the LITERACY-portal. Following two screenshots of these initial prototypes can be seen:

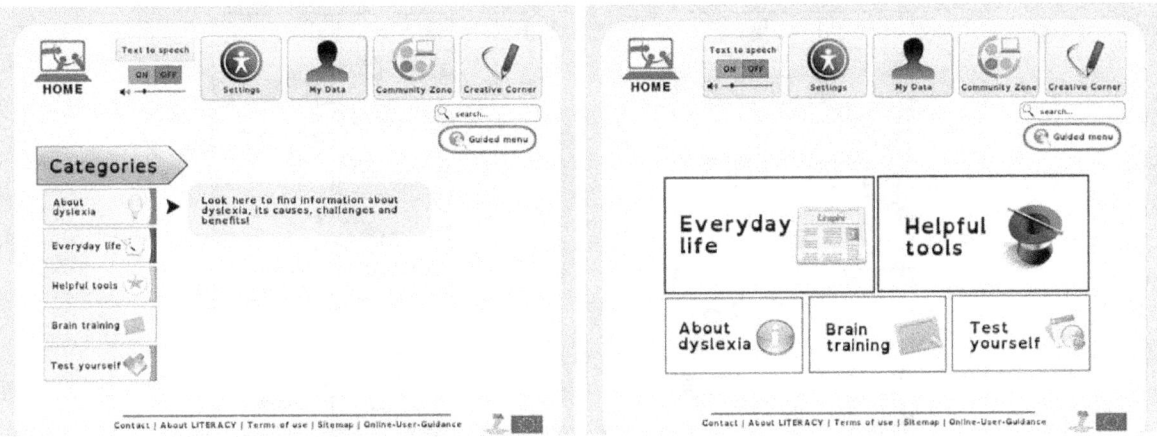

Figure 3: Initial design prototypes

Following these early design steps a meeting with external usability experts was arranged, which resulted in a redesign of parts of the portal. One of the key-modifications was the restructuring of the navigation for simplicity and resulting adaptation of the main-menu. Through some simple changes, which can be seen in figure 1, it was possible to keep the focus of the user on the main-menu while he is navigating the portal instead of splitting the focus between the top-menu and the main-menu. In the end this step did not only open up more space for content but also provides the user with a more consistent and clear experience in every area of the LITERACY-portal.

In order to not split the projects efforts on two different interface designs, vertical menu and grid menu, a second small scale testing of the menu-design was set up. The testing sessions were held face-to-face and utilized two simple clickable prototypes, which were generated by technical partners and translated into the native languages of the participants, Czech and Hungarian. The fact that the participants were able to do the testing in their native languages reduced the cognitive load and allowed the users to focus on the actual design. The result of this testing was that most of the 23 total participants favored the vertical style menu as it made it easier to navigate through the menu, orient oneself and get back on track if a wrong menu was entered. The following figure displays the results of this small scale testing session:

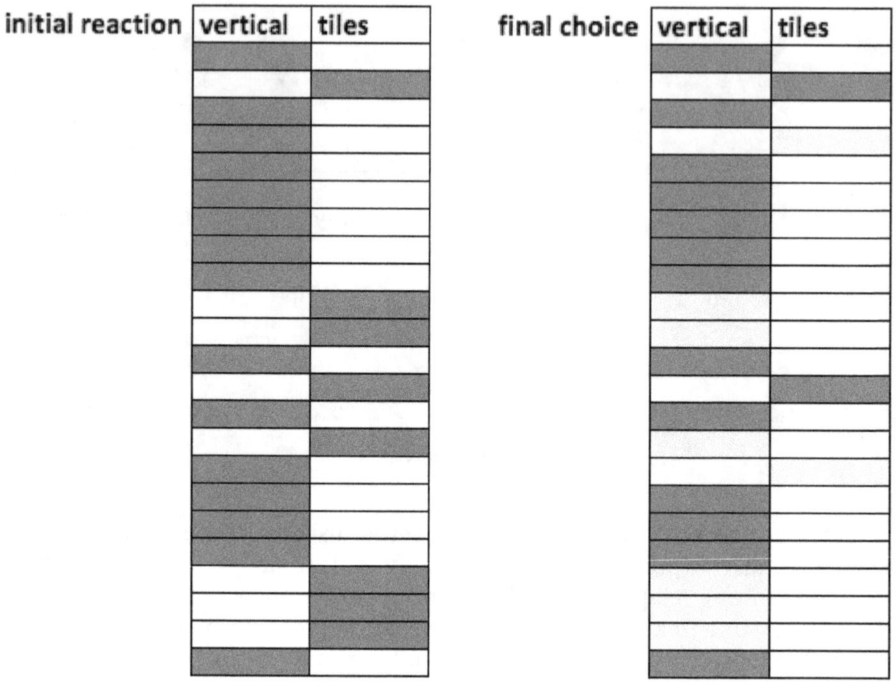

| initial reaction | vertical | tiles |
|---|---|---|
| | | |
| | | ■ |
| | ■ | |
| | ■ | |
| | ■ | |
| | ■ | |
| | ■ | |
| | ■ | |
| | | ■ |
| | | ■ |
| | ■ | |
| | | ■ |
| | ■ | |
| | ■ | |
| | ■ | |
| | ■ | |
| | ■ | |
| | | ■ |
| | | ■ |
| | | ■ |
| | ■ | ■ |

| final choice | vertical | tiles |
|---|---|---|
| | | |
| | | ■ |
| | | |
| | ■ | |
| | ■ | |
| | ■ | |
| | ■ | |
| | ■ | |
| | | |
| | | |
| | ■ | ■ |
| | ■ | |
| | | |
| | ■ | |
| | ■ | |
| | ■ | |
| | | |
| | | |
| | | |
| | ■ | |
| | ■ | |

Figure 4: Results of the screen-design testing

The left table shows the initial preference of the users based on the optical appeal of the menu. Green markings in the middle column indicate users that chose the vertical menu while the markings in the right column indicate users that chose the grid-menu. The table on the right displays the user preferences after they actually performed some simple tasks with both prototypes. Here the yellow markings represent users that this time preferred the other type of menu, while green markings indicate users that stuck with their initial opinion.

In a following step a testing was set up to find and chose suitable icons for the main menu as well as for the meta-menu in the top, cf. figure 1. A preliminary set of icons for each menu-item was established through the cooperation of the design team with specialists in usability, dyslexia and psychology. This testing-session was not executed through face-to-face meetings but rather with the help of specific web-based testing software that was accessible through a web-link. The software was created in cooperation with dyslexia experts in order to make it as accessible and easy to use as possible. Additionally it was translated into the native languages of the participants: Czech, Hungarian and Hebrew. The following figure shows some parts of the tool in different languages:

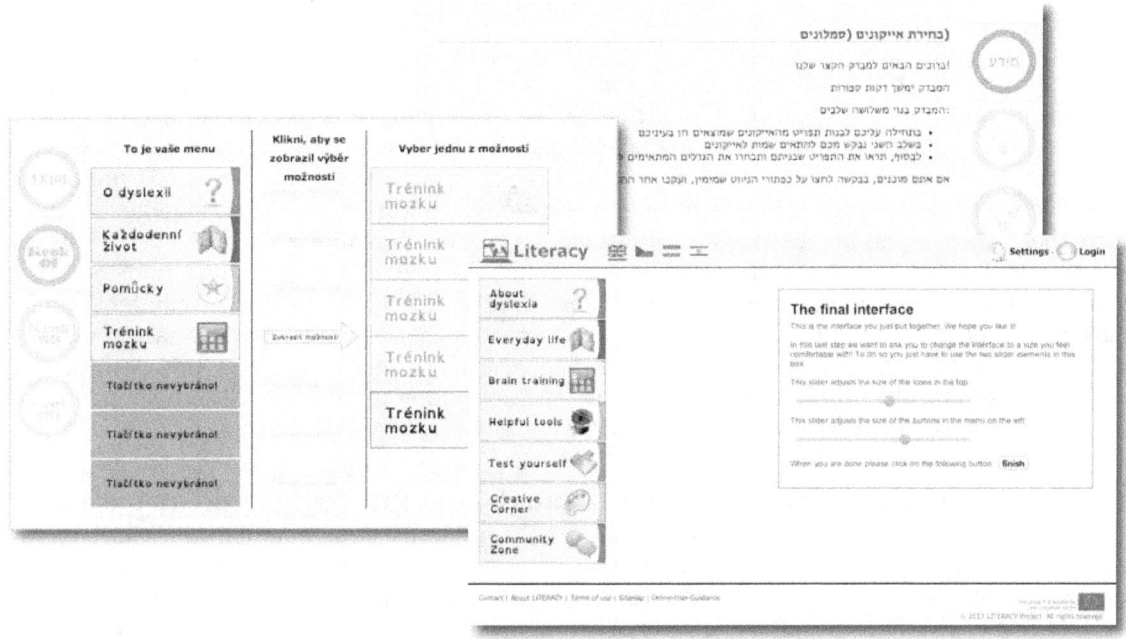

Figure 5: Icon-testing tool

In total 128 dyslexic users from Hungary, Israel and the Czech Republic participated in this testing session. The chosen icons can be seen in figure 1. In addition to the icon-preferences the tool also gave the users an option to adjust the size of the final menu, which can be seen in the bottom right screen of figure 4. This provided the design team with adequate size relations between different elements of the portal that are fitting for dyslexic users.

Accompanying to the described testing sessions surveys, interviews and face-to-face meetings with hands-on sessions were arranged and conducted with different dyslexics and stakeholders. These measures provided immediate feedback on planned testing sessions and helped improve them. Most notably the survey regarding the usage of community zone and creativity are worth mentioning. For this purpose two questionnaires were put together: one captured how dyslexics communicate online and which tools they prefer to use, while the other asked if the participants are creative, how they express it and if they use specific tools to do so. Overall 49 dyslexics participated in this survey. The following figure displays the age distribution of the participants:

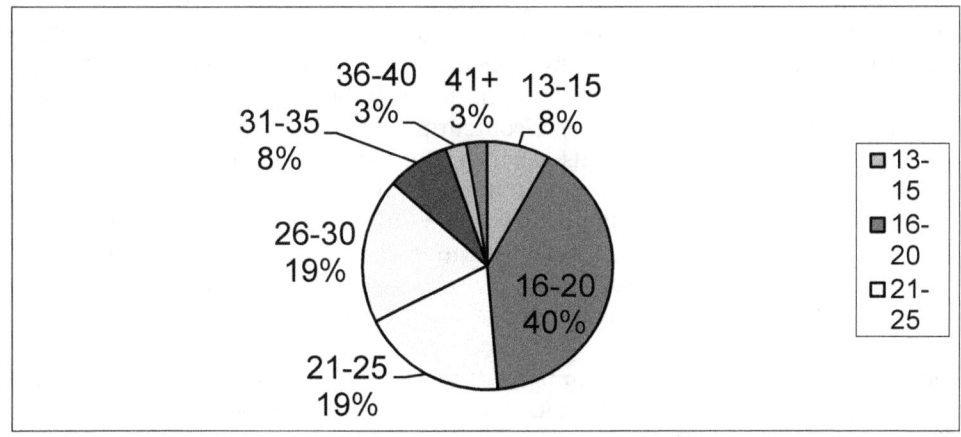

Figure 6: Age distribution of respondents

While the main target of this survey were young adults, it was important to also collect some data from other age groups in order to create specific tools or features that are targeted at older users. The results show that the respondents engage in creative activities. Only six respondents stated that they are not creative and creative efforts of the rest ranged from average to high level. All of the different age groups use ICT tools to support their creativity. A tendency of younger respondents on one hand using more tools, but on the other hand being less willing to learn about new ones was spotted. Additionally the respondents were rather willing to share their creations. Regarding the online social life of people with dyslexia, results say that Facebook is popular and only five of the respondents do not use it at all. However, questions on building an online community of people with dyslexia were not answered so clearly. Part of the respondents prefer open online groups, some prefer closed ones. Similarly, only a part of the respondents can imagine joining a self-help group for people with dyslexia. Active commenting received rather low scores, however, people often tend to at least skim through the comments and look for information in there, too. The respondents are also rather active in forums and various online communities.

## Social inclusion and self-empowerment through content, design and structure

One of the major goals of the LITERACY-project is to strengthen the social inclusion of people with dyslexia. Dyslexia itself does not necessarily cause people to be excluded from society and some dyslexics might not have trouble socializing, but there are still some handicaps and hurdles connected with it. Alan M. Hultquist describes it the following way: "As with any disability, dyslexia can lead to social, emotional and behavioral difficulties. These include trouble with peers, anxiety, depression and insecurity" (Hultquist, 2006). Therefore the LITERACY-portal strives to provide dyslexics with solutions and assistance to support their social inclusion, not only for face-to-face situations but also for the use of modern communication channels like social networks or instant messaging.

In the book "Interaction Design" Rogers, Sharp and Preece have following to say about "being social": "While face-to-face conversations remain central to many of our social interactions, the use of social media has dramatically increased. Many of us now routinely spend several hours a day communicating online". They also add that the "way we make contact, how we stay in touch, who we connect to, and how we maintain our social networks and family ties have irrevocably changed." (Rogers, 2013) Communication patterns have changed over the last years. Communication is fast, instant and often textual. Although this does not exclude dyslexics from actively participating, it nevertheless often gives them trouble. During the interviews conducted with dyslexics they were often asked how they deal with social media and how they communicate over the web. Not surprisingly they often responded that they use the same things others use: Facebook, Skype, instant messaging and audio-chats. Nevertheless they also mentioned their trouble with all these tools, which was mostly connected with overwhelming amounts of textual information.

The LITERACY-portal tries to target these issues in multiple ways. Firstly there are the two heavily interlinked areas "Community zone" and "Creative corner". The main objective of the Community zone is to help dyslexic users to interact with each other. It is through the Community zone that the LITERACY-portal becomes a "social" rather than an individualistic support tool. It is through the Community zone too that dyslexic users are called upon to become active by providing questions, comments, as well as responses from their particular, special life situation and perspective. In this way they are expected to support their peers by means that are truly complementary to the expert-content provided through the portal. It provides familiar, social tools such as Facebook and Twitter but also a forum and chat-module that will be explicitly managed by the LITERACY-partners to actively support initial community building.

The "Creative corner" on the other hand allows users to express themselves through creative means. The tools suggested in this area allow dyslexics to be creative and share their work with others on the portal or on the web in general. This provides an additional channel to get in touch with others, interact and communicate. For example, users can capture their life-stories and share with other how they master their challenges.

Another area, which is targeted to improve the social inclusion and help dyslexics with social interaction is the "Helpful tools"-section. It provides a multitude of assistive technologies, helpful software and tools, ranging from magnifiers or screen-readers to spell-checkers and mapping/organization software.

Lastly there exists a wide variety of interactive multi-medial e-learnings. These e-learnings provide tips and strategies about how to deal with everyday life situations and how to better process textual information:

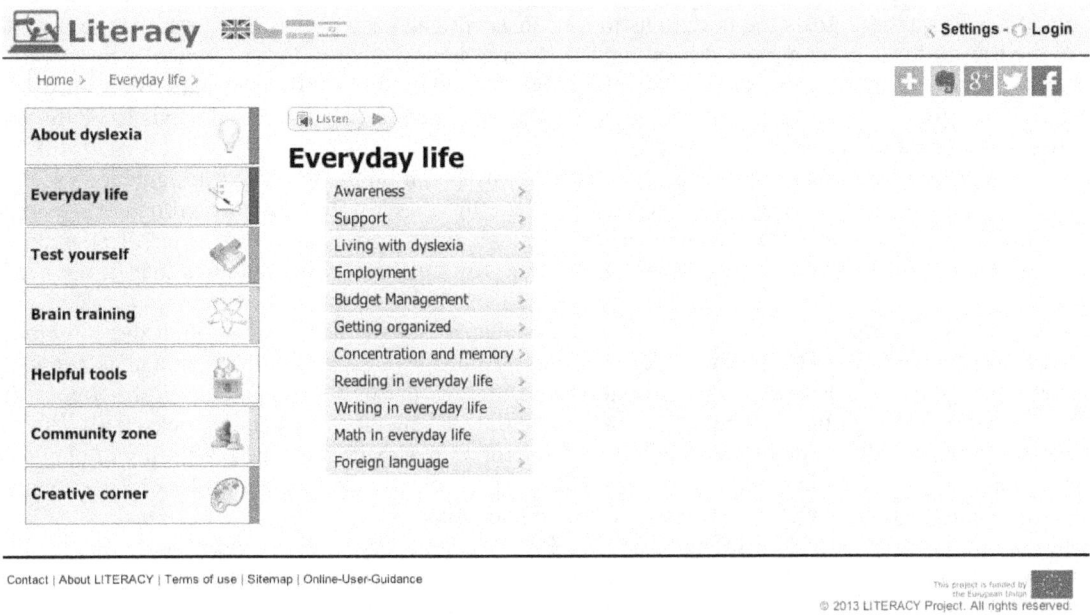

Figure 7: E-learning items

Figure 6 displays the second level menu for the "Everyday life"-section. Each of the items contains multiple e-learnings that provide tips and strategies about how to cope with certain situations or problems. Users can browse through the items independently, share them with their friends and even add their own comments, tips, suggestions or strategies to each item.

In contrast to the just described areas and solutions, which try to improve social inclusion through providing tips, strategies or tools, the "Brain training"-section aims to help dyslexics to improve their weaknesses in order to minimize their problems with social interaction. In his book "Dyslexia: A Practitioner's Handbook" Gavin Reid describes multiple cognitive skills associated with writing, like for example: organization, sequencing, identifying key-points, memory, grammar/syntax and translating a dyslexics often vivid imagination into written form (Reid, 2009). These are only some of the factors why dyslexics struggle with textual communication. In order to help the portals users to improve themselves in these areas there exist multiple trainings and interactive games within the "Brain training"-section. These trainings aim to help the users improve their skills, attention and memory and allow for progression based on the skill-level of the user.

An important part of the LITERACY-portals strategy to help dyslexic users to improve themselves and be successful is personalized content. The dyslexic user group is very heterogeneous. Not only do dyslexics have different forms of dyslexia but also individual strength and weaknesses. Additionally in 30% of the cases dyslexia occurs alongside other developmental disorders like dyspraxia, dyscalculia, dysgraphia or ADHD (Brunswick, 2009). Hence every user needs specific tools and trainings, catered to his or her specific needs, to achieve the best results. In order to provide the users with tools, trainings, tips and strategies based on their individual strength and weaknesses a self-assessment tool was implemented. A simple and autonomously performable three-step process assesses the user and ranks his skills in relation to himself. This means a user is not "judged" on how good or bad he did in comparison to standard-values but receives feedback where his personal strength and weaknesses lie in relation to himself. The system then suggests specific pars of the portal, for example a brain-training item or an e-learning on how to organize oneself, that fits the specific skills of the user.

## Conclusion

The LITERACY-portal strives to create a suitable environment for dyslexic users, which enables them to independently use and interact with its functionalities and in this way supports their social inclusion. In order to achieve these goals, the project decided to follow three simple principles: keep it simple, make it accessible and make it fun. To achieve these goals the portal has to be consistent and easy to use. This reduces the cognitive load and allows the user to focus on important things that help him to improve his skills. Additionally the portal needs to consider the specific needs of the dyslexic target group. Therefore the web-service has to be accessible and alternative channels to retrieve textual information need to be provided. Lastly the portal needs to be fun to use and allow the users to adapt it to their individual needs.

The design principle chosen to achieve all these goals is the human-centered design process. The HCD-process relies on consistent input from future end-users. Therefore the design is heavily influenced by suggestions and feedback of members of the targeted audience. The dyslexic users participated in a series of interactive testing sessions, interviews and surveys that allowed the design-team to implement functionalities that fit the needs of the target group.

The goal of supporting the social inclusion of dyslexic persons is achieved through the combination of a variety of means. Firstly the LITERACY-portal provides a multi-layered community area that allows users to interact with each other and also to share information and articles through social media. Furthermore the portal offers a variety of e-learnings that provide solutions, strategies and methods to handle tricky daily life situations dyslexics often struggle with. Through the "Brain training" section dyslexics have the possibility to play games that help them to improve cognitive skills like attention, memory or literacy, while the "Helpful tools" section provides a list of assistive technologies that might be helpful in certain situations.

In order to take the individual strengths and weaknesses into account, the portal also provides a short three-step assessment, which provides the user with a sub-set of the portal's contents that fits his/her specific profile. Further work will focus on contacting dyslexic users, observing and researching the ways in which they use the portal and further optimizing the portal to achieve its primary objective: Improved social inclusion of people with dyslexia.

**Acknowledgements**: This work was supported by the European Commission (Grant agreement no: 288596). The authors thank their consortium partners, in particular Sonia Martín-Roldán Pérez, Vera Vojtova, Kamila Balharová, Ján Struhár, Břetislav Beránek, Jakub Hrabec, Éva Gyarmathy, Bernard Lerer, Tsipi Egozi, Ofra Razel and Bracha Ehrman for their collaboration without which this paper could not have been written.

## References

Brunswick N. (2009). *Dyslexia: A Beginner's Guide* (pp. 15-19). London: Oneworld Publications
Dyslexia International asbl. *Dyslexia International - sharing expertise*, Retrieved from http://www.dyslexia-international.org/Educational%20Authorities/Statistics
Hultquist A. M. (2006). An Introduction to Dyslexia for Parents and Professionals (p. 38). London: Jessica Kingsley Publishers
The International Dyslexia Association (2007). *How Common Are Language-Based Learning Disabilities?*, Retrieved from http://www.interdys.org/FAQHowCommon.htm
ISO 9241 (2010). Ergonomics of human-system interaction – Part 210: Human-centered design for interactive systems.
LITERACY Project (2012). *Social Inclusion of People with Dyslexia*, Retrieved from http://www.literacyproject.eu/
Norman, D. A. (2002). *The design of everyday things* (p. 257). New York: Basic Books.
Reid G. (2009). Dyslexia: *A Practitioner's Handbook* (pp. 141-142). Hoboken: John Wiley & Sons
Rogers Y. & Sharp H. & Preece J. (2013). *Interaction Design: beyond human-computer interaction* (p. 101). New York:Wiley
Yin, R., K. (2009). Case Study Research: Design and Methods. Applied Social Research Methods. Vol. 5. USA: SAGE.

# 17 Convergence and Divergence: Accommodating Online Cross-Culture Communication Styles
Susan Simkowski & Bradley E. Wiggins, University of Arkansas USA

## Introduction

The process of media selection (social media, audio, video, websites, etc.) for online learners engaged in collaborative projects, especially when time and distance may separate the individual from assigned counterparts, is complex in that it relates to geography, an individual's level of proficiency in computer-mediated communication including social media, theories on media traits, and the linguistic and cultural nuances involved in a collaborative team.

Before entering into the primary theoretical discussion on factors and concepts which may ameliorate potential troubles that online learners as well as educators may encounter, it is advisable to review current perspectives on learning across cultures. Specifically, the current contribution offers a critical perception of online education at the threshold of a globalized community which is still separated by real world barriers as well as metaphoric ones. This chapter will detail the best practices to consider when traversing online education cross-culturally, especially when one wishes to have successful communication within one's own face-to-face team as well as with virtual counterparts.

## Cross-Cultural Learning

Learning styles, student strategies, and cognitive variations permeate the discourse on differences that exist between presumably dichotomous cultural structures (Wiggins, 2011). The literature on cultural dimensions such as individualist-collectivist, uncertainty avoidance, power distance, and as well masculinity touches on business, education, psychology, sociology, anthropology, and government. Common throughout the discourse is the reality of difference. While this difference between the various cultural dimensions exists, it does not suggest immutability.

## Student Learning Strategies

Acknowledging the dynamism of culture, Drake (2004) characterizes the introduction of international baccalaureate programs into the non-Eurocentric world as a source of potential dissonance. This argument rests on the reality of complex cultural differences which exist among various nations around the world. Indeed, among the Eurocentric nations, differences exist; however, these are differences in terms of being more or less of a particular cultural dimension, such as individualism, power-distance, or uncertainty avoidance.

Studies of students from Western and non-Western cultures propose that while some learners rely more on rote memorization (surface strategy), other learners enact a deep learning strategy (Ballard & Clanchy, 1984; Samuelowicz, 1987; Volet, Renshaw, & Tietzel, 1994). Three learning strategies relate to this discussion: surface, achieving, and deep.

A student maintaining a surface strategy meets minimal requirements stated by institutional curricular objectives and utilizes rote memory (Biggs, 1987; Hunt, 2003; King 1996). Conversely, an achieving strategy envisions a situation in which a student strives to get high grades and is generally as good a student as possible, even if the subject is of no interest to the student. A deep learning strategy is one focused both on competence and the process of relating new knowledge to previous knowledge. Research that has defined Western and non-Western cultures in terms of Hofstede's cultural dimensions (Hofstede, 1980; 2001; Hofstede & Pedersen, 1999), i.e. defining Western as individualist and non-Western as collectivist, has provided consistent distinctions in "learning, motivation for learning, learning strategies and goals or purposes of learning" (Brown et al, 2007, p. 593; Gabb, 2006; Ho & Chiu, 1994; Hwang, Francesco, & Kessler, 2003; Marsella, DeVos, & Hsu, 1985; Triandis, Bontempo, Villareal, Asai, & Lucca, 1988; Weisz, Rothbaum, & Blackburn, 1984). Indeed, significant cultural variations may be related to cognitive variations. By extension, these variations may characterize the nature of differences implied by cultural changes such as Western-style schooling (Cole, Gay, Glick, & Sharp, 1971).

## Cultural Awareness Training in the United States

As a feature of the cultural wealth of the United States, it is not surprising that its schools are becoming increasingly culturally and linguistically diverse. A testament to this trend is the increase in teacher preparation programs across the United States to train new and existing teachers in cultural awareness (Lim, Maxwell, Able-Boone, & Zimmer, 2008). What is lacking, however, is an understanding of effective social media design for e-learning content to be delivered to culturally and linguistically diverse audiences. According to the 2005-2009 American Community Survey, 12.4% of the US population, or 38,440,000 are foreign-born. Additionally, 19.6%, or 60,760,000 speak a language other than English at home (U.S. Census Bureau, 2009).

**Resources**. The United States spends approximately $631 billion for primary and secondary schools (Ruth, 2010). Despite this enormous expenditure, approximately 73% of high school students graduate as a nationwide average; in some regions the figure is around 50% or lower. According to the Sloan Consortium's report on K-12 online learning, primary school e-learning is still in its infancy (Allen & Seaman, 2009). However, the Sloan study noted that e-learning solutions are critical for poorer, rural school districts.

With some school districts seeing fewer qualified educators, online learning solutions may enable schools to draw on expertise located elsewhere and accessible online (Ruth, 2010). Patrick and Powell (2006) found that online course enrollments have increased in the United States by approximately 30% since 2003. This highlights the utilitarian aspect of online learning that is most beneficial to those students residing in rural areas or districts with educator shortages (Gibbs, Lane, & Lane, 2007). Picciano and Seaman (2009) reported enrollment in online courses had risen to over one million students. Watson, Gemin, Ryan, and Wicks (2009) also reported the growth of online learning in all but five states in the US. Similarly, Schaeffer and Konetes (2010) highlight the promise of online programs to provide opportunities for students to enroll in a wider range of courses not usually available at traditional schools.

**Calls for more research in e-learning design**. Rice (2009) surveyed distance education stakeholders to identify priorities in distance education for 2009-2014. The chief priority was 'evaluation of course design and delivery.' These influential online education stakeholders advocate research in effective course design and for online delivery and usage. Barbour and Reeves (2009) and Barbour (2010) endorse online course design to follow the structure of research methodology. Their recommended strategy shares similarities with the ADDIE model of instructional design which incorporates analysis, design, development, implementation, and evaluation (Dean, 2002), but involves iterative procedures to test and refine the course. Clearly, in order to maintain a productive and nurturing online learning environment for K-12, higher education, private sector and government training, more research is needed in course design.

The presence of collaborative teams with Global Online Learner Projects (GOLP), signifies an organizational endeavor to benefit from culturally diverse expertise. Such teams interact on a personal level within its own team and virtually with its globally distributed counterparts. The following three sections review the collected literature in order to provide a clearer understanding of the communication media selection for GOLPs. This review discusses three aspects of a GOLP's media selection which are (a) composition, (b) theories on media selection, and (c) intercultural significance.

## GOLP Composition, Location, and Need for Trust

The relationship between the composition and location of a GOLP determines much of the media selected for communication purposes. The combination of composition and location of a GOLP leads to a basic need to be able to trust both those within one's own GOLP and those located in another GOLP (Jarvenpaa & Leidner, 1998; Cho & Lee, 2008; Ulijn, O'Hair, Weggerman, Ledlow, & Hall, 2000). The following three subsections discuss this in greater detail. The subsections are as follows (a) heterogeneous GOLPs being more culturally aware than homogeneous GOLPs, (b) the location of the GOLP as a determinant in media selection given a need for trust, and (c) that the composition of a GOLP and its location generates a need for trust.

*Global Online Learner Projects Composition.* There is a greater chance for heterogeneous GOLP members to be more culturally aware than homogeneous GOLP members. In order to work effectively within culturally diverse teams, it is important to understand the nuances of the cultures with which one interacts (Timmerman & Scott, 2007; Jarvenpaa & Leidner, 1998; Shachaf, 2005; Uber Grosse, 2002; Hofstede, 1983; Hofstede, 2001; Beamer & Varner, 2008). Simply peruse the national presence for corporations with an international presence for a better understanding. For example, Starbucks takes a very different approach to its website in the United States than it does for Japan (starbucks.com). Information received by an individual is processed by a cultural frame which filters the message through an individual's cultural background (Maznevski & Chudoba, 2000; Matveev & Nelson, 2004). Given the challenges which heterogeneity poses members of a GOLP and given the GOLP's particular level of "virtualness," the team's composition is of much greater importance than where the individual members happen to be located geographically (Goodbody, 2005). With a solid understanding of intercultural communication issues and how best to resolve conflict (and/or how conflict is best avoided), the heterogeneous team tends to match or exceed the productivity of a homogeneous team (Maznevski & Chudoba, 2000). In part this is due to the cultural complexity of a heterogeneous team. Members of such a team often represent a breadth of linguistic and cultural diversity (Campbell, 2008; Shachaf, 2005). The next paragraph discusses the matter of GOLP location.

*Global Online Learner Projects Location.* The location of a GOLP often determines media preference given a need to formalize trust. Since GOLPs are dispersed all over the globe, separated from one and another GOLP by geography only, the increasing use of computer-mediated communication (CMC) and the Internet illustrates the ease by which technology can facilitate communication beyond national borders (Olaniran, 2004; Vallaster, 2005; de Vries, R., van den Hooff, B., & de Ridder, J. 2006). Asynchronous media tend to be the communication medium of choice especially among culturally diverse GOLPs (Timmerman & Scott, 2006). In written and spoken communication between GOLPs, the language is often English (Maznevski & Chudoba, 2000; Shachaf & Hara, 2005). Using email or social media such as Facebook or Twitter allows non-native speakers of English the opportunity to spell-check their messages prior to sending to other team members (Uber Grosse, 2002). In addition, the leanness of the email medium diminishes the chance for cross-cultural miscommunication (Goodbody, 2005; Martins, Gilson, & Maynard, 2004). Since the medium does not allow for the transference of non-verbal communication such as gestures, facial expressions, eye contact, and body language, the potential for a team member to misunderstand another member's message due to intercultural issues is greatly decreased (Shachaf, 2005; Timmerman & Scott, 2006). Global Online Learner Projects dispersed over various time zones tend to prefer asynchronous media (Shachaf, 2005; Jarvenpaa & Leidner, 1998). However, in order to ensure a good sense of collaboration and cohesiveness, especially when GOLPs use asynchronous media, Global Online Learner Projects must develop a level of trust and respect to compensate for the online nature of their collaborative projects (Jarvenpaa & Leidner, 1998; Martins, Gilson, & Maynard, 2004). The next paragraph discusses the issue of trust in greater detail as it pertains to a successful GOLP.

*Trust.* Team composition and its location lead to a need for good collaboration and trust in order to perform successfully. Though trust within the GOLP is likely to be neither permanent nor strong, it is necessary to develop trust given the shared objective of task completion (Lucas, 2012; Olaniran, 2004; Jarvenpaa & Leidner, 1998). Olaniran indicates that CMC's perceived inherent lack of a capacity to support rapport-building among GOLPs. Jarvenpaa and Leidner posit that strong bonds develop especially within teams consisting of diverse membership. Identity development within GOLPs is synonymous with successful team operation and prevents feelings of detachment or "deindividuation" (Matveev & Nelson, 2004; Søderberg & Holden, 2002; Jarvenpaa & Leidner, 1998). The next point discusses how GOLPs select media and how theories correspond to their media selection given cultural diversity.

## Media Traits Theories, Media and GOLP Structure, and Linguistic and Cultural Diversity

Some media traits theories do not illustrate a sense of rationale in determining a culturally diverse GOLP's media selection. These media traits theories consider individual media characteristics as determinants for selecting a given medium. The following subsections discuss (a) media traits theories, (b) the Adaptive Structuration Theory as it pertains to media selection for a GOLP, and (c) the aspect of linguistic and cultural diversity of GOLPs (DeSanctis & Poole, 1994; Shachaf & Hara, 2007; Cho & Lee, 2008; Timmerman & Scott, 2007; Søderberg & Holden, 2002).

*Media traits theories.* Research on media traits theories often disregards the potential impact of internal and external dimensions of culturally diverse GOLPs. Media traits theories on media selection focus on the function of media and communication task characteristics (Cho and Lee, 2008). Media Richness Theory (MRT) is a contingency theory which suggests that the richer the medium, the better it is to transfer ambiguous and/or complex messages (Russ, Daft and Lengel, 1990; Daft, Lengel, & Trevino, 1987; Shachaf & Hara, 2005). It was later revised to consider newer media (Martins, Gilson, & Maynard, 2004). Timmerman and Scott (2006) argue that communication over a wide range of media irrespective of richness is the end result because GOLPs span boundaries and cultures. Similarly, Maznevski and Chudoba (2000) found no connection between message traits and selected media. Media Accessibility Theory (MAT) proposes that media have accessibility traits which determine their use. Reliability, access speed, and availability all fall under this theory (Carlson & Davis, 1998). Maznevski and Chudoba found inconsistent similarities between media choice and message as explained by structural traits. Given the geographical distribution and cultural diversity of GOLPs, individual team members conduct themselves in numerous ways relative to their own social context. Shachaf and Hara (2007) developed the Behavioral Complexity Theory (BCT) to address aspects of global dispersion, cultural diversity, and preferred media characteristics of GOLPs. BCT focuses on media channel range and the flexibility of individuals. The next subsection details a GOLP's media selection in terms of its structure and the occurrence of successful communication.

*Media selection and adapted structure.* Given the available communication media, a GOLP adapts the selected medium/media to best suit its structure. Within the structure of communication media technology, successful communication occurs when interaction between GOLP members is well-planned and the selected media is well-adapted to the GOLP's structure. Managers of GOLPs often influence the selection of media in order to match the specific communication requirements of GOLPs (Martins, Gilson, & Maynard, 2004; Olaniran, 2004; Uber Grosse, 2002). Recalling Giddens's (1979) theory of structuration, the Adaptive Structuration Theory (AST) suggests that users of communication technology choose to adapt either a technology's role to the needs of the team, or, conversely, to adapt the team's structure to employ the technology in a amicable and conducive way (DeSanctis and Poole, 1994; Timmerman and Scott, 2006; Cho & Lee, 2008; Maznevski & Chudoba, 2000). For AST, in other words, individuals determine the outcome of technology efficacy (Timmerman and Scott, 2006; Cho and Lee, 2008). The next paragraph discusses the aspects of language and culture given the cultural diversity of GOLPs and how these impact the team's internal and external communication.

*Language and culture.* Linguistic and cultural diversity are features of GOLPs which form a subtext beyond theories of media traits. A GOLP's cultural and linguistic diversity is a benefit to the team in that the GOLP considers a task thoroughly instead of taking quick action due to its cultural composition. Regardless of the medium, communication tends to be smoother between peers and already acquainted individuals (Uber Grosse, 2002; Vallaster, 2005; Søderberg & Holden, 2002; Thomas, 2007; Ulijn, O'Hair, Weggerman, Ledlow, & Hall, 2000). Having access to a variety of communication channels is advantageous for GOLPs given the complexity of linguistic and cultural diversity (de Vries, van den Hooff, & de Ridder, 2006; Cho & Lee, 2008). The next section discusses the role of intercultural competency in GOLPs as it relates to successful communication given a wide range of media channels.

**Success Factors for GOLPs**

The literature suggests that if a GOLP has intercultural competency and is proficient in computer-mediated communication, like social media, the GOLP will select the best media (or combination of media) for the task at hand (Olaniran, 2004; Cho & Lee, 2008; Uber Grosse, 2002). It appears that intercultural competence and skilled handling of SM OR CMC correlate with a given GOLP's wide range of available media channels. The following subsections detail (a) intercultural competence as a success factor for GOLPs and (b) the opportunity for GOLPs to have access to wide range of communication media.

*SM OR CMC and intercultural competence.* Intercultural communication competence is a success factor for GOLPs when a wide range of communication media channels is available. An individual's culture impacts social interaction (Vallaster, 2005; Hofstede, 1983; Hofstede, 2001; Uber Grosse, 2002). A group's intercultural competence links with expressing messages clearly which yields a high level of team productivity (Matveev & Nelson, 2004; Hofstede, 2001; Hofstede, 1983; Timmerman & Scott, 2007). With a wide range of media channels available, GOLP members dispersed over a span of locations appropriate both rich and lean media for the given task at hand, but do not choose the media *because* they are rich, or *because* they are lean (Shachaf & Hara, 2007; Maznevski & Chudoba, 2004). A GOLP's selection of a specific computer-mediated form of communication results from the team's own cultural diversity and a desire to communicate effectively with other GOLPs (Campbell, 2008; Martins, Gilson, & Maynard, 2004). SM OR CMC technologies do not erode cultural boundaries due inherent media traits (Cho & Lee, 2008; Goodbody, 2005; Olaniran, 2004). Rather, GOLP team members who are knowledgeable of SM OR CMC technology and have intercultural competency reduce internal and external miscommunication (Ulijn et al., 2000; Olaniran, 2004). Successfully understanding the intended message for GOLPs denotes a sense of SM OR CMC technological skill coupled with cross cultural competency. In teams where individuals do not possess cross cultural competency, the intended communication suffers due to the complexities of intercultural communication (Uber Grosse, 2002; Shachaf & Hara, 2007; Shachaf, 2005). The next paragraph discusses the importance of media channel availability in terms of a GOLP's selection of a particular communication medium.

*Range of media channels.* Having access to a wide range of communication media is important for a GOLP when it selects a medium for a particular task. The medium is only as important as the message sent by a GOLP member (Timmerman & Scott, 2006; Maznevski & Chudoba, 2000). In culturally diverse GOLPs it is important for members to consider that the intended message has been understood (Goodbody, 2005). Adjusting one's own perspective to allow for successful communication across cultural boundaries is enhanced by the availability of multiple media channels (Reinsch and Turner, 2006). Access to multiple channels for communication furnishes the GOLP's communication efforts with a "heightened visibility" (Reinsch & Turner, 2006, p.350). In "multi-communicating" individuals within a GOLP increasingly use multiple media technologies in order to facilitate communication with other culturally diverse teams distributed around the world (Thomas, 2007; Campbell, 2008).

## Critique of the Literature

While some of the research studies drew conclusions based on actual global virtual teams, and the media they chose, other studies used virtual teams composed of students located in different countries (Timmerman & Scott, 2007). It seems that the educational impact of learning more about GOLP media selection, given the aspects discussed in this review, would increase by using data from real global virtual teams.

## The Premise and Application

What builds a sense of community better than local media? Print and, later, broadcast technologies, have been the source for local information for centuries (McLuhan, 1964). Generally speaking, radio stations have the mission of aligning itself to the community in which it serves (Simkowski, 2003). When radio broadcasting came about, news and information of interest could travel faster to those with a radio. Soon families made a habit of sitting in front of the radio listening to their favorite shows. Radio stations have built a sense of local community since the implementation of FCC in the guise as the FRC was to regulate radio to serve the public interest. This section addresses the implementation of radio, first in the form of broadcast radio, and, then, online radio as well as the application of a Global Online Learner Project in the guise of an online radio station.

Radio stations licensed by educational institutions (typically between 88.1 and 91.9 on the FM dial) can now be found to have a virtual presence in the form of a website (www.radio-locator.com). According to Hanley (2002), a National Public Radio board member, the most significant difference between commercial and non-commercial stations comes from the perspective of the FCC and the Internal Revenue Service. The legal prohibition to air commercials requires a very different business model. Commercial stations exist to deliver an audience to advertisers. Public stations exist either as subsidized activities, or they must create programming with enough audience to be sustained by grants and/or gifts from individuals. (Underwriting, while often compared to commercials, is legally a grant of support recognized on-the-air and possibly other ways). Self-supporting public radio stations, for example, are largely stations that deliver programming to a significant enough audience to garner financial gifts from that audience. Underwriting and grant support can be significant, but the largest source of public radio income is directly from listeners.

Thus, the balancing act for public radio station management is to present programming for a large enough audience, yet achieve public service for the medium. Serving a "small but loyal" audience usually means serving a small audience - and limits the amount of public service being done by a given station

(Hanley, 2002). In managing a public radio station, one must do well enough to deliver an audience and also have that radio service perceived as a good enough public service to deserve contributions for what most listeners receive for free. Hanley further stated that even stations that rely on subsidies eventually need to be accountable in the amount and significance of public service that is being performed, especially taking into consideration the perceived and potential community need.

There are about 10,000 radio stations of all types in the country (Petrizzi & Wright, 1977). According to the Corporation for Public Broadcasting (CPB) (2002), there are fewer than 800 public radio stations. The majority of public radio stations are owned by universities (417), followed by nonprofit community organizations (262). Only about 48 stations are owned by municipal entities or public school systems. Additionally, there are some radio stations owned by individual schools.

Public broadcasting stations provide services in education, programming, and staffing and operating for the community, similarly so can online radio. The Public Broadcasting Act, (1962) allowed public broadcasting to take risks that may be considered as creative or serve unserved and underserved audiences, particularly children and minorities. Thus, services become available to all the citizens of the United States. The bill was enacted by the Federal Government to ensure that Americans have access to public telecommunications services through all appropriate available telecommunications distribution technologies. Through this act, the vision of public radio is to be commercial-free and instructional, educational, and cultural in content.

*Radio* or radio spectrum is operationally defined for this study through the description from the FCC. Stations are full-power radio transmitters licensed by the FCC. Licensees are community organizations, colleges or universities, local authorities or state governments, which hold the FCC licenses. The FCC (2002) defined radio spectrum as follows:

> The radio spectrum is the part of the natural spectrum of electromagnetic radiation lying between the frequency limits of 9 kilohertz and 300 gigahertz. In the United States, regulatory responsibility for the radio spectrum is divided between the FCC and the National Telecommunications and Information Administration. (¶ 1)

To best put the definition in the vernacular, radio is designed to reach mass audiences with a signal that is transmitted from a central point and can be reached by persons around the standard radio receive equipment (Meyer, 1994). In turn, online radio can reach potentially a larger audience because it is not bound by terrestrial signal.

Unlike a licensed radio station, an online radio station can be set up and information disseminated rather inexpensively with no current regulations from the FCC. Similarly to broadcast radio, any individual with an internet connection can listen to an online radio station. In turn, individuals can rather easily start an internet or online radio "station." There are many services which charge little or nothing for one to upload audio content (spreaker.com, Live365.com, etc.). While many radio stations licensed to colleges have an online or internet presence, not all educational institutions have a licensed radio station. It was the desire of students within our university, which is does not have a traditional radio station, to have at least one online.

Students in two media communication courses (*Broadcasting in New Media* and *Survey of New Media*) were tasked with proposing an online radio station and creating its web presence. Additionally, students were required to get a "global perspective" and, in turn, a Global Online Learner Project was created. Students attained a global perspective by adding non-native English speakers or international students to their teams. Groups of three or four American students from a small southern public university were teamed up with international students who had a connection to the university. While the majority resided in Asian countries (Japan, South Korea, Vietnam), other countries included England, Mexico, and Spain. The American student population was 39 and the international population was 49, because each group had at least two international students.

Collaboration was typically either in the design or final stages. For example, the American students would ask questions what the international students would like to see and then the Americans would build it. The results would then be critiqued by the international students. It appeared during this initial GOLP that there was no online development between the American and the International students. Instead, students used social media to discuss what they liked and what need to be further explained. As the literature review indicates, the areas of linguistics and time difference were the biggest problem areas for the project. The objective of the assignment was to create a website or concept paper that brings the media communication students nearer to the goal of creating an online radio station. The purpose of the global connection was for

American students in a small southern town to understand the cultural nature of radio and the internet. Using social media to communicate, students were able to finesse the project, so that it met the needs of a global culture through the perspectives of these 49 international students.

**Remaining Research Questions**

Further research could delve deeper into analyzing media selection within the context of existing theoretical models and intercultural dimensions. When the authors included intercultural dimensions, they often chose the context dimension (high-context vs. low-context) and did not include other dimensions in their research (Hofstede, 1983; Beamer & Varner, 2008). Perhaps future research could test the validity (if any) of intercultural dimensions within a research framework probing the media selection of GOLPs. This data could illustrate the impact (if any) of the cultural aspect of GOLPs and their selection of media.

**References**

Beamer, L. & Varner, I. (2008). *Intercultural communication in the global workplace* (4th ed.). New York, NY: McGraw Hill.
Campbell, N. (2008, April 16). You've got mail! Using email technology to enhance intercultural communication learning. *Journal of Intercultural Communication*, 16. Retrieved October 5, 2008, from http://www.immi.se/intercultural/nr16/campbell-nittaya.htm
Carlson, J. & Davis, G. (1998). An investigation of media selection among directors and managers: From "self" to "other" orientation. *MIS Quarterly*, 22(3), 335-362.
Cardon, P. (2008). A critique of Hall's contexting model: A meta-analysis of literature on intercultural business and technical communication. *Journal of Business and Technical Communication*, 22(4), 399-428.
Cho, H. & Lee, J. (2008). Collaborative information seeking in intercultural computer-mediated communication groups. *Communication Research*, 35(4), 548-573.
Daft, R., Lengel, R., & Trevino, L. (1987). Message equivocality, media selection, and manager performance: Implications for information systems. *MIS Quarterly*, 11(3), 355-366.
DeSanctis, G. & Poole, M. (1994). Capturing the complexity in advanced technology use: Adaptive structuration theory. *Organization Science*, 5(2), 121-147.
de Vries, R., van den Hooff, B., & de Ridder, J. (2006). Explaining knowledge sharing: The role of team communication styles, job satisfaction, and performance beliefs. *Communication Research*, 33(2), 115-135.
Giddens, A. (1979). *Central problems in social theory*. Berkeley and Los Angeles: University of California Press.
Goodbody, J. (2005). Critical success factors for global virtual teams: Overcoming common obstacles to improve team performance. *Strategic Communication Management*, 9(2), 18-21.
Hofstede, G. (1983). The cultural relativity of organizational practices and theories. *Journal of International Business Studies*, 3, 75-89.
Hofstede, G. (2001). Culture's recent consequences: Using scores in theory and research. *International Journal of Cross Cultural Management*, 1, 11-30.
Inoue, Y. (2007, November 15). Cultural fluency as a guide to effective intercultural communication: the case of Japan and the U.S. *Journal of Intercultural Communication*, 15. Retrieved October 5, 2008, from http://www.immi.se/intercultural/nr15/inoue.htm
Jarvenpaa, S. & Leidner, D. (1998). Communication and trust in global virtual teams. *Organization Science*, 10, 791-815.
Lucas, S. E. (2012). *The art of public speaking* (11th ed.). New York, NY: McGraw Hill.
Martins, L., Gilson, L., and Maynard, M. (2004). Virtual teams: What do we know and where do we go from here? *Journal of Management*, 30, 805-835.
Matveev, A. & Nelson, P. (2004). Cross cultural communication competence and multicultural team performance. *International Journal of Cross Cultural Management*, 4(2), 253-270.
Maznevski, M. & Chudoba, K. (2000). Bridging space over time: Global virtual team dynamics and effectiveness. *Organization Science*, 11(5), 473-492.
McLuhan, M. & Gordon, W. T. (2013). *Understanding Media: The Extensions of Man : Critical Edition*. Berkeley, CA: Ginko Press.
Olaniran, B. (2004). Computer-mediated communication in cross-cultural virtual teams. *International & Intercultural Communication Annual*, 27, 142-166.
Reinsch, N., Turner, J. (2006). Ari, r u there? Reorienting business communication for a technological era. *Journal of Business and Technical Communication*, 20(3), 339-356.

Russ, G., Daft, R., & Lengel, R. (1990). Media selection and managerial characteristics in organizational communications. *Management Communication Quarterly*, 4(2), 151-175.

Shachaf, P. (2005). Bridging cultural diversity through e-mail. *Journal of Global Information Technology Management*, 8(2), 46-60.

Shachaf, P. & Hara, N. (2007). Behavioral complexity theory of media selection: A proposed theory for global virtual teams. *Journal of Information Science*, 33(1), 63-75.

Shachaf, P. (2005). Bridging cultural diversity through e-mail. *Journal of Global Information Technology Management*, 8(2), 46-60.

Simkowski, S.M. (2003). *Shifting or Drifting: Mission Statements and the Learning Organization*. Dissertation: Cardinal Stritch University, Milwaukee, WI.

Søderberg, A. & Holden, N. (2002). Rethinking cross cultural management in a globalizing business world. *International Journal of Cross Cultural Management*, 2(1), 103-121.

Timmerman, C. & Scott, C. (2006). Virtually working: Communicative and structural predictors of media use and key outcomes in virtual work teams. *Communication Monographs*, 73(1), 108-136.

Thomas, G. (2007). How can we make our research more relevant? Bridging the gap between workplace changes and business communication research. *Journal of Business Communication*, 44, 283-296.

Uber Grosse, C. (2002). Managing communication within virtual intercultural teams. *Business Communication Quarterly*, 65(4), 22-38.

Ulijn, J., O'Hair, D., Weggeman, M., Ledlow, G., & Hall, H. (2000). Innovation, corporate strategy, and cultural context: What is the mission for international business communication? *The Journal of Business Communication*, 37(3), 293-317.

Vallaster, C. (2005). Cultural diversity and its impact on social interactive processes: Implications from an empirical study. *International Journal of Cross Cultural Management*, 5(2), 139-163.

Wiggins, B.E. (2011). The impact of cultural dimensions and the coherence principle of multimedia instruction on the achievement of educational objectives within an online learning environment. PhD Dissertation, Indiana University of Pennsylvania, Indiana, PA.

# PART 3 MOBILE LEARNING

## 18 Using Digital Resources to Support Personalized Learning Experiences in K-12 Classrooms: The Evolution of Mobile Devices as Innovations in Schools in Northwest Ohio

Savilla Banister & Rachel Reinhart, Bowling Green State University, U.S.A.

The challenges facing the United States in educating its youth have been widely documented. The dropout rate in the past decades has been staggering, hovering around the 70% mark, with students of color and in lower socio-economic circumstances posting an even higher rate (Barton, 2005). Perhaps more troubling are the indicators that students who are staying in school until high school graduation are largely disengaged and disenfranchised with their experiences (Balfanz et al., 2007; Henry et al., 2012). Finally, emphasis on standardized tests that may or may not be relevant in determining how successful or productive students will be in our information-age world, have created an ambiance of confusion and stress for both teachers and students. (Au, 2011; Hanushek & Rivkin, 2010; Sahlberg, 2008) So, for all of the investment of time and money in public education for all of United States young people, in an effort to promote productivity and democracy, the results appear to be dismal.

But there are signs that major changes are coming to our educational institutions, changes that will drastically alter the traditional models that have long held across the years and have, for the most part, been resistant to promising models of reform. These changes are largely fueled by the reality of the digital world we now live in. Since the advent of the World Wide Web (circa 1995), the digital generation and exchange of information has become the norm. In the past decade, the interconnectivity and collaborative possibilities in the use, reuse, and co-construction of digital texts, images, audio, video, and databases (loosely identified as "Web 2.0" functionalities) has forced teachers to abandon their long-held positions as the ultimate possessors and distributors of knowledge. (Barnett, 2012; Drexler, 2010; Ertmer & Ottenbreit-Leftwich, 2010) Students come to school knowing that the "information is in the air" (Williams, Karousou, & Mackness, 2011) and that they have the ability to connect with experts around the world in multiple venues, in order to learn about all sorts of content, academic or practical.

Beyond the amount of resources available for learner consumption, in the support of educational growth, our digital tools now afford us the communicative and data-management power to truly provide individualized learning experiences for students. The United States Department of Education (US DoE) is supporting the Digital Promise initiative, using their League of Innovative Schools as a conduit to encourage implementations of powerful technologies to support meaningful learning. The US DoE's Office of Educational Technology is promoting strategies including one-to-one mobile devices for students, personalized learning networks, a national registry of learning resources, data management learning dashboards and competency-based education models to provide direction for dramatic changes in our nation's schools. (Hwang, Kuo, Yin, & Chuang, 2010; Miller & Lake, 2012; Wang & Liao, 2011)

So how are schools adapting to this new realization that they must embrace the educational possibilities of the digital age? This study sought to determine what regional K-12 schools in a Midwestern state were doing, as a result of these forces. Specific questions addressed in the study include:

1. What types of initiatives, related to the Digital Promise of DoE's Office of Educational Technology, are schools in this region exploring or deploying?
2. What are the identified priorities of these schools, specifically related to student learning outcomes?

In order to address these questions, an online survey (See Appendix A: Email and survey) was distributed through the Office of the Center of Excellence for 21st Century Educator Preparation of a state university. The survey was sent to principals of all schools within a 50-mile radius of the center with an email requesting completion of the online survey, or an option to complete the survey over the phone. Administrators were informed that they could pass the survey completion task on to another teacher/administrator of their choice, and that they would receive a follow up phone call in upcoming weeks, in order to acquire their responses, in the event that the online survey was not completed. As a perk for completing the 5-minute survey, principals were offered a complimentary registration to a full-day technology symposium being hosted at the university in the spring. Fifty-six administrators accepted this offer and attended the event later in the year.

Out of 657 school principals contacted, 96 completed the survey. This response rate of 14.6% represented a reasonable sampling of the schools in the region with 4 charter schools and 13 private schools in addition to 79 public schools in the response set. Surveys were not anonymous, but were confidential, as far as keeping individual responses from being distributed. Principals supplied their school names, addresses and an email contact, so that researchers might follow up on specific responses from their schools, and data was aggregated and shared back to the districts for comparison and conversation. This type of protocol was utilized to support a more open and collegial model of working towards meaningful change, grounded in the philosophy of the Open Source and Open Education mindsets.

Because the survey included items that were both quantitative and qualitative in the response choices, a mixed methods approach was used to analyze and report the findings. This paper will present descriptive statistics regarding the initiatives listed in the Exploring/Deploying item of the instrument ("Please Indicate the Initiatives that your school is either deploying or exploring."[1]), and then follow with a synopsis of the themes emerging from the open-ended items of
- What other initiatives (not mentioned above) are you investigating or implementing to support student learning?
- What are your highest priorities, connected to student learning, for your school/district at this time?

**Results**

In response to the survey item "Please Indicate the Initiatives that your school is either deploying or exploring," Table 1 summarizes the information shared by the schools. In this first item, principals were asked to use the initiative list provided, which included BYOD (Bring Your Own Device) or one-to-one mobile devices for students. If they were exploring or deploying this initiative in their school, they provided details, as to the type of devices they were supporting (laptops, tablets, handhelds). In addition, adoption of digital textbooks (in lieu of paper texts), flipped classroom models, incorporation of blended or online course options, the use of online assessment tools, a focus on individualized or differentiated instruction, and the alignment of their work with the Partnership for 21st Century Skills were included in the survey prompt.

Table 1: Indicate initiatives that your school is either deploying or exploring

|  | Not Familiar | Exploring (talking about implementation) | Deploying (Actually doing) | Total Responses | Mean |
|---|---|---|---|---|---|
| BYOD (Bring Your Own Device) | 20 | 40 | 30 | 90 | 2.11 |
| One-to-One Mobile Devices for Students (identify below) | 13 | 52 | 26 | 91 | 2.14 |
| Laptops | 6 | 30 | 41 | 77 | 2.45 |

---

[1] This item was slightly problematic, in that responders should have been offered the choice Neither Exploring or Deploying. In the survey, other than "not familiar," responders were inherently forced to choose some sort of allegiance to the initiative, as exploring or deploying. It is possible that they could have been familiar with the initiative, but not interested in exploring or deploying it. However, responders could have chosen not to select a response.

| Tablets (iPads, etc.) | 10 | 35 | 41 | 86 | 2.38 |
|---|---|---|---|---|---|
| Handhelds (iPods, cell phones, etc.) | 12 | 29 | 27 | 68 | 2.22 |
| Digital Textbooks (online academic resources) | 18 | 52 | 20 | 90 | 2.02 |
| Flipped Classrooms | 32 | 40 | 16 | 88 | 1.82 |
| Online or Blended Classes | 24 | 42 | 26 | 92 | 2.02 |
| Online Assessment Tools | 9 | 36 | 58 | 103 | 2.48 |
| Individualized/Differentiated Instruction | 3 | 30 | 68 | 99 | 2.64 |
| P21 (Partnership for 21st Century Skills) Alignment | 32 | 38 | 17 | 87 | 1.83 |

Table 2: Additional statistical analysis of exploring/deploying variance of items

| Statistic | BYOD | One-to-One | Laptops | Tablets | Handhelds | Digital Textbooks | Flipped Classrooms | Online or Blended Classes | Online Assessment Tools | Individualized Differentiated Instruction | P21 Alignment |
|---|---|---|---|---|---|---|---|---|---|---|---|
| Min Value | 1 | 1 | 1 | 1 | 1 | 1 | 1 | 1 | 1 | 1 | 1 |
| Max Value | 3 | 3 | 3 | 3 | 3 | 3 | 3 | 3 | 3 | 3 | 3 |
| Mean | 2.11 | 2.14 | 2.45 | 2.36 | 2.22 | 2.02 | 1.82 | 2.02 | 2.48 | 2.64 | 1.83 |
| Variance | 0.55 | 0.41 | 0.41 | 0.47 | 0.53 | 0.43 | 0.52 | 0.55 | 0.43 | 0.29 | 0.54 |
| Standard Deviation | 0.74 | 0.64 | 0.64 | 0.68 | 0.73 | 0.65 | 0.72 | 0.74 | 0.65 | 0.54 | 0.73 |
| Total Responses | 90 | 91 | 77 | 86 | 68 | 90 | 88 | 92 | 103 | 99 | 87 |

From these responses, top initiatives identified included:
- Individualized/Personalized Instruction (2.64)
- Online Assessment Tools (2.48)
- One-to-One Deployment Laptops (2.45)
- One-to-One Deployment Tablets (2.38)
- One-to-One Deployment Handhelds (2.22)

As Table 2 indicates, the variance and Standard Deviation for these items were minimal, ranging from 029-0.53 and 0.54-0.73, respectively. Using these initiatives as possible themes, qualitative analysis of the open-ended response items were examined to provide more descriptive details as to the actions and priorities of the school districts. These are summarized below.

Initiatives and Priorities
Common Core, Assessment and Yearly Growth
In the open-ended survey responses principals addressed these two questions:
A. What other initiatives (not mentioned above) are you investigating or implementing to support student learning?
and
B. What are your highest priorities, connected to student learning, for your school/district at this time?

In their responses, school leaders overwhelming expressed allegiance to the Common Core and to the state assessment system (soon to be online). Many mentioned the PARCC (Herman & Linn, 2013) assessments specifically and that they were to be completely online in upcoming years. The desire to have students and teachers perform well, as gauged by these standards, assessments, and value-added parameters was paramount among approximately 20% of the responses submitted in this area. The following quote is representative of the comments received:

Our focus has been directed at improving scores in the state mandated assessments. (OAA< OGT). We are also preparing for new statewide, end-of-course exams that will be implemented in the next few years.

The development of new learning standards, formative assessments, and preparation for online assessments (PARCC) is also a priority.

The implementation of Ohio's New Learning Standards (Common Core State Standards, Ohio Revised Standards), technology integration included in curriculum maps, measuring student growth, and evaluation are all connected in this plan.

**Focus on One-to-One**
Along with their commitment to the standards and legislated assessments, principals espoused a strong allegiance to innovation, personalized learning experiences for students and 21st century skills. They spoke of "giving our staff the tools for learning that allow them to teach our students the way the students are learning with their personal devices at home while all the while maintaining the high standard of excellence that we demand from both staff and students." The commitment to connect the curriculum to student success beyond the classroom was evident in the explanations associated with the one-to-one deployments, which were mentioned in detail, providing the names of the devices (Chromebooks, iPads, laptops, BYOD, cell phones, etc.). One school leader stated, "Our priority is that students will learn the curriculum necessary to be successful in life. We are preparing students for the future. We want to make sure our students are receiving the best education possible with the best tools that are available."

In other words, school principals connected one-to-one deployment initiatives to providing more personalized learning environment for students. One commented that, "We want to see more individualized strategies, one-on-one teaching time…we want to spend more time making learning relational, but also use higher level thinking skills." Another said, "We want to raise the rigor of our instruction in order to prepare our students better for life after high school. We are implementing a more challenging curriculum, and we need to do more with lesson planning and assessing learning objectives." Finally, a principal described their broader vision, explaining,

> Regarding student learning, our focus is on creating/maintaining student centered classrooms that foster and promote creativity, communication, and collaboration. Instructional goals should always include relevance; students should utilize 21st century learning skills to solve real world problems. Learning best takes place during the application of knowledge to accomplish real work.

These statements provide context for the infusion of the digital technologies in these schools. A context that connects curriculum and standards to meaningful, personalized learning. Of course, not all comments were as lofty and promising, as one principal noted, "…but we also need to work on getting more use of technology by our teachers in their instruction. We have gone to BYOD, but our students have indicated they see no value in bringing such devices to school because they can't use them in the classroom." This observation ties in to multiple comments related to professional development for teachers, and these will be unpacked and addressed in another article, as they are currently beyond the scope of this piece.

**Discussion**
While it is apparent that school leaders are working to accommodate the legislative demands of the national Common Core curriculum, online PARCC achievement testing and value-added criteria for teachers, they are doing so with an eye towards preparing students for a future outside these parameters and restraints. Implementing one-to-one mobile device initiatives, while providing an infrastructure for online testing (PARCC) and access to other state and national assessment systems, creates opportunities for teachers and students to individualize, customize and differentiate

instruction for students. Teachers continue to need professional development, not only to learn more about how to integrate the digital tools and resources being provided in their schools, but to "retool" as educators that facilitate personalized learning environments for all of their students. The interconnected, communicative, responsive, data-rich world in which we live now makes this possible. It is up to these pioneers to lead the way.

## References

Au, W. (2011). Teaching under the new Taylorism: High-stakes testing and the standardization of the 21st century curriculum. *Journal of Curriculum Studies, 43*(1), 25-45.

Balfanz, R., Herzog, L., & MacIver, D. J. (2007). Preventing student disengagement and keeping students on the graduation path in urban middle-grades shools: Early identification and effective interventions. *Educational Psychologist, 42*(4), 223-235.

Barnett, R. (2012). Learning for an unknown future. *Higher Education Researh and Development, 31*(1), 65-77.

Barton, P. E. (2005). One-third of a nation: Rising dropout rates and declining opportnities (pp. 1-47): Policy Information Center.

Drexler, W. (2010). The networked student model for construction of personal learning environments: Balancing teacher control and student autonomy. *Australasian Journal of Educational Technology, 26*(3), 369-385.

Ertmer, P. A., & Ottenbreit-Leftwich, A. T. (2010). Teacher technology change: How knowledge, confidence, beliefs, and cluture intersect. *Journal of Research on Technology in Education, 42*(3), 255-284.

Hanushek, E. A., & Rivkin, S. G. (2010). Generalizations about using value-added measures of teacher quality. *American Economic Review, 100*(May), 267-271.

Henry, K. L., Knight, K. E., & Thornberry, T. P. (2012). School disengagement as a predictor of dropout, deinquency, and problem substance use during adolescence and early adulthood. *Journal of Youth and Adolescence, 41*(2), 156-166.

Herman, J., & Linn, R. (2013). On the road to assessing deeper learning: The status of Smarter Balanced and PARCC Assessment Consortia CRESST Report 823 (pp. 20). Los Angeles: CRESST.

Hwang, G.-J., Kuo, F.-R., Yin, P.-Y., & Chuang, K.-H. (2010). A heuristic algorithm for planning personalized learning paths for context-aware ubiquitous learning. *Computers and Education, 54*(2), 404-415.

Miller, R., & Lake, R. (2012). Federal Barriers to Innovation (pp. 1-14). Seattle, Washington: Center for Reinventing Public Education.

Sahlberg, P. (2008). Rethinking accountability in a knowledge society. *Journal of Educational Change, 11*, 45-61.

Wang, Y.-h., & Liao, H.-C. (2011). Data mining for adaptive learning in a TESL-based e-Learning system. *Expert Systems with Applications, 38*(6), 6480-6485.

Williams, R., Karousou, R., & Mackness, J. (2011). Emergent learning and learning ecologies in Web 2.0. *International Review of Research in Open and Distance Learning, 12*(3), 1-11.

# 19 Evaluating the Nature Tour Mobile Learning Application
Jenni Rikala, University of Jyvaskyla, Finland

**Introduction**

The present paper focuses on the implementation process of the Nature Tour mobile application in Finnish basic education setting. The Nature Tour mobile application was developed in the project *Personal Mobile Space for learning and well-being* at the University of Jyväskylä, Finland (see Kankaanranta, Neittaanmäki & Nousiainen, 2013). The primary aim of the Nature Tour mobile application is to enhance outdoor learning experiences by helping the field trip documentation. Therefore, the aim of the present study is to explore what kind of impact the Nature Tour mobile application has on outdoor learning experience. This was examined with case study conducted on one given basic school in Central Finland in the autumn of 2012.

Outdoor learning is one of the most practical educational methods for teaching a unique natural phenomenon in the world (Tan, Liu, Chang, 2007). In outdoor learning approach, students learn through experiences and relationships in the outdoor environments where they can see, hear, touch and smell the real things (Priest, 1986). Modern information and communication technologies can enhance the quality and experiences of outdoor learning in many ways (Osawa et al., 2007). For instance, real-life observations conjoin with access to digital technology and contents can at the best help learners make distinctions among different species (Shih et al., 2011). In turn, mobile applications that give the learners an opportunity to collect the content and express themselves can have a positive effect on the study motivation and involvement (Huizenga, Hordijk & Lubsen, 2008). The benefits of using mobile devices in outdoor learning have been discovered in several studies. For instance, when learners are using mobile devices they can express their own perspectives more freely and choose their own preferred route and speed to learn (Shih et al., 2011). In other words, learning can be delivered 'just-in-time,' 'just enough,' and 'just-for-me' (Traxler, 2007). Hence, learning would be more enjoyable and challenging for learners. Therefore, especially the benefits to study motivation and learning achievements have been highlighted (e.g., Tan, Liu and Chang, 2007, Chen et al., 2008, Hwang, Shi and Chu, 2011). Also, considerable changes in teacher teaching and student learning have been reported (e.g. Zhang et al., 2010).

In this study, the feasibility as well as outdoor learning experiences were tested through a developed framework which includes the core characteristics of mobile learning. The teacher and student questionnaires were used to collect the data immediately after the experiment.

In the following sections the mobile learning framework, the developed mobile application, as well as the context of Finnish basic education are discussed. After this, the experimental investigation and the results are reported. Finally, the paper is concluded with reflective remarks.

## The Mobile Learning Framework

The first version of the mobile learning framework, which was tested with the case study related to the Nature Tour mobile learning application in early childhood education settings (see Rikala & Kankaanranta, 2014), advanced two theoretical frameworks introduced by Koole (2009) and Kearney et al. (2012). The framework consisted of two levels titled core level and medium level. The aspects such as context, time and space formed the core level of the framework. The medium level, in turn, comprised the other important aspects, which were the learner aspect, device aspect and social aspect. The study conducted on early childhood education settings indicated that the pedagogical aspect is one noticeable aspect and should be included in the framework (Rikala & Kankaanranta, 2014). The pedagogical aspect or pedagogical practices as those are titled in the revised version of the framework are highlighted, for instance, by Parsons et al. (2007), Nordin et al. (2010) and Ozdamli (2012) in their frameworks.

After an inclusive analysis of the various characteristics, a new framework is proposed (See Figure 1). The revised version of the framework separates the experience and mobile learning process. The experience is seen as the result of the mobile learning activity and mobile learning process. The characteristics that are incorporated to mobile learning experience are time-space, spontaneity and personality. The core characteristics of the mobile learning process, which are also affecting the mobile learning experience, are the learner, device and social aspect. These aspects are also intersecting, which means that when learners are conducting mobile learning activity, learners may move in within different physical and virtual locations and participate and interact with each other as well as with information and systems (Koole, 2009). The learner aspect refers to an individual learner's cognitive abilities, memory, emotions, possible motivation, attitudes, experiences, which are in a significant role in the learning process as Koole (2009) has highlighted in FRAME model. In the device aspect the physical, technical, and functional characteristics of the mobile device are emphasized as these characteristics influence the device usability, which in turn, influence the learner's experience (Koole, 2009). The social aspect, in turn, is associated with the process of social interaction and cooperation whose importance as part of the learning process cannot be underestimated (Koole, 2009).

The pedagogical practices strongly influence on the learning activity, mobile learning process, as well as how and what kind of mobile learning experience arises. In other words, the teacher's contribution is significant as the teacher is planning the situations in which the mobile application is used, the learning goals and contents and how learners are going to use mobile technology to achieve the learning goals; in outdoor learning approach to design the interactions with people, application, information, and natural resources. For this reason the pedagogical practices are included in the external level of the framework..

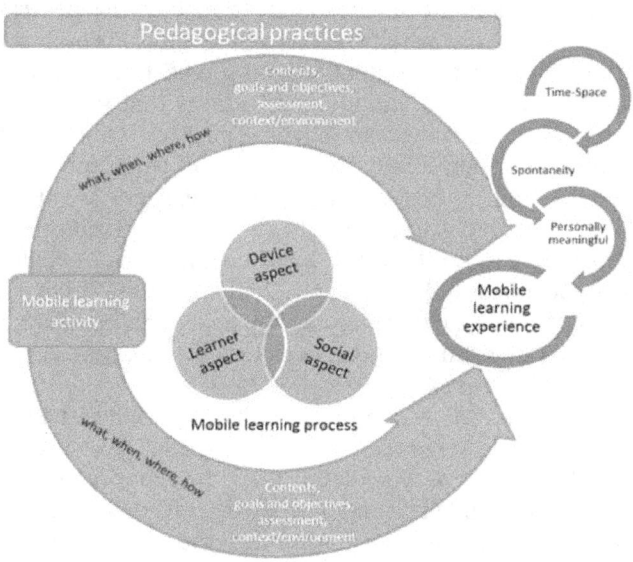

**Figure 1.** The mobile learning framework.

In this study, this mobile learning framework provides an evaluation framework, in which the learning experience and the feasibility of the Nature Tour mobile application are analyzed. The main interest is to explore what kind of impact the Nature Tour mobile application has on outdoor learning experience. The expected results are: 1) Mobile application can transcend spatial and temporal restrictions, i.e. support learning anywhere and anytime; 2) Mobile learning experience is personalized as well as motivating for learners; 3) Mobile devices and applications are easy-to-use, intuitive and help learners to concentrate on the task, not the device itself; 4) In mobile learning experience learners can exchange information and acquire knowledge with rich connections to other people and resources mediated by a mobile device; 5) The pedagogical practices influence on the learning activity, mobile learning process as well as mobile learning experience.

## The Nature Tour Mobile Application

The Nature Tour Mobile Application (Luontoretki in Finnish) (see Figure 2) was developed in the project Personal Mobile Space for learning and well-being at the University of Jyväskylä, Finland (see Kankaanranta, Neittaanmäki & Nousiainen, 2013). The primary objective of the mobile application is to improve children's outdoor learning experiences by helping the documentation of the field trips. The continuity of the learning experience can be promoted with activities before and after the field trip. For instance, before the field trip, children can familiarize themselves with plants, animals or fungi as the mobile application is associated with a web page which contains relevant information. After the field trip, the children can view the recorded observations and, for example, create stories. The web page also gives the opportunity to compare what species or phenomena have been observed across country.

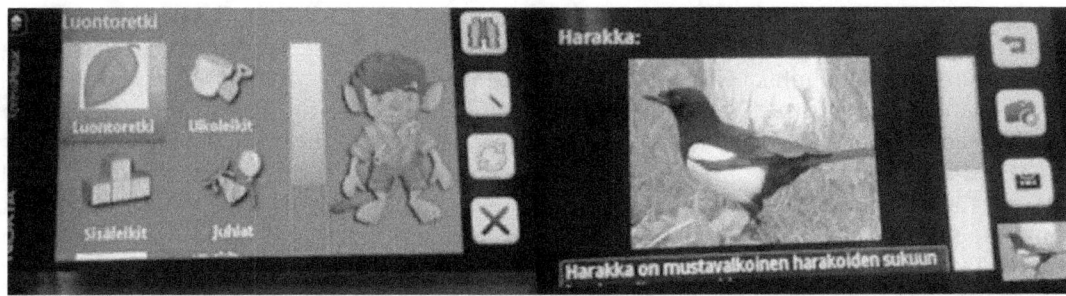

**Figure 2.** The Screen captures of the Nature Tour Mobile Application.

The function of the mobile application is to help recording observations during the field trip. The mobile application allows the user to save observations with photographs or audio recordings and to send these recordings to the web page, where they can be viewed later. The application contains category Nature Tour which includes the subcategories of different species. The user can have relevant information (e.g., picture and core information) about the species by choosing the species from the subcategories. The camera and record button give the user the opportunity to record observations. For instance, a child can try to take a picture of domestic bird (e.g. the great tit or mallard duck) or try to record it chirping or quaking. The application also contains other categories that allow the wider use of the mobile application in daily life. For instance, the application allows daily meteorological observations.

The mobile application requires the ability to read. The older children are able to use the application by themselves, but with younger children it requires adult guidance. Even though the application is designed to provide concrete experiences in nature, the teacher's contribution still is significant. The teacher plans the situations in which the application is used, the learning goals and how learners are going to use the application to achieve these learning goals. In other words, the application use requires balance between the curricula, student's needs and human interactions, in other words pedagogy. Hence, the application by itself does not guarantee the quality or meaningfulness of the outdoor learning experience. For instance, in outdoor learning approach it is important to design the activities and interactions with people and natural resources.

In other words, it is important to realize that technology-based activity does not exist ready-made in a piece of software. The same software can generate whole different activities in different classrooms and with different groups. Therefore, learning activities are always constituted through a situated interaction of the pupils, teachers and technologies. Thus, the learning culture impacts significantly on the use of technologies and softwares. (Mercer and Littleton, 2007.)

## Basic Education in Finland

In Finland children usually begin compulsory basic education in the year when a child has his/her seventh birthday. The role of basic education is to promote pupils' growth into humane individuals and ethically responsible members of society as well as to provide them with the knowledge and skills needed in life. After basic education, a young person can continue study (either general upper secondary school or vocational education and training) or enter working life. (Finnish National Board of Education, 2012)

The Finnish National Board of Education decides on the national core curriculum which includes the objectives and core contents of different subjects, as well as the principles of assessment and working approaches. The education providers (the local education authorities and the schools) usually draw up their own curricula on the basis of the framework of the national core curriculum. (Finnish National Board of Education, 2011)

The teachers, however, can choose their own teaching methods and have the freedom to select their own teaching materials to achieve the objectives stated in the curriculum. Some guidelines for choosing suitable methods are included in the national curriculum. The national curriculum, for instance, emphasizes the active role of the student. (Finnish National Board of Education, 2011)

Mobile technologies (especial tablet devices) have made an inroad in an educational context little by little in Finland too. There are for example projects funded by the Finnish National Board of Education that are aiming to bring updated information and action models to people implementing mobile technologies such as tablets at education (The Finnish National Board of Education, 2013). The aim is especially to integrate mobile devices into learning in such way that learning can happen in an authentic context (Silander, 2011). Unfortunately, many authorities and educators are not early adopters of these kinds of new technologies. The textbook still has a central role, and printed books are involved daily routines to teach different subjects in the curriculum. In other words, ICT has not widely integrated into schools and educational practices in Finland. For instance, there are large differences between regions, schools and grades in terms of educational use of ICT (Kankaanranta, Palonen, Kejonen & Ärje, 2011).

## The Study

The present study is an exploratory case study that examines the learning experience and the feasibility of the Nature Tour mobile application in one given basic education context in Central Finland. The case study is part of the TEKES (Finnish Technology Agency) funded project Personal Mobile Space for learning and well-being led by professor Pekka Neittaanmäki and Marja Kankaanranta, the University of Jyväskylä.

The main interest of the present case study is to explore what kind of impact the Nature Tour mobile application has on outdoor learning experience. The use of a case study method is appropriate as it can give understanding of perspectives, opinions and expectations of the smart phone usage and application as well as the learning experiences. At best the conclusions and explanations of the case study can be the most generalizable aspect of a case study. The collected data may be specific to a particular school, or student, or teacher, but the conclusions and explanations can be usable and generalizable in understanding how other schools, or students, of teachers work (Gillham, 2010, p. 12)

Nineteen second grade students (aged 7-8 years) and their teacher participated in the Nature Tour mobile application experiment in the autumn of 2012. The objective of the outdoor learning experience was to explore the local area trees. The aim was to record tree leaf observations with the Nature Tour mobile application. In other words, the mobile application helped to record observations during the field trip. These recordings were sent to the web page where they were printed out after the field trip. Based on the printed pictures the students tried to identify trees. The students also draw leaf structure pictures based on the printed pictures and constructed a memory game. In other words, the learning experience also included activities after the field trip.

The research data was collected with teacher and student questionnaires immediately after the experiment. The teacher questionnaire included fifteen open-ended questions of which fourteen thematically related to core characteristics of mobile learning (the context, time & space, device aspect, learner aspect, the social aspect and pedagogical aspect). The student questionnaire included fifteen questions of which one was open-ended, and others were scaled questions. The questions in the student questionnaire related to smart phone usage and especially to the learning experience.

# Findings

The Nature tour implementation was evaluated through a mobile learning framework (see Figure 1). The expected results were: 1) Mobile application can transcend spatial and temporal restrictions, i.e. support learning anywhere and anytime; 2) Mobile learning experience is personalized as well as motivating for learners; 3) Mobile devices and applications are easy-to-use, intuitive and help learners to concentrate on the task, not the device itself; 4) In mobile learning experience learners can exchange information and acquire knowledge with rich connections to other people and resources mediated by a mobile device; 5) The pedagogical practices influence on the learning activity, mobile learning process as well as mobile learning experience. These results are described and discussed in the following chapters.

## 1) Mobile Devices Can Transcend Spatial and Temporal Restrictions, i.e. Support Learning Anywhere and Any Time

In this experiment, the learning was extended outside the classroom. The objective was to explore local area trees and particularly tree leaves. The use of the application was also linked to classroom teaching and learning as the recorded observations were used after the field trip. The application, therefore, combined virtual and physical space as well as extended learning outside the classroom. According to the teacher, the implementation of the mobile application and linking its use as part of daily routines was easy. The experiment, therefore, indicated that the Nature Tour mobile application is easy to use and it at its best can support learning anytime and anywhere.

## 2) Mobile Learning Experience is Personalized and Motivating for Learners

The teacher commented that the application suited well for all students, and there was no need to adapt the use of application in any way. He also added that the application evidently increased student motivation as it made possible for every student to record their own observations easily during the field trip. The teacher also mentioned that the application allows the students to observe nature new and different way compared with the traditional field trip.

The students were very curious about the new approach that deviated from their routine exercises. 37% of the students reported that the experiment was great. 44% of the students, in turn, reported that the experiment was very nice. 13% of the students argued that the experiment was nice, and 6% of the students reported that it was OK. In other words, students viewed the experiment very positive, and nearly all (95%) of the students reported that they would like to use mobile application again.

The benefits that the teacher especially highlighted in his answers were related to the study motivation. The teacher commented: *"The students were able to work with their own material, and this clearly increased the student interest and motivation."* The teacher furthermore added that one of the best experiences for him was to observe the student enthusiasm and that the students were skillful and used mobile application without problems. As many as 84% of the students reported that the application inspired them to observe nature very much and 16% of the students reported that the application somewhat inspired them to observe nature. 89% of the students reported that the use of the application was interesting. In open-ended answers, the students for instance commented: *"It was fun to take pictures.", "It was nice to be on a field trip and to take pictures."*

In other words, learning experience was personalized and motivating for the students. In the field, the children were able to work their own pace and photograph things that they wanted. The students were motivated to observe nature and record their observations. The teacher commented, *"The students wanted to make observations and take good pictures without that teacher had to supervise them."*

### 3) Mobile Devices and Applications are Easy-To-Use, Intuitive and Help Learners to Concentrate on the Task, Not the Device Itself

All the students already had some experiences of mobile device usage. According to the teacher, the students were enthusiastic and liked very much that the mobile device usage was linked to teaching and learning. He furthermore added that the students reported that the use of the application was easy. This observation made by the teacher is also consistent with questionnaire answers. As much as 89% of the students agreed with the statement Nature Trip application was easy-to-use. Only 11% of the students argued that the application was not easy-to-use. Nor was the small screen problematic. As much as 89% of the students reported that viewing and reading the smart phone screen was easy.

No major technical problems occurred during the experiments even though the smart phones that were used in the experiment were loaned. These loaned smart phones have been utilized in several experiments that have an effect on their reliability. The answers also indicate that some minor problems with reliability occurred as 47% of the students disagreed with the statement The smart phone always functioned as I wanted. However, these problems did not interfere with the field trip as the teacher commented *"The field trip went well, and the students liked to use a mobile application. There were no problems."* Because the use of the device and application was easy for the students, and the instructions were clear, the attention was drawn to nature, not to other irrelevant things. In other words, the learners were concentrating on the task, not the device itself.

### 4) In Mobile Learning Experience Learners can Exchange Information and Acquire Knowledge With Rich Connections to Other People and Resources Mediated by a Mobile Device

In this experiment, the mobile technology was not used for mediate collaboration or social interactions. However, according to the teacher, the students eagerly showed their photographs to him after the field trip. The mobile application clearly encouraged social interaction with an adult. At its best, the application could promote dialogue and discussion, for instance, about species.

The application was mainly used to record observations with photographs. The application also contains information about species, but only 22% of the students reported that they used a lot of time to read information texts, and as much as 78% reported that they used no time or some extent time to read information texts. In other words, the students did not use the information texts of the mobile application to acquire new knowledge. However, the observations recorded during the field trip were utilized to acquire knowledge after the field trip. Hence, in a way, mobile technology helped students to acquire knowledge.

### 5) The Pedagogical Practices Influence on the Learning Activity, Mobile Learning Process as well as Mobile Learning Experience.

The experiment turned out to be successful especially because in the background of the implementation there was a well-defined pedagogical goal; learn to identify most common types of trees as well as investigate and compare leaf structures. According to the teacher, the clear pedagogical goal helped make the field trip situation more organized because the students were concentrating on the task not to other irrelevant things. The study, therefore, indicated that the technology use requires balance between the curricula, student's needs and human interactions, in other words pedagogy.

As the field trip situation was organized and the instruction was clear for the students, it was easier to guide students to search and observe nature more goal-oriented. At the same time, students were able to construct their own material and work with their own pace. The teacher argued that the mobile application use was beneficial in terms of teaching and learning. Application act as an aide, but also gave opportunity work different ways inside and outside the classroom.

## Conclusions

In this study, the main interest was to explore what kind of impact the Nature Tour mobile application has on outdoor learning experience. The Nature Tour mobile application experiment turned out to be a successful experiment. The experiment indicated that the Nature Tour mobile application is easy to use anytime and anywhere. The children were able to use the application outdoors without problems. Linking the use meaningfully into the classroom practices was also easy. All in all, the learning experience became meaningful as well as motivating for the students.

Hence, the mobile application brought motivating and engaging element in learning. The mobile technologies benefits' to study motivation have been highlighted in various earlier works (e.g., Tan, Liu and Chang, 2007, Chen et al., 2008, Hwang, Shi and Chu, 2011). In this experiment, especially the fact that the students were able to work with their own material increased the students' interest and motivation. The observation is consistent with Huizenga, Hordijk & Lubsen (2008) who argued that mobile applications that give the learner opportunity to collect the content and express themselves can have a positive effect on the involvement and motivation.

The experiment also indicated that the device and application are easy-to-use. All this combined with clear instructions and pedagogical goal made the learning process, and situation more organized and the students were concentrating on the task, not the device itself. It was also encouraging to find out that the Nature Tour mobile application stimulated interactions with the adults. Though, the social aspect is slightly questionable as the mobile technology was not used for mediating collaboration.

Traxler (2009) has argued that mobile learning is an inherently very noisy phenomenon where context is everything, and confounding variables abound. For this reason, the positive results may also be caused by some other factors. The novelty effect, for example, is one of the intrinsic shortages of mobile learning research. The novelty effect according to Cheung and Hew (2009) means that learners and teachers are more likely to use technology because it is new to them, compared with participants who have used technology for a longer period. Hence, the novelty effect may bias the results in some extent. For this reason, there should be longer-term experiments that would help to delimit the novelty effect. The repetition of the approach for a longer time would also give more evidence of the feasibility of the approach. Also, the learning outcomes and motivations as well as the effect of educational activity outside the classroom should be investigated more systematically. Shih et al. (2011) have argued that real-life observations conjoin with access to digital technology and contents can help learners to make distinctions, for example, between plants. In this study, it is impossible to specify the role of mobile application in the learning process, even though the teacher argued that the students learned the most common types of trees as well as leaf structure.

The experiment indicated that the pedagogical practices strongly influence on the learning activity, mobile learning process, as well as mobile learning experience. According to the teacher, the mobile application can act as an aid, but especially with young children there must be real-life observations and experiences for instance something concrete to touch, smell and in some cases to taste. The significance of the activity design and pedagogical practices increases because the application by itself does not guarantee the quality or meaningfulness of the outdoor learning experience. Even though the application is designed to provide concrete experiences in nature, the teacher is a person who plans the situations in which the application is used, the learning goals and how learners are going to use a mobile application to achieve these learning goals. In this experiment, especially the clear pedagogical goal made the activity organized and helped the teacher to guide the students to observe nature more goal oriented. As a consequence, students were motivated, engaged and were concentrating on the task and according to the teacher learned to identify the most common types of trees, to explore the leaf structure and to compare different types of leaves with each other.

## References

Chen, W., Tan, N., Looi, C.-K., Zhang, B.H., and Seow, P. (2008). Handheld computers as cognitive tools: technology-enhanced environmental learning. In, *Research and Practice in Technology Enabled Learning* (pp. 231-252), vol. 3, no.3.

Cheung, W.S., and Hew, K.F. (2009). A review of research methodologies used in studies on mobile handheld devices in K-12 and higher education settings. In, *Australasian Journal o Educational Technology* (pp. 153-183), 25(2).

Finnish National Board of Education. (2008). Education in Finland. Retrieved from http://www.oph.fi/download/124278_education_in_finland.pdf

Finnish National Board of Education. (2011). The Curriculum. Retrieved from http://www.oph.fi/english/education/basic_education/curriculum

Finnish National Board of Education. (2012). Basic Education. Retrieved from http://www.oph.fi/english/education/basic_education

Finnish National Board of Education. (2013). Oppimisympäristöhankkeet. Retrieved from http://www.oph.fi/oppimisymparistohankkeet

Gillham, B. (2010). *Case study research methods*. London: Continuum International Publishing.

Hwang, G.-J., Shi, Y.-R., and Chu, H.-C. (2011). A concept map approach to develop collaborative mindtools for context-aware ubiquitous learning. In, *British Journal of Educational Technology* (pp. 778-789), vol. 42, no. 5.

Huizemga, J., Hordijk, R., and Lubsen, A. (2008). *The world as learning environment: playful and creative use of GPS and mobile technology in education*.

Kankaanranta, M., Neittaanmäki, P., and Nousiainen, T. (Eds) (2013). *Arjen mobiilipalvelut -hankkeen oppimisen ja hyvinvoinnin ratkaisut. [Mobile solutions for learning and well-being]*. Univeristy of Jyväskylä.

Kankaanranta, M., Palonen, T., Kejonen, T., and Ärje, J. (2011). In, M. Kankaanranta (Ed.), *Opetusteknologia koulun arjessa* (pp. 47-76). Jyväskylä: Jyväskylän yliopisto, Koulutuksen tutkimuslaitos.

Kearney, M., Schuck, S., Burden, K. and Aubusson, P. (2012). Viewing mobile learning from a pedagogical perspective. In, *Research in Learning Technology*, 20.

Koole, M.L. (2009). A Model for Framing Mobile Learning, In Mohamed, A. (ed.) *Mobile Learning: Transforming the Delivery of Education and Training* (pp. 25-50). Edmonton, AB, CAN: Athabasca Univeristy Press.

Mercer, N. and Littleton, K. (2007). *Dialogue and the development of children's thinking : a sociocultural approach*. London New York: Routledge.

Nordin, N., Embi M. A., Yunus, M. Md. (2010). Mobile Learning Framework for Lifelong Learning. In, *Procedia – Social and Behavioral Sciences*, (pp. 130-138), volume 7.

Osawa, N., Noda, K., Tsukagoshi, S., Noma, Y., Ando, A., Shinuya, T., and Kondo, K. (2007). Outdoor Education Support System with Location Awareness Using RFID and Symbology Tags. In, *Journal of Educational Multimedia and Hypermedia* (pp. 411-428), vol. 16(4).

Ozdamli, F. (2012). Pedagogical framework of m-learning. In, *Procedia – Social and Behavioral Sciences*, (pp. 927-931), volume 31.

Parsons, D., Ryu, H., & Cranshaw, M. (2007). A Design Requirements Framework for Mobile Learning Environments. In, *Journal of Computers*, (pp. 1-8), vol 2, no 4.

Priest, S. (1986). Redefinging Outdoor Education: A Matter of Many Relationships. In, *Journal of Environmental Education*, (pp. 13-15) vol 17 no 3.

Rikala, J, & Kankaanranta, M. (2014). The Nature Tour Mobile Learning Application - Implementing the mobile application in Finnish early childhood settings. In, *Proceedings of the 6th International Coference on Computer Supported Education*, (pp. 171-178), vol 3.

Silander, P. (2012). Mobiilioppimisen malleja ja menetelmiä. Retrieved from https://docs.google.com/document/d/1XtSS_mfa8fXRT3WJtQRuU0_1qPL1yxiiupk7C-GQg0w/edit

Shih, J.-L., Chu, H.-C., Hwang, G.-J., and Kinshuk. (2011). An investigation of attitudes of students and teachers about participating in a context-aware ubiquitous learning activity. In, *British Journal of Educational Technology* (pp. 373-394), vol. 42(3).

Tan, T.-H., Liu, T.-Y., and Chang, C.-C. (2007). Development and Evaluation of an RFID-based Ubiquitous Learning Environment for Outdoor Learning. In, *Interactive Learning Environments* (pp.253-269), vol. 15, no. 3.

Traxler, J. (2007). Defining, Discussing and Evaluating Mobile Learning: the moving finger writes and having writ . . . . In, *The International Review of Research in Open and Distance Learning*, Vol 8, No 2. Retrieved from http://www.irrodl.org/index.php/irrodl/article/view/346/875

Traxler, J. (2009). Current State of Mobile Learning. In A. Mohamed (Ed.) *Mobile Learning: Transforming the delivery of Education and Training* (99. 9-24), Athabasca University Press, Edmonton, Canada.

Zhang, B.H., Looi, C.-K., Seow, P., Chia, G., Wong, L.-H., Chen, W., So, H.-J., Soloway, E., and Norris, C. Deconstructing and reconstructing: Transforming primary science learning via a mobilized curriculum. In, *Computers & Education* (pp. 1504-1523), vol. 55.

## Acknowledgements

I would like to express my sincere gratitude all the students and the teacher who made this study possible through their participation in the case study. The case study was part of the TEKES (Finnish Technology Agency) funded project *Personal Mobile Space for learning and well-being* led by professor Pekka Neittaanmäki and Marja Kankaanranta, University of Jyväskylä, Finland.

# 20 Design and Implementation of Strategies and Artifacts to Support Ubiquitous Computing In and Outside the Classroom: A reflective case study

Alan Amory, University of Johannesburg, South Africa

## Introduction

The chronicle presented here explores how the University of Johannesburg, South Africa, developed and implemented strategies and artifacts to support learning, using mobile devices both inside and outside the classroom. Herrington and Herrington (2007) argued that mobile technologies, allied with suitable theoretical frameworks, have the capacity to transform teaching and learning that is more than just a novelty and a tool for information redistribution. In this paper the context of the case study is given, followed by an exploration of a teaching and learning institutional policy and an associated framework for the use of ubiquitous computing. Thereafter, the development of mobile-friendly applications and strategies to support the use of mobile devices are presented. Lastly, the development of these approaches and assets developed are discussed in relationship to theories related to disruption (Christensen, 2008) and innovation (Crossan & Apaydin, 2010). Work described here should allow future researchers to investigate how "wireless, mobile technologies [might affect] the learning environment, pedagogy, and campus life" (Alexander, 2004). This narrative is about my reflections of the events associated with the development of strategies and artifacts for this project.

| Faculty | Enrolment |
|---|---|
| Art, Design and Architecture | 1 207 |
| Economic and Financial Sciences | 11 495 |
| Education | 3 886 |
| Engineering and the Built Environment | 8 323 |
| Health Sciences | 3 635 |
| Humanities | 6 827 |
| Law | 1 580 |
| Management | 8 320 |
| Science | 3 524 |
| Total | 48 797 |

**Table 1.** Headcount enrolment figures per faculty for 2013

## Context of the study

The University of Johannesburg is one of the largest residential South African universities, with four campuses situated in the greater metropolis of Johannesburg. Fifty-six percent of the student population of about 50 000 attend class on the Auckland Park Kingsway campus, 16.7 percent on the Auckland Park Bunting Road campus, 16.2 percent on the Doornfontein campus and 11.1 percent on the Soweto campus. In 2013 there were 48 797 registered students who studied in nine faculties (Table 1). As a comprehensive institution, the University of Johannesburg offers students scientific and technical study programmes, but it not aligned to a medical school. Of the 2013 student cohort 13.6 percent were postgraduate students. All the South African culture identities are part of the university and reflect regional diversity.

Teaching and learning activities are supported by Academic Support Services that include Academic Development and Support, the Library and Information Centre, the Internationalisation Office, Research and Postgraduate Studies, Community Engagement, and the Information and Communication Systems. In addition, the management of the institution includes activities associated with Human Resources, Institutional Advancement, Intuitional Planning, Evaluation and Monitoring, Operations and Administration (academic, central, corporate and general).

With respect to research production the university is one of the top six ranked institutions in South Africa. Over the past 5 years national research output has tripled at institutional level (from 326 to 873.91 units), and doubled at country level to 7.1% (873.91 of 12 363.81 units in 2012).

Information and communication technologies support all aspects of the work of the university, including student information, human resources and the financial system; and the use of web services for the institutional intranet and Internet, student portal and Edulink (the institutional Learning Management System – Blackboard). The University of Johannesburg's Internet includes a mobile component for access to pertinent information via cellular phones and other mobile devices.

## Teaching and learning philosophy

Amory, Gravett and Van der Westhuizen (2008) wrote a concept document for the University of Johannesburg to support 21$^{st}$ century teaching and learning. They argued that the institution needed to conceptualize students as becoming practitioners of a knowledge and professional domain, and suggested that recitation of information (an information-oriented position) approach limited learning, and that Information and Communication Technologies (ICT) should be used in innovative ways to enrich student experiences. These concepts formed the basis for the institutional teaching and learning philosophy policy, which included the following:

"UJ recognizes the complexity and rapidly changing nature of the social, economic and intellectual environment for which its students are being prepared. It is imperative, therefore, that teaching and learning at UJ should transform a primary concern with the transmission of knowledge (*learning about*) to a primary concern with the practices of a knowledge domain (*learning to be*). Therefore, in its teaching and learning activities and in the design of its modules and programmes, and within the parameters of reasonably practicable implementation, it recognizes the need:

- For teaching to be concerned with the enabling of learning that supports *social* and *individual* knowledge constructions;
- For learning to be concerned with the transformation of *information into knowledge*, and for such knowledge to encompass more than mere learning about the facts, concept systems and processes of a particular knowledge domain, but to equip students with an enquiring mind;
- For students to engage meaningfully and willingly with learning content that is part of a *learning task* within a learning environment that supports collaboration, and for its students to act purposefully in such an environment;
- For teaching and learning to nurture the traits of *thinking* and the various practices of a particular knowledge domain; and
- For students to experience knowledge not as a mere static product of information production and consumption, but as a process and *instrument of inquiry* to solve problems."

(University of Johannesburg Senate document SEN 252/2008, p. 5, my emphasis)

## Case themes

At the start of 2012 three events influenced the use of technology to support teaching and learning in the institution:
- The leadership of the Information and Communication Systems, Library and Information Services, and learning technology components of Academic Development and Support – the Centre for Academic Technologies – divisions changed.
- The Vice-Chancellor appointed a consultant to support the use of ICT more broadly in the institution.
- A new committee was established to oversee the closer integration of ICT into institutional practices (IT Advisory Committee).

The core objectives that arose from these changes were to support the development of a 21st skilled academia, alignment of the use of technology in teaching and learning to institutional policies, development of "finger-ready" applications to support the widespread use of mobile devices by staff and students, and providing ubiquitous access to information to the university community. However, to realize these aims, the institution needed to address a number of issues. Professional development in the use of ICT in teaching, learning and assessment was limited to training academic members of staff in the use of Blackboard, the institutional Leaning Management System. This could be viewed as a *learning from technology* position (Jonassen & Reeves, 1996) contrary to the institutional teaching and learning philosophy that posited a *learning with technology* approach. Therefore, a new framework was developed to align teaching and learning practices with the institutional *learning with technology* teaching and learning philosophy (Theme 1). As a result, the skill development sessions for staff and students and professional workshops on learning with technology for academic members were redesigned and aligned with this new framework (Theme 2). The institutional Internet provided resources to the wider community, to potential students who wished to be part of the UJ community, and to staff and registered students (multiple audiences both inside and outside the institution). Student notices, resources and management tools were part of the Student Portal and online teaching tools were available through the Edulink portals. The look-and-feel of these two portals reflected interface designs prevalent before the advent of mobile devices. The introduction of mobile devices into the system required the development of portals for use by mobile devices and allowed a redesign of information architecture (Theme 3). A number of issues were related to ubiquitous access to information, including the institutional network, e-books and devices for underprivileged students managed by the IT Advisory Committee (Theme 4).

## Theme 1: Learning with technology framework

It is well understood that collaboration is an important component of learning (Piaget, 1977; Vygotsky, 1978). Today, social media is an integral part of social dialogue and collaboration (Moran, Seaman, & Tinti-Kane, 2011). Amory (2012) posited that authentic learning tasks (Brown, Collins & Duguid, 1989; Newmann, Bryk & Nagaoka, 2001; Reeves, Herrington & Oliver, 2004; Smeets, 2005) promote effective learning, especially when constructed as the *object of the activity* (Engeström, 1987; Leont'ev, 1978; Vygotsky, 1978). Furthermore, Amory suggested that educational technologies should act as tools to facilitate knowledge construction, thus supporting a *learning with technology* position (Jonassen & Reeves, 1996). Therefore, the learning with technology framework integrates collaboration (C), authentic learning (A) and tool/technology (T) into a framework (Table 2). This CAT framework makes use of the authentic task definition from the work of Reeves et al. (2004) rather than the more recent conceptualization by (Herrington, Reeves, & Oliver, 2010) that uses abstract concepts, which might be difficult to grasp for lecturers not well versed in educational theories.

| Collaboration | Authentic learning | | Tool/Technological |
|---|---|---|---|
| We learn from each other | Have real-world relevance | Provide opportunity for reflection | Information stream |
| Social media connects us | Are ill-defined | Are integrated across different subject areas | Enabler of communication |
| | Are complex | | Empowering collaboration |
| Together we create new ideas, connections and products | Provide opportunities to examine from different perspectives | Are integrated with assessment | Information transformation tool |
| | | Yield polished products | Professional tool |
| Course facilitators create environments for social change | Provide opportunity for collaboration | Allow for competing solutions and outcomes | |

**Table 2.** The Collaboration-Authentic learning-Tool/technology framework

The tool/technology part of the framework includes ways in which technology can be used in the classroom and also embraces the concept of explicit and implicit tool mediation (Wertsch, 2007). Explicit mediation involves the intentional introduction of a tool into an existing activity that is obvious. Implicit mediation involves language and higher order cognitive actions that are not always obvious. The CAT framework posits the unit of analysis is learning, and not the use of technology (Amiel & Reeves, 2008) and thereby notions of e-learning and m-learning, which explore electronic text and mobile devices respectively, to support learning are re-imagined as tools that mediate learning outcomes.

### Theme 2: Skill and professional development

Prior to 2012 two routes were available to aid the academic community: student and staff technical support, and training workshops. A new approach to provide staff and student technical skills is centered on a single help desk, supported by a modern "ticketing" software system to monitor, manage and track queries. In addition, self-service and online resources to develop technical skills are part of the approach. The first is a mobile application for smartphones that include solutions to the problems most often experienced by staff and students (uHelp – Mobile – see below). Additional support from this application can be obtained by sending an SMS or email to the help desk, or by making a phone call. Other self-development services available are comprehensive websites to help staff involved in the development of Blackboard modules (uHelp – Web and Blackboard on-demand). Therefore, support is provided via a mobile app, websites, and multiple routes to an integrated help desk where, when necessary, problems might be solved through one-on-one interactions (Fig. 1). To support Information and Communication Technology (ICT) literacy a number of interventions were developed. During the First Year Seminar (orientation), workshops on ICT and tablet use are provided. These are extended to a number of workshops available during timetabled term time to both students and staff (Fig. 1).

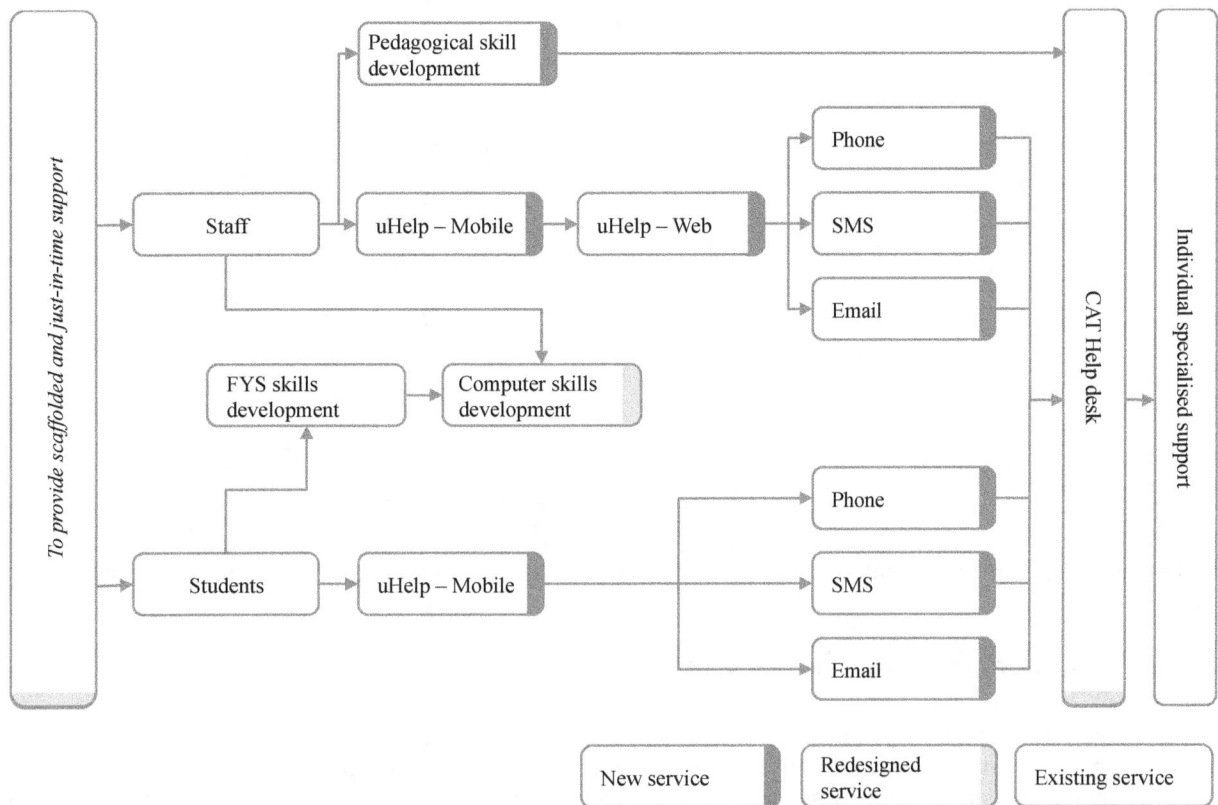

**Figure 1.** Redesign of support and skill development services for staff and students to support computer literacy and skill development

For the support of teaching with technology new staff development workshops were developed, tested and implemented (Fig. 2). The introduction of the CAT framework to academic members included the distribution, via paper and online documents, of an easy-to-read z-folder that was summarized in a single page handout. In addition, a number of workshops were developed to explore the CAT framework, authentic learning, use of social media in teaching and learning, and the pedagogical use of mobile devices in the classroom. The intention of the workshops is to model the CAT framework approach to support contemporary pedagogical approaches that are aligned with the institutional teaching and learning philosophy.

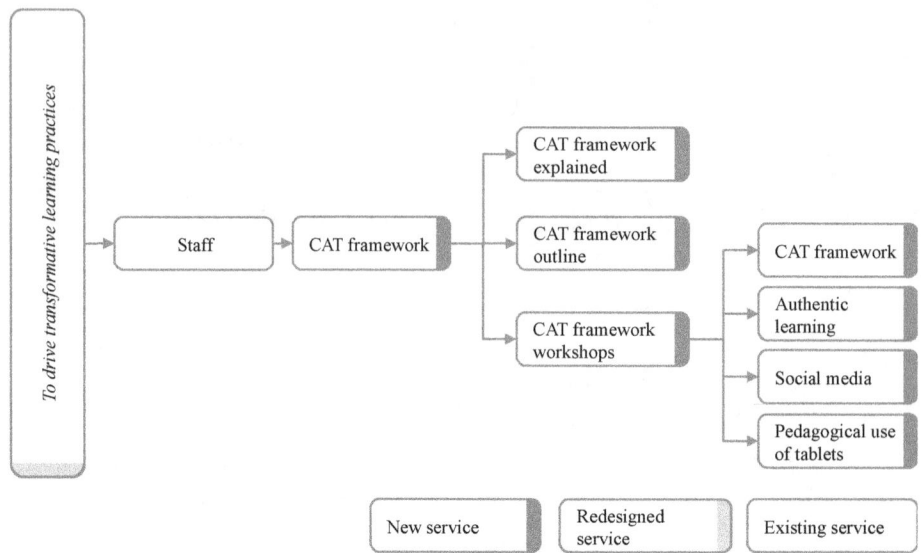

**Figure 2.** Outline of professional development opportunities to support the transformation of teaching practices

## Theme 3: Resources for mobile devices

To realize the vision of a totally connected UJ community, it was necessary to re-imagine ways in which the community interacted with institutional resources when connected via smartphones and tablets. Therefore, over the past two years the Centre for Academic Technologies created new "finger-ready" tools to support the move to a mobile world. These tools include a phone application uGo (ugo.uj.ac.za) and the staff and student portal uLink (ulink.uj.ac.za).

The production and release of these tools support the reconceptualization of the institutional Internet and intranet resources. First, the Internet faces outwards to provide information and a rich user experience to all external visitors. Second, streamlined access to institutional resources is via a smartphone application (uGo) (described below). uGo is available as native iOS and Android apps, and as a mobi site for all other smartphones. Within uGo there are a number of interrelated components (uConnect) that support prospective students as they move through the institutional application, admission and registration processes. Third, uLink provides an integrated environment to support all members of the UJ community in their interactions with all its digital assets. Lastly, graduates move back to uConnect as they graduate and become part of our alumni. Therefore, the Internet faces outward and uLink faces inward. uGo and the associated uConnect components support transitions into and out of the UJ community. The development of uGo and uLink are briefly described.

### uGO

Part of the strategy was to provide just-in-time support to staff and students via mobile devices. In addition, it became necessary to give staff and students mobile access to Blackboard, and to provide mobile access to important institutional data. A number of different avenues were explored to rapidly create an institutional mobile application that allowed the integration of such components. After a presentation of Blackboard Central to the IT Advisory Committee and a successful application to the Members of the Executive Committee to divert funds to this project, the development of uGo was initiated. Within six months the University of Johannesburg released a mobile application for iOS, Android and Blackberry smartphones and an Internet site designed for mobile devices, which provided access to Blackboard Mobile application, study programmes offered by the nine faculties, library information, staff directory, news, emergency contact numbers and uHelp – the just-in-time support tool (Fig. 3).

To provide a mechanism to better manage processes associated with student application, admission and registration a number of resources were specifically designed for the next version of uGo. These components were conceptualized to support the life cycle of students entering and leaving the institution. In addition to the application, admission status and registration process, other components that are part of the processes of entry into the university, were included: institutional social media handles collected into a single component, an easy to use component to calculate the Admission Point Score required for entry into the university, access to surveys and tests required to be completed prior to registration and activities associated with the First Year Seminar (Fig. 3). These components guide potential students during the process of becoming part of the university community and also as they move to the world of work (graduation and Alumni).

**Figure 3.** Version 1 and 2 of the mobile application uGo

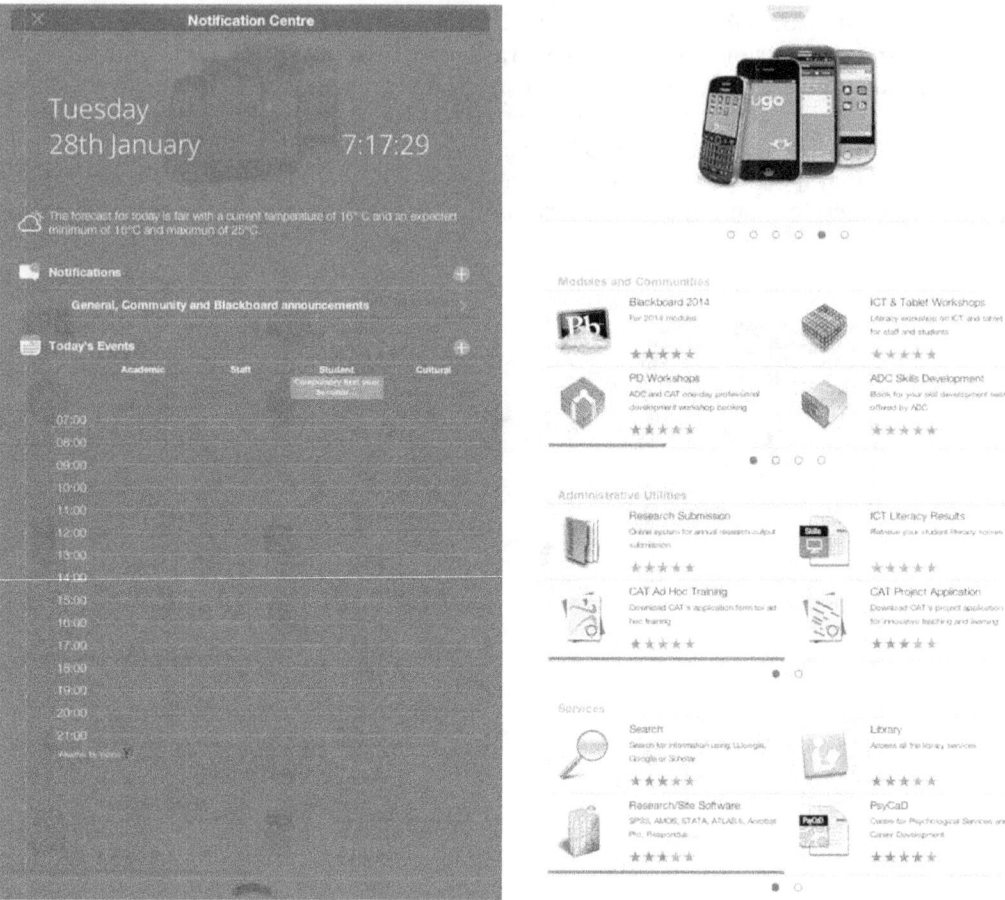

**Figure 4**. The institutional portal, uLink, designed for mobile devices

| Modules and Communities | Staff | Student | Administrative Utilities | Staff | Student | Services | Staff | Student |
|---|---|---|---|---|---|---|---|---|
| **Blackboard 2014** Link to all your 2014 modules | ✓ | ✓ | **Research Submission** Online system for annual research output submission | ✓ | | **Search** Search for information using UJoogle, Google or Scholar | ✓ | ✓ |
| **Blackboard Modules 2013** Link to all your past modules | ✓ | | **Class Timetable** Find the times and venues for your lectures | | ✓ | **Library** Access all the library services | ✓ | ✓ |
| **ICT & Tablet Workshops** Booking for literacy workshop on ICT and tablet use for staff and students | ✓ | ✓ | **Assessments Results** Get your assessment results | | ✓ | **Health Services** Available campus health services | | ✓ |
| **PD Workshops** ADC and CAT one-day professional development workshop booking | ✓ | | **ICT Literacy Results** Retrieve student computer literacy scores | | ✓ | **Emergency Contacts** Emergency telephone numbers | ✓ | ✓ |
| **ADC Skills Development** Book for your skills development sessions offered by the Academic Development Centre | ✓ | ✓ | **Academic Record** Get a copy of your academic record | | ✓ | **Campus Timetables** Timetable for each campus | ✓ | ✓ |
| **Research Workshops** Book for a research development workshop | ✓ | ✓ | **Academic Timetable** The academic timetable for 2014 | | ✓ | **Regulations** University rules for students | | ✓ |

| Service | ✓ | ✓ | Service | ✓ | ✓ | Service | ✓ | ✓ |
|---|---|---|---|---|---|---|---|---|
| **How to use Blackboard** Teach yourself to use Blackboard | ✓ | ✓ | **HR Self-Service** Manage your leave and other HR issues | | ✓ | **Research/Site Software** SPSS, AMOS, STATA, ATLAS.ti, Acrobat Pro, Respondus | | ✓ |
| **MS Office Training** Online MS Office training modules | ✓ | ✓ | **Financial Verification** Verify your financial status for registration | | ✓ | **PsyCaD** Centre for Psychological Services and Career Development | ✓ | ✓ |
| **Skills Development Manuals** Download manuals on how to use a computer or your tablet | ✓ | ✓ | **CAT Ad Hoc Training** Download CAT's application form for ad hoc training | | ✓ | **UJ's Bus Services** Schedules for transport between campuses | ✓ | ✓ |
| **uHelp** Online resource to solve your immediate technical problems | ✓ | ✓ | **ITS iEnabler** Registration, e-payments and contact details | | ✓ | **UJDigispace** Search our institutional archive | ✓ | ✓ |
| **Announcements** Important community and module announcements | ✓ | ✓ | **Examination Timetable** Times and places for your examinations | | ✓ | **Student Labs** Information about UJ's student computer laboratories | | ✓ |
| **Attendance Register** With a code you can register your class attendance | ✓ | ✓ | **CAT Project Application** Download CAT's project application form for innovative teaching and learning | | ✓ | **100 Tips** 100 tips for students by students | | ✓ |
| **Mendeley** A free reference manager and academic social network | | ✓ | **Examination Results** Get your most recent examination results | | ✓ | | | |
| **Academia.edu** Helps you follow the latest research | | ✓ | **HEDA** Higher Education Data Analyser Portal | | ✓ | | | |
| **LinkedIn** Manage your professional identity and build your professional network | | ✓ | **Bandwidth Usage** Your Internet usage | | ✓ | | | |
| **CAT Framework** Read CAT's framework | | ✓ | **Financial Statement** Manage your university financial accounts | | ✓ | | | |

**Table 3.** uLink components available to staff and students

## uLink

Apart from the uGo mobile application it was necessary to design, develop and deploy a portal for staff and students accessible by mobile devices and desktop computers. uLink was created to give staff and students access to their particular resources. uLink includes a Notification Centre, the Banners, Modules and Communities, Administrative Utilities, and Services (Fig. 4). The Notification Centre provides important messages to the community and a summary of events for the day. Staff members who access uLink from their desktop or laptop computers can post new notifications and/or events. The main interface of uLink includes a banner at the top of the page and services and tools organized into the three groups: modules and communities, administrative utilities and services (Table 3).

### Theme 4: Infrastructure and the IT Advisory Committee

The IT Advisory Committee played pivotal roles in many of the processes associated with the introduction of mobile devices to students, including:
- Wi-Fi connectivity in all libraries, open areas in all student residences, all first-year teaching venues, student centres, at least two open areas per campus and Council Chamber and conference venues;

- Setting minimum specifications for handheld devices;
- Provision of a mobile device to those students without financial means to acquire a device; and
- Provision of electronic textbooks (e-books) for the library and to students.

Two important developments are discussed in more detail.

The tender processes for the procurement of devices started in 2012. However, during the evaluation of the submitted tenders, the committee conflated two issues: procurement of the device with access to e-books. Members of the tender committee argued that the devices would be useless is they did not include digital versions of the textbooks. This is a *learning from technology* position, is contrary to the institutional teaching and learning philosophy and based on an instructivist teaching paradigm. It is disappointing that after six years of engagement with the university community, some academic members were ill informed of the institutional teaching and learning philosophy. However, a positive outcome was the re-evaluation of policies related to textbooks and digital resources managed by the library. Library staff members undertook a review of all prescribed textbooks and academic members were encouraged to prescribe textbooks available in print and e-format. Furthermore, the use of open access books was encouraged and all purchases made by the library would consider e-books first.

In October 2013 the IT Advisory Committee proposed that a pilot study be undertaken to evaluate the use of mobile devices in the classroom. However, the value of a pilot project was challenged at the Senate Teaching and Learning Committee and was not accepted by the Vice-Chancellor who requested that the use of mobile devices be compulsory for all 2014 first-year students and provided substantial funding to support the initiative.

## Assertions and generalizations

In January 2014 the University of Johannesburg became the first South African institution to fully embrace the use of mobile devices for teaching and learning. The development of the CAT framework, provision of skill development to staff and students and professional development to academic members, a just-in-time help system, deployment of smartphone applications and an institutional portal designed for use by mobile devices, infrastructure development to support ubiquitous access, development of policies to support the use of e-books, and provision of devices to underprivileged students created a coherent ecosystem for *learning with technology*.

The introduction of mobile devices into the classroom is a disruptive event (Christensen, 2008) as a disconnection now exists between learning and students' expectations, and between the academic teaching paradigm (mostly instruction) and the presence of a device in the classroom. Furthermore, this disruption is not low-level (engaging existing clients), but the development, exploration and use of a different teaching paradigm (authentic learning tool-mediated knowledge construction). Further research needs to be undertaken to understand this disruption, especially when the unit of analysis is not the students or teacher, but the job of learning and teaching with a mobile device (Christensen, 2008).

Crossan and Apaydin (2010) posited that innovation is a critical component of any organization and is part of gaining a competitive advantage. They present a multidimensional framework to explore organizational innovation (Fig. 5) that includes three components: determinants of innovation, innovation as a process and innovation as an outcome. With respect to leadership, top management was instrumental in driving institutional policies and processes, and provided appropriate funding to support both infrastructure and resource development. However, the complex relationship described in the framework between leadership, the managerial levels and processes are more complex than reported in the case study. Crossan and Apaydin (2010, p. 1171) proposed the "dynamic innovation capabilities reside in managerial levels" that include "mission/goals/strategies; structures and systems; resource allocation; organizational learning and knowledge management tools; and culture". Yet, in this study, leaders of the Information and Communication Systems, Library and Information Services, and Centre for Academic Technologies with the Vice-Chancellor appointed consultant and chairperson of IT Advisory Committee drove innovation.

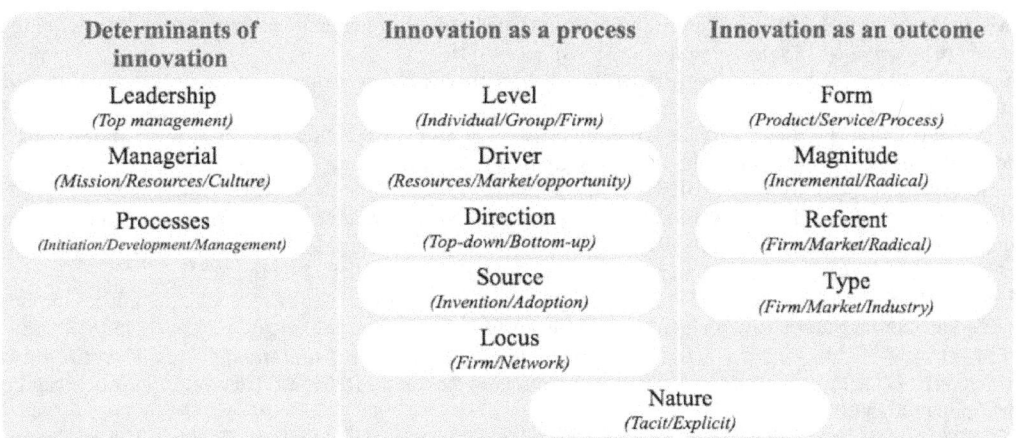

**Figure 5.** Multidimensional framework of organizational innovation (redrawn from Crossan & Apaydin, 2010)

The *level* of the innovation is aligned to individuals, groups or institutional processes. In this case the innovation mainly revolved around individuals. The *driver* and *source* of this innovation made use of internal knowledge and resources to provide the best learning experience for the students and, therefore, included an external driver – market opportunity. The *direction* included top-down and bottom-up activities but the integrated approach was a bottom-up innovation. The *locus* of the innovation was a closed process as it was internal to the institution.

Outcomes include service-, process- and business model innovations (*form*) that have the potential to induce radical changes to current teaching and learning practices (*magnitude*). While many learning organizations have explored the use of mobile devices in teaching and learning with technology as the unit of analysis, the approach at the University of Johannesburg argues that the unit of analysis is learning. Therefore, the innovation is different from other approaches and the *referent*, which defines the newness of the outcome, it still to be determined. Yet, this referent dimension, according to these authors, is related to the *magnitude* that in this case is viewed as radical innovation. The *type* of the innovation is related to technical (services to the community) or administrative (relates to work activity) innovation. In this case the innovation is both technical and social. Finally, the *nature* of the innovation is both tacit (products) and explicit (process).

While this multidimensional framework for organizational innovation allows for the careful analysis of innovation, this case study clearly shows that without change agents, working top-down and bottom-up, little innovation could have taken place, especially in a complex environment as an institution of higher education. Future research should investigate how the introduction of mobile technologies into the classroom, allied to the CAT learning framework, would affect the learning environment, pedagogy, and campus life at the University of Johannesburg.

## References

Alexander, B. (2004). Going nomadic: Mobile learning in higher education. *Educause Review*, *39*(5). Retrieved from http://www.educause.edu/pub/er/erm04/erm0451.asp?bhcp=11

Amiel, T., & Reeves, T. C. (2008). Design-based research and educational technology: Rethinking technology and the research agenda. *Educational Technology & Society*, *11*(4), 29–40.

Amory, A. (2012). Tool-mediated authentic learning in an educational technology course: a designed-based innovation. Retrieved from http://www.tandfonline.com/doi/abs/10.1080/10494820.2012.682584

Amory, A., Gravett, S., & Van der Westhuizen, D. (2008). Teaching and learning at the University of Johannesburg: a position paper. Retrieved from https://152.106.6.200/handle/10210/4270

Brown, J. S., Collins, A., & Duguid, P. (1989). Situated cognition and the culture of learning. *Educational Researcher*, *18*(1), 32–42.

Christensen, C. (2008). Disruptive innovation and catalytic change in higher education. In *Forum for the Future of Higher Education* (pp. 43–46). Harvard Business School.

Crossan, M. M., & Apaydin, M. (2010). A multi-dimensional framework of organizational innovation: A systematic review of the literature. *Journal of Management Studies, 47*(6), 1154–1191.

Engeström, Y. (1987). *Learning by expanding: An activity-theoretical approach to developmental research.* Helsinki: Orienta-Konsultit.

Herrington, A., & Herrington, J. (2007). Authentic mobile learning in higher education. Retrieved from http://researchrepository.murdoch.edu.au /5413/1/authentic_mobile_learning.pdf

Herrington, J., Reeves, T. C., & Oliver, R. (2010). *A guide to authentic e-learning.* New York: Routledge.

Jonassen, D. H., & Reeves, T. C. (1996). Learning with technology: Using computers as cognitive tools. In D. H. Jonassen (Ed.), *Handbook of research on educational communications and technology* (pp. 693–719). New York: Macmillan.

Leont'ev, A. N. (1978). *Activity, personality, and consciousness.* Englewoods Cliffs: Prentice-Hall.

Moran, M., Seaman, J., & Tinti-Kane, H. (2011). Teaching, learning, and sharing: How today's higher education faculty use social media. Babson Survey Research Group. Retrieved from http://files.eric.ed.gov/fulltext/ED535130.pdf

Newmann, F. M., Bryk, A. S., & Nagaoka, J. K. (2001). *Authentic intellectual work and standardized tests: Conflict or coexistence* (p. 47). Chicago: Consortium on Chicago School Research. Retrieved from http://ccsr.uchicago.edu/publications/p0f02.pdf

Piaget, J. (1977). *The development of thought: Equilibration of cognitive structures.* Oxford, England: Viking Press.

Reeves, T. C., Herrington, J., & Oliver, R. (2004). A development research agenda for online collaborative learning. *Educational Technology Research & Development, 52*(4), 53–65.

Smeets, E. (2005). Does ICT contribute to powerful learning environments in primary education? *Computers & Education, 44,* 343–355.

Vygotsky, L. S. (1978). *Mind in society. The development of higher psychological processes.* Cambridge, MA: Harvard University Press.

Wertsch, J. V. (2007). Mediation. In H. Daniels, M. Cole, & J. V. Wertsch (Eds.), *The Cambridge companion to Vygotsky* (pp. 178–192). New York: Cambridge University Press.

# PART 4 GAMING

## 21 Using a Game-Based Approach to Design a Rich Media Learning Environment

Min Liu., Jason A. Rosenblum, Lucas Horton, & Jina Kang, The University of Texas at Austin, USA

In this paper, we will examine game-based learning by describing a learning environment, *Alien Rescue*, that combines game elements, play, and authenticity in the real-world for the purpose of engaging students' learning of science and enhancing student motivation. This game-like environment uses play to organize meaningful player experiences. It further situates this experience through the perspective of scientific inquiry in ways that help students learn the language of science through role-play in a science fiction fantasy setting. We will discuss the design of the environment and present research conducted. Our goal is to provide research evidences and explore the theory, design, and research behind a science-learning environment that is informed by a game-based learning approach.

## Literature Review

Games and game-like environments can provide students with opportunities for experiential, authentic learning. Gee (2003) provided a framework to understand how commercial games can foster learning in ways that are grounded within principles such as situated meaning, multimodal literacies, active learning, and knowledge transfer. Games expose players to context-sensitive dialogue and in the process, "pu[t] language into the context of dialogue, experience, images and actions," (Gee, 2008, p. 36) a process that Gee describes as creating situated meaning. According to Gee (2008), games are able to promote the acquisition of situated meaning by embedding knowledge within specific contexts and by relating the language used in them to "actual experiences, actions, functions, and problem solving" (p. 36). Games thereby represent knowledge in the form of game assets, visual representations, and interactions that form what Gee (2003) describes as a "semiotic domain" that presents "any set of practices that recruits one or more modalities...to communicate distinctive types of meanings" (p. 18). Semiotic domains can be construed as game environments, each of which embodies what Gee describes as a "design grammar" (p. 99). In doing so, these environments embody Squire's (2006) notion of a "designed experience" (p. 19) through which players construct their own understanding of the game space.

According to Squire (2006), designed experiences enable players to "learn through a grammar of doing and being" (p. 19-20) while enabling them to participate in "ideological worlds" that offer spaces for inquiry. Squire found that disadvantaged minority middle-school students who played *Civilization* (1991) turned their game play experience into a historical simulation through which they inquired into historical differences between European and African American colonization practices. Similarly, Egenfeldt-Nielsen (2011) studied the effects of student gameplay of *Europa Universalis* on learning of history, as measured by retention and motivation (Egenfeldt-Nielsen, 2011).

Games such as *Civilization* and *Europa Universalis* thus present opportunities for learning both as an outcome of game play and as a platform for critical inquiry into sociocultural issues. However, games can also help students develop critical media literacies around the design and play of games (Squire, 2005). Additionally, by studying the discourse in forums within *World of Warcraft*, Steinkuehler and Duncan (2008) found that students demonstrated a range of scientific literacies through collaborative and scientific discourse and this process led students to develop "scientific habits of mind " (p. 535) by socially constructing knowledge, using systems-based reasoning and by using feedback and counterarguments in their discourse.

Games designed to support curriculum are also used to create spaces for immersive, experiential learning. *Quest Atlantis* (*QA*) is a 3D multiuser virtual environment (MUVE) in which students must play within a quest-based system to solve problems and save an endangered world (Barab, Thomas, Dodge, Carteaux, & Tuzun, 2005). QA is designed to create a space that encourages players to become immersed within a rich context for game play that involves student role play in which students "must apply conceptual understandings to make sense of and, ultimately, transform the context" (Barab et al., 2005, p. 97) of their game play experience.

*Alien Rescue* (*AR*), the game-like environment under investigation, incorporates a variety of game-like strategies to foster play. *AR* positions learners as novice scientists tasked with the problem to find new homes for several alien species and in doing so provides a meaningful, "designed experience" within a fantasy-based context that provides a space for scientific inquiry. *AR* thereby uses authentic scientific problem-solving strategies as a design grammar in an immersive, 3D environment to situate problem solving and promote ludic play (Liu, Horton, Kang, Kimmons, & Lee, 2013).

We are interested in investigating the efficacy of this game-like environment as a learning tool and its impact on students' learning. The overall research goal that guides this line of research is to examine the effect of this game-like environment on students' learning. We present the findings of three studies that used *Alien Rescue* with sixth graders, the targeted audience.

## Description of the Research Context

All three studies used the same environment, *Alien Rescue* (http://alienrescue.edb.utexas.edu), which engages sixth-grade students by challenging them to solve a complex problem. Students must use the tools, procedures, and knowledge of space science to learn about our solar system and apply processes of scientific inquiry. It is designed as a space science curriculum unit for approximately 15, 50-minute class sessions and is aligned with both National Science Standards and Texas Essential Knowledge and Skills (TEKS).

The design of *Alien Rescue* for this age group is grounded by the creation of a learning environment that is rich in what Malone and Lepper (1987) described as a "Heuristi[c] for designing intrinsically motivating instructional environments" (p. 248). Malone and Lepper recommended that game environments incorporate four elements that help keep players motivated: challenge, curiosity, control, and fantasy. *Alien Rescue* incorporates various game attributes such as challenge, control, fantasy, interaction, communication, mystery, role-play, representation, goals, sensory stimuli, adaptation, and 3D, as suggested by Malone and Lepper and other researchers (Garris et al., 2002; Wilson et al., 2009) in game-based learning.

The program begins with the narrative of the central problem. Each of six alien species, each displaced from a distant galaxy, needs to find a new home because their homes have been destroyed. Students learn this narrative by watching a video that is presented through a television news format. The video then situates students in the role of young scientists who are asked to join a United Nations rescue operation. After students view the video, they begin to work as space scientists aboard a fictional space station see Figure 1 [b]). Once they emerge in the station, they are free to explore the 3D environment and examine five separate rooms contained in the station: the Alien Database (see Figure 1 [c], [f]), Probe Design Center, Probe Launch Center, Mission Control Center, and the Communication Center (see Figure 1 [a], [d], [e]). In addition, students are given a set of persistent tools through a toolbar that is placed at the bottom of the screen. This toolbar enables them to use tools such as the Solar System Database, Concept Database, Notebook, Periodic Table and Spectra (see Figure 1 [e]). These interactive multimedia tools are designed to help students (a) share cognitive load, (b) support cognitive processes, (c) support cognitive activities that would otherwise be out of reach, and (d) support hypothesis generation and testing, using Lajoie's (1993) four conceptual categories (see Table 1).

Table 1

*Descriptions of Cognitive Tools Provided in Alien Rescue*

| Tool Categories | Tool Functions |
|---|---|
| **Tools sharing cognitive load** | |
| Alien Database | Provides information via 3D imagery and text, on the aliens' home planet, their journey, species characteristics, and habitat requirements. |
| Solar System Database | Provides information on selected planets and moons within our solar system. Data is intentionally incomplete to support the ill-structured nature of the problem-solving environment and foster the need for hypothesis testing. |
| Missions Database | Provides information on past NASA missions, including detailed descriptions of probes used on these missions. |
| Concepts Database | Provides instructional modules on selected scientific concepts using interactive animations and simulations designed to facilitate conceptual understanding. |
| Spectral Database | Provides information to help students interpret spectra found in the Alien Database. |
| Periodic Table | Provides an interactive periodic table of the elements. |
| Spanish/English Glossary | Provides Spanish translations of selected English words found within the program. |
| **Tools supporting cognitive process** | |
| Notebook | Provides a notebook to store student notes about their research findings. |
| Notebook Comparison Tool | Helps students to compare information from multiple notebook entries so that students can detect similarities and differences among the information in the entries. |
| **Tools supporting otherwise out-of-reach activities** | |
| Probe Design Center | Provides information on real scientific equipment used in both past and future probe missions. Students construct probes by deciding probe type, communication, power source, and instruments. |
| Probe Launch Center | Provides an interface for launching probes. Students check designed probes and choose which probe(s) they want to launch according to the budget. |
| **Tools supporting hypothesis testing** | |
| Mission Status Center | Displays the data collected by the probes. Students analyze and interpret this data in order to develop a solution. Equipment malfunction can occur, and poor planning may lead to mission failure and budget waste. |
| Message Tool | Provides students with ability to send and receive text messages received from the Interstellar Relocation Commission Director as well as the aliens. The Message Tool also includes the Solution Form. |
| Solution Form | Provides students with a way to submit their solution for each alien species. Students must also use the form to provide a rationale for their choice of alien habitat. Teachers can review and critique these solutions. |

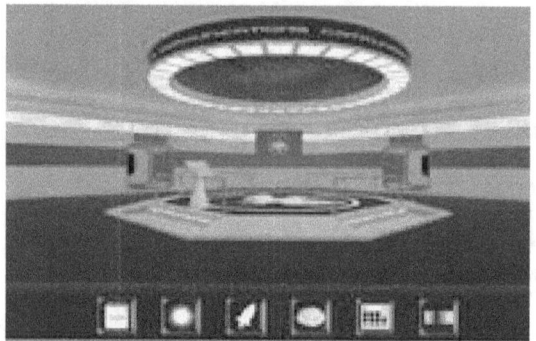

a. Students find themselves as scientists aboard an international space station.

b. The introductory video introduces students to the problem of relocating homeless aliens.

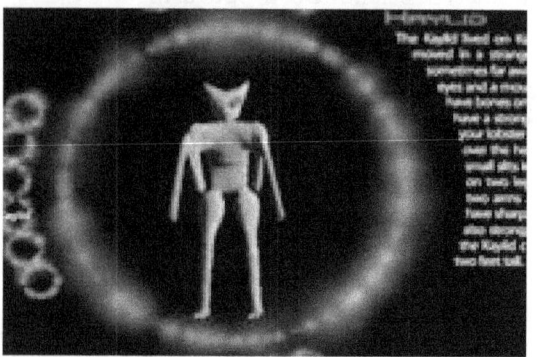

c. One of the alien species is depicted in the Alien Database.

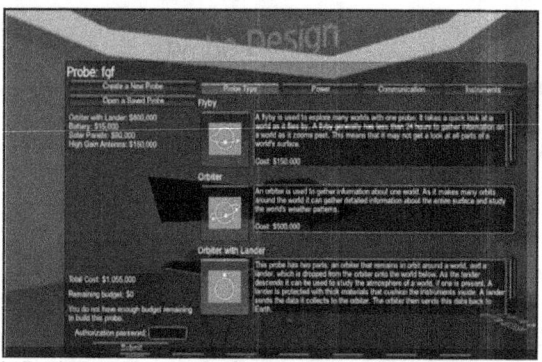

d. Students select probe design options based upon hypotheses.

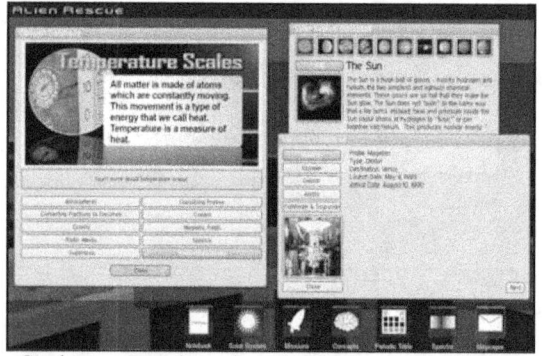

e. Students use tools such as the Concept Database, Solar System Database, and Mission Database.

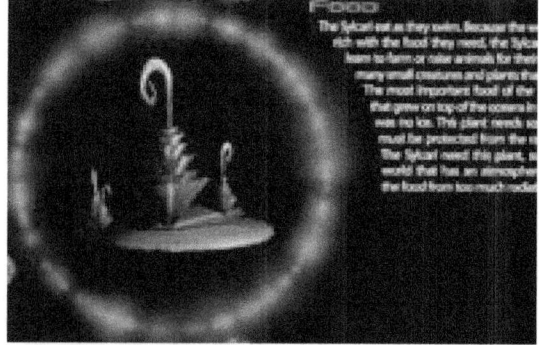

f. Food of one of the alien species is depicted in the Alien Database.

*Figure 1:* Screenshots of tools in *Alien Rescue* to support scientific inquiry.

## Previous Research Findings

Two studies have been conducted to examine *Alien Rescue* and students' learning. The first study examined sixth graders' science learning, their motivation, and the relationship between students' motivation and their learning of science after using *Alien Rescue* (Liu, Horton, Olmanson, & Toprac, 2011). A total of 220 sixth graders participated in the study. The analysis of the results showed that students significantly increased their science knowledge from pretest to posttest after using the program ($F(1,142) = 320.94$, $p < .01$, $ES = .69$), they were motivated and enjoyed the experience, and a significant positive relationship was found between students' motivation scores and their science knowledge posttest scores ($F(2, 129) = 23.17$, $p < .01$).

In the second study (Kimmons, Liu, Kang, & Santana, 2012), the relationship between sixth graders' science learning and their attitudes was further examined with a different student population ($n=478$). The findings indicated that students' science knowledge increased significantly from pretest to posttest by 30 points (out of 100, $t(478) = -31.28$, $p < .01$). Moreover, female students, on average, had higher gain scores than male students by 3 points. This finding indicated that program use had a significant effect on student achievement. In addition, student attitude towards the learning environment was associated with achievement ($F(2, 467) = 3.35$, $p < .05$). Attitude appeared to be a stronger contributing factor than other variables (e.g. gender, teacher) to achievement scores ($\beta = .05$, $t(384) = 5.8$, $p < .01$), with the exception of the pretest score.

In both these studies, qualitative data were also included. The analysis of student open-ended responses indicated students often used the word "fun" to describe their experience with *AR*. A few of typical comments from the sixth graders include: The program was "freaking awesome!!!" "so unique," "sooooooooo cool!!!!" and "soooooooooooooooooooooooooooo FUN!!!!!!!!!!!!!!!!" Figure 2 presents a word cloud of students' responses to the question "how do you describe *AR* to a friend" in Study 1 or "what do you think of *AR*?" in Study 2.

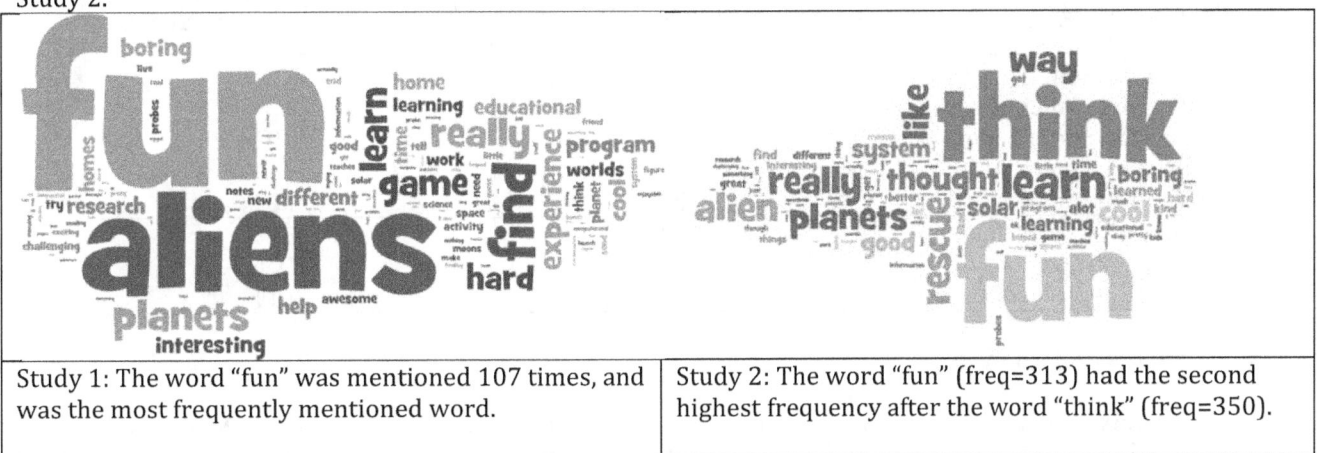

| Study 1: The word "fun" was mentioned 107 times, and was the most frequently mentioned word. | Study 2: The word "fun" (freq=313) had the second highest frequency after the word "think" (freq=350). |

*Figure 2.* Sixth graders' responses in a word cloud.

## The Present Study

To further this line of inquiry, we recently collected data from sixth graders in two different schools. We asked the following research question: "What is the effect of this game-like environment on sixth graders' science learning and what do they learn by using the environment?"

### Participants and Setting

All sixth grade students from two public middle schools in a mid-sized southwestern city in the U.S. participated in this study (see Table 2). The participating population included talented and gifted (TAG) students, regular education students (RegEd), English as a Second language (ESL)/English Language Learners

(ELL) students, and students with special needs. These sixth graders used AR in their daily 50-minute science classes as their curriculum for space science for three weeks. All students had their own computer to use but also worked in small groups; a recommended instructional strategy for implementing AR. Five sixth-grade science teachers taught these intact classes. These teachers had received training previously on how to use the environment and this was their second year using the environment in place of regular textbooks as their space science unit.

Table 2
*Demographics of the Participating Schools*

| Student Ethnicities | School 1 ($n$=130 approx.) | School 2 ($n$=300 approx.) |
|---|---|---|
| White | 65.6% | 51.8% |
| African American | 4.3% | 10.3% |
| Hispanic American | 24.9% | 25.7% |
| Asian/Pacific Islander | 2.0% | 6.9% |
| Native American | 0.5% | 0.5% |
| Multiracial | 2.5% | 4.8% |
| Economically disadvantaged | 22.6% | 21.1% |
| At-risk | 27.9% | 20.9% |
| Limited English Proficient | 2.1% | 2.1% |

**Data Sources and Analysis**

A mixed-methods design was employed with two data sources: 1) science knowledge test and 2) open-ended question responses. Students' learning of science was measured by their understanding of the various scientific concepts introduced in AR. The tests reflect what the designers and subject matter experts consider to be important knowledge for the students to acquire after completing the curriculum. It includes both factual knowledge and application questions, and was used in previous studies with similar samples using the same learning environment (Kimmons et al., 2012; Liu et al., 2011). One test included 20 items ($r$= .87) for School 1 and the other included 18 items ($r$= .72) for School 2 (The science teachers in School 2 made a slight modification to the test provided by the researchers to fit their curriculum unit.) This test was administered before and after the implementation of *Alien Rescue* to measure any change. After the students completed AR, they were asked to respond to the following open-ended questions: "What did you learn from *Alien Rescue*?" and "Tell us how much you liked *Alien Rescue* as compared to other science activities? Why."

An ANOVA with repeated measures was conducted with gender as a between-subjects independent variable and time of testing (pretest and posttest) as the repeated measure within-subject variable for each participating school. The dependent variable was students' science knowledge test scores. Responses to open-ended questions were analyzed using a constant comparative method of analysis (Lincoln & Guba, 1985; Strauss & Corbin, 1990) and a multi-level coding scheme by Miles and Huberman (1994). We first cleaned responses, eliminating blanks responses or those without meaning. We then consolidated all responses from both schools in one spreadsheet. Next, we read each response and chunked the data line-by-line. Relevant information was extracted through a systematic and iterative examination of the raw data. A list of codes describing the data emerged. We then compared the codes so that similar codes were combined, different ones were separated, and categories emerged at the next level (Creswell, 2009). This iterative analysis continued until it became apparent the emerged codes and themes represented the data adequately and no new codes emerged to support our research question. Two researchers were involved in the process of coding, checking, and verifying codes, categories, and themes until a 100% inter-rater reliability was reached.

## Findings

### Results from Quantitative Data

For School 1, the two-factor mixed ANOVA with repeated measure indicated that there was a main effect for the time of testing: $F(1,112) = 153.02$, $p < .01$, ES = .58. The correct responses in the science knowledge test increased significantly from pretest to posttest for both male and female students; and the average gain score from pretest to posttest was 24.29 with $M_{male} = 23.34$ and $M_{female} = 25.78$. There was not a significant two-way interaction between gender and time of testing (see Table 3). There was also not a gender main effect: $F(1,112) = 1.21$, $p = .27$, ES = .01; however, it is worth noting that female students had 2.44 higher gain in points than their male counterparts.

For School 2, the two-factor mixed ANOVA with repeated measures indicated that there was a main effect for the time of testing: $F(1, 255) = 132.62$, $p < .01$, ES = .34; and for gender: $F(1, 255) = 9.72$, $p < .01$, ES = .04. The correct responses in the science knowledge test increased significantly from pretest to posttest for both male and female students (see Table 3); and the average gain score from pretest to posttest was 13.31 with $M_{male} = 12.28$ and $M_{female} = 14.46$. It is worth noting female students had 2.18 higher gain in points than their male counterparts. There was not a significant two-way interaction between gender and time of testing.

Table 3
*Students' Science Knowledge Test Scores*

| Science Knowledge Score (% on 0-100 scale) | Boys | | Girls | | Total | |
|---|---|---|---|---|---|---|
| | n | M (SD) | n | M (SD) | n | M (SD) |
| School 1 | 69 | | 45 | | 114 | |
| Pretest | | 57.17%  (22.61) | | 52.11%  (13.76) | | 55.18%  (21.69) |
| Posttest | | 80.51%* (18.55) | | 77.89%* (22.55) | | 79.47%* (20.17) |
| School 2 | 134 | | 123 | | 257 | |
| Pretest | | 49.54%  (21.81) | | 41.82%  (19.7) | | 45.85%  (21.15) |
| Posttest | | 61.82%* (19.18) | | 56.28%* (16.28) | | 59.17%* (18.03) |

*Significantly different from the pretest, $p < .01$. Only those who completed both pre- and posttests were reported.

### Results from Qualitative Data

Sixth graders were asked to describe the specific information and skills they learned from working in AR. The analysis of this qualitative data in their open-ended responses resulted in a total of 515 units. These units were tallied given the codes describing the data. The emergent themes and representative quotes are presented in Table 4. The students stated they learned about our solar system (the planets, moons, and their characteristics) (51%); the scientific instruments (creating and launching probes and various instruments needed for each type of probe) (16%); alien species (8%); scientific concepts such as magnetic fields, gravity, and temperature scales (7%); problem solving (4%); conducting research (4%); managing a budget (2%); and working with others (2%). "Nothing" comprised about 4% of the responses.

Table 4
*Student Responses to "What did you learn from Alien Rescue?"*

| Categories | % (total units=515) | Sample Quotes |
|---|---|---|
| Solar System related | 50.87% | I learned many different facts about the moons and planets in our solar system that I haven't known before, and some were quite interesting. I enjoy learning about outer space, therefore I thought that *Alien Rescue* was a neat game that could help us learn about the solar system. |
| | | I learned a lot of the moons of our different planets. I also learned what living things need to survive, like an atmosphere, solids or gasses and all that different stuff. I learned a lot of different characters about the different planets in our solar system. |
| | | I have learned a LOT of information about our solar system, and become more analytical. |
| Scientific Instruments related | 15.73% | Different moons from planets. How magnetic field works. I also learned how the different instruments work for probes. |
| | | *Alien Rescue* made me familiar with scientific tools/equipment to measure information from an area. |
| | | I learned a lot about the different instruments that were used on the probes we made. For example, I never knew that the different types of cameras were specifically meant to find certain pieces of information. If I had not known that I would be sending a wide angle camera to find something very specific. |
| Aliens related | 7.77% | The many kinds of alien names. I also learned what they eat and what kind of elements so they can breath on a planet. |
| | | That different aliens need different kinds of atmospheres and different kinds of environments.....It's so cool. |
| | | I learned that aliens need certain things to breath in the air so they can live. I also learned that some aliens need to live on a place where they can dig under ground and build there homes. I also learned a little bit about planets. |
| Scientific Concepts related | 7.18% | I learned mostly about magnetic fields, gravity, elements and the solar system. |
| | | Each planet, moons, surface, atmosphere, magnetic field, |

| | | |
|---|---|---|
| | | elements, gravity, and temperature. |
| | | I learned about a new temperature scale called "Kelvin." |
| Problem Solving | 4.08% | I learned about how to use information to solve problems. |
| | | I learned a lot about planets and how to design probes, eliminate choices, and go for the best possible answer. |
| | | From *Alien Rescue* how to really research and find information using tools and solve problems. |
| Doing Research | 3.88% | I've also learned what I call "matching skills". Such as having to match the aliens' specific needs to a planet or moon that provides those needs. |
| | | How to match up my facts to what I already know. I also learned about the solar system characteristics. I learned different things about the planets I didn't know. |
| | | There is a lot of research that is in this process. |
| Managing budget | 2.33% | I learned more about the make-up of planets and materials on them. I also learned about the different tools. Also that probes cost a lot. |
| | | I learned about different instruments that gather information about other worlds. I learned that $10,000,000 doesn't go very far when you are researching other worlds. Lastly, I learned how to read a barometer. |
| | | That if we need to send aliens to different worlds it would require extreme funds and research. That we need to be prepared for something like this at any moment. |
| Working in groups | 1.94% | It taught me to work with my group and find informative facts. It taught me more information about the planets in our solar system. |
| | | I also learned that you have to trust people to help you find information instead trying to do the work all by yourself. |
| | | *Alien Rescue* helped with my skills with working together with my group. |
| Other (including fun, note-taking) | 1.94% | I also learned that science can be fun. I love science. About the weird aliens that will some day come to our solar system and our planets. |
| | | I learned how to take good notes. |

| | | |
|---|---|---|
| | | I learned that taking notes and looking over them can be very important when it comes to solving problems like this one. |
| Nothing | 4.27% | Nothing |

Note: Students' responses often reflected more than one coding unit. In providing sample quotes in the table, quotes were placed in the primary code to show sample responses.

The sixth graders at School 1 were also asked "Tell us how much you liked *Alien Rescue* as compared with other science activities [on a scale of 1-5]? Why?," 37% ($n = 44$) of the students responded "very much," 32.8% ($n = 39$) responded "much," 16.8% ($n = 20$) responded "somewhat," 9.2% ($n = 11$) responded "not much," and 4.2% ($n = 5$) responded "not at all." That is, close to 70% of the sixth graders liked *Alien Rescue* as compared to other science activities. The top four reasons for their rating are: "fun" 25% ($n = 36$), "learn" 15.3% ($n = 22$), "game" 7.6% ($n = 11$), and "group work" or "collaboration" 6.9% ($n = 10$). Sample responses include:

- It was a <u>fun</u> way to explore astronomy.
- I like *Alien Rescue* much more than other science activities because we're not just sitting at our desk doing work that must be done on our own, it's a <u>fun</u> activity that ties in with what we're learning.
- *Alien Rescue* was better than other activities because I liked <u>learning</u> about the different things. *Alien Rescue* gave us a chance to work independently on a project by ourselves. I also liked that we could work with different people. <u>Collaboration</u> caused us to debate and come up with more correct answers than if we were working by ourselves.
- Because *Alien Rescue* you can <u>learn</u> what scientist really do and how they learn about all the planets.
- It was interactive. *Alien Rescue* was also like a video <u>game</u> and I really like things like that.
- I liked *Alien Rescue* more than other science activities because it was a <u>group</u> project, we got to do it on the computer, and it was like a video <u>game</u>.

## Discussion

### Students' Learning as Supported by Game-Based Approaches

Sixth graders often referred to *Alien Rescue* as a game. However, did they learn as a result of playing *AR*? Results from quantitative and qualitative data of the present study clearly indicate that sixth graders have acquired significantly more science concepts after playing *Alien Rescue* and they were able to articulate what they learned. In addition to content knowledge about our solar system and scientific concepts, the students learned about the processes of using scientific instruments, conducting research, managing a budget, and applying important problem solving skills. In addition, they acquired interpersonal skills by working with other students, skills that are crucial for what the Partners for 21st Century Skills (n.d.) characterize as "21st century readiness." The findings of our present study support the findings from our previous research in which students demonstrated a gain in science knowledge after they used the program. Moreover, the findings from this series of three studies suggest that playing *Alien Rescue* can encourage positive learning outcomes, and are thus consistent with findings from other game-based learning research (Barab et al., 2005; Egenfeldt-Nielsen, 2011; Ketelhut 2007; Squire, 2006). Notably, in all three studies female students had a slightly higher gain score than their male counterparts. In our two previous studies, we also found a positive relationship between students' learning and their attitude and motivation. Additionally, female students in Study 2 had fewer negative comments than male students in describing their experiences with *AR*. These findings are encouraging, given the documented research showing a decline in students' motivation to learn science during the middle school years (Eccles & Wigfield, 2002; Lepper, Iyengar, & Corpus, 2005; Osborne, Simon, & Collins, 2003).

### Learning Through an Authentic, Experiential, and Playful Experience

Games are appealing because they are fun to play. For middle school students, the process of having fun can engage them in deeply meaningful ways (Gee, 2003). In investigating sixth graders' experiences with *Alien Rescue*, a recurring theme is that they had fun while learning. This theme is consistent with our intention to deliver a playful experience in an intentional problem-based narrative in *AR*. Our prior research indicates that *AR* has created an authentic, playful, and experiential learning experience for middle school students (Liu et al., 2013).

Authenticity is achieved by placing students in the role of young scientists and charging them with the task of saving distressed aliens. This central problem is presented through a compelling introductory video to create a sense of urgency (see Figure 1 [b]). As scientists, the students are challenged to find new homes for the aliens by engaging in the process of scientific inquiry: identifying the problem, researching, forming hypotheses, testing and validating their hypotheses, and justifying their rationales. Thus, the problem-solving process requires students to think and act like scientists and communicate with each other, thereby demonstrating scientific literacy. In addition, students use a variety of media-rich tools designed to assist learning (see Figure 1 [c], [d], [e] [f] & Table 1). Learning therefore occurs as a result of solving a complex problem. Such processes encourage and support active learning and multimodal literacies development (Gee, 2003, 2008). It is necessary to point out that although various tools are available for students to use, they must decide which tools to use, when, and why. There are six different types of alien species for students to rescue and each species has its own unique characteristics. Moreover, there is not one single correct answer to the central problem. Some answers are more optimal than others. It is therefore up to the students to present evidence and justify their problem solution with a rationale. These complications present a challenge to sixth graders that encourages them to control their own learning path.

In *Alien Rescue*, real-world scientific inquiry is coupled with a more playful experience and delivered through a 3D immersive, discovery, and sensory-stimuli-rich approach (see Figure 1 [a], [c], [f]). *Alien Rescue* thus presents a game-like, problem-based learning (PBL) environment that promotes a ludic approach to support learning. When students enter the program, they are not given explicit instructions on how to begin problem solving. They must explore and discover the available tools, understand their functions and determine when to use which tool at the time. This design evokes uncertainty, mystery, and curiosity, important game attributes (Malone & Lepper, 1987; Wilson et al., 2009). As discussed in the study by Liu and her colleagues (2013), two aspects of the program are notably important in creating a fun experience: (a) the use of the Alien Database and (b) the Probe Design and Launch tools. The Alien Database presents information about each of the six alien species, including details about their physique, nutritional needs, and habitats. This detail is packaged into an interactive 3D tool that is designed to help establish a sense of fantasy (see Figure 1 [c] & [f]). For sixth graders, the task of helping the alien species is an engaging and enjoyable part of the process. This fantasy-based approach is important to help motivate students and develop a sense of helping others as shown in this study. Of the responses in the category of learning about alien species (see Table 3), 35% of the units are about helping aliens as shown in such responses as "I liked that I can help the species find a new and right world that works," and "That there really could be aliens out there. Also that we need to help them if they every come for our help." The theme of "saving aliens" was also found to resonate more with girls than boys (Kimmons et al., 2012).

Interactive elements such as the Probe Design and Launch Tools and Alien Database (see Figure 1 [c], [d] & [f]) foster experiential learning that is authentic, fun, and collaborative. As one teacher commented on her experience in using *AR*, "The interactive graphics, databases, and discovery learning format provided my students with innumerable hours of higher-order thinking opportunities. The program required them to collaborate with their classmates, plan probe missions, and learn about the needs of alien species."

Notably, the ethically conscious game, *Fate of the World* (*FOTW*) purposefully crafts a possibility space in which learners act to solve environmental problems, while *Quest Atlantis* (*QA*) provides a space in which learners must act as agents of social change in a troubled world. Similarly, *AR* positions learners as scientists on board a space station, who are being asked to help six alien species that have come seeking help (Liu et al., 2011). Thus, *FOTW, QA,* and *AR* all challenge students to tackle socially important problems that provide rich contexts for play, situated in fictional game-like settings. In *AR*, students must also acquire a working literacy of the scientific method through a discovery-based approach in which they must apply the scientific method to research, form hypotheses about possible alien habitats, launch probes to collect data, and validate their working hypotheses. This student experience is highly collaborative and situated in a classroom context. Thus, the peer-based process students adopt when playing *AR* help them acquire scientific literacies that in some ways parallel the process the students used to acquire "scientific habits of mind" in Steinkuehler and Duncan's study (2008, p. 530).

In conclusion, this game-like environment uses play to organize meaningful player experiences. The findings of this study confirmed our previous research and provided further evidence to show that the design of an engaging, interactive environment using a games-based approach can help students have fun while learning.

## References

Barab, S., Thomas, M., Dodge, T., Carteaux, R., & Tuzun, H. (2005). Making learning fun: Quest Atlantis, a game without guns. *Educational Technology Research and Development, 53*(1), 86-107. doi: 10.1007/BF02504859

Civilization [Computer software]. (1991). Alameda, CA: MicroProse.

Creswell, J. W. (2009). *Research design: Qualitative, quantitative, and mixed methods approaches*. Thousand Oaks, CA: Sage Publications.

Eccles, J. S., & Wigfield, A. (2002). Motivational beliefs, values, and goals. *Annual Review of Psychology, 53*(1), 109–132.

Egenfeldt-Nielsen, S. (2011). *Beyond edutainment: Exploring the educational potential of computer games*. Retrieved from http://www.lulu.com/shop/simon-egenfeldt-nielsen/beyond-edutainment-exploring-the-educational-potential-of-computer-games/ebook/product-17534578.html. doi: 10.1.1.93.4661

Europa Universalis [Computer software]. (2000). Stockholm, SE: Paradox Development Studio.

Fate of the World [Computer software]. (2011). UK: Red Redemption, Ltd.

Garris, R., Ahlers, R., & Driskell, J. E. (2002). Games, motivation, and learning: a research and practice model. *Simulation & Gaming, 33*(4), 441–467.

Gee, J. P. (2003). *What video games have to teach us about learning and literacy*. New York, NY: Palgrave Macmillan. doi: 10.1145/950566.950595

Gee, J. P. (2008). Learning and games. In K. Salen (Ed.), *The ecology of games: Connecting youth, games, and learning* (pp. 21–40). Cambridge, MA: MIT Press. doi: 10.1080/13691180802552890

Gentile, D. A., Choo, H., Liau, A., Li, D., Khoo, A., Sim, T., & Fung, D. (2011). Pathological video game use among youths: A two-year longitudinal study. *Pediatrics*, 127, 2.

Ketelhut, J. D. (2007). The impact of student self-efficacy on scientific inquiry skills: An exploratory investigation in River City, a multi-user virtual environment. *Journal of Science Education and Technology, 16*(1), 99–111.

Kimmons, R., Liu, M., Kang, J., & Santana, L. (2012). Attitude, achievement, and gender in a middle school science-based ludic simulation for learning. *Journal of Educational Technology Systems, 40*(4). 341-370. doi: 10.2190/ET.40.4.b

Lajoie, S. P. (1993). Computer environments as cognitive tools for enhancing learning. In Lajoie, S. P., & Derry, S. J. (Eds.), *Computers as cognitive tools* (pp. 261-288). Hillsdale, NJ: Lawrence Erlbaum Associates.

Lepper, M. R., Iyengar, S. S., & Corpus, J. H. (2005). Intrinsic and extrinsic motivational orientations in the classroom: Age differences and academic correlates. *Journal of Educational Psychology, 97*(2), 184–196. doi: 10.1037/0022-0663.97.2.184

Lincoln, Y. S., & Guba, E. D. (1985). *Naturalistic Inquiry*. Thousand Oaks, CA: Sage Publications.

Liu, M., Horton, L., Kang, J., Kimmons, R. & Lee, J. (2013). Using a ludic simulation to make learning of middle school space science fun. *The International Journal of Gaming and Computer-Mediated Simulations*. 5(1), 66-86. DOI: 10.4018/jgcms.2013010105

Liu, M., Horton, L., Olmanson, J., & Toprac, P. (2011). A study of learning and motivation in a new media enriched environment for middle school science. *Educational Technology Research and Development, 59*(2), 249–265. doi: 10.1007/s11423-011-9192-7

Malone, T. W., & Lepper, M. R. (1987). Making learning fun: A taxonomy of intrinsic motivations for learning. In Snow, R. E., & Farr, M. J. (Ed.), *Aptitude, Learning and Instruction* (Vol. 3). Hillsdale, NJ: Erlbaum.

Miles, M. B., & Huberman, A. M. (1994). *Qualitative data analysis* (2nd ed.). Thousand Oaks, CA: Sage Publications.

O'Neil, H. F., Wainess, R., & Baker, E. L. (2005). Classification of learning outcomes: Evidence from the computer games literature. *The Curriculum Journal, 16*(5), 455-474. doi: 10.1080/09585170500384529

Osborne, J., Simon, S., & Collins, S. (2003). Attitudes towards science: A review of the literature and its implication. *International Journal of Science Education, 25*(9), 1049–1079. doi: 10.1080/0950069032000032199

Partners for 21st Century Skills. (n.d.). Retrieved from http://www.p21.org/

Rideout, V. J., Foehr, U. G., & Roberts, D. F. (2010). Generation m2: media in the lives of 8- to 18-year-olds. *Kaiser Family Foundation.* Retrieved from http://www.kff.org/ entmedia/upload/8010.pdf

Squire, K. (2005). Toward a media literacy for games. *Telemedium, 52*(1&2), 9-15.

Squire, K. (2006). From content to context: Video games as designed experiences. *Educational Researcher, 35*(8), 11. doi: 10.3102/0013189X035008019

Steinkuehler, C., & Duncan, S. (2008). Scientific habits of mind in virtual worlds. *Journal of Science Education and Technology, 17*(6), 530-543. doi: 10.1007/s10956-008-9120-8

Strauss, A., & Corbin, J. (1990). *Basics of qualitative research: Grounded theory procedures and techniques.* Thousand Oaks, CA: Sage Publications.

Tarng, W., & Tsai, W. (2010). The design and analysis of learning effects for a game-based learning system. *Engineering and Technology, 61,* 336-345. doi: 10.1.1.192.8685

Video games have 'role in school'. (2006). Retrieved October 2, 2006, from http://news.bbc.co.uk/2/hi/technology/5398230.stm

Wilson, K. A., Bedwell, W. L., Lazzara, E. H., Salas, E., Burke, C. S., Estock, J. L., & Conkey, C. (2009). Relationships between Game Attributes and Learning Outcomes: Review and Research Proposals. *Simulation & Gaming, 40*(2), 217-266.

Wittgenstein, L. (2009). *Philosophical investigations.* London: Wiley-Blackwell. (Original work published 1953)

# 22 Development of a Gaming Instructional Material and Design Framework for "Exploration Activities" in Science

Hodaka Taguchi & Toshiki Matsuda, Tokyo Institute of Technology, Tokyo, Japan

## Introduction

In Japanese upper secondary schools, students are required to learn at least one subject from "Basic Physics," "Basic Chemistry," "Basic Biology," and "Basic Earth Science" in science education (Ministry of Education, Culture, Science, Sports and Technology [MEXT] 2009). In these subjects, "Exploration Activities," such as "energy and motion of the object," are required for each content unit. In the Exploration Activities, students are expected to understand domain-specific knowledge better and to cultivate their scientific ability to explore phenomena.

Exploration Activities are required for the following reasons (Central Council for Education 2008). Firstly, according to a survey by the National Institute for Educational Policy Research [NIEPR] (2007), most Japanese upper secondary school students believe that science is useless in daily life, and they do not want to work in jobs that require learning outcomes of science education. Secondly, MEXT's National Course of Studies has focused on cultivating students' abilities of self-learning and problem-solving (MEXT 1998, 1999), but student achievement in these areas remains insufficient. In order to improve this situation, the current National Course of Studies adopts the following three instructional steps for every subject area: "Step 1: Understand fundamental knowledge and train basic skills well" –> "Step 2: Utilize acquired knowledge and skills in problem-solving" –> "Step 3: Perform Exploration Activities."

However, it is doubtful that Exploration Activities in science will play the expected role in the new curriculum because such activities were already introduced in the previous curriculum (MEXT 1999), but they did not achieve their objective, as mentioned above. In addition, the government-authorized textbooks do not provide appropriate examples; instead, they present examples of laboratory experiments for students to collect and analyze quantitative data only by following the textbook's instructions and questions. Thirdly, in Japanese school culture, teachers tend to emphasize preparation for college entrance examinations. They tend to instill domain-specific knowledge and give problems that have a specific correct answer. In addition, Matsuda (2012a) found that few student teachers in a teacher training course for certification to teach secondary school science could create appropriate lesson plans for Exploration Activities. Problems in the plans they created included inappropriate choices of problems, topics not related to daily life, problems with only a single correct answer, and a teacher-centered instruction style.

The point of Exploration Activities is not to teach new scientific knowledge, but to instruct students on how to solve problems scientifically using the learning outcomes of science education. In this process, they may acquire new scientific knowledge but should not memorize it, because they will be able to acquire it again whenever necessary. We consider that students need to learn methodologies of scientific problem-solving that include identifying problems in daily life and understanding and trying to solve them scientifically; moreover, they should gather data, not by conducting laboratory experiments, but by reading reliable sources on others' work, such as on Web or in books. We also consider that appropriate problems for Exploration Activities should not have a single correct answer because students need to explore cases in which there are two or more possibilities or even opposing hypotheses.

To realize the policy for Exploration Activities described above, Mio and Matsuda (2012) proposed a gaming material for science and technology communication concerned with the Great East Japan Earthquake that took place in March 2011. The topic of the gaming material is "sending food to a quake-stricken area," and it is realized by Katto and Matsuda (2012). In addition, Katto et al. (2013) developed a gaming material about "installing solar panels in an apartment."

These materials were developed according to the design framework for Information Studies (Hirabayashi & Matsuda 2011), a compulsory subject area for informatics education in Japanese upper secondary schools. Matsuda (2014) improved the design framework as shown in Figure 1, based on the materials, which were created for many domains. He also stated that problem-solving in daily life should be performed on the basis of his framework because most problems in daily life are solved by analyzing data collected neither by experiments in a laboratory nor through surveys conducted by the problem solver, but rather data collected from the Web, books, and so on. On the other hand, he also stated that the framework should be extended by adding tasks and ways of viewing and thinking dependent on each subject area.

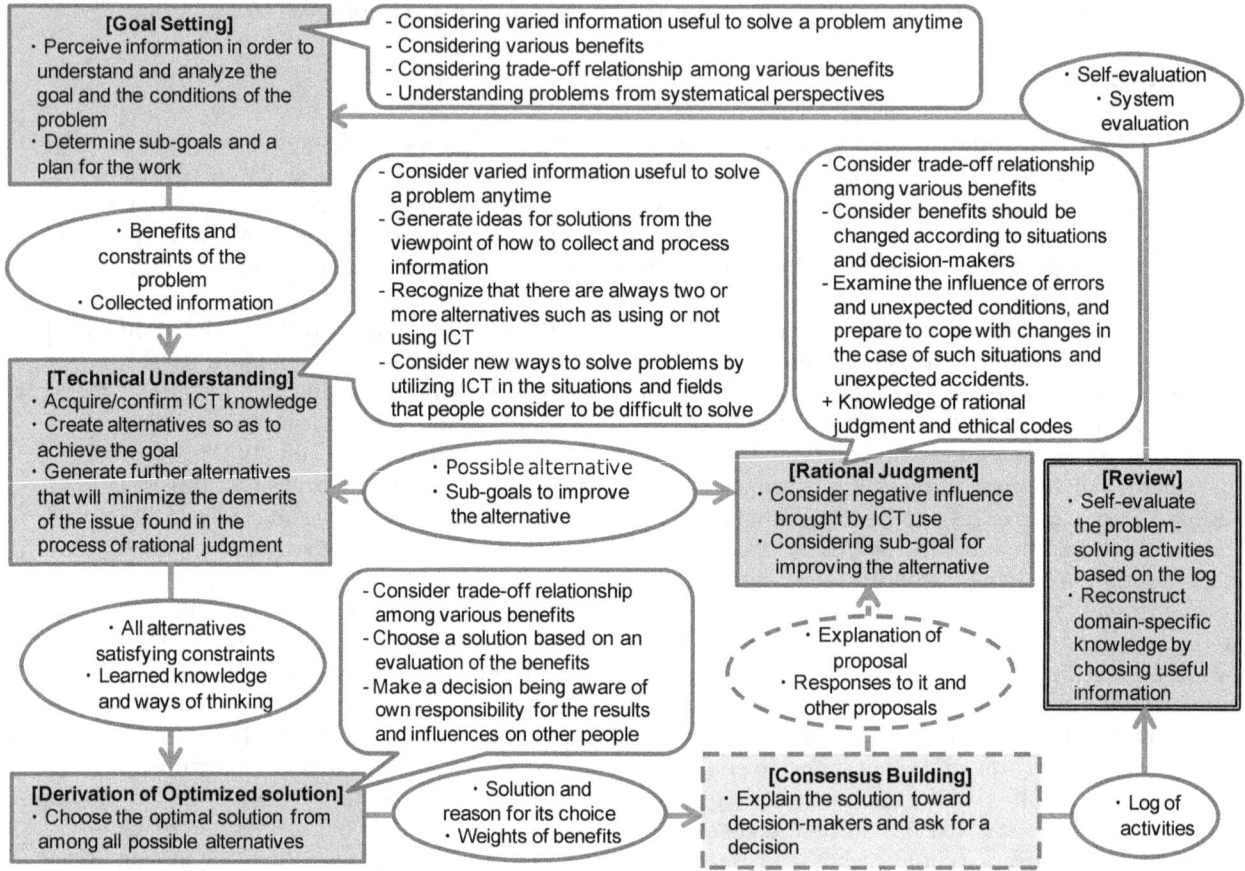

**Figure 1**: Matsuda's (2014) Design Framework of E-learning Materials for Information Studies

## Purpose

In this study, we examine the teaching methods of Exploration Activities, and for this purpose, we develop an e-learning game material to help students conduct such activities, using our proposed design framework for gaming materials of Exploration Activities. To create the design framework, we examine which tasks and ways of viewing and thinking should be added to Matsuda's (2013a) framework for scientific problem-solving. The topic of our gaming material is "earthquake disaster prevention" because this topic was used in the teacher training course mentioned above, in which student teachers make lesson plans.

## Design Framework of E-learning Materials for Scientific Exploration Activities

As mentioned previously, a framework of Exploration Activities in science should be similar to Figure 1. However, it is necessary to extend the activities to include scientific tasks and ways of viewing and thinking in each process. Therefore, we developed the framework shown in Figure 2 based on the following discussion.

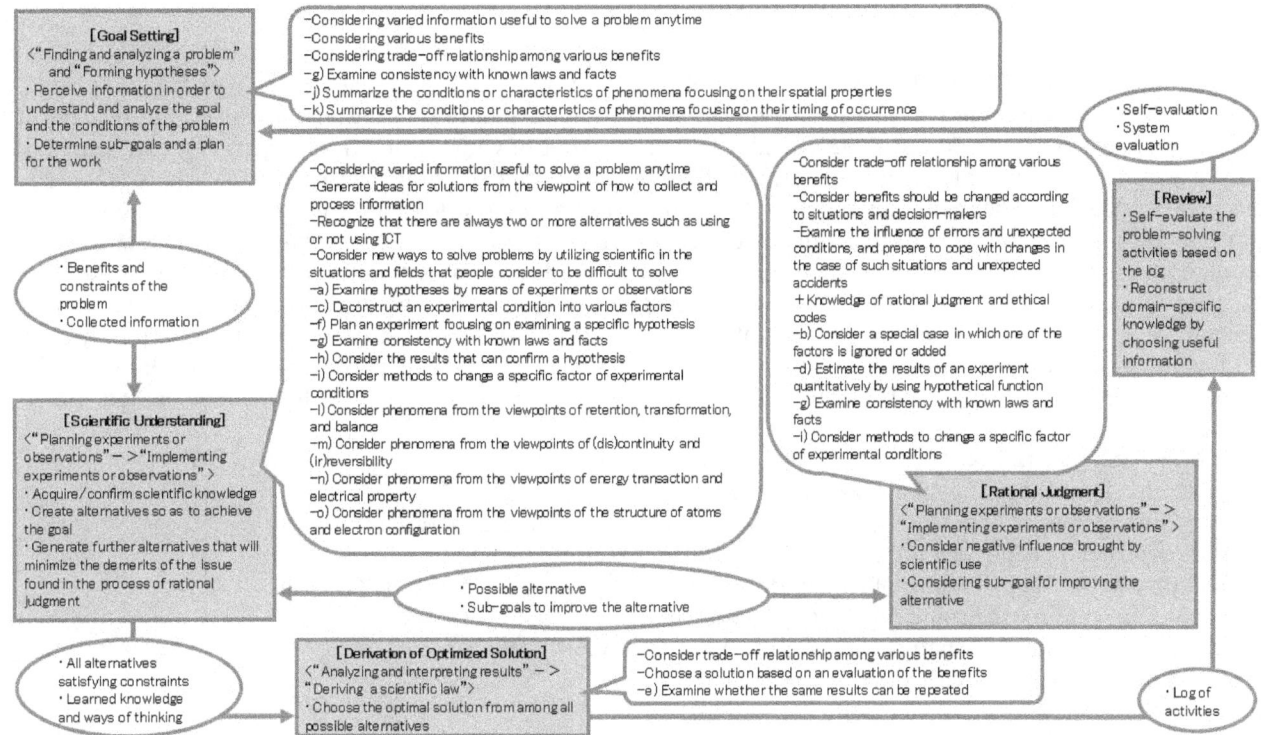

**Figure 2:** Our Framework for Designing Gaming Materials for Exploration Activities in Science Education

## Procedural Knowledge: Script Knowledge of Scientific Problem-Solving

The problem-solving process of Figure 1, shown as rectangle elements, corresponds to the design process described in ITEA's (2007) technology standard and is sufficiently general and useful for problem-solving activities in daily life. However, the tasks in each process are largely those necessary to consider how to utilize information and communication technology (ICT) in problem-solving activities. On the other hand, the guidebook of the National Course of Studies for Science Subjects (MEXT 2009) explains that scientific problem-solving is fundamentally performed by the following procedure: "Identifying and analyzing a problem" -> "Forming hypotheses" -> "Planning experiments or observations" -> "Implementing experiments or observations" -> "Analyzing and interpreting results" -> "Deriving a scientific law." In order to show commonality between these two processes, we matched them as follows and showed the relationship explicitly in each process (rectangle). We do not consider that "Planning experiments or observations" and "Implementing experiments or observations" match the technological understanding process and rational judgment process, respectively. Instead, we consider that technological understanding is a process to create ideas and alternatives, and rational judgment is a process to examine and check them.

- "Finding and analyzing a problem" and "Forming hypotheses" = goal setting
- "Planning experiments or observations" -> "Implementing experiments or observations"
      = Technological understanding and rational judgment
- "Analyzing and interpreting results" -> "Deriving a scientific law" = Derivation of optimized solution

In addition, we rewrote "technological understanding" as "scientific understanding" and changed "ICT" to "science and technology." However, this rewrite does not mean that Exploration Activities in science do not require the utilization of ICT. On the contrary, as we mentioned previously, these activities should emphasize not performing laboratory experiment but collecting published data from the Webs, books, and so on. Therefore, "technology" in the revised framework includes ICT, and informatic and systematic ways of viewing and thinking should be used in each process, in addition to scientific ways of viewing and thinking, as shown in the balloons in Figure 1.

## Scientific Ways of Viewing and Thinking

Although MEXT (2009) stated that promoting students' utilization of scientific ways of viewing and thinking is one of the objectives of science education, it did not explain explicitly what these scientific ways of viewing and thinking are. Perhaps, MEXT's idea is that the ways of viewing and thinking are not teachable but acquired naturally through performing scientific Exploration Activities. However, we do not support this idea because it is based on behaviorism and is overly optimistic. Rather, our idea is based on Bruer's (1993) statement that domain-specific knowledge, meta-cognitive skills, and general strategies are all elements of human intelligence and expert performance. As Matsuda (2013b) explained, ways of viewing and thinking correspond to meta-cognitive skills and should be taught explicitly as viewpoints or checkpoints that evaluate and conceive of solutions. Therefore, we adopt Matsuda's (2012b) scientific ways of viewing and thinking, as shown in Table 1. Hereafter, we discuss which ones should be utilized in each process as well as their integration into the informatic and systematic ways of viewing and thinking shown in balloons in Figure 1.

**Table 1**: Matsuda's (2012b) Scientific Ways of Viewing and Thinking

| |
|---|
| a) Examine hypotheses by means of experiments or observations. |
| b) Consider a special case in which one of the factors is ignored or added. |
| c) Deconstruct an experimental condition into various factors. |
| d) Estimate the results of an experiment quantitatively by using hypothetical function. |
| e) Examine whether the same results can be repeated. |
| f) Plan an experiment focusing on examining a specific hypothesis. |
| g) Examine consistency with known laws and facts. |
| h) Consider the results that can confirm a hypothesis. |
| i) Consider methods to change a specific factor of experimental conditions. |
| j) Summarize the conditions or characteristics of phenomena focusing on their spatial properties. |
| k) Summarize the conditions or characteristics of phenomena focusing on their timing of occurrence. |
| l) Consider phenomena from the viewpoints of retention, transformation, and balance. |
| m) Consider phenomena from the viewpoints of (dis)continuity and (ir)reversibility. |
| n) Consider phenomena from the viewpoints of energy transaction and electrical property. |
| o) Consider phenomena from the viewpoints of the structure of atoms and electron configuration. |

To identify scientific problems and form hypotheses for scientific problem-solving, we should focus on differences and inconsistencies between phenomena and scientific facts or laws. Therefore, in the Goal Setting process, as a special viewpoint for "Understanding problems from systematical perspectives," we added (g) as a scientific way of viewing and thinking. From a similar viewpoint, we added (j) and (k) to find and summarize the purposes and conditions of problems systematically.

The main purpose of the scientific understanding process is to generate ideas or alternatives for examining hypotheses and understanding collected data. To generate ideas for collecting data for examining hypotheses, it is necessary to use appropriate scientific concepts or factors in confirming/acquiring scientific knowledge. To this end, (f), (g), and (h) are necessary. In addition, corresponding to the domain of problems, (l), (m), (n), and (o) must be used. Then, (c) and (i) are needed to analyze data or create a plan for an experiment. If no appropriate data can be collected, (a) should be used.

The main purpose of the rational judgment process is to critically review the results produced by the scientific understanding process. For this purpose, (b), (g), and (e), should be used. In addition, (d) may be useful to check the results quantitatively and inductively.

Decisions in the derivation of an optimized solution process are not necessarily scientific but technological. Therefore, we consider that no scientific ways of viewing and thinking need to be added.

#### Domain-Specific Knowledge of Science

Domain-specific knowledge is modeled through the semantic network (Collins & Quillian 1969). As long-term memory is not lost but temporarily unavailable, Matsuda (2013b) emphasized the importance of knowledge chunking as well as the direction and strength of connections among various pieces of knowledge. To promote knowledge chunking, teachers should teach students ways to summarize and acquire related knowledge. Then, to promote the useful reconstruction of acquired knowledge, they should provide students with problem-solving tasks in authentic contexts. This is because, in general, domain-specific knowledge is taught using a buildup approach, but in real situations, people do not use knowledge in this order.

The gaming material requires the following domain-specific knowledge: mechanisms of tsunamis and snow avalanches, relationships between rock falls and sediment disasters and strata, and dangerous chemical substances and fire material. When students learn about these topics from a textbook, they begin by looking at the keywords "rock fall" related to disaster phenomena. Next, they learn about how rock falls occur. Finally, they learn about cases of actual damage caused by rock falls.

On the other hand, when students estimate the risk factors of a given area, they need to pay attention to the features of the area and identify dangerous factors based on these features. Then, they must examine their own hypotheses and confirm the correct risk factors based on collected data and their existing knowledge of mechanisms or characteristics of disaster occurrences. Finally, the students need to look for data concerned with other factors to confirm the safety level of the area. Therefore, teachers need to provide students with opportunities to reconstruct knowledge (re-connection) in a manner analogous to real life situations.

## Development of a Gaming Instructional Material

The problem for the gaming material is to discuss "an earthquake disaster that will happen in a specific district." As a typical case, we chose Ota-ku, Tokyo, and guided the students to consider risk factors that might lead to disasters if a large earthquake were to strike the region. However, the purpose of the activity is not to teach about the risk factors in this specific area. Rather, the goal is for students to practice deducing risk factors scientifically for an unfamiliar place when they travel. Therefore, the game prompts students to form hypotheses about the risk factors of a specific area by choosing from several possible factors that can cause earthquake disasters and other natural disasters in general, and to explain the reasons for their choices based on science. Further, it requires students to examine whether the risk factors they do not choose are appropriately left out.

The basic method of hypothesis testing is to search for information on the Internet and to consider causal relationships between the disasters and the ratio/scale of risk factors on the basis of statistical data. We also expect the students to learn the relationships between settings they actually see or visit in everyday life and risk level as explained by the collected data, because Ota-ku, Tokyo, is their hometown.

#### Goal Setting Process

In the Goal Setting process, at first, the game instructs students to discuss "an earthquake disaster in Ota-ku, Tokyo," and explains the procedure of the Exploration Activities (Figure 3). Then, the students are prompted to collect information to understand the problem according to the procedure in Figure 3. They learn about the estimated probability that an earthquake with a magnitude greater than 7.0 will occur in the Tokyo area within the next 30 years. In addition, using a risk map created by the Tokyo Metropolitan Government Bureau of Urban Development (Figure 4), they find Ota-ku's risk level. Next, they are guided to set the sub goal of "studying why Ota-ku is dangerous" and create a plan for forming and examining a hypothesis about Ota-ku's risk factors (Figure 3). This part of the activity is intended to promote students' utilization of scientific ways of viewing and thinking (i) for finding the relationships between geographic features and risk levels while comparing Ota-ku to other areas. Moreover, they are prompted to describe the reasons for positing their hypothesis.

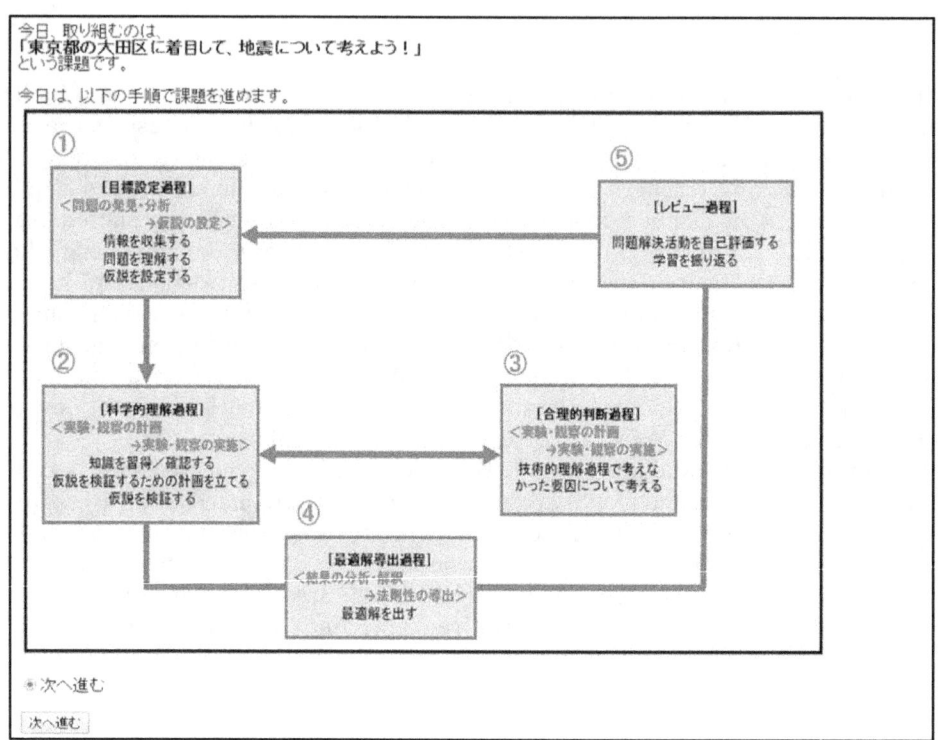

**Figure 3:** Explaining the Procedure of the Exploration Activities.

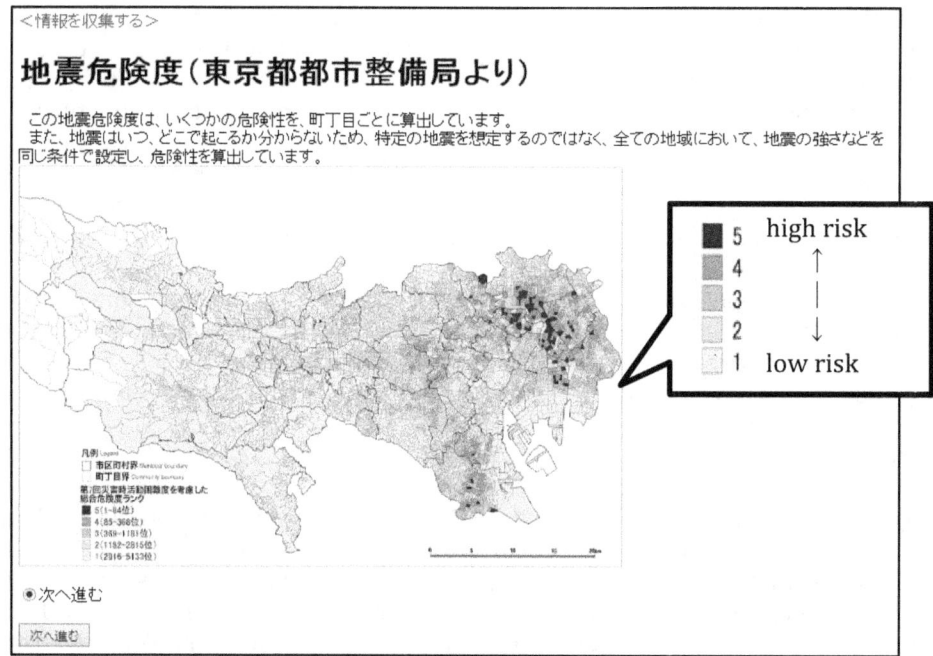

**Figure 4:** Risk Levels of the Earthquake Disaster in Tokyo.

## Scientific Understanding Process

In the Scientific Understanding process, at first, the students are required to make a plan to examine their hypothesis as shown in the task list. Here, they need to consider how to collect a variety of information with appropriate methods by utilizing informatics and systematic ways of viewing and thinking. Therefore, the game asks the students to select a method for collecting information from "a textbook," "library books," "the Internet," or "newspapers and magazines" (Figure 5). In addition, it prompts them to consider and describe the merits and demerits of each method. Though the game leads the students to collect information online because various agencies provide up-to-date information, the instructions also advise them to pay attention to the reliability of the information they find. Next, it prompts them to analyze and interpret the data found on web pages prepared in the game (Figure 6) to examine each factor of their hypothesis. This task guides the students to use scientific ways of viewing and thinking (a), (f), and (h).

**Figure 5:** Making a Plan to Examine the Hypothesis.

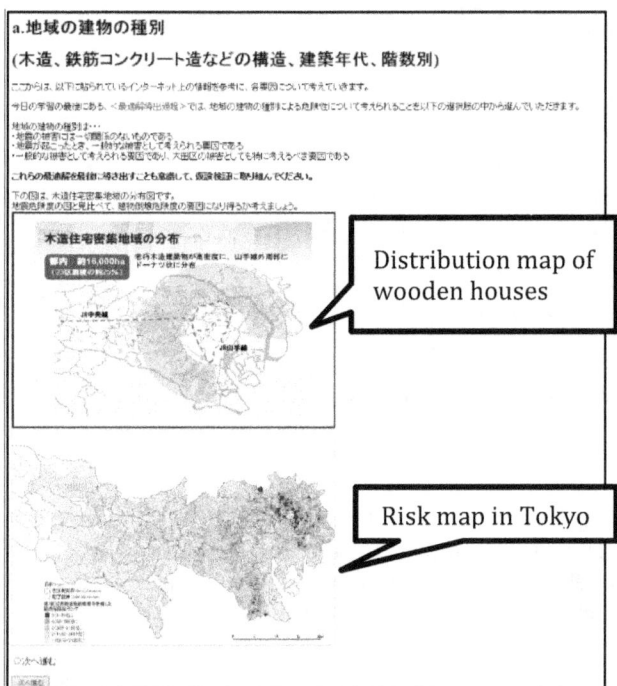

**Figure 6:** Example of Checking a Factor of a Hypothesis.

## Rational Judgment Process

As a result of the Great East Japan Earthquake in March 2011, many unexpected phenomena caused further damages. Therefore, in the Rational Judgment process, it is important for the students to consider rebuttals to their hypotheses and to verify their reasoning used in the Scientific Understanding process from a critical perspective. First, the game instructions tell the students to consider whether the risk factors they did not include in their hypothesis can indeed be neglected in the region, bearing in mind that if the range of the hypothesis is too narrow, unexpected crises can occur. In this way, the students are prompted to use scientific ways of viewing and thinking (b) and (i) to consider what particular influences exist under the specialized/generalized conditions. Moreover, (d) and (g) promote their recognition of the importance of quantitative analysis as well as simple true/false discussion and both the integrity and consistency of the whole logic.

## Derivation of an Optimized Solution Process

In the Derivation of an Optimized Solution process, the students are prompted to determine the risk level of each factor in Ota-ku, Tokyo, based on the learner's hypothesis and reasoning performed in the Scientific Understanding process and the Rational Judgment process. Finally, they are asked to label each factor as one from the following three choices: "×: It is not related at all to the earthquake damage," "△: In general, it causes earthquake disasters but not in this area," and "○: It causes earthquake disasters in Ota-ku, Tokyo."

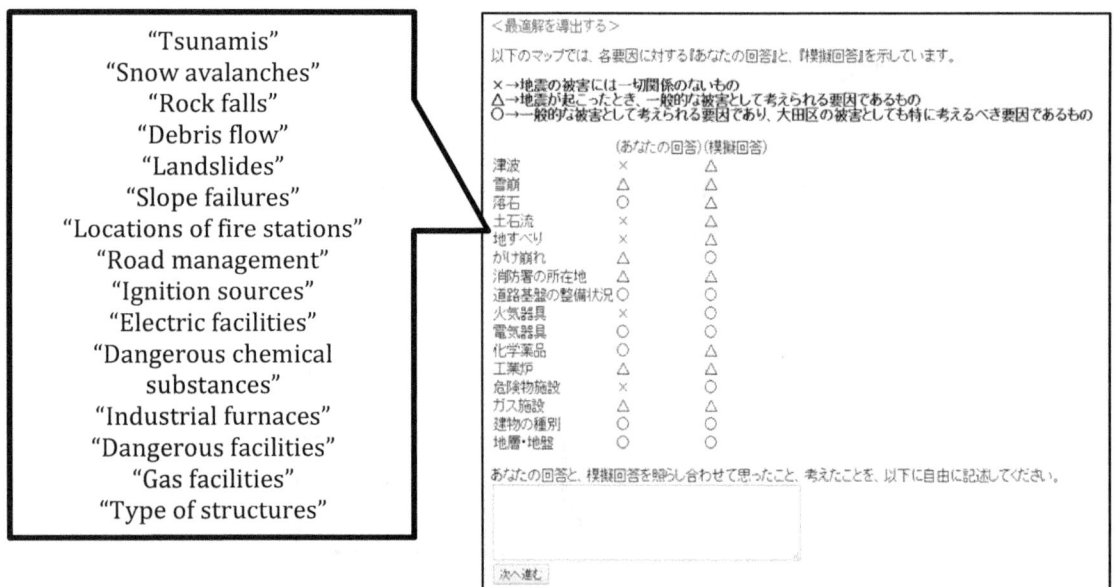

**Figure 7**: Comparing Student's Conclusions with an Example Answer.

## Review Process

In the Review process, at first, each student's conclusion is shown to him/her in contrast with an example answer (Figure 7). Then, we prompt the students to use scientific way of viewing and thinking (e) to discuss the shown table and describe their opinions. Finally, they reconstruct their domain-specific knowledge through self-evaluation activities and a post-questionnaire.

## Evaluation of the Gaming Instructional Material and Framework

In May 2014, we conducted a session with the gaming material for eight persons who are teachers at the Tokyo Tech High School of Science and Technology or student teachers at various universities. We asked them to complete pre- and post-questionnaires on their opinions about the e-learning material before and after using it.

**Table 2**: Results of the Post-Questionnaire (Frequency of Answers)

|  | strongly disagree | disagree | agree | strongly agree |
|---|---|---|---|---|
| Q1. This gaming material is a good example of a lesson that makes students understand learning outcomes of science education are useful in everyday life.. | 0 | 3 | 5 | 0 |
| Q2. This material helps you make a lesson plan for earthquake disaster prevention. | 0 | 1 | 4 | 3 |
| Q3. This material helps you make a lesson plan for Exploration Activities in science. | 0 | 1 | 7 | 0 |

Table 2 suggests that the game can help teachers create lesson plans for earthquake disaster prevention and science Exploration Activities. However, we need to improve it to better help students see the usefulness of studying science for application in everyday life. To this end, we discuss the points of improvement based on the participants' responses to the post-questionnaire. Because we conducted a formative evaluation while developing the prototype gaming material for nine student teachers who took our pre-service teacher education course of science in January 2014, we refer to its results. According to the results of this evaluation, 4, 9, and 5 students answered positively to Q1, Q2, and Q3, respectively. Therefore, our game was effective regarding the contents of Q3 but not Q1.

Firstly, we need to pay attention to the time limitations of actual lessons. According to the participants' opinions, the game took too much time and the repetition of similar activities felt boring because the game asked students to discuss every factor concerned with earthquake disasters in either the Scientific Understanding process or Rational Judgment process. To allow the students to learn by self-pacing, we need to set some factors as compulsory and others as optional, taking into account whether enough time is available, according to their choice of factors to include in the hypothesis.

Secondly, the game was improved to encourage students to utilize scientific ways of viewing and thinking explicitly; it was subsequently evaluated better in regard to Q3 than it was previously in the results of formative evaluation. However, it was insufficient to instruct explicitly how to utilize scientific domain-specific knowledge. Therefore, we need to explain how to utilize and memorize domain-specific knowledge, such as how to utilize knowledge about the mechanisms of tsunamis and snowfall corresponding to geographic features of each region.

Thirdly, we are considering conducting collaborative exploration learning activities to promote students' utilization of scientific ways of viewing and thinking. When we conduct trial lessons, we will examine a case to discuss the differences in students' results in the Derivation of an Optimized Solution process.

## Future Directions

In this study, we developed gaming materials and a design framework. However, we should improve this framework by performing trial lessons with the gaming materials as well as by developing new gaming materials. Moreover, to utilize the learning outcomes of science education, learning outcomes of technology education, especially technological ways of viewing and thinking, should be utilized as well. This means that we need to discuss a design framework of gaming material for project learning in STEM education.

## Acknowledgements

This research was supported by JSPS KAKENHI Grant Numbers 23501137 and 26350313 and the foundation for the Fusion of Science and Technology (FOST).

## References

Bruer, J. (1993). *Schools for Thought: A Science of Learning in the Classroom*, Cambridge, MA: The MIT Press.
Central Council for Education (2008). *The Report on the Next Revision of the National Course of Studies for Primary and Secondary Schools*. Retrieved from http://www.mext.go.jp/a_menu/shotou/new-cs/news/20080117.pdf
Collins, A.M. and Quillian, M.R. (1969). Retrieval time from semantic memory. *Journal of Verbal Learning and Verbal Behavior*, 8 (2), 240–247.
Hirabayashi, S. and Matsuda, T. (2011). Constructing Design Principles for Developing Gaming Instructional Materials for Making Cyber Ethics Education Authentic, *Proceedings of E-Learn 2011*, 1280–1288, AACE: Chesapeake, VA.
International Technology Education Association (2007). Standards for Technological Literacy: Content for the Study of Technology. Retrieved from http://www.iteea.org/TAA/PDFs/xstnd.pdf
Katto, Y., Matsuda, T., and Endo, S. (2013). Considering Science and Technology Communication Literacy for All and Developing an E-learning Material to Cultivate it. *Technical Report of Japan Society for Educational Technology*, JET13-2, pp. 1–8.
Katto, Y., Matsuda, T., and Endo, S. (2012). Development of a New High School Instructional Material for Engineers' Moral Education that Emphasizes Anticipated Responses to Hidden Risks. *Technical Report of Japan Society for Educational Technology*, JET12-5, pp.97–104.
Matsuda, T. (2014). Improving the Design Framework of E-learning Game Materials for Information Studies: Consideration of a Student Model, The 12th Hawaii International Conference on Education, pp. 2129–2141.
Matsuda, T (2013a). Improving Design Framework of E-learning Game Material for Information Studies-Based on a Student Model Representing Learning Outcomes of Informatics Education-. *Technical Report of Japan Society for Educational Technology*, JET13-4, pp.57–64.
Matsuda, T (2013b). A Simulated Teaching Game for "Instructional Method of Information Stuides" -Introducting a Learner's Model to Show Results of Instruction as Feedbacks-. *Technical Report of Japan Society for Educational Technology*, JET13-1, pp.345–352.
Matsuda, T (2012a). Improvement of IAG system in Order to Cultivate Student Teacher's Ability Prompting Leaners to Utilize Mathematical Views and Ways of Thinking in Problem-solving. *Technical Report of Japan Society for Educational Technology*, JET12-1, pp.277–284.
Matsuda, T. (2012b). Design Principles of Problem-based Instruction in "Mathematics I" and "Introduction to Sciences": S&G Views. Japan Association of Simulation and Gaming, Proceedings of the 2012 Spring National Conference, pp. 71–76. (in Japanese)
Ministry of Education, Culture, Science, Sports and Technology (2009). National Course of Studies for the Upper Secondary Schools from http://www.mext.go.jp/a_menu/shotou/new-cs/youryou/kou/kou.pdf.
Mio, A. and Matsuda, T. (2012). Science Communication Gaming Material for Cultivating Scientific Views and Ways of Thinking on the Topic of Earthquakes Disaster. *Linkoping Electronic Conference Proceedings 73*: 355–362.
National Institute of Educational Policy Research (2007, April). Investigations of Academic Ability and an Attitude Survey on the Feelings of Children with Regard to their Studies at Upper Secondary School Level in 2005. Retrieved from http://www.nier.go.jp/kaihatsu/katei_h17_h/h17_h/05001000040007004.pdf.

# 23 Serious Game Gademavo: How to enhance students' ability in taking decisions in a complex world

Anne-Dominique Salamin, University of Applied Sciences Western Switzerland, Switzerland

## Introduction

More than 19000 (27% of all Swiss UAS students) learners enrol every year in the different curricula proposed by the University of Applied Sciences Western Switzerland2. This university offers students strong references to the real professional world, either by linking the teaching laboratories with real experiments or by developing projects with professionals in action. Since 2004, an e-learning centre has been in charge of developing and conducting research in blended learning, along with new innovative training means.

The average student age at the HES-SO is 25, and most students attending a Bachelor curriculum belong to the "digital natives" generation. It can be noticed that the distinguishing features of their learning process is strongly influenced by technology, private and public multi-tasking, and the abundance of images to which they are submitted. This type of student shows short attention spans, they are zappers, they need a variety of small activities, preferably in a visual form, to maintain their attention. Some of the specific learning characteristics of this generation present a positive influence on the learning process. The students of this generation tend to show a natural capacity for using technology, not attempting at apprehending and mastering it, but instead they experiment with it and achieve great success, they appreciate being considered as co-experts in their courses, achieving results through cooperation and they get deeply involved when producing contents available for all. The "digital natives" appreciate horizontal hierarchical interactions and stop considering the professor as the only source of knowledge, and see him as a more experienced person with whom to cooperate.

Whether we use the term Student 2.0, the Now Generation3, Generation Y, the famous «theorized digital natives" so-called by Prensky (17), every professor will immediately pinpoint the idiosyncrasies. For such students, the act of thinking has become more important than knowledge itself, beliefs take the upper-hand on facts, the attention span has decreased dramatically, collaboration during the learning process reaches out world-wide, authority has no genuine hold on them.

## New competence

In the HES-SO environment, the crossroad for some of these features (horizontal interacting between professor-student, high level of computing literacy, little appetence for theoretical reasoning) results in a strong demand from the students to have access to modelized methods, directly transferable into the practical world, thus avoiding preliminary reflexion, which is time consuming and which generates insecurity and risks.

In a professional environment, a number of situations involve strict and common-to-all applications of procedures, in order to secure the excellence of the job to be achieved. Thus, it is highly recommended that nurses performing a health care action all undergo the same steps. It seems logical to solve a physics or maths problem by applying the same method and similarly the security rules in a firm must be applied in the same way by all.

However, the real professional environment for which the UAS students are trained, reaches way beyond the simple application of pre-established formulas. The main difference between an adapted professional and a competent professional lies not only in the application of principles, but also in "engaging or activating several types of knowledge, in a particular situation and in a given context", as analysed by Le Boterf (3). Thereby he distinguishes three factors resulting from competence, the will to act concerning

---

[2] Quoted in this document as HES-SO
[3] The young generation, everything and right away

context and individual motivation, the power to act referring to work organization, and the action taking which "implies knowing how to combine and rally pertinent resources. The latter constitutes a relevant theoretical frame which guides the transfer of knowledge from the professor to the student, the future professional.

Additionally, the current complex and changing world, requires active professional to dispose of a range of know-how in order to build a solid future (15). Among the know-hows required, we can identify the ability to comprehend problems arising in hitherto unseen contexts, the ability to identify, hierarchize and select relevant information, the ability to imagine alternative processes, even iconoclastic ones, and the ability to take adequate decisions, which all represent a central asset, in the process of choosing among critical items when taking action. Nevertheless, problem solving applied to cases closely related to real life, suitable strategy elaboration and decision communication, are seldom taught as such in the Swiss UAS curricula.

Therefore, we decided to create a serious game intended to train students to surpass their spontaneous approach when applying procedures and to develop their sense of analysis, as well as their ability in taking decisions.

## Gaming as a tool for alternative learning

Truly there is a consensus that serious games represent an efficient means for learning, although thorough studies on this matter remain insufficient. Some studies aim at demonstrating that gaming and its resulting pleasure make it a tool unsuitable for knowledge acquisition, quoting for example the philosopher Alain, who assumed, in 1932, that only what is painfully learnt can be memorized. This belief has evolved, but remains significant in tertiary education. University is still considered as a place where effort must be endured, where knowledge is transmitted vertically by an expert professor addressing the students-learners, who listen. In tertiary teaching, a vector for elitist perspectives, basing its laurels on fundamental or applied research, where reason and pure logic prevail, gaming as a means for learning remains a hard to imagine orientation.

However, the public, its expectations and capabilities having greatly evolved, it seems beneficial that pedagogical objects should equally evolve.

**Learning factors**

The quality of the learning process, its transferability from a theoretical to a real situation is multifactorial.

Several writers have pondered about the importance of motivation in the learning process. Thus, Nuttin (14) considers motivation as « any emotional tension, any feeling likely to trigger and support an action towards a goal ». His theory differentiates between two types of motivations :

- ✓ *intrinsic motivation* : when only interest and pleasure in the action drive the individual
- ✓ *extrinsic motivation*: when circumstances external to the individual underpin his action: positive or negative reward, pressure from the group etc.
- ✓ *amotivation* : when the individual, overpowered by uncontrollable factors, has the impression he cannot predict the consequences of his actions.

The coupling of need-interest also provides a better response: a learning object becomes more interesting when responding to a need, a desire, an urge, a pleasure etc.

We also wish to quote Viau (23) to remind us of some conditions for motivation during the learning process
- o make sense from the student's point of view
- o offer variety, and bond with the upcoming scheduled activities
- o represent a challenge which can be addressed and solved thanks to perseverance
- o be authentic and represent a real situation in every day or professional life.

- spur a cognitive activity from the learner, in which he must find links with previous activities, organize material, rely on prior knowledge etc.
- give a sense of responsibility to the learner by encouraging personal choice making
- favour interaction and collaboration among the learners
- comprise clear instructions
- be feasible during the given time

Tardif (21) heightens that « Situated learning » fits into pedagogical environments which take into consideration the students' preoccupations, the logic of their questioning. The knowledge built-up and the competence developed in such a context are very significant and, rather than being an abstract learning process, become learning in the action and from the action.

As for Piaget's studies (16), they show that any new knowledge is the result of an individual learning experience, relying on adaptation and assimilation notions which shape the adaptation process. The new knowledge only becomes effective when it is reassembled to integrate the learner's ideational network

Giordan (2) postulates that this adaptation alters the thinking schemes and, very frequently, comes to oppose the learner's prior knowledge. The latter learns by solving the cognitive conflict.

Finally, cultural constructivism reminds us that cultural influences (customs, tools, languages, etc.) can influence the learning process. Generally, tools used by the learners, affect their way of thinking, and therefore all cognitive operations produced. The computer, the Internet, video games have contributed in shaping the habits and the acting and thinking behaviour of students currently enrolled in university curricula.

Prenzky (15), in his theory on serious games, remarks that « the "stuff" to be learned — information, concepts, relationships, etc. — cannot be just "told" to these people. It must be learned by them, through questions, discovery, construction, interaction, and, above all, fun."

Again here we find the notion of interaction with knowledge, challenge and building-up mentioned by Viau (23).

This brief theoretical enlightening tends to show how serious games, as a fun tool, enables setting up trials, supports motivation and encourages the learning progression, as understood by the constructivism approach.

Subsequently, we wondered if students' expectations could meet with institutional conditions, to show sufficient ground for the development of such a tool.

## The digital natives' expectations

The « digital native » student in Switzerland, as in Europe, spends part of his leisure time playing video games. The increase in platforms (smartphones, tablets, laptops, game consoles) has contributed to a widespread use of video games among a public reaching far beyond the intensive players.

A survey conducted in Europe in 2012 by the Interactive Software Federation of Europe draws up the profile of the European gamer, sampling 16 European countries and 15'142 persons aged from 16 to 64, among which 650 people in Switzerland. The results for this country show that more than 25% of the gamers belong to the Y generation. Globally, 41% are gamers, among which 45% are women. 30% play on their smartphones or tablet and 20% game more than once a week.

In parallel, in May 2013, the e-learning centre HES-SO Cyberlearn launched a survey to gather digital native students' expectations in order to guide its future developments. The survey was launched early May 2013, on Cyberlearn's homepage during two weeks. The student population totals 20'000. We calculated the representative sample as follows: P (percentage): 50%, M (students population size): 17430, C (confidence level): 95%. E (error margin): 5%. Depending on the settings chosen, the size of the representative sample is of 376, and 800 students answered the questionnaire.

Most students generally study at a bachelor level (89%), a lower percentage is enrolled in master studies (8%) (3%: else). They are mostly between 18-26 years old (81%) (26-35 years old: 16%, older: 3%). 55% of them are women, 45%, men.

Among this student population, 59 % like to interact with their colleagues, 38 % get deeply involved in the class learning activities, and 31% prefer their professor to organize the learning activities.

When these students are asked as « digital natives », which items they wish to be made available to them in order to improve their learning process (in class or outside class), among a variety of possible answers, 10% choose serious games as a means for learning. It is relevant to link this answer to the one obtained in the European survey mentioned above, where 11% of the participants, when asked "what words do you associate with game?" attribute the words "informative/**educational**" to video games, thus pointing out the interest and evolution in the way gaming can contribute to a pedagogical input.

Thus, resorting to serious games makes it possible to take advantage of the distinctiveness of this new public in order to make it progress. As Prensky (18) points out: « students will not have short attention spans for learning if the approaches you take really engage them. It is possible to get learners of all ages totally involved in learning any subject matter ».

Prensky (18) adds that : « Using [serious games] may, however, mean re-thinking much of what you believe about teaching and training. » Indeed, this is where the shoe pinches, rather than arguing about true effectiveness issues in teaching or jeopardizing the academic reputation of a university delivering tasteless education, or being compromised by an amusing, light-hearted and entertaining teaching approach.

## The Gademavo game

The e-learning Center HES-SO Cyberlearn has, therefore, decided to refer to an actual case in order to estimate the possible benefits brought forward by using games in some of its university courses, by developing a simulation game. We have developed a game centered on problem solving and decision making, in a context closely related to real life professional situations, which the students might come across after graduation. Our objective is three-fold:

- Engage the student,
- Contribute to the development of the student's ability to make decisions in a complex environment.

Gademavo enables students to be confronted to a practical case connected to the professional context for which they are training. It concerns UAS students and aims at spurring their ability to solve problems and take suitable decisions in a graphic environment calling upon their future professional insertion.

Gademavo is available in French and English and can be freely used by all interested professors by accessing this address http://cyberlearn.hes-so.ch/gademavo.

The case to be solved is presented with the help of numerous multimedia resources and different mechanisms enabling the student to ponder about the proposed issue, while providing different game options (scoring of points, of objects, etc.). The students can freely choose from a range of several different cases set up previously.

Every game is used in a blended learning context, thus in connection with classroom teaching. It is particularly suitable for teaching involving analysis in steps and problem solving.

The game itself comprises an administrative interface, where the professor can customize the game parameters for the desired professional context and for the gaming procedures he wishes to adopt (interface, awards, game mode) and a client interface, in which the students can play.

**Integrating the game in the classroom**

The game is used in a blended learning context. Gademavo is a multi-platform game, and can, therefore, be used on a computer, as well as a portable, a laptop, a tablet such as an ipad or even on a smartphone.

The professor needs no computing competence to generate a game customized to his teaching context. He designs the case, related to his teaching field, creates or re-uses resources possibly illustrating the case (with the help of the Cyberlearn center, if so wished), structures the game for a specific class and defines the parameters (layout adapted to professional context, choice of a mini-game where points can be scored, etc.). He then launches the game in class and lets the students use the game at their own pace during two or three class sessions.

The game takes place in four rooms (meeting room, oval room, situation room and decision room) and lasts about 6 hours altogether. The students are invited to work during class during 2 sessions and outside the classroom for the remaining time. The 3rd session is used by the professor for feedback, per group and per class.

Although this is not a multi-user game, the students work in groups. They choose the case to be treated, listen to the client/patient, select the resources which they think are appropriate, analyse further resources, score points and collect useful objects by answering questions on the topic covered by the game, or by playing a mini-game proposed to them by the professor. They can ask other groups for help inside the game. The group which provides help scores extra points, the group receiving help does not evolve.

In Version 1 of the game, the students must ask the right questions and analyse documents with the help of tools commonly used for problem-solving in a non-gaming environment. They can then send the produced documents to their professor directly from the game. In Version 2 of the game, some simple and efficient tools are proposed inside the game to avoid having to quit the interface and to proceed with the analysis, thus providing complete immersion.

**Game procedure**

✓ *First room : Meeting Room*

Figure 8 : Meeting Room

Once the game is launched, the student group finds itself in the meeting room, the first room in the game.

*Pedagogical intention*

As the game is a template which can be customized to various professional contexts (health, computing, communication etc.), we gave priority to the office metaphor which can easily be proposed for different professions (legal office, physiotherapist office, communication agency etc.). We have then parcelled the different steps. The first room allows the game to start.

In this room, the students can :

- ✓ form the group,
- ✓ choose to purchase help from a « wizard »,
- ✓ choose the case they wish to analyse among the « clients/patients »
- ✓ score points and win objects by answering quizzes.

✓ **Second room : Oval Room**

Figure 9 : Oval Room

### Pedagogical Intention

In this room, the first expected action is to furnish the room, display diplomas on the wall, before the « client/patient » is willing to talk. These actions cost points. Once everything is set-up, icons appear when clicking on the « client/patient » who orally explains which actions must be taken. These icons give access to audio, video and text files which illustrate the case. Some of the information can be useless, some is without interest, but some is relevant. The students must select the three most pertinent information, which is automatically placed in a safe and remains accessible throughout the game. From here, access to the other resources is denied.

This selection process constitutes the first step in a problem solving procedure: selecting pertinent information among a large range of choices.

In this room, the students can :

- ✓ furnish the room,
- ✓ watch resources which explain the case,
- ✓ select relevant resources.

✓ **Third room : Situation Room**

Figure 10 : Situation room

*Pedagogical intention*

In this room, the students can access different, but minor scale, resources, which shed a new light on the case (e.g. medical context, blood results, x-rays, etc.). In order to look at these resources, the students need the appropriate devices (microscope, x-ray machine etc.). These devices can be won when completing quizzes. If the required devices are missing, the students can return to the meeting room and complete more quizzes with the hope of winning more devices, or they can ask other groups to lend them the missing devices.

This procedure boosts the students to go over some quizzes again and so to go deeper into the underlying theory of the exercise, and this provides a new opportunity to understand the case thanks to a new type of resource: the useful samples.

In this room, the students can:

- ✓ select samples,
- ✓ view the samples.

✓ **Fourth room : Decision Room**

Figure 11 : Decision room

*Pedagogical intention*

In this room, the students must take a first decision to submit to the « client/patient » in order to find a solution adapted to his problem. The students must select some analysis items and link them to three questions: what is the problem, what is the objective aimed at by treating this case, and what are the actual measures to be taken to reach the objective and solve the case. This choice is then automatically proposed to the client/patient who will provide a brief feedback. If the choice is « perfect », the game ends and the scores, as well as the final decision taken, are sent to the professor. If the choice is not « perfect », the students continue their effort by working on two more decisions. When three wrong combinations are selected, the game is over and lost. The game was designed for 270 possible combinations from which the students can select their propositions.

This procedure enables students to modelize the case by synthesizing, structuring and organizing the disparate data they usually have to deal with, which represents a truly adequate method for problem solving and decision taking. In Version 2 of the game, this feature becomes more sophisticated, by asking students to describe in more detail the solution they propose concerning the decisional choice made earlier on.

In this room, the students can:

- ✓ select and organize the elements of the decision taking,
- ✓ select and send the professor the documents produced to achieve their personal analysis procedure (in Version 2, the students can create these documents in Gademavo)

- ✓ submit their decision to the « client-patient » three times.

We plan a follow-up of the game through an assessment to favour reflexion on the actual learning achieved (metacognitive process)

**Acceptance and impact of the game on students**

In a first phase, we tested the game with students and adapted it according to their remarks. From March 2013, we will conduct a study to assess the impact and acceptance of the Gademavo game with two classes of the second year Bachelor in Economics, as part of a course for communication inside the firm. The first class counts 60 full-time students, split into two groups, and the second class counts 30 part-time students.

We will assess the following features :

- ✓ game acceptance,
- ✓ interest in the game,
- ✓ full completion of the game,
- ✓ time needed for taking the correct decision,
- ✓ number of points scored
- ✓ competence improvement between the beginning and end of the test.

We also wanted to evaluate to what extend the knowledge proposed in a formal manner during the course is grasped better or differently when using a game, and to check whether it has turned into competence applicable on the field. Indeed, as Bellotti, Kapralos, Lee, Moreno-Ge and Berta (1) proclaim « An important aspect in the evaluation of serious games, like other educational tools, is user performance assessment». At the end of the game, a questionnaire is sent to all students, members of the group to assess their expertise, to measure both, the theoretical level (linked to the quizzes completed in the game) and the competence level in problem solving and decision taking. Bellotti, Kapralos, Lee, Moreno-Ge et Berta (1) highlight that « the measure of the person's performance through a test is a more objective assessment of the game. ». Since the game is played in groups, it is enlightening to perform an individual assessment to find out if there are differences in the individual level of competence among the participants of a same group.

## Conclusion

Serious game is merely one of the numerous resources, which encourages the digital native student to part from its regurgitation position, preferred in the traditional model « I tell you, you tell me, and I grade you ». The idea is not to replace the course with a type of resource adapted to the educational challenge raised by the students 2.0, but rather to vary the means used to address the acquisition of new knowledge.

By adopting a critical and engaged attitude, based on reflexion, on decision taking, on collaboration when addressing knowledge, a tool such as Gademavo plays its part in setting-up a tertiary educational teaching method, renewed, efficient and adapted to the current world and to the competence requirements of the future environments.

## References

Bellotti, F. , Kapralos, B., Lee, K., Moreno-Ger, P., Bera, R. (2013) *Assessment in and of Serious Games: An Overview.* Advances in Human-Computer Interaction Volume 2013, Article ID 136864.http://dx.doi.org/10.1155/2013/136864.

Giordan, A., de Vecchi, G. *Les origines du savoir*. Delachaux, Neuchatel, 1987, réédition Ovadia 2010.

Le Boterf, G. (1997). *De la compétence*. Paris: Editions d'organisation.

Le Boterf, G. (2000). *Construire les compétences individuelles et collectives*, Paris: Éditions d'organisation.

Callois, R. (2001, 1981). *Man, Play, and Games* in Champaign: University of Illinois Press.

European summary of 2012 ISFE Consumer Study
http://www.oecd.org/edu/school/programmeforinternationalstudentassessmentpisa/34473687.pdf.

Fabricatore C. (2000). *Learning and videogames: an unexploited synergy* in Learning Development Institute. www.learndev.org/dl.

Freinet, C. (1964). *Tome 2 : Les invariants pédagogiques*.

European summary of 2012 ISFE Consumer Study
http://www.oecd.org/edu/school/programmeforinternationalstudentassessmentpisa/34473687.pdf.

Jonassen, E. , MAHWAH, NJ., LAWRENCE ERLBAUMHILL, M. (2005). *More colleges offering video game courses* in Handbook of Research on Educational Communications and Technology (2nd ed., pp. 571-581).

Gee, J. P. (2003). *What video games have to teach us about learning and literacy (2nd ed.)* in New York: Palgrave Macmillan.

Montessori, M. (1912). *The Montessori Method.* New York: Frederick A. Stokes Company. Full text available online at http://digital.library.upenn.edu/women/montessori/method/method.html.

Natkin S. (2004). *Jeux vidéo et médias du XXIe siècle* in : Paris: Vuibert, 112 p.

Nuttin, J. (1991). *Théorie de la motivation humaine du besoin au projet d'action.* Paris : PUF.

OCDE Collectif (2004). *Résoudre des problèmes, un atout pour réussir. Premières évaluations des compétences transdisciplinaires issues de PISA 2003.*

Piaget J. (1936). La naissance de l'intelligence chez l'enfant. Paris : Delachaux et Niestlé. http://www.fondationjeanpiaget.ch/fjp/site/textes/VE/JP36_NdI_avpropos_intro.pdf

Prensky, M. (2001*). From Digital Game-Based Learning* in Ed. McGraw-Hill

Prensky, M. (2001). *Digital Natives, Digital Immigrants 1 et 2.* In : On the horizon (MCB University Press. Vol. 9 N° 5).

Rieber, L. P., SMITH, L., & NOAH, D. (1998). *The value of serious play.* In : Educational Technology, 38(6), 29-37.

Sauvé, L., KAUFMAN, D. (2010). *Jeux et simulations éducatifs. Etudes de cas et leçons apprises.* In : Presses de l'Université du Québec.

Tardif, J. (1992). *Pour un enseignement stratégique: L'apport de la psychologie cognitive (French Edition).* Editions Logiques. http://www.usherbrooke.ca/ssf/veille/bulletin-perspectives-ssf/novembre-2011/le-ssf-veille/jeux-serieux-apprendre-en-jouant-jusqua-luniversite/. http://www.ccdmd.qc.ca/correspo/Corr5-3/Viau.html.

# 24 Learning Geosciences in Virtual Worlds: Engaging Students in Real-World Experiences

Reneta D. Lansiquot, Janet Liou-Mark, Reginald A. Blake,
The City University of New York, United States

## Introduction

Recent global and national environmental crises remind us of how vulnerable we are to natural disasters and also how critical comprehensive geosciences knowledge is to our survival. Unfortunately, an acute crisis remains in graduating science, technology, engineering, and mathematics (STEM) majors in the United States, which is even more pronounced among the geosciences. Since the 1950s, fewer undergraduate and graduate degrees have been granted in the geosciences than in any other STEM field. The American Geosciences Institute (2011) reports that, over the past 18 years, only 11%–15% of seventh and eighth graders formally take a year of earth science. This low percentage is due to the integration of earth science components in the general science curriculum, thus partially fulfilling the earth science requirement.

Nonetheless, formal and informal geosciences education is as dismal in New York State as it is nationally. In New York City, middle school students have to take the Earth Science Intermediate Level Science Test (ILST) while high school students take the Earth Science Regents Examination. Both the test and the exam are based on the Earth Science Core Curriculum which is based on Standards 1, 2, 4, 6, and 7 of the New York State Learning Standards for Mathematics, Science, and Technology:

- Standard 1: Students will use mathematical analysis, scientific inquiry, and engineering design, as appropriate, to pose questions, seeks answers, and develop solutions.
- Standard 2: Students will access, generate, process, and transfer information using appropriate technologies.
- Standard 4: Students will understand and apply scientific concepts, principles, and theories pertaining to the physical setting and living environment and recognize the historical development of ideas in science.
- Standard 6: Students will understand the relationships and common themes that connect mathematics, science, and technology and apply the themes to these and other areas of learning.
- Standard 7: Students will apply the knowledge and thinking skills of mathematics, science, and technology to address real-life problems and make informed decisions.

In general, the students are tested on their major understandings, skills, and real-world applications drawn from the following eight subject areas: 1. Size, Shape, and Composition of Earth; 2. Mapping; 3. Rocks and Minerals; 4. Weathering, Erosion, Deposition, and Landforms; 5. Earthquakes and Plate Tectonics; 6. Earth History; 7. Meteorology and Climate; and 8. Astronomy.

At project initiation, the New York state-wide pass rates of students who scored at Level 3 and 4 for the ILST was 30%, but the mean ILST pass rate for the two middle schools that are a part of this project was only 20%. The New York statewide pass rate of students who scored between 85%–100% on the Earth Science Regents Examination was 5%, and the mean Earth Science Regents Examination pass rate for the two high schools in this project was 2%. These statistics highlight the poor geosciences knowledge of our students.

In order to meet state and city standards, students must be able to demonstrate conceptual understanding by using a concept accurately in order to explain observations and make predictions and by representing the concept in multiple ways (through words, diagrams, graphs or charts, as appropriate). Both aspects of understanding —explaining and representing — are required to meet this standard. City performance standards call for teachers to frame questions to distinguish cause and effect. Students should be able to identify or control variables in experimental and non-experimental research settings, as well as work individually and in teams to collect and share information and ideas. Computer simulations can help students gain interdisciplinary problem-solving strategies (Cabo & Lansiquot, 2013).

## Engaging Virtual Experiences in the Geosciences

Effective educational models, such as computer simulations, should allow for multiple representations of content. Our virtual-world geoscience simulations allow students to enjoy experiences not normally available in an urban classroom (e.g., hiking up a mountain with their teachers and classmates) while learning technical content, thus enhancing the learning experience. Moreover, virtual worlds are persistent, multidimensional, graphical environments consisting of open communities in which people can establish a sense of presence, learn, socialize, and collaborate (Downey, 2012; cf. Schroeder, 2008; Spence, 2008). Since academic success is socially motivated, computer-supported collaborative learning is one of the most promising ways to improve teaching and learning (Lipponen, 2002). To promote inquiry and engagement, we used Second Life, a three-dimensional online virtual world so that students could experience the impossible in a classroom setting exploring geosciences concepts by, for example, following a trail up a mountain and taking weather readings on the way to the top. Blended learning in online virtual worlds can help create and support a sense of class community that keeps students engaged to develop advanced geosciences knowledge (Atkinson, 2008; Russell, 2007). This type of online interaction is more explicit because students can see virtual avatars of each other (see Figures 1 & 2) that gestures, rather than needing to rely on purely text-based interactions (Lansiquot, 2012). We used Second Life to create, design, and program three-dimensional geosciences modules. Accompanying lesson plans were based on New York State Standards and New York City Performance Standards. We used mathematics components to underpin and elucidate geosciences concepts.

The geosciences modules were developed with detailed explanations of the lesson plan's engagement with student learning and explicit expected outcomes. Specifically, students were expected to understand the following: Weather patterns become evident when weather variables are observed, measured, and recorded. These variables include air temperature, air pressure, moisture (relative humidity and dew point), precipitation (rain, snow, hail, sleet, etc.), wind speed and direction, and cloud cover. Weather variables are interrelated. For example, temperature and humidity affect air pressure and the probability of precipitation. Air temperature, dew point, cloud formation, and precipitation are affected by the expansion and contraction of air due to vertical atmospheric movement.

We developed the mountain weather module activity to include:
1. Initial exploration with guiding questions
2. Teams for detailed data collection (field campaign)
3. Presentation of data and initial explanations by team
4. Hands-on activities to explore theory behind each concept

This module also includes an accompanying mountain weather lesson plan for teachers that cover the following five concepts: 1) drop in pressure with altitude, 2) drop in temperature with altitude, 3) behavior of dew point and relative humidity with altitude, 4) behavior inside the cloud, and 5) climate changes over the back of a mountain.

After the students collect their data, reflection on the process of measuring and collecting include initial discussion and exploration, detailed exploration and initial analysis, and learning and applying the theory (see Lansiquot, Blake, Liou-Mark, & Vant-Hull, 2012).

*Figure 1.* Student avatar hiking up trail on geosciences virtual island, terra-formed for exploration and data collection.

*Figure 2.* Student avatar exploring wind patterns on the geosciences island virtual peninsula.

    Building on the mountain weather lesson, the sea breeze lesson engaged students in the concepts that land heats and cools more rapidly than water; warm air expands, spilling excess air at the top onto neighboring regions and creating a circulation; the effect of air being spilled from a warm onto cooler regions is low pressure in warm regions and higher pressure in cooler regions; and air will move from regions of high to low pressure.

Our sea breeze module activity includes:
1. Exploring wind patterns, first attempt at explanation
2. Using instruments, measure pressure, temperature
3. Graphing of data, second attempt at explanation
4. Appling pressure blocks to explain phenomena
5. Appling concepts to sea breeze day/night, peninsula versus coast

## The Study

Geosciences virtual modules were created by a team consisting of a geosciences faculty, post-doctorate scientist, technical writing specialist, learning specialist, mathematics educator, and two high school science teachers. High school students explored mountain weather and sea breeze patterns with their classmates.

A sample of 17 high school students was recruited from City Polytechnic High School of Engineering, Architecture, and Technology (City Poly) located downtown Brooklyn, New York. Two females and 15 males participated in the two-day module testing. There were six ninth graders and ten eleventh graders, and they were either enrolled in a Chemistry course (15) or Living Environment course (2). All the students were not planning to take the New York State Regents for their respective science class.

Based on student observations, during the spring 2012 mountain weather module pilot study, we realized that students should first be allowed to become familiar with the virtual world, to explore our geosciences island, and simply play. In the fall 2012, the cohort of high school students explored the virtual geosciences island for two hours. During a subsequent extended two-hour class session, students completed the mountain weather module. Finally, during the last two-hour class session, students completed the sea breeze module.

## Findings

A paired-samples $t$-test was conducted to compare the pre- and post-knowledge tests for the mountain weather module. There was a statistically significant difference in the scores for the pre-test (M=3.1, SD=1.3) and post-test (M=4.8, SD=1.9); $t(17)= 4.9$, $p<.01$. These results suggest that the exploratory exercises in an online virtual world had increased students' knowledge of mountain weather. A paired-samples $t$-test was also conducted to compare the pre- and post-knowledge tests for the sea breeze module. There was a statistically significant difference in the scores for the pre-test (M=7.0, SD=2.8) and post-test (M=8.3, SD=3.1); $t(16)=2.6$, $p<.05$. These results suggest that the exploratory exercises in an online virtual world had increased students' knowledge of mountain weather and sea breeze in geosciences concepts.

The results from the module feedback survey showed that City Poly students strongly felt that they had a better understanding of mountain weather and sea breeze and that the geosciences concepts were interesting. They strongly felt they had learned something new about the geosciences and they did not find the modules too challenging. Table 1 summarizes the mean responses from both module feedback surveys (see Bong 2002, 2004).

Table 1.
*Mountain Weather and Sea Breeze Modules Student Responses*

|  | Mountain Weather Module Mean (n=17) | Sea Breeze Module Mean (n=16) |
|---|---|---|
|  | 1=strongly disagree and 7=strongly agree | |
| I have a better understanding of the concept after completing the geosciences module. | 5.88 | 6.00 |
| The geosciences module was challenging. | 4.35 | 4.63 |
| The geosciences concepts in the module were interesting. | 6.24 | 5.53 |
| I had a difficult time focusing on the module. | 2.53 | 3.53 |
| I learned something new about the geosciences through the module. | 6.35 | 6.06 |

**Some anecdotal responses regarding the mountain weather module included:**

What did you like best about the module?
*The fact that it was like exploring real stuff without the fear of heights.*
*I like exploring the world and looking around.*
*I liked learning how clouds are formed. It is very hands-on and interesting. I like this format learning*
*It kept me entertained.*
*The physical example of a cloud in Second Life.*
*I liked how I learned that when the altitude increases, the temperature decreases.*
*It made this class more interesting and it made it feel like real life.*

What was the most important thing you learned?
*The dew point was where clouds form or the ingredients needed to form it.*
*The most important thing that I learned was how certain objects are used and that they measure.*
*Learned how clouds forms*
*Clouds form when the dew point reaches a certain temperature*
*I learned about the temperature and wind on a mountain*
*The most important thing was learning about the altitude and pressure, temperature etc.*

**Some anecdotal responses regarding the sea breeze module included:**

What did you like best about the module?
*I like the visual aid help me understand sea breeze better.*
*The fact that it had these data that could be recorded in different areas.*
*What I liked the most is being able to use Second Life to understand these concepts.*

What was the most important thing you learned?
*How pressure works because of the wind and other factors*
*I learned what a barometer is and what it measures.*
*The direction of wind in certain locations*
*I learned how temperature and pressure is related.*
*I learned about the temperature of places near the beach.*
*I learned temperature is higher on land.*

## Discussion

Recreating the concept of mountain weather in a virtual world was challenging. There were many concepts and components that needed be covered in order to provide an educational experience to students. The simulation had to be created in such a way that students who interacted with it could observe key components and collect relevant data. Students needed to be able to provide accurate results and a conclusion explaining their understanding of mountain weather and sea breeze. Creating each component required the use of a different feature in Second Life. The features used have been broken up into feature-based solutions. For example, scripting in Second Life is the solution to creating the five following integrated tools that students used to observe their environment:

1. Altitude meter: Contains a get z-axis script and convert the height, the z-axis height into meters.
2. Thermometer: Contain a get z-axis script. The script calculates the altitude traveled up, then calculated the temperature (i.e., air temperature drops 1 degree Celsius every 100 meter altitude increase).
3. Pressure meter: Builds on the altitude meter, since air pressure is reduced when altitude increases.
4. Relative Humidity meter: Similar to the other tools, the relative humidity meter has a get z-axis script; as altitude increases, relative humidity does too.
5. Dew Point calculator: This was the most difficult tool to program because it requires student input. The tool asks student for the relative humidity and temperature and calculate the dew point after both variables have been provided.

Programming the aforementioned tools necessary for students to observe and collect data was not as straightforward as we anticipated because physics and mathematical calculations are not precise in Second Life. These tools did not have a "tangible" object associated with them (see tools in the bottom left of Figures 1 & 2).

Creating a mountain in Second Life was the simplest part of this project. As we had a region with terra-forming rights, creating a mountain is as easy as raising the terrain with a few simple clicks. A hiking path could be paved for students as a trail guide. To make the simulation more realistic, trees and other plant life were also easily added. We applied two terrain textures. The windward side of the mountain had to be textured with a green terrain; the leeward side had to be textured with a dry desert-like texture. This provides a visual understanding of how mountains, or more specifically, rain affects an entire region.

Rain and wind are necessary to portray clouds. Particles in Second Life are created using scripting. Particles were the most time-consuming component to complete in order to provide the visual effects of mountain weather and sea breeze. Particle clouds were placed over the mountain. Rain particles were programmed to fall from the clouds, but required input from either another object or an avatar, such as a touch, via mouse click. For mountain weather, wind was portrayed simply by displaying the slow movement of cloud and/or rain particles over the x-axis or y-axis. For sea breeze, wind was portrayed by placing flags along the peninsula so that students are able to more clearly see the direction of the wind (see Figure 2).

We created object boards that display diagrams of how mountain weather works, including billboards with information that also linked to websites and played videos. We also created an information center (a shed at the base of the mountain) for students to obtain their tools. With these tools, students are able to explore the mountain climate changes on the island as a weather model. Students were able to hike up the trails with their teacher and classmates and take readings along the way provided by the scripted tools. With this information, students are also able to form conclusions and understand how mountain weather works. Additional media were also provided in this online virtual world.

## Conclusions

We plan to continue the concept design for a natural disasters module. This module will include three-dimensional simulations of an earthquake, hurricane, tsunami, and volcano. These natural disasters in the virtual world will simulate ground-based sensing, and will be incorporated into a new interdisciplinary course at the College. Unfortunately, in addition to Second Life as a deployment environment becoming less predictable, we also have limited virtual space. In lieu of purchasing more virtual islands, and incurring additional costs, we moved over to an open-source application that will allow for the creation of islands, as needed.

OpenSimulator is an open source multi-platform, multi-user 3D application server. Hosted on our college server system, it can be used to create virtual worlds that can be accessed through a variety of clients. OpenSimulator will allow faculty to customize their worlds using the technologies they feel work best – its framework is designed to be easily extensible. In addition, by gaining control of the server side component of these virtual environments, public schools will be able to refine and add additional capabilities, scale as needed, and have better control of student and teacher access. We have archived and moved our geosciences island from Second Life to OpenSimulator.

## References

American Geosciences Institute (2011). *Status of the geoscience workforce 2011*. Retrieved from http://www.agiweb.org/workforce/reports.html.

Atkinson, T. (2008). Second Life for educators: Myths and realities. *TechTrends, 52*(5), 26-29.

Bong, M. (2002). Predictive utility of subject-, task-, and problem-specific self-efficacy judgments for immediate and delayed academic performance. *Journal of Experimental Education, 70*(2), 133-162.

Bong, M. (2004). Academic motivation in self-efficacy, task value, achievement goal orientations, and attributional beliefs. *Journal of Educational Research, 97*(6), 287-297.

Cabo, C., & Lansiquot, R. D. (2013). Development of interdisciplinary problem-solving strategies through games and computer simulations. In R. D. Lansiquot (Ed.), *Cases on interdisciplinary research trends in science, technology, engineering, and mathematics: Studies on urban classrooms* (pp. 268-294). New York: IGI Global.

Downey, S. (2012). Visualizing taxonomy for virtual worlds. *Journal of Educational Multimedia and Hypermedia, 21*(1), 53-69.

Lansiquot, R. D. (2012). Real classrooms in virtual worlds: Scaffolding interdisciplinary collaborative writing. In A. P. Ayala (Series Ed.) *Smart innovation, systems and technologies: Vol. 17. Intelligent and adaptive educational-learning systems: Achievements and trends* (pp. 269-292). New York: Springer.

Lansiquot, R., Blake, R., Liou-Mark, J., & Vant-Hull, B. (2012). Experiencing the impossible: Designing virtual modules in the geosciences. In P. Resta (Ed.), *Proceedings of the Society for Information Technology and Teacher Education International Conference 2012* (pp. 4142-4145). Chesapeake, VA: AACE.

Lipponen, L. (2002). Exploring foundations for computer-supported collaborative learning. In Proceedings of the *Conference on Computer Support for Collaborative Learning* (pp. 72-81). Boulder, CO: International Society of the Learning Sciences.

OpenSimulator. (2013). Retrieved from http://opensimulator.org.

Russell, D. (2007). GEOWORLDS: Utilizing problem-based scenarios in Second Life to develop advanced geosciences knowledge. In T. Bastiaens & S. Carliner (Eds.), *Proceedings of World Conference on E-Learning in Corporate, Government, Healthcare, and Higher Education 2007* (pp. 1813-1818). Chesapeake, VA: AACE.

Schroeder, R. (2008). Defining virtual worlds and virtual environments. *Journal of Virtual Worlds Research*. Retrieved from http://journals.tdl.org/jvwr/index.php/jvwr/article/view/294

Second Life. (2013). Retrieved from http://www.secondlife.com.

Spence, J. (2008). Demographics of virtual worlds. *Journal of Virtual World Research*. Retrieved from http://journals.tdl.org/jvwr/index.php/jvwr/article/view/360

## Acknowledgements

This material is based upon work supported by the National Science Foundation under Grant No. 1108281.

# 25 Video Game Genres and What is Learned From Them
Eddie Gose & Michael Menchaca, University of Hawaii, USA

## Introduction

In an industry grossing over $9.5 billion in 2007, computer and video games have become a popular pastime for players of all ages in Western and Asian societies ("The Entertainment Software Association - Industry Facts," 2012). It is predicted that by 2017 the video game global market will reach $78 billion ("DFC Intelligence - DFC Intelligence Forecasts Worldwide Online Game Market to Reach $79 Billion by 2017," n.d.). Video games are found everywhere from video game parlors, computers, tablets, and even cellular devices. People are growing up playing video games and current research indicates video games may be affecting the way people learn (Chazerand & Geeroms, 2008; James Paul Gee, 2007b, 2007b; Prensky, 2003).

Video game players, also known as gamers, use cognitive skills to pass stages, beat monsters, solve puzzles, or beat games. Gee (2003) describes a video game as a world that a gamer integrates and participates in, a realm only available via games. In order to progress in games, players must be able to make decisions, attain information, complete complex tasks, and manage resources. Video games have also become a mainstream form of entertainment even encroaching onto television, music, and movies. The average age of a gamer is 35 years old and they have played video games for an average of about twelve years. Pew Internet and American Life Project reports nearly 99% of teen boys and 94% of teen girls are playing video games (Lenhart, Kahne, Middaugh, Macgill, Evans, & Vitak, 2008).

The attention so far in this literature review has been about the aggressiveness and the social science behind how video games affect people. Researchers are demystifying the notion that video games are more than just violence and mindless activity, they are currently finding that learning occurs during game play (Gee, 2007a, 2007c; Shaffer et al., 2004). The current generation of serious games include powerful simulations of real-world systems that activate critical thought and decision making (J. P. Gee, 2003; Jenkins, Klopfer, Squire, & Tan, 2003). Video games may be used as a highly effective learning tool to satisfy the demands of learners who want to be interested and engaged with the curricular content (Prensky, 2003). This section on learning through video games will focus on the research and analysis of how video games are affecting learning.

## Statement of the Problem

A review of current literature revealed a lack of research on the topic of video game genres with practically no research on video game genres and learning. The current trend of video game research is based on studies that focused on a particular video game and not the video game genre that it belongs to. In the real world, video game titles have a shelf life governed by its popularity. If the game becomes boring, obsolete, or replaced with a newer version, then that video game is put aside and becomes a distant memory. Video game genres tended to stay the same no matter what game title was released under a particular genre. The purpose of this study was to explore video game players' identification of video game genres and what they have learned from playing the genres.

## Research Questions

RQ1. What are the video game genres identified and defined by video game players?
RQ2. What are the learning constructs (skills, abilities, and/or dispositions) identified and defined by video game players from playing the different video game genres?

## Conceptual Framework

The theoretical framework to study perceptions of learning came from George Kelly's (1963) Personal Construct Theory (PCT). In this particular study, the qualitative portion identified the different elements (video game genres) and learning constructs (skills, abilities, and/or dispositions). PCT was developed to measure participant knowledge through a psychological process known as a repertory grid. The repertory grid is a tool used to qualitatively identify elements and constructs. Working within the framework of PCT, the research aimed to survey video game players' identification of video game genres and to also identify perceived learning constructs from playing those genres.

Working within the framework of PCT, this research aimed to survey video game players' identification of video game genres (elements) and identification of perceived learning constructs from playing those genres. This first step required the use of two focus groups. Both focus groups were asked to identify and define what video game genres they could identify. Once that data was collected, they were then asked to identify and define what were they have learned from playing the different video game genres. Once the data had been collected from both groups, two follow up interviews were conducted to ensure accuracy of results.

## Participants

Eight undergraduate and graduate students (18-25 years old) attending a Research I University were interviewed in the focus group phase of the study. The students were affiliated with the video game playing club and officially recognized by the University system as a registered independent organization. The school is a public institution of higher education and the school is classified as a Research I university on the Carnegie Classification of Institutions.

As recommended for qualitative research (Daniel, 2011; Merriam, 2009), the researcher employed purposive sampling in which participants were chosen based on certain criteria. Theoretical sampling of this particular set of subjects were chosen based on theoretical categories which provided a certain polar type (Eisenhardt, 1989). Rather than using a sampling of the general populous, the researchers utilized purposive sampling because of the participants' knowledge, experience, and expertise as members of a specific target population. The eight participants fit the description of a video game player who is in an institute for higher education and is a member of a video game playing organization. On a side note, only one individual was female while the rest of the participants were male. Of the two focus groups, one individual from each group was later asked to participate in the one-to-one interview portion of the study.

## Findings

Because PCT has been successful in other exploratory studies, this study utilized PCT to answer the research questions on identifying and defining the different video game genres and identifying and defining the learning constructs generated from each video game genre.

For research question number 1: What are the video game genres identified and defined by video game players? The RepGrid was used to draw out the participants' identification and definition of the elements. The theme was video game genres and the element or sub-theme was a video game genre. The researcher asked for consensus of each identified element so that all of the major video game genres were recorded. Along with identifying each element, each group was asked to define each element. Examples of some of the elements were real time strategy, puzzle, sports, and first person shooters. Specific video game titles were not included as elements, but were recorded as examples that could be used in the survey tool. Along with using the RepGrid tool to identify the elements for the first research question, the researcher also facilitated for group effect for the best results possible (Carey & Smith, 1994; Kelly, 1963).

In regards to the first theme of video game genres, the focus groups and interviews reported twelve sub-themes. Those sub-themes were the different video game genres identified which were role-playing games (RPG), massively multiplayer online role-playing games (MMORPG), first person shooter (FPS), sports, puzzle, real-time strategy (RTS), action, turn based, simulation, fighting, kinetic controlled, and casual (see Table 1). The participants also provided the definitions for each video game genre. Video game title examples were also provided to help clearly exemplify what video game titles associated with a video game genre. Evaluating different video game genres is an important first step in gaining a better understanding how these genres relate to different learning from playing video games.

Table 1. Identified video game genres, definitions, and examples.

| Video Game Genre | Definition | Examples |
| --- | --- | --- |
| Role playing games (RPG) | A game in which players take on the role of a hero or character who engages in an adventure | Final Fantasy, Knights of the Old Republic, Mass Effect, Dragon Age |
| Massively multiplayer online RPG (MMORPG) | Online role playing games (RPG) which allow large amounts of gamers to play in an evolving virtual world at the same time via the internet. | World of Warcraft, EVE Online, DC Universe Online |
| First person shooter games (FPS) | Video game genre centered on a weapon-based combat through a first person perspective. | Counter Strike, Battlefield, Call of Duty |
| Sports games | Video game genre that simulates the practice and play of any traditional sports. | FIFA Soccer, Madden NFL, NBA 2K |
| Puzzle games | Video games that emphasize puzzle solving. | Bejeweled, Tetris, Solitaire |
| Real time strategy (RTS) | Time-based video game genre that centers around resource and building management. This genre utilizes war game type of gameplay. | Starcraft, Age of Empires, Warcraft |
| Action games | Video game genre that physically challenges the video game player's character. | Grand Theft Auto, Ratchet and Clank, Super Mario |
| Turn based games | Video games that involve a mix of strategy and tactics to beat opponents, in a pattern of turn taking. | X-COM, Final Fantasy Tactics, Shining Force, Monopoly, Rampart |
| Simulation games | Video games that depict real world situations, physics, and events. | The Sims, Ace Combat, Gran Turismo, Rollercoaster Tycoon |
| Fighting games | Video game genre which one video game player battles another (artificially controlled and/or player controlled) character. | Smash brothers, Street Fighter, Marvel vs. Capcom, Tekken |
| Kinetic controlled games | Video games that utilizes a player's physical movements to actively control the in game character. There is usually of a movement peripheral that records the player's movement to interact with the game's mechanics | Rock Band, Just Dance, Championship Sports |
| Casual games | Video games that are simple games with simple rules that may be played with no complex time commitment required, and played by a mass audience of casual gamers | Pac-Man, Pinball, FarmVille, Plants vs. Zombies, PopCap Games |

The second research question in the study was: What are the learning constructs (skills, abilities, and/or dispositions) identified and defined by video game players from playing the different video game genres? The RepGrid was used to draw out the participants' identification and definition of the learning constructs from playing the different video game genres. The identification of the elements used in the RepGrid was used to determine what the participants had learned from playing the different video game genres. Learning constructs were then defined. Once again, the identification of the learning concepts was derived from the same highly specialized group of individuals, that their identification and definitions for each learning concept is interpreted as expert opinion. Thus, research question number two was answered.

Table 2 shows the comprehensive list of all learning constructs. The theme of learning constructs had nineteen sub-themes. The sub-themes are highlighted in the table under the heading of Learning Construct. There were eleven learning constructs that were supported by the focus groups and interviews. Those included conflict management, communication skills, crafting, critical thinking, attention to detail building management, hand-eye coordination, how to be competitive, interpersonal skills, map awareness, and conduct research. There were eight other learning constructs supported by at least one of the groups and both interviews. Those included coding/computer programming, creating a community, economics, reading comprehension, resource management, strategy, spatial thinking, and time management. The comprehensive list of nineteen learning constructs compiled from this study is a first attempt at identifying what people are learning from playing different video games. Its significance to the current body of video game research is that this study is classifying different learning constructs not done before by other researchers.

Table 2. Identified learning constructs and its definitions.

| LC# | Learning Construct | Definition |
| --- | --- | --- |
| LC01 | Coding/computer programming | is the process of editing or writing source code to modify gameplay in a video game. |
| LC02 | Conflict Management | is the process of limiting the negative aspects of conflict. This process includes dealing with disputes in a rational, effective, and fair way. The aim of conflict management in a video game environment usually involves problem resolving abilities and good negotiating skills to resolve conflict within a game or between real life players. |
| LC03 | Communication Skills | is the ability to convey information to another person or a group of people. |
| LC04 | Creating a Community | is the process of developing and/or maintaining a small group of individuals to start conversations around specific tasks, hobbies, interests, organizations, or a video game. |
| LC05 | Crafting | is the method to which a video game player learns to produce items (blocks, tools, materials, armor, etc.) for game use or trade. |
| LC06 | Critical thinking | is the method to which a video game player learns to reason at a high level of thought. |
| LC07 | Attention to detail | is the method to which a video game player learns to concentrate on the important details necessary to completing or accomplishing different tasks. |
| LC08 | Building management | is the method to which a video game player learns to develop certain structures in order to create products necessary for economical success or growth. |
| LC09 | Hand-eye coordination | is the coordinated control of eye movement with hand movement as part of completing everyday tasks. |
| LC10 | How to be competitive | is the practice and use of strategies, a video game player strives to achieve above normal success. |
| LC11 | Interpersonal skills | is life skills used every day to communicate and interact with |

|      |                       | others.                                                                                                                                                                                                                      |
|------|-----------------------|---|
| LC12 | Map awareness         | is the ability to learn a map's terrain or environment, while always knowing the position of where you are on the map; map awareness also allows you to take advantage of certain positions in a map to maximize task success. |
| LC13 | Conduct research      | is the ability to search for different resources to learn more about a certain topic to achieve success. |
| LC14 | Economics             | is the social science that studies the behavior of individuals, groups, and organizations, when they manage or use scarce resources, which have alternative uses, to achieve desired ends. |
| LC15 | Reading comprehension | is the act of understanding what you are reading. It is an active and intentional process that occurs during and after reading a particular piece of writing or text. |
| LC16 | Resource management   | is the ability to efficiently and effectively deploy resources to maximize success. |
| LC17 | Strategy              | is the ability to make up a plan designed to achieve a goal. |
| LC18 | Spatial thinking      | is the ability to record information about one's environment and its spatial orientation. |
| LC19 | Time management       | is the act or process of planning and exercising conscious control over the amount of time spent on specific activities to effectively and efficiently complete tasks. |

## Conclusions

The conclusions of this study addressed each of the research questions. They were derived from the data collected. Game based learning is a growing field of study. There are both proponents and opponents arguing about the benefits of playing video games. The purpose of this study was to explore what types of learning occurs when playing video game genres as opposed to single video game titles.

The findings of this study indicated that there are several major video game genres identified by video game players. Those video game players in this study were considered to be educated, expert consumers of video game playing. This study provided us with a list of twelve video game genres and their definitions. The video game genres identified were role playing games (RPG), massively multiplayer online role playing games (MMORPG), first person shooter (FPS), sports, puzzle, real time strategy (RTS), action, turn based, simulation, fighting, kinetic controlled, and casual.

The research supported that video game players were learning different constructs from playing the identified video game genres. There were a total of 19 learning constructs identified and defined. The learning constructs were coding/computer programming, conflict management, communication skills, creating a community, crafting, critical thinking, attention to detail, building management, hand-eye coordination, how to be competitive, interpersonal skills, map awareness, conduct research, economics, reading comprehension, resource management, strategy, spatial thinking, and time management. Exploring learning constructs from playing video game genres provided a more generalized list of learning constructs. This comprehensive list of learning constructs could be used to test specific game titles or other sub video game genres. This is the next step the researchers will continue examining.

Future research needs to build and expand on these findings to add to the new topic of video game genre based learning. In addition to identifying and defining different game genres and learning constructs, the researchers will continue this research by explore what are the similarities found between each of the video game genres with the learning constructs identified. It is logical that the researchers will continue to study the differences and similarities between the video game genres and learning constructs, but to also examine other populations of video game players. The researchers have hypothesized that different groups of video game players may identify different video games and learning constructs.

In conclusion, the researchers will use the findings of this research to continue with the PCT framework to create a survey tool that will produce a survey tool that will evaluate and assess each video game genre and how it relates to the learning constructs. With that type of data, similarities and comparisons could be analyzed and discussions could focus on how it may be used in educational settings. This will hopefully provide a framework for educators that may want to use video game genres as a learning tool in their classrooms. This proposed framework will serve as a guide for evaluating different video game genres, assessing each genre as it relates to one or more learning constructs, and integrating these genres into classroom curricula. By understanding the intricacies of video game genres and learning constructs as defined in this study, educators would be more prepared to make educated, student-centered decisions when selecting examples of. In addition, the findings of this study lend themselves to furthering the body of knowledge in video game research with the hopes of confirming the assertion that video games can be a principal tool for teaching and learning in the 21st century.

## References

Anderson, C. A., & Dill, K. E. (2000). Video games and aggressive thoughts, feelings, and behavior in the laboratory and in life. *Journal of Personality and Social Psychology, 78*(4), 772.

Anderson, J., & Barnett, M. (2011). Using Video Games to Support Pre-Service Elementary Teachers Learning of Basic Physics Principles. *Journal of Science Education & Technology, 20*(4), 347–362.

Bailey, K., West, R., & Anderson, C. A. (2010). A negative association between video game experience and proactive cognitive control. *Psychophysiology, 47*(1), 34–42.

Chazerand, P., & Geeroms, C. (2008). The business of playing games: players as developers and entrepreneurs. *Digital Creativity, 19*(3), 185–193. doi:10.1080/14626260802312616

Daniel, J. (2011). *Sampling Essentials: Practical Guidelines for Making Sampling Choices*. SAGE Publications.

DFC Intelligence » DFC Intelligence Forecasts Worldwide Online Game Market to Reach $79 Billion by 2017. (n.d.). Retrieved April 11, 2014, from http://www.dfcint.com/wp/?p=353

Dunbar, G., Hill, R., & Lewis, V. (2001). Children's attentional skills and road behavior. *Journal of Experimental Psychology: Applied*, *7*(3), 227–234. doi:10.1037//1076-898X.7.3.227

Eisenhardt, K. M. (1989). Building theories from case study research. *Academy of Management Review*, 532–550.

Gee, J. P. (2003). What video games have to teach us about learning and literacy. *Computers in Entertainment (CIE)*, *1*(1), 20–20.

Gee, J. P. (2007a). *Good Video Games and Good Learning* (1st ed.). Peter Lang Publishing.

Gee, J. P. (2007b). *What Video Games Have to Teach Us About Learning and Literacy.* (2nd ed.). Palgrave Macmillan.

Green, C. S., Pouget, A., & Bavelier, D. (2010). Improved Probabilistic Inference as a General Learning Mechanism with Action Video Games. *Current Biology*, *20*(17), 1573–1579. doi:10.1016/j.cub.2010.07.040

Jackson, L. A., Witt, E. A., Games, A. I., Fitzgerald, H. E., von Eye, A., & Zhao, Y. (2012). Information technology use and creativity: Findings from the Children and Technology Project. *Computers in Human Behavior*, *28*(2), 370–376. doi:10.1016/j.chb.2011.10.006

Jenkins, H., Klopfer, E., Squire, K., & Tan, P. (2003). Entering the education arcade. *Computers in Entertainment (CIE)*, *1*(1), 8.

Kelly, G. (1963). *A Theory of Personality: The Psychology of Personal Constructs*. W. W. Norton & Company.

Lenhart, Amanda, Kahne, J., Middaugh, E., Macgill, A., Evans, C., & Vitak, J. (2008, September 16). Teens, Video Games, and Civics: Teens' gaming experiences are diverse and include significant social interaction and civic engagement. Pew Internet & American Life Project. Retrieved from http://www.pewinternet.org/~/media/Files/Reports/2008/PIP_Teens_Games_and_Civics_Report_FINAL.pdf.pdf

Mayo, M. J. (2007). Games for science and engineering education. *Communications of the ACM*, *50*(7), 30–35.

Merriam, S. (2009). *Qualitative Research: A Guide to Design and Implementation* (3rd ed.). Jossey-Bass.

Prensky, M. (2003). Digital game-based learning. *Computers in Entertainment (CIE)*, *1*(1), 21–21.

Shaffer, D., Squire, K., Halverson, R., & Gee, J. P. (2004, December). Video games and the future of learning. Retrieved from http://www.cwrl.utexas.edu/currents/fall05/payne.html

Squire, K. (2011). *Video Games and Learning: Teaching and Participatory Culture in the Digital Age*. Teachers College Press.

The Entertainment Software Association - Industry Facts. (2012). Retrieved September 28, 2012, from http://www.theesa.com/facts/index.asp

www.ingramcontent.com/pod-product-compliance
Lightning Source LLC
Chambersburg PA
CBHW081841230426

43669CB00018B/2774

*9781939797155*